Give Me Shelter

STUDIES IN CANADIAN MILITARY HISTORY
Series editor: Dean F. Oliver, Canadian War Museum

The Canadian War Museum, Canada's national museum of military history, has a threefold mandate: to remember, to preserve, and to educate. Studies in Canadian Military History, published by UBC Press in association with the Museum, extends this mandate by presenting the best of contemporary scholarship to provide new insights into all aspects of Canadian military history, from earliest times to recent events. The work of a new generation of scholars is especially encouraged, and the books employ a variety of approaches – cultural, social, intellectual, economic, political, and comparative – to investigate gaps in the existing historiography. The books in the series feed immediately into future exhibitions, programs, and outreach efforts by the Canadian War Museum. A list of the titles in the series appears at the end of the book.

Give Me Shelter

The Failure of Canada's Cold War Civil Defence

Andrew Burtch

UBCPress · Vancouver · Toronto

21 20 19 18 17 16 15 14 13 12   5 4 3 2 1

Printed in Canada on FSC-certified ancient-forest-free paper
(100% post-consumer recycled) that is processed chlorine- and acid-free.

Library and Archives Canada Cataloguing in Publication

Burtch, Andrew Paul
    Give me shelter : the failure of Canada's Cold War civil defence / Andrew Burtch.

(Studies in Canadian military history, ISSN 1499-6251)
Includes bibliographical references and index.
Issued also in electronic formats.
ISBN 978-0-7748-2240-4 (bound); ISBN 978-0-7748-2241-1 (pbk.)

    1. Canada. Civil Defence. 2. Civil defense – Canada – Planning – History – 20th century. 3. Cold War. 4. Canada – Military policy – History – 20th century. I. Title. II. Series: Studies in Canadian military history

UA929.C2B87 2012   363.35097109'045   C2011-907393-5

Canadä

UBC Press gratefully acknowledges the financial support for our publishing program of the Government of Canada (through the Canada Book Fund), the Canada Council for the Arts, and the British Columbia Arts Council.

This book has been published with the help of a grant from the Canadian Federation for the Humanities and Social Sciences, through the Aid to Scholarly Publications Program, using funds provided by the Social Sciences and Humanities Research Council of Canada.

Publication of this book has been financially supported by the Canadian War Museum.

UBC Press
The University of British Columbia
2029 West Mall
Vancouver, BC V6T 1Z2
www.ubcpress.ca

For Virginia and Graham –
the only people with whom I would want to share a fallout shelter.

Contents

List of Illustrations

Acknowledgments

THIS BOOK IS A STUDY of what happens when you ask people to consider the unthinkable: the devastation wrought by nuclear war, and what, if anything, could be done to prevent unnecessary loss of life. It is the product of a prolonged research project that began at Carleton University during my doctoral studies, and it has been shaped and encouraged on its way from concept to manuscript by a wide community of professionals, scholars, family, and friends. Much of what stands out in the work is the result of their support – any errors of commission or omission are mine.

I owe my greatest debt of gratitude to Norman Hillmer, whose understanding of the historical profession helped steer me towards this promising topic in the first place. His sharp editorial commentary helped to shape my inquiry, reasoning, and improve my writing over the course of several years. In addition to his astounding assistance during the writing of this manuscript, he provided invaluable editorial suggestions as it evolved to its present form. He kept me motivated, and, in return, I added to his insanely busy schedule. Words hardly suffice to express the depths of my appreciation, but here goes: I thank him for his mentorship and the advice he offered during many leisurely Sunday walks through the neighbourhood but, above all, for his patience, friendship, and unwavering support.

During the process of writing this manuscript, support, advice, and encouragement from the Department of History at Carleton University was always forthcoming and helpful, especially from Aleksandra Bennett, Fred Goodwin, Duncan McDowall, James Opp, John Walsh, and Susan Whitney, among others. Joan White and Regina Aulinskas, who have shepherded many students through the department, have my deepest respect as well as my apologies for any trouble I caused in my time there.

None of this work would have been possible without the patience and service offered by the staff at Library and Archives Canada, whose quick review and release of the many once-restricted files used in this work greatly accelerated my research. At the Directorate of History and Heritage, Steve Harris and his staff also provided helpful direction and timely access to documents in their research centre. Staff librarians and archivists at the Canadian War Museum's

Military History Research Centre provided essential interlibrary loan service and pointed out interesting files and photographs. Image research was greatly assisted by Jennifer Devine at Library and Archives Canada, Janet Lacroix at the Canadian Forces Photo Unit, Suzanne Dubeau at the Clara Thomas Archives and Special Collections at York University, and Susan Kooyman at the Glenbow Archives in Calgary. Deep underground and safe from nuclear attack, the staff and volunteers of the Diefenbunker Museum in Carp, Ontario, offered access to their archives and their recollections of emergency planning.

Along with being Canada's national museum for military history, the Canadian War Museum is a terrific place to work. Since 2006, I have had unparalleled opportunities to meet with veterans and serving members of the Canadian Forces as well as members of the public who have been touched by war. It is a humbling experience that has enriched my understanding of Canadian military history. My colleagues in Research and Exhibitions provided great support as I developed this project, offering commentary on chapters or ideas, suggesting new avenues of inquiry, and recommending other sources. Thanks go to Laura Brandon, Tim Cook, Amber Lloydlangston, Peter Macleod, Jeff Noakes, and Cameron Pulsifer. Dean Oliver unfailingly supported my studies, encouraged my efforts to complete this manuscript, and shared important and much-valued advice about research and publishing.

I would like to express my gratitude to Emily Andrew, Senior Editor at UBC Press, who offered essential guidance at each of the many stages on the way to publication. Her passion for historical scholarship shines through in her work. Special thanks are due to this manuscript's reviewers, whose thoughtful comments and suggested revisions were enormously helpful in completing this work. The copy editor, ever patient, caught weaselly errors of grammar and reason (including this one!), while Megan Brand, UBC Press's production coordinator, turned out a quality finished product. The assistance of the Social Sciences and Humanities Research Council (SSHRC) was simply indispensible. A SSHRC Canada Graduate Scholarship first helped me through my doctoral studies, and their Aid to Scholarly Publications Program helped make the publication of this work possible, as well as many others in Canada.

I should close with a word of thanks to my friends and colleagues, including Jesse Alexander, Martin Auger, Greg Donaghy, Serge Durflinger, Jason Ginn, Andrew Godefroy, Richard Goette, David Hood, Andrew Iarocci, David Meren, Omar Khan, Christopher O'Brien, Michael Petrou, Christine Rivas, Ryan Shackleton, Ryan Touhey, Jim Whitham, James Wood, Morgan Wright, Stacey Zembrzycki, and many, many others who acted as valuable sounding boards whenever asked on a wide variety of subjects. My mother and father, Leslie and

Terry Burtch, kept me in touch with family and offered tremendous support and much love. My wife, Virginia Miller, is my greatest supporter, a terrific editor, scholar, and teacher and an unequalled partner. Graham, our son, makes me hope for a world without fear of nuclear war.

Abbreviations

ARP	Air-Raid Precautions
CBC	Canadian Broadcasting Corporation
CCCRH	Canadian Committee for the Control of Radiation Hazards
CCEP	Cabinet Committee on Emergency Plans
CD	civil defence
CDO	Civil Defence Order (1959)
CDC	Cabinet Defence Committee
CFMM	Canadian Federation of Mayors and Municipalities
CGS	Chief of the General Staff
COG	Continuity of Government
COSC	Chiefs of Staff Committee
CVB	Central Volunteer Bureau
DRB	Defence Research Board
DSO&P	Directorate of Survival Operations and Planning
EASE	Experimental Army Signals Establishment
EMO	Emergency Measures Organization
FAP	Financial Assistance Program
FCDA	Federal Civil Defense Administration (United States)
FRG	Federal Republic of Germany
GOC	General Officer Commanding
GDR	German Democratic Republic
GWCDC	Greater Winnipeg Civil Defence Committee
IACCEP	Interdepartmental Advisory Committee of Emergency Planning
ICBM	Intercontinental ballistic missile
ISD	Information Services Division
NATO	North Atlantic Treaty Organization
NORAD	North American Air Defence
NSAWS	National Survival Attack Warning System
PMQ	Permanent married quarters
RCAF	Royal Canadian Air Force
SMTP	Special Militia Training Plan
WBC	War Book Committee

Give Me Shelter

Introduction

AT 10:20 A.M. ON 23 April 1952, an atomic bomb detonated in the centre of Ottawa. The force of the blast toppled the Parliament buildings, and the intense heat turned even the sturdiest towers into burnt-out shells. Shock waves burst underground water mains throughout the city, causing insurmountable difficulties for the city's meagre firefighting forces. Twenty-five percent of the residential neighbourhoods near to ground zero were destroyed, and fire threatened the remaining homes. The bridges across the Ottawa River and the neighbouring city of Hull were almost completely destroyed, and flames ravaged the Gatineau Hills. By mid-afternoon, thousands of the homeless crowded into the fairground at Lansdowne Park to receive food and water. As sunset approached, the fires still burned, and 25,000 people were counted dead at the end of the first day, 50,000 were injured, more than half seriously, and over 105,000 were without shelter.[1]

This was one scenario devised for an exercise by Canada's federal civil defence organization, an agency created in the early days of the Cold War to develop strategies to protect civilian population and infrastructure in the event of a nuclear war. Under the shadow of the atomic bomb, civil defence (CD) plans reached into every corner of daily life. From 1948 to 1963, Canada's CD planners attempted to bring the message of preparedness to every citizen with the use of public exercises, publicity campaigns, and educational programs. Yet, in spite of the great risks facing Canadians, the public largely rejected CD. Its failure hinged on the nature of the relationship between the state and its citizenry, the government's inadequate plans, and the balance of civil-military relations in Canada during the Cold War.

Civil defence planning in Canada took shape over three stages, distinguished by the reach of CD policy into the public sphere and the strategy for defence crafted under each plan. The first stage lasted from 1948 to 1954, during which planners articulated a strategy of self-help for targeted Canadian cities, based loosely on the model of rescue, first aid, and firefighting that British and German cities had adopted to combat the bombing campaigns of the Second World War. While planners recognized the power of the atomic bomb, they concluded that it was just another bomb, albeit a powerful one, and they believed a country

FIGURE 1 AND 2 (*facing page*)   Parliament Hill and the National War Memorial, destroyed by the atom! *Source:* Library and Archives Canada/National Defence collection/Accession 2008-0377-R112/No. Z-9436-1-A, No. Z-9436-2-A

could absorb its blow and survive. The federal government attempted to place most of the responsibility for organizing and financing CD on the shoulders of the target cities. During the self-help stage, recruiting, public education, and training were directed at enlisting the residents of Canadian cities as volunteer firefighters and wardens who could save life and property in their community.

Civil defence's perception of the atomic bomb as simply another weapon disappeared forever in 1952, when the United States successfully detonated the hydrogen bomb, prompting a revolution in CD planning. What point was there in fighting fires when the entire city would be cratered? A new stage of civil defence planning was thus defined by the evacuation strategy, which gradually replaced the notion of self-help from 1954 to 1959. The evacuation policy required preparations within target cities so that they could secure their citizens' co-operation for an orderly exodus within three hours of an attack warning. It also demanded provisions to feed, shelter, and care for nuclear refugees in reception areas in rural municipalities surrounding the target city. Civil defence publicity and recruiting expanded accordingly from the cities into the countryside. With federal and provincial assistance, Canadian cities carried out major CD exercises involving tens of thousands of people in urban and rural areas. The policy encountered major obstacles as evacuation warning times drew shorter and as the sinister threat of radioactive fallout, which was expected to irradiate much of the populated areas of the country, came to be better appreciated by CD officials and the public alike.

The last phase of CD, which took effect in 1959, shifted the focus from an evacuation to a "national survival" strategy. The problem of fallout was not easily resolved, nor, because of its unpredictable nature, could CD planning be confined any longer to target areas. To prepare a capable warning system and to develop a network through which civil authorities could co-ordinate the survival and reconstruction effort, the federal government devised a comprehensive national survival program. It contained provisions for Continuity of Government measures, which were designed to ensure that the basic machinery of government could withstand the disruption of attack and continue to direct the country's wider survival efforts. The public was instructed to build fallout shelters within their homes that they could use to survive the most lethal period of radioactive fallout following a nuclear attack. Unlike previous plans, which had concentrated on recruiting and publicity in a handful of cities across the country, the national survival plan that unfolded required that all citizens take on some responsibility to defend their homes. By 1962, however, CD was fading away, its plan rejected or ignored by the public, underfunded, and increasingly irrelevant as relations improved between the East and the West.

The obligations of citizenship formed a major theme of CD policy and publicity in Canada during the early Cold War. Canada's CD structure, like that of the United States and the United Kingdom, depended on the voluntary participation of its citizens in local CD organizations and the relationship – the implicit contract – between the state and its citizens. The international literature of citizenship studies is wide and varied, sparked by post-Second World War reflections on the relationship and exchanges between the individual, the community, and the state.[2] In Canada, the trajectory of these studies has flowed in two directions: the first examining the evolution of the political and social rights associated with changing citizenship regimes and the second dissecting the concept of citizenship as a form of belonging to the national polity, and its relationship and relevance to fragmented regional, ethnic, and linguistic identities.

Citizenship became a national project of the federal government in the immediate aftermath of the Second World War. The passage of the Canadian Citizenship Act into law on 1 January 1947 created the legal definition of

Canadian citizenship as a birthright – distinct from the status that Canadians already possessed as British subjects.[3] The new legislation was enacted during a time when the relationship between Canadians and the state was substantially changing, heralded by the massive social welfare program brought into effect at the end of the Second World War. The federal government, greatly strengthened by the wartime centralization of economic and constitutional power, expanded its support for social security to meet the expectations of a public weary of the deprivation and uncertainty caused by over a decade of depression and war.[4]

The social welfare program sought actively to use the power of the state and its public monies to provide individuals with protection against want. In so doing, it effectively changed the nature of the contract defining the network of social relations between the public and its government.[5] The Keynesian "civic bargain" was a system in which the universal contribution of taxes by the population undergirded political and legal rights with universal coverage of social welfare. This influential relationship characterized the citizen-state nexus throughout most of the Western world from 1945 to the 1970s, when it began to erode under economic pressure and social divisions.[6] State responsibility for social welfare was complemented by similar forays into publicly funded cultural projects and the efforts of immigration officials to define who counted as a citizen and who did not.[7] The policies of public agencies in these years exercised influence over not only the relationship between the citizen and the state but also the relationships between citizens within their communities.[8] As political scientists have observed, state agencies have the potential to write their priorities into the social fabric of the country. The state defines and redefines not just the rights privileged to citizens but also the obligations expected of them.

After 1948, as Civil Defence Canada struggled to obtain public recognition, build its base of volunteers, and ensure that Canadians would comply with the policies developed to protect them, its officials developed a prescriptive, obligation-based model of citizenship. The concept of citizen-as-defender was in many respects a traditional ideal in Canada, with several historical precedents. During the siege of Quebec in 1759, when the parish church bells sounded the alarm, it was the legal obligation of every loyal Canadien to rush to the scene of a fire with leather bucket in hand and work together to prevent flames from spreading.[9] Popular memory of the War of 1812 credits the volunteer militia made up of average Canadian citizens, not the professional British forces, with saving Upper Canada from invasion.[10] The "militia myth," the pervasive belief that volunteer forces were equal to standing military forces, had more to do with nationalist feeling and public disdain for professional soldiering than with the militia's actual ability to defend the country. In practice, the belief that rapidly

trained and minimally equipped citizens could adequately defend the homeland bred complacency in defence preparations at the cost of military preparedness and effectiveness. Yet the ideal of the citizen-as-defender endured during
the first half of the twentieth century, when hundreds of thousands of Canadians
enlisted during both World Wars – only a tiny proportion of whom had any
previous military experience – creating a popular memory of "democratic armies" of volunteers marching to victory against autocratic enemies with huge
professional forces.[11] Civil Defence Canada's recruiting strategy was intimately
bound to this concept of a citizen's obligation to serve in defence of his or her
country.

The campaign for a Cold War civil defence had the ambition of preparing
the populace, in the midst of optimistic post-war reconstruction, to absorb
unimaginable damage and civilian casualties, in a country that had not seen a
major war fought on its soil for over 100 years. Civil defence officials believed
that their plans had little chance of succeeding unless the population prepared
itself for the worst, well in advance of the outbreak of the next war, because
there would be no comfortable period of mobilization in which the country
could transition from peacetime to wartime. These same officials attempted
to instil the concept of participation in CD as a civic virtue – a responsibility
towards which every patriotic Canadian would have to contribute if the country
was to withstand an attack using weapons that could transform cities into craters
and scatter lethal radiation everywhere.

Civil defence's appeal to civic virtue coloured virtually every contact between
the Canadian CD organization and the public. These points of contact surfaced
at CD exhibits, recruiting drives, an extensive publication program, civil defence
exercises, and at hundreds of lectures in church basements, movie theatres, and
mock shelters. The post-war concept of citizenship depended on the defence
of public rights, but public duties figured heavily in the citizen-state relationship.[12] The Canadian government demanded support from the public for CD
in the name of national security. The fact that most citizens refused to take
responsibility for this duty is remarkable, suggesting that they were unwilling
to fulfill their obligation to defend the country. Yet Canadians could not imagine
how a defence was possible, and they believed that the actions of the government, whether through a change in foreign and defence policies or a publicly
subsidized shelter construction program, would have more impact than the
gestures of private citizens. The reverse proved true. Without the public's consent,
the government's CD efforts could not succeed.

Since so many Canadians perceived survival as a responsibility of the government, the limits of government planning and policy making in the nuclear age
constitute another major theme of this work. The atomic bomb was considered

FIGURE 3   Civil defence training officer Lieutenant-Colonel W. Arthur Croteau points to ground zero of an atomic explosion over Ottawa during a 1952 map exercise in Hull, Quebec. *Source: Toronto Telegram*, Clara Thomas Archives, York University

to be a threat to national security, but it was one that the federal government attempted to solve through planning. The national civil defence organization that resulted was a by-product of such thinking. Civil defence planning entailed preparation for disaster under the rubric of old and new government responsibilities, such as communications, health care, and transport. The planning process involved many government departments with competing interests, and this confusion led to much discussion and little action.

Once the federal government decided on a firm course of action, CD policy became politicized as planners and their political masters solicited the co-operation of provincial and municipal governments. With a few exceptions, the provinces refused Ottawa's requests to finance CD efforts and pointed to the federal government's constitutional responsibilities for the defence of the country. The municipalities were early adopters of CD, and in some cases they moved ahead of the federal government to create some form of defence against the atomic bomb, but most balked when they learned of the heavy costs that would be needed to ready their cities and maintain a large body of volunteers.

Intergovernmental battles over CD, often toxic in nature, undermined public confidence and forced Civil Defence Canada into a steady retreat from its first principle that the provinces and municipalities needed to assume most of the responsibility for emergency preparations. The federal treasury amended the CD financing rules to provide incentives to other governments to prepare for disaster. As a result, federal funds initially provided half, and then three-quarters, of the cost of CD in Canada. Civil defence officials in the federal office, who were determined at first not to work directly with the municipalities, soon found that, if they did not, no city in Ontario or Quebec would have even the rudimentary tools needed to build their defence. The Canadian government took on ever-greater responsibility for emergency planning and never achieved the full co-operation of the provinces or municipalities in civil defence.

Disputes between Canada's levels of government created a CD system that was unable to respond quickly to the changing threats posed by the arms race. The technology of nuclear weapons and their delivery systems underwent several revolutionary advancements during the Cold War – none more important than the development of city-killing hydrogen bombs and the creation of inter-continental ballistic missiles to deliver them. Civil defence plans lagged embarrassingly behind these developments. Secrecy shrouded nuclear weapons, leading to delays in the disclosure of their effects to CD agencies in Canada and the United States. This delay, in turn, complicated strategies for public protection. Compounding this central difficulty was the task of developing a practicable plan that the provinces and municipalities would accept. Moving from an atomic defence to a thermonuclear defence took nearly two years, while the introduction of the missile threat threw the Canadian system into a frenzy of confused activity and planning adjustment that lasted right up until the Cuban Missile Crisis very nearly made any further discussion of the issue meaningless.

The relationship between civilian and military authorities in the preparation of CD measures is the third major theme of this work. Questions frequently emerged during federal and provincial disputes about whether or not support for a CD organization was a matter of self-help or national defence. This question also plagued CD and military planners within the federal government when they mapped out which government departments would fulfill CD tasks. What if preparations did not work, and CD measures could not protect Canadians? If Civil Defence Canada was the country's last line of defence, did the military have any responsibility to support or, if necessary, supplant the CD organization if it proved incapable of fulfilling the tasks assigned it?

Civil defence planners worried that the public might perceive CD as a military endeavour. Greater involvement by the armed forces in CD would have seemed to say that it was a military solution to a military threat and, therefore, a federal responsibility. As a result, the provinces and municipalities would have abandoned their organizations. Moreover, greater involvement from the military would have posed the risk of alienating support from voluntary civilian associations whose participation in CD was essential to local organizations' success. After all, if soldiers could be paid to assume rescue duties, why should the public do the job for nothing? Military involvement also blurred the line between community preparedness and national defence. Civil defence officials were concerned that it would prevent potential volunteers from registering, lest they be conscripted or placed under military command. Canada's senior CD officials, most of whom were retired military officers, were asked not to invoke their old ranks, and debates persisted over whether to change the name of Civil Defence Canada to "Civil Disaster." Despite these worries, in the end Canada's CD agency was only too glad to accept greater support from the military in shoring up the country's passive defences.

It was the military, in fact, that was most reluctant about its involvement in CD planning and organization. They were absorbed in the building and maintenance of a professional standing armed force whose aim was to fight alongside Cold War allies overseas. The Korean War, and the immense government investment in rearmament, helped the armed forces to achieve this goal. The Canadian Chiefs of Staff Committee viewed support for CD as an obligation that could irreparably damage their ability to support Canadian units stationed with NATO forces in France and West Germany, which was the West's strategic deterrent to war. For most of the 1950s, the military fought to stay out of CD plans, with the exception of providing warning to Canadian cities.

Plans for national survival after 1959 altered this balance significantly. Local CD agencies had proven unable to attract and retain the volunteer manpower that most observers believed was necessary to save lives in a nuclear war. The military was forced to take on full responsibility for rescue and re-entry, which was formerly the task of volunteers. The Canadian army's reserves were stripped of their role as reinforcements for a future war in Western Europe and instead tasked with saving lives and fighting fires. The new civil-military relationship was uneasy and short-lived, as militia volunteers lost interest in "snakes and ladders" exercises, and the public grew wary of the risks posed by giving the military too much authority in an emergency.

While in the past decade historians have begun to build a richer understanding of Canada's own Cold War home front, focusing particularly on the national security state as it affected immigration and political culture, CD has escaped the attention of all but a few.[13] With the exception of an unpublished organizational survey written for the fiftieth anniversary of Emergency Preparedness Canada, there is not an official history of Canadian civilian defence planning for today's revisionists to revise.[14] This work is the first to present the history of Canada's CD agency and plans in the early Cold War.

This work is the result of research conducted primarily at Library and Archives Canada (LAC), using the files of the federal government departments directly and indirectly concerned with planning Canada's CD policies. The manuscript group collections at the LAC contain many references to CD, specifically the prime ministerial fonds, the files of cabinet ministers such as Paul Martin and Douglas Harkness, and the files of senior CD staff involved in planning and training. This research has been complemented with work in the files of professional and voluntary associations who pledged their support to community CD, such as the files of the Imperial Order Daughters of the Empire, the Canadian Federation of Mayors and Municipalities, and other groups.

The Department of National Defence's Directorate of History and Heritage in Ottawa retains the seven-volume diary of Major-General Frank Worthington, who held the post of federal civil defence co-ordinator from 1948 until his retirement in 1959. These volumes contain reflections that are indispensible for the study of CD in Canada. The Canadian War Museum's Military History Research Centre's archival and library collections were also exploited for original oral histories, training manuals, and personal document collections. Similar research was performed in the Doug Beaton Library at the Diefenbunker Museum in Carp, Ontario.

There is an enormous body of North American literature dedicated to the study of the Cold War, and yet only a few of these texts examine CD. This is at once remarkable, considering the heated public debates held in Canada and the United States about CD during the early Cold War, and unsurprising, since the vast bulk of Cold War historiography has focused on the foreign policies and military strategies of the United States and the Soviet Union. It was only in the late 1970s and early 1980s, coinciding with a renewed public discussion of the alleged benefits of a CD program, that the literature began to engage civil defence as a domestic aftershock of the Cold War.

The dominant school in the American literature about CD efforts emerged as part of the studies that addressed larger questions about how the atomic bomb and the concept of security were synthesized into American culture. Most American historians contend that federal and state governments deliberately misrepresented the effects of the atomic bomb and the feasibility of CD measures in order to reassure the public that they could survive a nuclear attack.[15] This act of deception, they allege, resulted in a "false consciousness." The public, deceived into believing that they could survive, supported American foreign policies against the Soviet Union.[16] These authors build on the arguments of revisionist foreign policy historians such as Gabriel Kolko, who examine the economic underpinnings of American foreign policy to expose a self-interested, aggressive diplomacy aimed at asserting US hegemony in the world by cowing allies and threatening the Soviet Union.[17] With a few exceptions, most of the work done on civil defence in the United States castigates the program as an illiberal form of government control managed by the military and CD advocates, avoiding the study of the evolution of civilian defence policies. These historians work to correct the conception that Cold War America was uniformly quiescent, conservative, and in favour of the arms race.

Paul Boyer's 1985 work remains one of the most influential historical assessments of the Cold War's cultural impact.[18] The author, who was an active participant in the American disarmament movement in the 1960s, wrote at a time of renewed opposition to nuclear arms in the United States. Boyer investigates how the American public came to accept the atomic bomb, along with its horrific effects, as part of their lives during the Cold War. He examines articles published in leading American periodicals and magazines by American scientists, works of science fiction dealing with atomic war, and other cultural forums to determine how "Americans first confronted the bomb, struggled against it, and absorbed it into the fabric of the culture."[19] He contends that government officials who emphasized the useful applications of the atom, and the atomic scientists and intellectuals who portrayed a destructive atomic future, used fear to gain legitimacy.[20]

Particularly relevant to Boyer's argument was the body of literature that emerged after the Second World War from the medical community. Psychologists and sociologists wrote many reports in the post-war period indicating the dangers posed by mass panic and hysteria. Studies such as the one produced by Irving Janis, a Yale psychologist, advised that preparedness for nuclear war could serve to "inoculate" the public against emotional overreaction to the bomb. These studies, paired with optimistic training booklets and films such as *Duck and Cover,* form the bedrock of Boyer's thesis: "Reassuring and interconnected messages, emanating from so many authoritative sources as the decade ended, contributed powerfully to the emergence of a decisive and unsettling new stage in America's cultural and political engagement with atomic weapons."[21] His argument that CD was a means to regulate "atomic anxiety" has become an influential interpretation of CD's role in America's Cold War.[22]

Scholars have built on works about the atomic question to examine other aspects of normative Cold War culture. The revisionist school's early portrayal of the Cold War is not marked by economic prosperity but, rather, by repression and imperilled liberalism and is characterized by atomic and anti-Communist paranoia. The apparatus of this system, the argument goes, was regulated by the agents of state authority who employed fear, whether through CD exercises or in chasing real and imagined subversives, to contain domestic cultures of dissent.[23]

In Canada, there is no evidence to suggest that CD planners operated in the service of such a conspiratorial agenda. While officials were as concerned about public hysteria as their allies to the south, they always opted to disclose, rather than censor, whatever information they had about nuclear weapons and used fearful imagery and rhetoric to underline the severity of the consequences arising from a nuclear exchange.

Investigation into the major themes of this work was inspired by Laura McEnany's examination of American CD agency and its impact on American family life.[24] She argues that the voluntary participation of the public in CD raised questions about the responsibilities of citizens and the state in homeland defence. McEnany interprets CD as a point of contact between the relatively peaceful Cold War home front and the reality of international confrontation with the Soviet Union.[25] McEnany explains how the American government applied CD concepts to export responsibility for defence to private citizens, effectively creating a grassroots approach to national security. This process, she argues, transformed the American family into a paramilitary reserve and created a system designed to protect itself from external invaders and crush subversives within.

McEnany recognizes that the work of civil defence was two-tiered: the first a secretive and bureaucratic policy-planning process and the second constituting the work necessary to enlist the public to adopt the prescribed measures. McEnany found that the civil defence publicity used to promote the concept of "self-help," with its emphasis on individual responsibilities and the defence of a distinctive way of life, "subtly transformed civil defense from a list of tasks into a set of desirable personality traits."[26] Almost unique among CD studies, McEnany's perspective takes pains to illustrate that CD planners were genuinely concerned about the public and were often frustrated and puzzled by the hostile or apathetic reception that their plans received in the public. In this work, Canadian CD publicity is examined through the same lens, revealing what Canadian officials expected of their volunteers and, just as importantly, what type of volunteers were most sought after.

A study of the American literature brings out some of the common themes in North American CD measures, but this is first and foremost a national study. Canada's proximity to the American superpower was a defining influence in post-war life. Nowhere was this effect as evident as in defence. The fortunes of the Second World War brought Canada into the American orbit and resulted in joint defence planning. After the war, continuing binational discussions and a growing network of liaisons and memorandums of understanding served to cement the relationship, leading to ambitious radar warning lines and the North American Air Defence treaty in the 1950s. Civil defence was no exception to this trend. The two countries shared similar vulnerabilities – densely populated industrial target areas surrounded by rural countryside; divisions of responsibility for emergency planning between federal, territorial, and municipal governments; and a populace complacent about the need for emergency preparedness in a nuclear age.

Canadian CD authorities, realizing their shared problems, consulted from the outset with their American counterparts, who were better funded and had greater access to intelligence about nuclear weapons and the Soviet threat. In 1951, this relationship resulted in a formal accord with the United States that mandated that, in the event of an atomic attack or major disaster, the two countries' CD agencies would operate as if there were no border. In the interim, Civil Defence Canada borrowed heavily from their colleagues down south, reprinting American publications in whole or in part under Canadian letterhead, soliciting material from American specialists for publications in federal and local CD bulletins, and observing American nuclear tests and exercises.

While elements of Canada's CD strategies were inspired by events in the United States, the Canadian government did not automatically ape American plans. Civil Defence Canada carefully weighed and tested each strategy against the special circumstances of Canada's climate, politics, and means before reaching decisions on policy. Especially in the case of fallout shelters, the public noticed large discrepancies between Canadian and American plans, and, more often than not, turned to the more readily available American designs and demanded the Canadian government mark buildings that could serve as group shelters. However much Canadian CD authorities cherished their relationship with the United States, Canada's decisions about CD plans and priorities were not crafted in Washington. This work examines the rise and fall of Canada's civil defence.

Canada's civil defence program failed for a constellation of reasons. Successive governments pursued and altered CD and drafted plans behind closed doors, but they never provided the public with the tools required to create a meaningful defence. Civil Defence Canada and its officials meanwhile limped by on a fraction of a percentage of the billions of dollars committed to the military defence of the country during the same period. This support was insufficient to provide the public with concrete evidence of the progress in implementing CD measures for their defence and made it an easy target for criticism and ridicule. In the public eye, air-raid sirens, additional fire trucks, and do-it-yourself shelter designs were no match for Soviet thermonuclear bombs and intercontinental ballistic missiles, and they were never enough to convince Canadians that their contribution to CD would satisfy the public good. Civil defence was remembered by the public most often when international crises made the theoretical threat of annihilation in war frighteningly real, and it was forgotten just as quickly when these menaces passed.

1
From World War to Cold War, 1945-50

THE SECOND WORLD WAR ended with mushroom clouds over the Japanese cities of Hiroshima and Nagasaki. The atomic bombing of Japan killed more than 100,000 and injured a further 90,000 people. The intense light and heat released by the blasts created horrific burn injuries, and thousands of people displayed devastating symptoms of radiation poisoning. The atomic weapon cast a long shadow over the world. Its terrible potential threatened the future survival of civilization itself. Atomic bombs, and their massively more destructive thermonuclear cousins, reshaped international relations, military strategy, and the manner in which the world imagined its future. As military professionals around the world struggled to incorporate the weapon into their plans, governments looked on at the ruins of Hiroshima and Nagasaki and were forced to grapple with the prospect of the destruction of civilian targets on a massive scale. The defence of the homeland – civil defence (CD) – was part of their answer.

The Second World War had proven the extent of the civilian home front's vulnerability to enemy action. Most countries threatened by enemy attack have not only relied on active military defences to close with and destroy attacking forces, such as fighter aircraft and anti-aircraft weaponry, but also possessed "passive" defences, whose purpose was to absorb damage caused by the attack. Civil defence encompassed those passive defences that were concerned with minimizing risk to the population and infrastructure and that included professional and volunteer firefighters, police, wardens, nurses, engineers, and other trades that could rescue the injured, provide first aid to wounded civilians, and shelter the homeless. The Canadian government, drawing on the experience of the United Kingdom, maintained an Air-Raid Precautions (ARP) organization from 1939 to 1945, although an attack against Canada was considered increasingly unlikely as the war drew on. The substantial challenges posed by creating and maintaining an effective wartime civil defence organization figured heavily in post-war planning.

In this context, the Canadian government wrote plans for its post-war civilian defence organization in 1947. Planners believed that preparation was a prudent investment that might save Canadian lives and industrial potential in the event of another world war. Yet CD preparations for nuclear war proved more contentious, complicated, and costly than the government had anticipated, particularly during the economic transition from wartime conditions to peace.

Wartime ARP

Canada's Cold War CD plans were initially drawn from the ARP system created in the United Kingdom immediately preceding the Second World War. The Canadian government's plans for passive defence began in August 1936, in response to international rearmament. The organization existed only on paper until August 1939, when it became clear that Canada would soon be involved in a war with Germany. Wartime ARP was managed by the Department of Pensions and National Health, a post that was administered by Ian Mackenzie. Mackenzie had served as the minister of national defence from 1935 to 1939. Prime Minister William Lyon Mackenzie King had transferred him to the health portfolio because he lacked confidence in the minister's ability to administer defence efforts under the pressures of a total war.[1] When the war arrived, Mackenzie delegated his authority over ARP to provincial premiers in the Maritimes and in British Columbia, who formed provincial ARP committees to protect the population on the coasts.[2] The provincial organizations in turn advised municipalities in vulnerable areas to set up their own ARP organizations, drawing volunteers from the public. The federal government provided money to these areas to purchase fire prevention and safety equipment. In addition, the federal ARP organization distributed reprints of training manuals and information pamphlets published by its British counterpart, which was further along in its preparations because of the enormous public anxiety that had developed in the interwar period over the potential threat of enemy air attacks. British preparations met their first tests in 1940, when the first German bomber raids struck the United Kingdom. British ARP workers gained operational experience in firefighting, first aid, and rescue from responding to the German bombing runs during the Battle of Britain.[3]

In Canada, voluntary ARP organizations were established in Halifax, Saint John, Quebec City, Montreal, Vancouver, and Victoria, the cities that the military assessed as the communities most vulnerable to aerial or naval bombardment.[4] ARP efforts were intensified in June 1940, following the German breakout on the Western front and the fall of France.[5] Provincial premiers or designated officials were given authorization to conduct air-raid drills and blackout or dimout exercises, so long as they did not interfere with the activities of the local military forces.[6] Ontario and Quebec were the least enthusiastic about their newfound responsibility for ARP, but under wartime regulations they had little choice but to formally accept the duties. Only fourteen voluntary ARP organizations were established in Ontario in 1940. Citizens who joined ARP or Civilian Protection Committees in these provinces did so as much out of imperial sentiment as fear. For example, in Verdun, Quebec, most of those individuals who first joined were British-born Canadians with a keen attachment to the cities in Britain under threat from Nazi bombers.[7]

Coastal areas in the Maritimes and in British Columbia, on the other hand, embraced ARP because the threat from enemy action appeared to be credible. The Halifax branch manager of the Canadian Bank of Commerce recalled how quickly the city had dimmed its lights and adopted other wartime measures for the home front, its officials recognizing the threat from German submarines.[8] The Japanese attack on Pearl Harbor in December 1941 frightened municipal and provincial authorities, who argued that ARP organizations made up of volunteer firefighters were insufficient to protect the industrial port cities. F. Maclure Solanders, commissioner of the Saint John Board of Trade, wrote to the prime minister to assert that his city's industrial contribution to the war demanded protection from modern anti-aircraft and coastal gun emplacements, not unarmed citizen volunteers.[9]

On the Pacific coast, British Columbians blacked out their windows at night because they feared attack by Japanese submarines or airplanes. Provincial officials in Alberta were also concerned about their vulnerability because of the work that was underway to build the Alaska Highway through their territory. The premier of Alberta, William Aberhart, wrote to William Lyon Mackenzie King on 16 April 1942 to demand additional military protection and resources for the ARP, because "the citizens of this province have been warned continually by persons in authority of the danger of attack from the Japanese bases established in the Aleutians as well as by carrier-based planes off the Pacific Coast."[10] The federal government rejected the request because Alberta was too far inland to be attacked by air. Air-raid wardens in other inland cities pestered the military for additional training and material to better defend the homes in their communities. Ottawa's ARP Executive Committee asked the military to train its wardens on the light machine guns that they planned to mount on the rooftops of public buildings. Such requests were universally rejected on the grounds that wardens, however determined to protect civilians, were not soldiers.[11] The government did not intend to divert resources from the Atlantic and European theatres of war where they were needed most, even if local communities believed that they were at immediate risk from enemy attack. ARP organizations were therefore dependent on local interest and resources in order to thrive during the war.

Attracting and retaining the interest of volunteers in the ARP organization during the war was a consistent problem. The fear of attack prompted communities across the country to take some form of precautions. At its peak, 634 ARP units operated across the country, staffed by approximately 218,511 volunteer and paid personnel, but these numbers were highly fluid from month to month.[12] Many of the most senior volunteers were veterans of the First World War seeking to contribute to the war effort.[13] Participation in the ARP organization did not translate into compliance with ARP directives. Public interest in following the rules fluctuated depending on the overall direction of the war and the proximity of the threat to Canada. Results consequently varied across the country. Local officials in many parts of the country were frustrated by the unwillingness of civilians to abide by blackout regulations or to pay any attention to local ARP exercises.[14] There was, for example, a long chain of correspondence between the RCMP, ARP officials, and the Military District Command in the Gaspé region over whether or not drivers who failed to observe roadblocks or dim their headlights should be charged. In the end, no action was taken, but the correspondence reveals some of the confusion and irritation over the civilian population's inability to comprehend risk.[15] In many centres with ARP organizations, officials considered publicity to be the answer to a wide range of problems, including raising public awareness and ensuring compliance with ARP measures.

Publicity for the ARP organization resembled the publicity drives developed during the war to influence Canadians to purchase Victory Bonds, support salvage drives, and abide by rationing regulations. Like the merchant marine, industrial workers, and salvage-savvy housewives, ARP was publicly touted as a fourth arm of the armed services.[16] Convincing the public of the possible threat from distant enemy aircraft, however, remained a sizeable obstacle. As a way of reminding the public about the threat of bombers, the Royal Canadian Air Force (RCAF) stations in Canada sometimes contributed "bombers" to blackout exercises and mock air raids, but the most popular method was to draw attention to the good work of the ARP organizations in Britain during the nightly air raids. For example, in March 1943, Stanley Lewis, the mayor of Ottawa, addressed a "monster rally" to discuss his experience while caught in a London air raid.[17] The rally, and others like it, was held to win over a skeptical public and to persuade idle volunteers that their contribution was valuable and still needed.[18] As Allied fortunes improved by the end of 1943, the public became less convinced of the need for the organization.

In August 1943, W.C. Mainwaring, chairman of the British Columbia ARP Advisory Council, pleaded with Ian Mackenzie, who represented British Columbia's interests in the Cabinet, for a strong federal government message in support of provincial ARP measures. He lamented that favourable war news in Europe and Alaska and negative press editorials about the ARP had caused the public and ARP personnel in the province to become "alarmingly apathetic."[19] A month later, Lieutenant-General Kenneth Stuart, Chief of the General Staff (CGS), advised Mackenzie that the publicity battle was already lost. "Nothing short of a strong statement," Stuart argued, would do much good, "and it then becomes tantamount to crying wolf."[20] Local military and ARP officials continued to publicly stress the need for ARP measures and exercises, but plans were already well under way to dismantle the organization. The Canadian Chiefs of Staffs Committee (COSC) concluded in November 1943 that most of Canada was probably immune to attack. Ontario, Quebec, and Alberta were removed from the vulnerable areas list – these provinces demobilized their ARP units in 1944.[21] The following October, the COSC ruled that an attack on British Columbia was considered "possible but highly improbable." The Cabinet War Committee concluded several days later that the Department of Pensions and National Health should discontinue support for ARP in Canada.[22] General demobilization of ARP volunteers did not occur until March 1945. The Cabinet War Committee gave a reprieve to certain areas, such as Halifax, where war risks remained. This decision proved to be wise because volunteers in the Halifax ARP organization saved many lives when they evacuated residents of Bedford Basin away from a burning storage depot for naval ammunition. It exploded shortly afterwards.

The organization was officially disbanded by an Order-in-Council issued on 11 September 1945, after hostilities were fully ended. Not everyone was convinced that dismantling the entire ARP organization was a good idea. In January 1945, Brigadier-General Alexander Ross, a highly decorated veteran of the battle of Vimy Ridge in the First World War, and Mackenzie's director of ARP from 1943 to 1945, contemplated the future of continental defence. In a letter to Mackenzie, Ross argued that it "might be considered advisable" to maintain a skeletal CD organization for post-war defence arrangements and offered his services for future consideration.[23]

Others were more vocal and lobbied for continued vigilance. In an editorial in *The Post: Official Organ of the Civil Defence Guild of British Columbia,* one ARP advocate denounced the government's decision to disband the organization. To *The Post* editorialist, the detonation of the atom bombs over Japan clearly signaled a new era:

> Every week we read in the Press of the diabolical inventiveness of scientists and ordnance experts in producing newer and more lethal weapons with ranges of over 3000 miles. Does anyone doubt that these weapons will soon be in the hands

of all nations and that in a war of the future they will be mainly directed against civil populations? Does anyone doubt that, if there is another war, air attack on civilians will be intensified and whole cities will be suddenly destroyed long before the main armies come to grips, let alone the reserve forces? Does anyone think that should the Four Horsemen again be let loose on an unhappy world that any country would have as much as one month's grace to perfect its Civil Defence?[24]

Like Ross, the editorialist considered that a small, well-trained cadre, in co-operation with the armed forces, local police, and firefighting organizations, would be a sufficient basis on which to train the rest of the population in the event of a future war. However, in the relatively optimistic atmosphere of the immediate post-war period, ARP organizations and their promoters had already been forgotten.

Atomic Anxiety, 1946-48

In the glow of victory, the Canadian government turned its attention to winning the peace, through extensive social spending. Defence planning after the war was accordingly cautious, frugal, and attentive to the demands of a war-weary public. Proposals from the military for a large standing peacetime force to support the United Nations were rejected out of hand by Prime Minister Mackenzie King, who believed the government should plan "on the basis of a better order of things and not assume serious obligations as suggested."[25] The Cabinet Defence Committee (CDC) decided in September 1945 that there was no reason to reassess future defence needs.[26] Despite the Soviet Union's international espionage efforts, posturing at the United Nations, and invective towards the West, few Canadian observers seriously believed that the Russians had any intention or ability to start a war until their own crumbling economy was in order.[27]

The detonation of the atomic bomb, however, had ignited the public's imagination, and it was accompanied by a torrent of speculation about what the weapon's power meant for military strategy and international relations. In 1946, American journalists published the first bestselling books about the atomic bomb and its unexpected radioactive side effects. John Hersey's narrative *Hiroshima* was the most influential of these books, describing the carnage and chaos caused by the bomb in unflinching tones. Hersey vividly captured the personal and social effects of radiation poisoning on Japanese civilians with painstaking and tragic detail.[28] His account, originally serialized in *The New Yorker* and later published in book form, was widely read and distributed.

A more chilling perspective of future warfare was found in David Bradley's account of the first post-war atomic bomb tests in the Pacific. Bradley described the lethal radioactivity that coated warships after the tests. He was convinced that defence against the atomic bomb was impossible and that "the devastating influence of the bomb and its unborn relatives may affect the land and its wealth – and therefore its people – for centuries through the persistence of radioactivity."[29] Other authors, predicting the future character of war, resorted to rhetorical device to describe scenes that had previously been the domain of science fiction.

Some of the early debates about atomic weapons filtered into parliamentary proceedings about Canadian defence policy. The modest establishment of the post-war armed services was designed to furnish Canada with a well-balanced army, air force, and navy, which would train volunteers as they joined to fight in any future conflict. The foremost duty of the permanent force was to defend Canadian territory under the conditions of the Canada/US Basic Security Plan, which was agreed to at the Permanent Joint Board of Defence.[30] Douglas Abbott, the minister of defence, defended this "flexible" policy, which he argued could meet the challenges posed by changing international conditions and military technology. Abbott dismissed opposition demands for a greater defence investment by stating that if a war broke out in the next few years, any Canadian contribution would not have any "perceptible effect."[31] Quoting a widely read article published by the famous German physicist and pacifist Albert Einstein in the *New York Times* magazine, Co-operative Commonwealth Federation critic Henry Archibald agreed with the minister and argued presciently that "a few more tanks or a few more aeroplanes is useless ... where will your army be? It will be away out somewhere with all the cities and communications cut out behind it."[32]

The Canadian government and its armed services worried that extensive media coverage, and the failure of early efforts to institute international control over the atom, would lead to unchecked "atomic anxiety." Beginning in 1947, the government considered the revival of a civilian defence organization to meet the hazards of the new weapons.[33] In March, the COSC asked the newly created Defence Research Board (DRB) to investigate civilian defence measures conducted during the Second World War.[34] As research progressed, Brooke Claxton, who succeeded Abbott as minister of national defence in 1946, unveiled the government's first statement of post-war defence policy in the House of Commons.[35]

Though Ottawa hoped to preserve peace, Claxton informed the House that the lack of progress at the United Nations in 1946 demanded that the government prepare an insurance policy in the event of war. Last on the list of his department's long-term objectives was the "organization of government departments and civilian agencies capable of putting into immediate effect a plan for civil defence."[36] Claxton promised the House of Commons that Canada's CD would be based on a firmly grounded, practical planning process based on reliable intelligence, which would not entertain hysterical diatribes about "push-button wars" and other future threats featured in press accounts. However, the minister dismissed the opposition's suggestions for concrete, visible defence projects, such as national first aid training, as premature.[37]

The DRB's initial research led the board to recommend to Claxton that steps should be taken to assign authority and responsibility for "planning civil defence arrangements in light of recent scientific developments in war."[38] The recommendation attracted the attention of cabinet ministers and Lieutenant-General Charles Foulkes, CGS. Claxton was convinced that planning for civil defence should proceed "without delay," but he did not want to provoke public alarm about nuclear war preparations. Dr. Omand Solandt, chairman of the DRB, an accomplished expert in operational research and the only Canadian to accompany the British mission to Japan to investigate the effects of the Hiroshima bombing in November 1945, agreed with Claxton's cautious approach. Solandt advised that the planned CD agency should act as a limited advisory body to hospitals and industry about the location of those buildings that would likely be near target areas. Foulkes wanted a stronger organization and better intelligence about the atomic bomb. The general was particularly concerned about

alarmist statements being made in the press concerning the effects of atomic bombs in which people were being told that there was no defence against these weapons, thus building up a defeatist attitude in the country. He felt that someone in authority should be in a position to give information to groups of informed people that steps are being taken to protect the country in the case of another war.[39]

The minister of health, Ian Mackenzie, agreed with Foulkes, but disagreed with the DRB, which had concluded earlier that the Department of National Defence should not co-ordinate the activities of the CD agency. Mackenzie contended that CD was not simply an issue of public welfare but, rather, a matter of national security best handled by the armed forces.[40] Mackenzie's advice, based on his own frustration in dealing with unco-operative provinces about ARP during the war, went ignored. The unresolved questions about whether CD was a civilian or military, federal or provincial, responsibility created numerous obstacles to planning and preparations in the following years. In the initial planning discussions, however, alleviating the public's concern about the bomb without creating a panic was more important than clarifying roles and responsibilities.

Mackenzie perhaps also had in mind a disturbing article in *Maclean's* magazine. Colonel Wallace Goforth produced a short piece in October 1947 entitled

"If Atomic War Comes."[41] The author was ideally placed to comment as he was partly responsible for the creation of the DRB and had benefitted from his own personal experience in armament research during the Second World War and from his access to Solandt. As a result, Goforth's article contained the most accurate predictions about the trouble the Canadian government would encounter when preparing civilians for war. On the first page of his article, a crude drawing of an atomic fireball was superimposed on an aerial photograph of Winnipeg's downtown core. Concentric rings illustrated blast damage leading two-and-a-half miles from ground zero, and the image's caption explained that a bomb dropped over Portage and Main streets would kill 40,000, injure 60,000, and render 200,000 homeless.

Goforth estimated that if even twenty-five bombers managed to penetrate Canada's non-existent anti-aircraft defences, seventeen major centres would be destroyed, and the largest electric power plants and industries would cease production. Canada would suffer 1,450,000 killed and wounded right away, with a further 650,000 rendered homeless. Casualties would clog the hospitals. Canada would be back at its beginnings, Goforth explained: "The bleeding remnant of this Dominion would be set back economically and socially to the equivalent of its position at Confederation 80 years ago."[42] Goforth wrote his article to sway public opinion in favour of establishing an effective CD agency over the next ten years. He derided such fantastic options as rebuilding cities into subterranean "rabbit warrens" and, instead, offered an accurate prediction that some government facilities would be forced to go underground. He doubted that any government, whether federal or municipal, had the patience, foresight, and budget to adopt long-term protective measures. He predicted that the main impetus for a future CD organization would come from service clubs, women's institutes, chambers of commerce, and other "public-spirited" associations devoted to the welfare of their cities, much as had been the case during the Second World War.[43]

The COSC forwarded the DRB's final report to the CDC on 22 April 1948. The DRB presented more conservative recommendations for action in CD than Goforth had suggested. The DRB believed that international conflict in the future would include aerial attacks against continental North America and sabotage by enemy spies. Therefore, it was essential to begin planning for CD. The DRB defined civilian defence as "all those defensive measures that can be taken by or on behalf of the civil population to ensure that when such an attack is made the will to resist is maintained, and the economic and social organization of the community will function effectively in support of offensive operations."[44] The DRB had examined the state of plans in the United States and the United Kingdom and advised against importing either country's plan unaltered.

Canada's unique climate, and the division of authority over health services between the federal and provincial governments made it necessary to develop an independent CD policy.

Most importantly, the DRB recommended that CD should not be planned locally, as it had been during the Second World War. The problems that an atomic blast would cause meant that CD preparations and operations could not be limited to any one city. Efforts would have to be supervised and co-ordinated over a wider area through national, centralized planning. However, constitutional restrictions on federal powers forced the DRB to recommend that responsibility for the organization and operation of CD agencies had to remain at the provincial and municipal levels, unless the federal government was prepared to intervene extensively in areas of provincial control, such as health, welfare, and disaster relief, or in areas of municipal control, such as firefighting and policing. It was clear that the federal government was not pre-pared to do so.

The authors of the DRB report ultimately assigned federal responsibility for CD planning to both civilian and military authorities. The DRB researchers concluded that the armed forces, and especially the army, would have to carry out CD tasks, including rescue and emergency medical treatment immediately following an attack. They argued that the CD agency should be created within the Department of National Defence since plans could be shared directly with the COSC and the CDC, and approved internally, without the need to pass controversial legislation through the House of Commons.

As a first step, the DRB urged the immediate appointment of a civilian advisor to assist the minister of national defence in CD matters. The ideal candidate required military experience and an acumen for administration and public rela-tions. The advisor would be responsible for federal planning but would also delegate action to other government departments and agencies as often as pos-sible, precluding the need for a large support staff.[45] Cabinet approved most of the DRB's recommendations because no major expenditures or alarmist meas-ures were required immediately. Rapid progress would be impossible in any case, since responsibility for federal CD planning alone was divided between no less than twelve government departments and agencies, with plenty of op-portunities for bureaucratic impasses.[46]

A suitable appointment for the position of the CD advisor was not found until 7 October 1948, when Claxton selected retired Major-General Frederic Frank Worthington. He was a career army officer, a veteran of two world wars, and an advocate for military innovation who was directly responsible for the formation of the modern Canadian armoured corps during the Second World War. He came to Claxton's attention as a result of his command of the Pacific

FIGURE 4   Major-General F.F. Worthington, February 1951. *Source:* Library and Archives Canada, PA-141059

Coast Militia Rangers volunteer home defence force at the end of the war. Also of note were Worthington's capable post-war efforts as commissioner of the Canadian Red Cross during the Fraser River Valley flood in June 1948, where he supervised the distribution of food aid.[47] Worthington was suitable for the post because he was a distinguished veteran, a proven leader, and an administrator who had demonstrated his active interest in civilian defence.[48]

Claxton announced Worthington's appointment on 19 October 1948. When first approached by the press, Worthington stressed that he planned to establish something resembling a permanent disaster committee as a "sensible precaution," but not one that was worth getting excited over.[49] Press editorials welcomed Worthington's appointment and approved of his experience, but they were critical of the government's emphasis on general planning and questioned whether there would be time in a future war to translate plans on paper into action that would save lives.[50] Worthington's work to create such a plan meant reaching agreement within the federal government and with the provinces about the form and function of a Cold War CD organization. It is doubtful that Worthington realized the long, complicated, and painful task that was set before him.

Worthington's Plan for Civil Defence

In early November 1948, Worthington moved with his wife, Clara, who went by the name "Larry," from their home in British Columbia to Ottawa, where he met with Claxton to develop an outline for a Canadian CD organization to discuss with the provinces. Provincial support and, more importantly, participation were vital if his agency was to become effective. Claxton and Worthington agreed to pursue the decentralized CD plan approved by Cabinet in 1947. The federal agency would provide training and educational materials, gather intelligence about threats, and provide information and warnings about attacks to the provincial agencies for transmission to the concerned municipalities. Canadian cities would be directly responsible for recruiting and maintaining their own organizations, and their activities would be overseen and co-ordinated by provincial CD agencies.[51] After meeting with Claxton, Worthington departed on a cross-country tour to meet the provincial premiers and convince them to support the federal CD concept.

Worthington's meetings with the premiers in November-December 1948 had two aims. The first was to obtain their provisional support for the federal concept of the national organization. The second was to ensure that no individual province would implement its own civil defence plans prematurely, without federal input.[52] The proposed organization received a mixed reception from the provinces. The premiers of New Brunswick (J.B. McNair), Nova Scotia (Angus L. Macdonald), and Manitoba (D.L. Campbell) offered their full support for a decentralized civilian defence organization. Macdonald and McNair, in particular, welcomed the renewed federal interest in CD, since both men had been involved in the wartime ARP.[53]

The remaining provinces offered conditional support. Leslie Blackwell, Ontario's attorney general and an amputee from the First World War, agreed with Ottawa's proposed layout in principle. He told Worthington that Ontario would defer participation until it could evaluate a full and official federal policy. He gave Worthington his assurance that CD could be rapidly organized in the province once the proposed federal-provincial arrangements were finalized.[54]

Alberta's premier Ernest Manning was anxious to have an agency in place as soon as possible, but only on condition that the federal government assume the entire responsibility for planning, co-ordination, and organization. Manning explained that the municipalities would not otherwise follow the provincial government on what they believed to be a matter of national defence. He suggested that the government's best solution was to appoint experienced federal employees as heads of regional civil defence agencies, which would encompass multiple municipalities.[55] A centralized organization, he believed, would prevent regional parochialism in planning. By contrast, Saskatchewan's representative demanded a strong provincial voice in civil defence decisions, while Quebec officials were alone in refusing to extend any support to the program. Premier Maurice Duplessis stated that Quebec would decide when the time was appropriate to take any action for CD.[56] Duplessis and the other provincial representatives required little prompting to acknowledge threats against the civilian population. Only Prince Edward Island believed that it was immune to attack, but the premier agreed with Worthington that a CD organization in the province might be useful to prevent public hysteria if other areas in the country were bombed.

Worthington had been cautioned by the deputy ministers for national health and welfare, Dr. Graham Cameron and Dr. George Davidson, that the provinces would not want to provide any money in support of the proposed agency. Therefore, Worthington wisely avoided the subject in his initial discussions, seeking mainly to obtain general support.[57] Only BC premier W.B. Black raised the question, declaring that the federal government should pay the full bill for CD. Several provincial representatives argued that measures to prepare for natural disasters should take priority over measures for nuclear war. They reasoned that most of the population would volunteer their time to an organization designed to defeat a threat that they understood. Although they were approached individually, the provinces had already reached a consensus that investment in a program with peacetime applications would produce greater dividends than a standing force to meet a threat that might never arrive.

Most provincial governments informed Worthington that they wanted greater support for infrastructure improvements, especially the standardization of firefighting equipment across the country. In Canada, every municipality purchased its own firefighting equipment and frequently bought the cheapest material, which often proved incompatible with those in other cities. As a result, over fifty types of fire hose and hydrant couplings were in use in Ontario alone. In the event of a conflagration covering a wide area, municipalities whose stock of couplings was insufficient or destroyed would find themselves with hydrants that they were unable to use, since their neighbours used different equipment.[58] To his credit, Worthington took up this question with the Canadian Standards Association (CSA), with the assistance of Ontario fire marshal and wartime

ARP warden W.J. Scott. By 1950, the CSA grudgingly adopted the "Worthington" standard of fire hose coupling, prompting an extensive refitting of fire hydrants across the country. Saskatchewan's and British Columbia's demands for CD assistance were more extensive because they hoped federal money would build a more elaborate highway network and more hospitals, both of which would be useful during an attack but fell under provincial jurisdiction. Worthington received their proposals with heavy skepticism: "It rather smacks to me of endeavouring to obtain something for the Province under the guise of Civil Defence without too much expense, although ... the Trans-Canada highway certainly is important ... for any type of defence."[59]

Over the course of his two-month tour of the provinces, Worthington met with representatives of national volunteer organizations to negotiate their support for civil defence. The co-ordinator was most interested in obtaining the co-operation of the Canadian Red Cross and St. John Ambulance, since both groups had first aid and disaster response plans already. He would determine later how their organizations could be linked to the municipal CD organizations.[60] The last step in Worthington's intelligence gathering was to examine organizations in other countries, especially those of the United Kingdom and the United States. In early January, Worthington flew to London to meet with Sir John Hodsoll, the director general of Civil Defence Training in the Home Office and spent a week meeting with British civilian and military officials concerned with different elements of CD planning. In early February, Worthington went to occupied Germany to examine their anti-aircraft fortifications and air-raid bunkers, but was dismayed to learn that they had been demolished.[61] Worthington concluded his travels with a short visit with representatives of the Office of Civil Defense Planning in Washington to examine the American CD organization. Armed with new-found intelligence from abroad and support for the proposed CD program from the provinces, however provisional, Worthington returned to Ottawa and prepared to draft his report for Claxton.

Worthington worked with the deputy minister of defence, C.M. Drury, to produce final recommendations to the Cabinet on 17 March 1949. His report provided a basic plan for the organization of CD in Canada, which formed the basis for all future administration and planning. Worthington argued that a National Office of Civil Defence should be established immediately as a section of the Department of National Defence, with its responsibilities closely related to CD organizations already operating in the United Kingdom and the United States. Worthington informed Claxton that "the basic fundamentals of civil defence as provided by the British system have been adopted. The terminology leans slightly towards the United States due to the fact that Canada is geographically joined to the United States and for an emergency we must ensure joint understanding of methods and means adopted for the overall benefit of both countries."[62] The national office would be designed to meet "present requirements," meaning that it would carry on with the minimal staff for immediate planning. Worthington recommended that the federal CD agency should have directors to oversee three major activities: plans and operations, technical services, and training. The federal office would be headed by a civil defence co-ordinator, who would be accountable to the minister and responsible for developing national policy, co-ordinating activities with other government departments, provincial and municipal governments, public and private agencies including industry, and liaising with his British and American counterparts.[63]

The co-ordinator's responsibilities were consistent with the overall role envisioned for the federal CD office – namely to act as an advisory and co-ordinating body while urging existing federal government departments to use their resources to contribute to national preparations for civil defence, "these problems being simply an extension of the department's normal functions."[64] The national office, for example, would rely on intelligence from the COSC and the DRB to ensure that its policies would not conflict with existing or future mobilization plans for the army, navy, or air force.

The three proposed divisions would operate in a similar fashion. The director of plans and operations was tasked with co-ordinating plans with other agencies and departments, working closely with other divisions to develop and implement plans. Organizing the medical, hospital, and health aspects of civil defence fell under this directorship. The Department of Health and Welfare would provide advice about patient care and hospital policy, the Department of Transport would provide information to establish proposed evacuation and dispersal plans, and the RCAF would provide the infrastructure for the all-important early warning system.[65]

The role of the director of technical services was to supervise the technical aspects of the future CD programs. The office was meant to develop and approve designs for shelters or other tools for public protection against the effects of atomic, biological, and chemical warfare. Worthington called on the DRB and the Department of Reconstruction and Public Works to assist his technical services division with shelter designs and strategies for housing refugees from stricken cities as well as to develop a national communication system to co-ordinate resources in the event of an attack.

The training division was to develop and maintain a curriculum that focused on leadership training for wardens and rescue teams. In his report, Worthington proposed that this program could lead to a chain of national, regional, and municipal CD schools to train professional planners and volunteers alike in basic principles. The training director would also work to produce promotional material for the Department of National Defence's public relations group, for use in public education about "the risks involved and the means of self-protection in order to minimize panic and loss of life."[66] This material was sent to provincial CD agencies for national distribution.

Worthington's plan could not account for the forms that the provincial organizations would take, since most of the premiers he spoke with were reluctant to appoint provincial CD directors. This, in turn, formed a possible impediment to the effective formation of municipal units because Worthington's office was constitutionally bound to channel all information for the municipalities through the provinces. Without provincial directors, he could not be assured that federal resources and information would find their way to the cities. Worthington's planning did not include specific provisions for the cities because the federal government could not dictate municipal affairs. He hoped that the federal and provincial governments would negotiate a solution to the constitutional obstacles standing in the way of rapid progress, before the cities, acting from anxiety or public pressure, acted independently to create local CD organizations.

Worthington believed that his plan, which reflected many of the DRB's original recommendations, would prevent duplication of effort, unnecessary expenses, and conflict with provincial rights. The final phase of his program assumed that a sufficient number of leaders and key personnel would be trained to take part in exercises and, if necessary, to facilitate the rapid recruitment of volunteers to meet a wartime emergency. The final phase required interoperability between the Canadian and American CD organizations. The close proximity and shared infrastructure of North American target cities necessitated the mutual support and co-operation of the agencies across the border.[67] Worthington concluded his report to Claxton with the assurance that if his plan was approved by Cabinet, Canada's CD would be ready when required. However, the gatekeepers to Cabinet approval had their doubts about the viability of Worthington's plan.

Civil Defence Delayed ... and Then Accelerated

Claxton presented Worthington's program to the CDC on 21 March 1949. There it met with considerable criticism from Brigadier J.D.B. Smith, the committee's military secretary. Smith rightly noted that there was no evidence in Worthington's report of any agreement between the government departments about how to proceed, despite Worthington's considerable provincial and international consultations. Smith proposed the formation of a Joint Civil Defence Planning Staff. This staff would define the object of CD plans, determine the effective preparations needed, and make the final organizational recommendations.[68] A.D.P. Heeney, clerk of the Privy Council and Cabinet secretary, agreed and recommended the formation of an interdepartmental sub-committee of the Cabinet War Book Committee to reach agreement among the interested departments and agencies. Heeney noted a tension in the government's motives:

> The whole matter is complicated not only because of interdepartmental rami-fications but also because of the direct interest and responsibility of the provinces and of the local authorities. It will be hard to give the appearance of doing enough to satisfy the ebb and flow of public opinion and at the same time to provide against an emergency a really useful organization.[69]

Worthington was frustrated that the Cabinet did not act on his recommenda-tions immediately, and he held numerous meetings with representatives from concerned government departments in anticipation of Cabinet's approval. On 21 June 1949, he asked Norman Robertson, the chairman of the Cabinet War Book Committee, to form the sub-committee that Heeney had proposed. Robertson expanded the committee to admit deputy ministers from the Departments of National Defence, National Health and Welfare, Transport, Reconstruction and Development, Public Works, Veterans Affairs, Justice, and the Post Office.[70]

Worthington chaired the first meeting of the Sub-Committee on Civil Defence on 8 September and was not encouraged by the results. The deputy ministers in attendance agreed that a plan should be finalized, agreed to examine those areas that fell under their department's mandate, but rejected the idea of ap-proaching the provincial governments as being premature.[71] Worthington left the first meeting vexed by the sub-committee's cumbersome structure, which in his view neglected provincial interests in vital areas and would ultimately delay the implementation of his recommendations. He informed Claxton about these problems, but the minister was apparently satisfied with the progress. Claxton told Worthington not to worry about the time element.[72]

Strangely, it was municipal activity, not Soviet saber-rattling, that motivated the federal government in late 1949 to tackle the CD planning task with more speed. In the preceding year, Worthington had made contact with Churchill Mann, a gregarious retired general who had served on Lieutenant-General Harry Crerar's staff through Normandy and who had also been involved with the Canadian Red Cross after the war.[73] Toronto's city council had approached Mann to chair their Civil Defence Planning Committee after the Ontario Parliament passed its first CD legislation. The provincial CD bill reformed existing fire safety regulations and permitted the province to co-operate with the federal government and other provinces in fire equipment standardization, but it also prompted some municipalities to begin organizing CD in their communities.[74] Mann produced Toronto's first plan using wartime Canadian and British publications, and early post-war American reports and pamphlets, to suggest measures that would protect Toronto against atomic attack and sabotage using a blended force of CD volunteers and local militia forces. On 23 September 1949, he completed the first draft of his plan and contacted Worthington's office to obtain the federal government's input.[75]

The following day, US President Harry Truman announced to the public that the Soviet Union had successfully detonated their first atomic bomb in Semipalatinsk, in what is now Kazakhstan.[76] The news caused Worthington great concern, though not because of the obvious implication that the United States' confident monopoly over atomic weapons had just crumbled. The co-ordinator worried that other municipalities, influenced by public anxiety, would follow Toronto's lead and create their own CD corps without federal guidance. His concern was perhaps misplaced, since Mann had complained to Worthington previously about the disinterest of Toronto's city council in the impending atomic threat. Nevertheless, Worthington persuaded Mann to stop his activity until a federal plan had been worked out. The general feared that Toronto's planning might highlight to the press the federal CD program's lack of progress.[77] Worthington used Mann's example to prod his colleagues on the Sub-Committee on Civil Defence for visible progress in CD planning, before the municipalities attempted it on their own.[78]

His remarks proved prescient. A week later, Vancouver's mayor authorized a local organization because "the people were getting restive and a great deal of pressure was being brought on the city council."[79] As Worthington had feared, Toronto and Vancouver's planning and approaches already appeared to be at odds with one another. While Toronto gave the responsibility for CD to a retired general, Vancouver's Police Commission took on the job. The commission's draft plan overestimated the extent of damage a single atomic bomb would cause to Vancouver, and federal planners became concerned that their report, if unchanged, would only further incite public alarm. Worthington went to Vancouver to urge the Police Commission to adopt Toronto's draft plan and appoint an experienced co-ordinator, the retired Air Vice-Marshal F.V. Heakes. Heakes had been among the first Canadian representatives of the Canada-US Permanent Joint Board and had been responsible for the air defence of the shipping locks at Sault Ste. Marie, Ontario, during the war.[80] After the war, he was involved with the handling of refugees during the Fraser River Valley flood. Heakes agreed to take on the CD post because, as he explained to Worthington, he had been "a little bored" since his retirement.[81]

To the Sub-Committee on Civil Defence, Worthington argued forcefully that it was only a matter of time before Vancouver and Toronto's efforts would be duplicated elsewhere. He was able to point to examples in the United States, where their central planning had to be revised as the result of individual cities' pursuit of irrelevant preparations without reference to the federal government. Chicago's experience was cited as an example. That city's planning staff had shifted their emphasis in emergency planning towards countermeasures for biological warfare, based on a specious claim that the atomic bomb was obsolete.[82] The time had arrived for a federal plan to be developed in co-operation with the provinces in order to ensure an integrated and even approach to civilian defence that would avoid hysteria and heavy financial commitments before an emergency arose.

On 20 October, the Canadian armed forces disclosed their revised expectations of attack to the CD planning committee, lending additional weight to Worthington's concerns. The Soviet Union's newly revealed atomic capability led the COSC to conclude that the Soviet Union would soon be able to initiate long-range atomic strikes against urban and industrial areas using one-way bomber attacks that would break down civilian morale and cripple Canada's military potential.[83] Worthington used the opportunity offered by the COSC's estimate to reform the Sub-Committee on Civil Defence and to submit a plan for immediate action to accelerate CD development.

Worthington successfully recast the immediate and long-term objectives of the federal CD office to parallel the new military planning assumptions and public anxiety over the atomic bomb.[84] He recommended to Claxton that the time had come to involve the provinces, the municipalities, and outside agencies such as the Canadian Red Cross and St. John Ambulance in a joint planning process, with clear divisions of responsibility.[85] The threat also demanded that CD organizations be developed in Halifax, Quebec City, Montreal, Ottawa, Toronto, Hamilton, Windsor, Sault Ste. Marie, Sarnia, Winnipeg, Edmonton, Vancouver, and Calgary – all cities that could be considered to be targets for Soviet bombers because they were hubs of communication or industry, major population centres, or all of the above. Co-operation from these cities and their provincial representatives was required immediately to develop a nation-wide warning system, plans for blast shelters in target cities, national co-ordination of the medical and fire services, and the construction of stockpiles of medical and alimentary provisions to support internally displaced persons.

In order to be fully effective, federal, provincial, and municipal plans would need to consider the preparations conducted in the United States, especially in the case of border cities such as Windsor, Sault Ste. Marie, and Sarnia. The only immediate federal expenditure would be for the development of civil defence bulletins and advisory warnings to pass to the provinces and municipalities to guide their planning and the execution of the immediate priorities. The financial estimates could be revisited later on a cost-sharing basis once the immediate priorities had been planned with the provinces.[86] If no action was taken, Worthington warned, public apprehension and overreaction to the atomic threat would continue. There would likely be criticism of the federal government "for not taking the initiative and giving some guidance."[87]

Claxton submitted Worthington's suggestions to the CDC for approval, recommending another round of provincial consultations to resolve the pressing problems that he had identified. His most important recommendation was that the federal government should formally request each province to appoint a provincial civil defence co-ordinator to liaise with Worthington, begin planning for provincial services, and provide guidance to municipalities that were anxious to begin some form of preparation.[88] Civil defence planning, cautious and halting during the first years of the Cold War, took another small step forward into the public arena.

Over the following year, Worthington concentrated on the mobilization of provincial allies to support joint projects, and he obtained the co-operation of the RCAF in planning for an early warning system. He also initiated discussions with the Canadian medical profession to obtain their support for a plan to disperse new hospital construction away from likely blast areas in target cities. Worthington's progress continued to be limited by a lack of formal channels of communication between his agency, other government departments, and their provincial counterparts. Another obstacle to properly co-ordinating activities across the federal government was the reluctance of senior civil servants to co-operate without a ruling from Cabinet about their specific responsibilities.[89]

Support from Cabinet was no more forthcoming. Worthington had hoped that the CDC would approve the organization that he had spent nearly two years crafting in interdepartmental committees. He aimed to gain leverage with other government departments that had been reluctant to offer their full co-operation and be able to set the provinces and communities across the country into action. Worthington's diary provides insight into the CDC's deliberations and how apparently out of touch the Cabinet was with the projected level of threat to Canada.

By his own account, Worthington's presentation to the CDC in March 1950 was disastrous. Prime Minister Louis St. Laurent examined his proposed plan silently before making "rather a long dissertation on the impracticability of building a lot of underground shelters in the city."[90] Defence minister Claxton had provisionally approved Worthington's plan, and during the meeting he attempted, unsuccessfully, to persuade St. Laurent, who Worthington believed had little interest in military affairs, of the plan's validity and the limited risks to the government of adopting it.

Worthington insisted that it was necessary to study the subject before a war since measures could not be put into effect after a bomb had fallen. St. Laurent moved on to the early warning system and suggested that planning would be acceptable as long as it did not involve more than "looking around until such time as war might come."[91] Worthington interjected that the installation of an early warning system after the war had started was utterly meaningless, and he added that the Americans would do it for Canada if Cabinet refused. An unidentified member of the committee reiterated that the Canadian CD program would have time to mobilize and plan after war was declared. An incredulous Worthington responded: "I was willing to lay my life [sic] that if war came an attack on this country would come with little or no warning." When asked whether evacuation plans were necessary, he replied that having a plan to evacuate the living before an attack would be easier and more hygienic than having to clean up the dead afterwards. An embarrassed Claxton intervened to "smooth the ruffled feathers."[92]

As the discussion continued, it became apparent that the government was opposed to taking any action that might provoke undue public alarm. Lester B. Pearson, the secretary of state for external affairs, argued that the draft letter to the provinces concerning the need for CD was too alarmist and might frighten people. Worthington countered by claiming that the people were more likely to be frightened by a lack of direction. St. Laurent calmly ignored Worthington's bluster and demanded a redrafted letter. Norman Robertson, Heeney's successor as Cabinet secretary, suggested instead that the military should take over civil defence. This would eliminate the need to involve the provinces and enable the government to keep planning in private for a while longer. Claxton and Worthington both leapt to the defence of the military, which had already considered and rejected extensive involvement in CD. They asserted that one of the principal tasks of civil defenders was to provide for the protection of civilians so that the armed forces would be free for military operations against the Soviet Union.

Despondent, Worthington asked Cabinet if it had decided to reject his plan, but the CDC did not send him away empty-handed. The committee record noted that they approved Claxton's planned organization, authorizing the defence minister to deal directly with the provinces and for Worthington to work with provincial CD chairmen.[93] In discussing the committee's decision with his staff, Worthington clarified the government's instructions. Cabinet had merely permitted further planning activities and consultation with provinces and national agencies. The Sub-Committee on Civil Defence was forbidden to offer "firm commitments" to anyone.[94] Worthington later reflected that the prime minister had no idea what CD was and had likely not been briefed on any of the pressing matters that the advisor had come to discuss. Worthington remarked sourly that nothing short of a catastrophe would secure any more support from Cabinet, and he discounted their concerns about unnecessarily frightening the public. He added to his diary that "the only frightened people I knew of were sitting in the room."[95]

Conclusion

Early threats of atomic annihilation in the post-war period inspired the federal government, some provinces, and several cities to establish a peacetime civil defence organization. Yet the form that Canada's civil defence would take, and the extent of its responsibilities, was far from settled during the five years following the end of the Second World War. Planners drew on Canada's wartime passive defence, and from similar organizations in the United Kingdom and the United States, to draft initial plans, but these conflicted with the federal government's post-war priorities, provincial rights, and the Canadian military's mobilization plans. In 1949, Worthington's CD office used the period following the detonation of a Soviet atomic bomb, which brought about independent, unsanctioned civil defence planning in Canadian cities, to accelerate federal plans. Civil defence's meagre progress was characteristic of the Canadian government's hesitant and cautious awakening to the stakes of the Cold War conflict. The federal leadership's priorities were firmly set on domestic reconstruction and not on rearmament, and this focus did not change until the government's position was overtaken by events overseas. Canada had pledged support for collective security in both the United Nations and in NATO by 1949, but this commitment did not translate into any substantial infusion of funding for the armed forces, nor was it matched by any concrete civil defence preparations. Everything changed with the Communist invasion of South Korea the following year, which forced CD to expand past the planning table and reach into Canadian communities as the Canadian government raced to rearm in preparation for a third world war.[96]

The Korean War and the Trouble with Civil Defence, 1950-53

THE INVASION OF SOUTH KOREA by Communist-controlled North Korea on 25 June 1950 took Canada by surprise. The United States-led war and the massive Chinese intervention that followed shocked the Canadian government onto a Cold War footing. The urgency of the crisis forced the government to set its post-war agenda of demobilization and reconstruction aside. Cabinet ministers dusted off wartime economic controls, the RCMP sniffed through the civil service for possible Communist infiltrators, and Parliament supported huge budgetary increases for a rearmament program that reactivated the Canadian defence industry and doubled the size of the Canadian armed services.[1] In the atmosphere of crisis in the fall and winter of 1950-51, fearing that the conflagration in Korea was just the opening act for an offensive in Western Europe, military and government planners pushed forward with contingencies for another world war.

Civil Defence Canada benefitted from the rearmament program, moving to a new department and receiving new spending powers. Provinces and municipalities undertook extensive civil defence (CD) preparations that reached into the communities for volunteers. Rapid expansion, however, brought about protracted debates over fiscal and constitutional responsibility for CD. The resources required to develop plans and infrastructure to deal with an atomic attack exceeded what the provinces and municipalities could reasonably afford to pay. The provinces instead demanded money from Ottawa, while regional and local CD organizations languished in a state of inaction and confusion. Civil defence was kept alive in many communities only through the effective leadership and strong personalities of full-time and volunteer co-ordinators, most of whom were retired senior military officers. For these newly minted civic leaders, progress in CD was most evident when the public's attention was keenly focused on the possible consequences of nuclear war. As the Korean War settled slowly into an armistice, even the best CD co-ordinators' personal charm and leadership proved insufficient to sustain public interest in war preparations.

Civil defence planners made little progress in the first few months of the Korean War, as the government struggled to piece together a brigade of volunteers to contribute to the UN mission. Defence minister Brooke Claxton, assisted by the federal CD co-ordinator F.F. Worthington, hosted the first Dominion-Provincial Conference on Civil Defence in Ottawa. The conference, which sought agreement between the federal and provincial representatives on areas of responsibility in CD planning, was inconclusive. The provinces generally refused to co-ordinate CD among their municipalities, and the federal government did not offer financial incentives for the provinces and municipalities to begin serious planning for war.

Worthington used the summer of 1950 to refine his plans for a Canadian CD organization. As a result of his study of British and American preparations, Worthington envisioned a system based on local target surveys, which divided the country into "target areas," "cushion areas," and "reception areas." Defining regions of the country in these terms had an important effect on CD funding, planning assumptions, and public acceptance. Target areas comprised the big cities – major population or industrial centres such as Montreal or Sudbury whose destruction would jeopardize the Canadian war effort. Target cities required organizations that were capable of taking immediate action to minimize destruction, including the establishment of extensive rescue, firefighting, engineering, and first-aid capabilities to co-ordinate evacuation and rescue civilians trapped in crumbling or burning buildings. Cushion areas were towns and villages that surrounded cities in a fifty-mile concentric ring outside the area of devastation. Civil defence operations in these towns depended on sufficient personnel and good communication across municipal boundaries so that they could supply reinforcements to rescue efforts within the burning cities and accommodate displaced persons for immediate treatment and evacuation to outlying areas.

Outside the target and cushion areas, which together formed a "civil defence zone," the reception area needed volunteers to provide long-term relief. These volunteers would register and billet displaced and injured people evacuated during the post-attack period. Underlying Worthington's plan was the promise of military support. In the event that all three area organizations failed, the armed forces would have to be called in as a last resort. Civil Defence Canada promoted Worthington's plan in *Civil Defence Manual no. 1: Organization for Civil Defence,* the first official Canadian CD manual published for public distribution. They released it in the fall and winter of 1950, just as the situation in Korea reached its nadir.[2] The first printing, distributed free of charge to the provinces and municipalities, was totally exhausted by January 1951.[3] According to Ontario's provincial secretary, Arthur Welsh, Canadian municipalities had been "crying for guidance" about how to prepare their communities for war, a possibility that seemed ever more likely after the Chinese army marched into Korea, throwing the UN force back on its heels.[4]

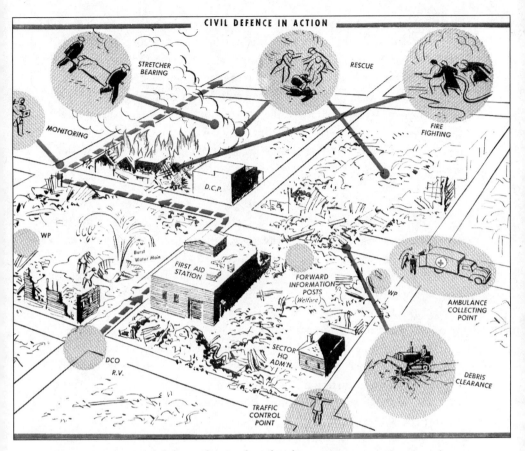

FIGURE 5   Most civil defence planners based early strategies on wartime experience. The target area operations shown here resembled wartime Air-Raid Precautions work in the United Kingdom. *Source: Operations and Control of the Civil Defence Services.*

Rearmament and Civil Defence

The allied reversal in Korea in October 1950 prompted a re-examination of Canada's defence policies. Like US policy makers, Canadian officials interpreted the Chinese assault as a feint designed to distract the West and divert scarce resources from the Soviet Union's real target: Western Europe. At a midnight Cabinet meeting on 28-29 December, ministers were informed that the Russians would be capable of launching an assault against Europe as early as May 1951. Brooke Claxton and Lester Pearson sombrely warned their colleagues that "the only safe assumption is that the period of greatest danger has already begun."[5] In response to the crisis, Canadian defence spending increased to its highest ever: $5 billion over three years, resulting in new equipment, extensive recruiting, and a new Department of Defence Production, overseen by C.D. Howe to co-ordinate the effort. Howe, a successful businessman-turned-administrator, had overseen Canada's industrial and economic effort during the Second World War, and though he was unconvinced that the setbacks in Korea warranted the alarm they received, he easily stepped back into his wartime role. Howe showed how the Korean War had changed the government's attitude towards military spending when he remarked that "if the army decides they want a gold-plated piano ... we buy the gold-plated piano."[6] The armed services had seen their numbers and budgets cut to the bone during the government's post-war de-mobilization. Now they had a licence to spend money.[7]

Buried in the torrent of defence spending for the Korean War was $700,000 that Claxton had allocated to CD for the 1951-52 fiscal year. The federal government's first financial commitment also guaranteed that Worthington could depend on greater budgetary support in the future. He immediately prepared an ambitious five-year plan to "fully" prepare Canada for atomic attack. His principal objective was to recruit a wartime CD organization that was supported by 200,000 volunteers working in every Canadian target city and every population centre with more than 10,000 inhabitants. He also requested authority from the federal government to pay 33 percent of the costs for fire hose conversion, to supply financial incentives for the public to begin converting their basements into shelters, to build national stockpiles of medical supplies, bedding, food, and other essentials for the wounded and homeless, and to provide training equipment to CD volunteers.[8]

However, $700,000 was not nearly enough to complete all of these tasks. Claxton used Worthington's plan to make a case before the Cabinet Defence Committee (CDC) for more robust CD funding on 20 February 1951. He asked for $1 million for training equipment; 16,000 uniforms for volunteers; 400 fire pump trucks; an additional $900,000 for the stockpiling program; $350,000 for the construction of a national CD college, which was to be completed by 1952; and $250,000 for rescue equipment and warning sirens. An investment of $5 million, Claxton advised, could purchase and stock 1,000 group shelters for the public.

The defence minister admitted, however, that these programs could not begin until he reached a cost-sharing agreement with the provinces. His most im-mediate priority was to obtain financial assistance for training aids, provincial CD schools, and educational materials. Civil Defence Canada obtained more money, but only a fraction of Claxton's $6,476,000 estimate survived the CDC's review, a surprising defeat for his department during the spending boom that occurred between April and December 1951, when the cost of the rearmament program averaged $5.5 million per day.[9] Claxton's failure to obtain more money for CD, however, reflected government plans to build up Canada's air defences and contribute to a credible military deterrent to Soviet expansion in Europe. Claxton and his armed forces advisors agreed that Korea was a sideshow to a coming Soviet gamble over Germany.[10] The critical workload faced by the Department of National Defence in co-ordinating recruitment and rearmament to support operations in Korea as well as NATO's commitment to Western Germany knocked CD to the bottom of Claxton's list of priorities. In the shuffle, Civil Defence Canada was as much a casualty as a beneficiary of rearmament. The burden of preparing cities for possible destruction was gladly shifted onto the provinces, and Claxton happily shifted his CD responsibilities onto one of his Cabinet colleagues.

As a result of Worthington's emphasis on welfare, public health, and rescue planning, representatives from the Department of National Defence persuaded Cabinet's War Book Committee to transfer the main role of CD organization and planning to the Department of National Health and Welfare. The CDC agreed that the Department of Health and Welfare's already "extensive relations with provincial and municipal authorities" could accelerate CD progress. Privy Council Order 985 authorized the departmental handover of CD to Health and Welfare. The change was announced to the provinces at the second Dominion-Provincial Conference on Civil Defence on 23 February 1951.[11]

In his opening comments to the assembled provincial delegates, Claxton claimed that CD was outside the Department of National Defence's mandate, which dealt "only with matters relating directly to military defence."[12] The purpose of the meeting, however, was to determine financial responsibility for CD. Cash-strapped municipalities had examined the government's municipal guide and were already in rebellion. In November 1950, the Canadian Federation of Mayors and Municipalities (CFMM), which had at first supported federal plans, changed their minds about paying for local CD once they realized the complexity of the job and the costs that they would have to absorb.[13] Provincial delegates who hoped for a government announcement increasing their share of spending were disappointed. The federal government did commit funding to cover some costs, including the provision of more training aids and manuals, radiological detection equipment and protective uniforms and badges for volunteers, and warning systems for cities with a population over 20,000. The government committed to build and maintain a national stockpile of medical equipment at no cost to the provinces. The federal government also agreed to pay a third of the overall costs of purchasing fire equipment and provincial standardization programs. The remainder of the bill for CD would rest with the provinces and municipalities.[14]

The shift to the Department of National Health and Welfare received national press coverage, much of which was favourable. Headlines praised the government's decision to transfer the agency, and the leadership of Paul Martin, the health and welfare minister, as a timely move that would ensure that CD did not get buried under conflicting priorities in the Department of National Defence. Martin's takeover drew even greater attention because a secret list of seven Canadian atomic targets was circulated at the Dominion-Provincial Conference of Civil Defence.[15] The CFMM, apparently mollified by federal commitments to a greater share of CD expenditures, issued a statement demanding action from the provinces and promoting the municipality's key role in co-ordinating CD. Local CD planning, the executive stated, was "in conformity with the Canadian pattern and tradition," and it developed "initiative and esprit de corps which are absolutely essential for effective civil defence."[16]

The *Globe and Mail* cautiously approved of the new CD arrangement in the hopes that it would give direction to a public that "must know exactly what is expected of it." The editors argued that Martin's appointment made good sense because of the essential nature of the services that welfare agencies could deliver in an emergency.[17] Martin made a gracious speech directed at the provinces during the conference, but he was not altogether pleased with his new responsibility, which he believed to be a distraction from his goals to improve national health programs.

In private, Martin thought CD a "frustrating assignment" and a "real headache."[18] His years as head of the federal CD organization were marked by heated public battles with the provinces, especially Ontario and Quebec, which refused to increase their commitments to CD following the 1951 conference. Both provinces' representatives attacked the federal government in the press and denounced the costs of CD to the provinces. They argued that the federal government had abandoned its constitutional responsibility to pay the entire costs of Canada's national defence – and what was a nuclear CD program if not a contribution to national defence?[19]

In late February, Ontario Premier Leslie Frost and Provincial Secretary Arthur Welsh defended the paltry $25,000 budget that they reserved for CD committees and blamed the federal government for not presenting a credible plan earlier. The provincial opposition joined in the attack against the federal CD program: "Ottawa kicks civil defense around and clearly implies it is unimportant ... Yet it then tells us to tighten our belts and dig up five billions [sic] for the defense program."[20] Neither Welsh nor Frost mentioned the federal government's new financial commitments or made reference to any of the admittedly limited progress made in federal planning.

At first, the Quebec government appeared more co-operative than their Ontario counterparts, passing the first legislation in Canada to create a provincial CD organization. Even the federal government had not passed legislation through the House of Commons to establish its CD office, as had the United Kingdom.[21] The Quebec law appointed a co-ordinator and authorized Quebec municipalities to enter into regional CD arrangements and commit expenditures, subject to the approval of the Municipal Commission of Quebec.[22] Paul Sauvé, Quebec's minister for youth and social affairs, a senior member of Duplessis's Cabinet and the minister responsible for CD, signalled that the law's passage did not mean his province was going to accept a major share of the cost of CD. It was Quebec's stated position that the federal government was shirking its constitutional responsibility at a time when tax dollars were being spilled into national defence. Bill 73 committed Quebec to do the bare minimum asked of it by the federal government. Sauvé justified the bill as a confidence-building measure, passed "to assure those who elected us that we accept the full measure of responsibility under *normal conditions*."[23] Normal conditions included natural disasters and floods but not nuclear war, and Quebec's position on this central point did not change over the next decade.

Civil Defence in Winnipeg

The attention given by the press to federal-provincial infighting about CD concealed progress elsewhere. Some provinces and their municipalities chose to invest in their own CD organizations without waiting for a national consensus. Organizations such as the one that developed in Winnipeg benefitted from capable leaders and modest aims. In November 1950, the Manitoba legislature formed a Provincial Civil Defence Control Committee that consisted of the premier, the minister of CD, and the minister of health. The province envisioned a system that prepared the public for civil disaster and atomic attack and encouraged regional planning in spite of the provincial Cabinet's qualms about the long-term costs of such a program.[24]

In December 1950, Winnipeg was the first city to form an operational CD organization, an initiative perhaps prompted by the disastrous Red River floods that year. Representatives of eighteen municipalities, including Winnipeg, St. Boniface, and Assiniboia, agreed to incorporate a large regional organization – the Greater Winnipeg Civil Defence Committee (GWCDC), under the control of Winnipeg Alderman J. Gurzon Harvey.[25] The larger organization was created because municipalities in the greater Winnipeg area had already established small-scale CD groups after the outbreak of hostilities in Korea. Officials in Winnipeg, encouraged by Ottawa, argued that the GWCDC would prevent the inefficiency and overlapping effort that would likely result if each municipality continued to plan in isolation. The mayor of St. Boniface, George C. Maclean, called an emergency meeting of all citizens to vote on the creation of a CD organization in July 1950. The citizens in attendance voted unanimously in favour of creating an organization that would protect against "fire, flood, or invasion perils."[26] A.C. Delaney, Manitoba's first provincial CD co-ordinator, brokered the arrangement as his first task.[27]

Winnipeg's city council appointed Major-General M.H.S. Penhale as the director of the Winnipeg Metropolitan Civil Defence Board in June 1951. Penhale had just retired from a long career in the Canadian army where he had served in both World Wars. In the Second World War, the heavy-set general had commanded the 3rd Canadian Infantry Brigade during the invasion of Sicily. His last years before retirement were spent as the General Officer Commanding Western Command. He was chosen for the CD position because of his role in co-ordinating the army's disaster response during the Red River flood. A shrewd organizer, if procedure-bound, Penhale spent the first few months of his appointment meeting with different members of the various community associations to obtain their support.[28] The Manitoba government had hoped that CD could be organized to act as a civilian force responding mainly to peacetime natural disasters, but in 1951 Penhale found the nuclear threat more pressing. He provided lectures to municipal councils that composed the Greater Winnipeg CD area and offered assessments of the roles they were likely to play in a nuclear emergency. For example, Penhale told representatives from Fort Garry to prepare their citizens to form a reserve mobile rescue column. He believed Fort Garry was sufficiently distant from an atomic bomb blast in Winnipeg for its uninjured volunteers to re-enter the blast area and dig out survivors. Penhale's presentation so impressed an official from the University of Manitoba that he offered to enlist 475 of his students.[29]

The federal guidelines for local organization asked local co-ordinators to refrain from premature public recruitment. Federal planners instead suggested that local CD officials contact existing voluntary service clubs in their community, preferably local chapters of national organizations. From November 1950 to January 1951, Worthington had met and brokered agreements with the Boy Scouts Association of Canada, the Canadian Legion, the Canadian Red Cross, and St. John Ambulance to provide volunteers and training in first aid and rescue to municipal CD groups. As a result of their national membership and community-oriented mandates, these were the only voluntary associations chosen to sign formal agreements with the Canadian government.[30] The CD agreement struck with the Canadian Red Cross and St. John Ambulance also had a subtle, but lasting, effect on the Canadian health care system. Under the terms of the agreement, the Canadian Red Cross was given sole responsibility for the creation of a nationwide blood collection and transfusion service, ending a dispute between the Canadian Red Cross and St. John Ambulance over blood services in Canada.[31]

Many other professional and volunteer associations offered their services to assist the country to prepare for disaster or nuclear war. Worthington, the Department of National Defence, and Paul Martin received dozens of letters from veterans' associations and religious and secular charitable groups all anxious to play a role, including the Canadian Corps Association Quebec Command, the United Church of Canada, the National Council of Jewish Women, and the International Order of Odd Fellows.[32] Medical associations such as the Victorian Order of Nurses and the Canadian Osteopathic Association clamoured to participate as well.[33]

Penhale met with some early opposition from the Winnipeg school board, particularly from Joe Zuken, a long-time board trustee and labour activist, who deplored Civil Defence Canada's intrusion into Winnipeg's daily affairs. At board meetings, he moved to oppose CD exercises and activities in Winnipeg. He viewed Penhale's CD as "a military proposition directed by a military man."[34] To Zuken, CD was nothing more than creeping militarism directed at the Soviet Union, designed to increase the young's fears of the bomb and deluding them into believing that a future war could be survived. In the anxious, anti-Communist atmosphere of the early 1950s, however, few in Winnipeg were inclined to listen to Zuken. The local press named Zuken "Moscow's Man" and characterized his opposition to CD as pro-Soviet rhetoric.[35]

Local service organizations, with their pre-existing memberships and links to the community, were early targets for CD organizers.[36] Penhale made his first request for assistance to Winnipeg's Central Volunteer Bureau (CVB). He believed that the Winnipeg office was perfect for recruiting because it co-ordinated all voluntary activities for the city on a block-by-block grid, supervised by 300 women living throughout the city's neighbourhoods. The volunteer bureau's members filled the rolls of his female warden service, and the CVB kept a survey book of the addresses and contact numbers of public-spirited men and women living on every block of the city. The CVB also kept listings of women with occupational experience in welfare work. These were ideal volunteers because the CVB charter encouraged any activity "operating for the public good and provided no commercial gain is derived."[37] After an agreeable first meeting in July 1951, Penhale delegated responsibility for the co-ordination of all of Winnipeg's service clubs and voluntary agencies to the administrators of the CVB and invited its president to represent social services on the Winnipeg Metropolitan Civil Defence Board.[38] Through the CVB, Winnipeg's CD organization soon received offers of assistance from the Canadian Legion and the Boy Scouts as well as from local employers such as the Hudson's Bay Company and Eaton's. It was not until September 1951 that the city embarked on its first recruiting campaign directed at the general public.

Penhale was pessimistic about the prospects of his first public recruiting campaign, given the reluctance of certain "community leaders" to offer their support to his organization publicly. He had hoped to enlist prominent members of the community to head branches of the CD organization, but he had little success. Penhale's request to a local judge to become the chief warden for Winnipeg was rejected by Chief Justice Ken Williams on the basis that judges should not be involved in "extraneous activity." Williams was sympathetic to Penhale's pleas for assistance but unmoved. In his diary, Penhale bitterly observed that this attitude was "very disappointing and indicative of a certain complacency which is evident in the minds of many of the more prominent people ... They really do not expect to be involved in serious trouble, and feel that having had a flood that a repetition of such a disaster, or anything like it, is unlikely."[39] The retired general was further discouraged by Winnipeg mayor Garnet Coulter's unwillingness to make radio broadcasts in support of CD during the September 1951 recruiting campaign. Penhale reluctantly agreed to be the spokesman for local publicity but only after it was made clear to him that there was no alternative.[40]

In Ottawa, Worthington's own impatience with the federal government's lack of public support for CD led to a brief but widely reported outburst directed at his minister. At a press conference held to introduce the visiting Swedish director-general of civil defence, Ake Sundelin, Worthington faced questions from reporters asking why Canada's progress had been allowed to lag so far behind the Swedish organization, which had a budget of $30 million and over 900,000 compulsory CD workers.[41] Worthington angrily pointed through his open window to the Parliament buildings and snarled: "The trouble lies behind you!"[42] He later confided to his journal that he "blew his top" and that his remarks were inspired by a similar outburst from Millard Caldwell, the director of the United States Federal Civil Defense Administration, who urged the US government to either "speed up civil defence or kill it."[43] The incident was reported in most major newspapers across the country. George Davidson, the deputy minister of welfare and Worthington's immediate superior, was furious. Worthington was called into Paul Martin's office, where he was told to retract his comments or face early retirement.[44] Several days later, Worthington offered

FIGURE 6   Students at a 1951 rescue exercise work to liberate a "casualty" from under a beam. *Source: Toronto Telegram*, Clara Thomas Archives, York University

a feeble "clarifying statement," which explained that the federal government was not the problem but that "the public itself must be aroused to get behind civil defence."[45]

The federal civil defence co-ordinator was promptly sent out of Ottawa on a cross-country tour to assess the progress of local CD directors. He arrived in Winnipeg just as Penhale launched the city's first public recruitment campaign.[46] Perhaps stung by Worthington's criticism, Paul Martin joined the general in Winnipeg to voice his support for the campaign, challenging residents to meet the city's goal to recruit 7,000 volunteers. Civil Defence Week opened in Winnipeg on 22 September 1951 and rapidly attracted volunteers. The campaign concentrated on Winnipeg's vulnerability to aerial attack and natural disaster. Penhale placed an important emphasis on the value of CD to combat events such as the flooding that had recently affected the city and adjoining areas. If the public had not read about the campaign in the newspaper or heard about it on the radio, the city's first air-raid siren, purchased and installed at federal expense, wailed every day from 26 September to 29 September. Elaborate demonstrations of local army units' anti-aircraft artillery drills, blasts from the air-raid siren, and mock air raids complete with searchlight exercises led some citizens to volunteer, but many others jammed police station switchboards to find out if an attack was underway.[47]

Fourteen hundred women of the CVB supported the campaign. They established 142 registration booths across the city. Their organization proved to be an asset, registering 3,900 volunteers from the general public and 2,000 others from Winnipeg service clubs. Volunteers were drawn from the Lions Club, the Rotary Club, the Federation of French Canadian Women, the B'nai B'rith Winnipeg Lodge, the St. Andrew's Home and School Association, the Fort Garry and St. James Kiwanis Clubs, and various local industries.[48] During the Civil Defence Week, 7,300 volunteers came forward.[49] The success of the Winnipeg campaign was all the more considerable because it was conducted on an incredibly sparse budget. Prior to the campaign, the Winnipeg Civil Defence Board's Advisory Committee reported that the municipal budget had not funded CD publicity. The committee approached local firms to donate funds for advertising, and the Hudson's Bay Company offered one of their own newly hired public relations experts, Frank Walker, to help co-ordinate CD publicity.[50] Fortunately, local radio stations offered free broadcasting time for Civil Defence Week.

Municipalities elsewhere in Canada did not meet with the same success. C.H.F. Fletcher, the CD co-ordinator for Windsor, Ontario, vented his bitter disappointment not just about the small number that his organization attracted but also about their low standing in the community. Fletcher had asked for 3,000 volunteers in his campaign, but only 600 came forward. He noted sourly that "most of these were industrial workers."[51] Like Penhale, Fletcher wanted men from the community who would be able to offer leadership and guidance in an emergency. Industrial workers were neither as eminent nor as experienced as the "business and professional men" that Fletcher had hoped to attract. His complaint was standard fare for CD organizers across the country, who grumbled about not being able to attract the right kind of volunteer. Fletcher's disparaging comment about industrial workers neglects the fact that these men probably volunteered to join because of the federal government's early initiatives to organize industry for CD. The remark does, however, imply that "business and professional" men were more likely to be leaders because they were rooted in the community, better educated, and held a higher social position. Civil defence co-ordinators rarely discussed the role of working-class volunteers in the defence of the city, but the distinction offers some interesting insight into how the concept of social prestige, which undergirded some recruiting campaigns, may have had a role in their failure. All citizens had a responsibility to support their local CD corps, but organizers did not value all volunteers equally.

In Winnipeg, Penhale's troubles really began once his organization grew in size. While the past experience of the Red River Valley flooding and the conflict in Korea fuelled interest in CD, he was faced with the long-term problem of obtaining sufficient funds to train and equip his largely volunteer force and of devising exercises and activities for the volunteers to keep their interest from waning. The issue of financial responsibility for CD had been simmering since the federal government first ventured into the field in 1948, but it rapidly gained in importance as municipalities began to assess how much nuclear preparedness would cost their communities. The resulting friction between different levels of government led to press skepticism about the federal government's motives and effectiveness in planning for a realistic civil defence.

Civil Defence in Montreal

In other municipalities, a lack of capable leadership and over-ambitious programs left some organizations stranded. The early failure of CD planning in Montreal provided another federal-provincial flashpoint. One of the more heavily publicized intergovernmental clashes over financial responsibility for CD occurred over Montreal's budget for its planned organization. With the highest population density in the country, a thriving financial centre, and port facilities, Montreal was considered one of the top three targets for a Soviet attack on Canada, along with the locks at Sault Ste. Marie and the port of Halifax.

In early 1951, Montreal's municipal council created a Municipal Committee for Civil Defence and appointed Brigadier J. Guy Gauvreau as the local co-ordinator.[52] Gauvreau had deep roots in Montreal. During the Second World War, he had commanded the Fusiliers Mont-Royal and had participated in the campaign in northwest Europe, but was taken out of the fight with grave injuries when his jeep hit a landmine in October 1944. After the war, he served on the executive of the Montreal Tramways Company. In contrast to Worthington and Penhale, who were also fellow retired generals-turned-civil defence planners, Gauvreau was remarkably young, just thirty-six when he took on the CD post, but Worthington predicted that Gauvreau would be a capable organizer who could secure co-operation from his municipality and the province.[53]

In August 1951, Gauvreau made public his first plan and draft budget for a projected organization with 60,000 volunteers, and in so doing he caused the province and the federal government great embarrassment.[54] Gauvreau, perhaps because of his experience on the executive board of the Montreal Tramways Company, envisioned a massive restructuring of the roadways in and around Montreal to allow the easy evacuation of the population and re-entry of rescue personnel. His plan included digging railway and highway tunnels under the St. Lawrence River, the construction of extra bridges, and the excavation of a massive transport tunnel and shelter in Mount Royal. Gauvreau's ambitious scheme took into account the minimum infrastructural improvements that residents of Montreal island would need to escape the city centre, in the event that it suffered total destruction from a single atomic blast. Gauvreau had concluded that determined volunteer wardens and firefighters alone would not materially improve Montreal's chances of survival.

The $363 million price tag horrified Worthington, Martin, and provincial officials and drew instant media attention.[55] If necessary, Gauvreau conceded, the city could survive with the mere investment of $18 million. Camillien Houde, Montreal's boisterous mayor and, initially, a CD enthusiast, promptly rejected municipal responsibility for preparations, asserting that "it was not the City of Montreal which declared wars, hence the incurrence of defence costs were outside the field of municipal responsibility."[56] As a result of Montreal's size and importance as a potential target, and the Quebec government's intransigence on the CD file, Martin took the unusual step of negotiating directly with the Montreal Metropolitan Civil Defence Committee. He managed to convince city council representatives to invest the $75,000 originally allocated from municipal coffers in order to keep the skeleton of the organization alive "at all costs."[57] With provincial officials, the minister was more candid:

> It would not be possible for the federal government to entertain expenditures ... as payment for the projects outlined since, in each case, these are public improvements and not directly associated with Civil Defence. Undoubtedly many of these improvements would be extremely valuable in the event of a disaster but their main function would be for the improvement of the metropolitan area under normal conditions.[58]

Worthington had no sympathy for Gauvreau. In a meeting following the release of the Montreal CD budget, the federal co-ordinator was critical of his wish list and observed that Gauvreau might as well have asked for the moon. Civil defence was not a total failure in Montreal regardless of its financial woes. By early 1952, Gauvreau claimed to have recruited 10,000 individuals. In fact, this number included all municipal officials and employees with some role in disaster planning, including police and fire services. Only 3,000 had genuinely volunteered for CD and, of these, only 1,000 were trained. Based on these numbers, Worthington optimistically reported that local activity and interest indicated that, with limited federal assistance, the organization could thrive without a multi-million dollar investment. Compared to other major cities, which had not even begun to organize, Montreal's accomplishments were still impressive. Worthington hoped that Montreal's organization could be preserved in order to promote CD elsewhere.[59] Gauvreau was not disappointed with his time as co-ordinator – the brigadier instead left CD planning for more lucrative work as the vice-president of DOW Chemical Limited. Gauvreau failed where Penhale had succeeded, perhaps because he painted a starker picture of what it would realistically cost for a Canadian metropolis to survive an atomic attack. Where Penhale had started small, building his organization from a small group of volunteers that already existed in the community, Gauvreau had looked to what the city would need in the near future and designed an organization to fit. Gauvreau's plan, unlike Penhale's, was too expensive to survive long.

The Cities Rebel

Montreal's complaints over the lack of federal aid were matched by similar rumblings from municipalities across the country that demanded federal and provincial money for local civil defence. Civic authorities in Stratford, Ontario, sent Prime Minister St. Laurent a resolution demanding that the federal government assume the full costs for CD because of its constitutional responsibility for national defence and the imminent possibility of war.[60] The resolution alone would not usually have obtained much attention, but when it began to be endorsed by multiple towns and cities across Ontario, Civil Defence Canada took notice. Newspaper editors and municipal councillors raised similar concerns about the ability of municipalities to pay for CD as well as about the propriety of asking them to do so. One editorialist in Creston, British Columbia, speculated that unless sufficient funds were found, rural cities and towns would be within their rights to turn away refugees from bombed cities.[61]

Civil defence funding embarrassed Martin again in November 1951. Several days after the minister informed a large audience in London, Ontario, that Canadian CD had entered its "operational phase" in Windsor, Montreal, Winnipeg, and Halifax, Windsor's city council held a noisy session where a majority of councillors endorsed the Stratford resolution.[62] Although the government's official list of targets in Canada was still a closely guarded secret, Windsor controller Lawrence Deziel believed that so few Canadian cities would be targeted that the federal government could easily bear the costs for municipal preparations. The city council compromised and kept CD alive on the condition that the federal government pay a quarter or more of the costs of its administration.[63]

There was a rising consensus among municipalities in the fall of 1951 that at the very least some form of cost-sharing program was required to keep interest in the CD organization alive. This sentiment was reflected in renewed criticism from the CFMM in a statement presented to Prime Minister Louis St. Laurent. The federation's executive endorsed municipal responsibility for some aspects of CD, but only if Ottawa committed to pay for most of the costs of organization.[64] The CFMM's executive contended that the federal government's financing structure, which demanded that the provinces and municipalities pay first before receiving an unspecified percentage of federal compensation, served only to undermine the federal government's claim that there was actually an urgent need for CD.[65] The CFMM executive also proposed that a National Committee on Civil Defence be established, bringing in municipal representatives to the existing dominion-provincial committee. They believed that municipal representation in CD policy formation "would make CD, nationally and locally – a truly joint project of the citizens of Canada and in which every Canadian has a great and vital stake."[66]

The provinces indicated their deep dissatisfaction with the existing formula for CD financing. With a few notable exceptions, most provinces had refused to commit any significant money to provincial programs or provide support to growing municipal agencies. Saskatchewan's minister responsible for CD, J.H. Sturdy, complained to Martin that Saskatchewan's investment was based on the assumption that the federal government would eventually reconsider and commit more funds to regional preparations.[67] Saskatchewan had inaugurated educational programs, including rescue and fire safety courses for high school students. Delays in the provision of federally produced training aids led J.O. Probe, the province's CD co-ordinator, to offer his resignation. Worthington's quick intervention secured necessary training aids and prevented Probe's departure. He would not have been replaced had he resigned.

By early 1952, the financial crunch was keenly felt by Winnipeg's organization. Penhale pleaded for support from Rhodes Smith, Manitoba's attorney general, because Winnipeg's city council was unable to finance local CD beyond the basic organization and planning. Penhale's budget for 1952 included $142,000 to carry out existing activities as well as to build a control centre and improve Winnipeg's radio communications. Without these modest improvements, the warning and rescue systems would have been dependent on easily severed landlines in an emergency.[68] None of the paltry $26,000, which had been reserved for CD in Manitoba reached Winnipeg, and Smith rejected Penhale's request for a $50,000 infusion in April 1952.[69] Federal planners observed municipal dissatisfaction and financial starvation with increasing concern. They recognized that continued disputes over financial responsibility would severely damage the federal government's credibility and overshadow major investments elsewhere, such as the drug stockpiling program. Worthington argued for a program that would match funds to resolve the impasse over CD, and he eventually got it.

Financial Support for Civil Defence

On 27 March 1952, Martin revealed to provincial ministers in charge of CD that the federal government had committed $1.4 million for per capita grants in 1952-53. The minister cautioned that the money would be paid out to each province for specific CD projects proposed by the municipalities, forwarded by the provinces, and approved by the federal government. The Department of Health and Welfare insisted on federal approval to prevent CD funds from being spent on general infrastructure projects such as highways, bridges, or railways. The funds made available to each province were calculated according to populations living in target or non-target areas, at 14 cents and 8 cents per person, respectively. Under the federal scheme, Ontario and Quebec would receive the most money, approximately $450,000 each. Prince Edward Island, with its small population, was eligible for only $7,000. These were paltry sums paid out from a meager federal budget. Nonetheless, they represented a significant policy reversal, and the matching funds were the best that Martin could squeeze out of the government's otherwise lush rearmament program.[70]

Worthington was pleased with the announcement, but he had hoped for more. He wanted safeguards written into the matching plans agreement to ensure that municipalities would reap the greatest benefit. These safeguards included provisions to reach separate agreements with municipalities in Quebec or Ontario, whose progress was severely limited by the provincial legislatures' refusal to fund any CD project. Davidson rejected Worthington's proposed changes and underlined that the primary purpose of the program was not to enhance CD in the municipalities but, rather, to embarrass provincial governments into investing funds into their CD programs. If municipal funds were matched directly, Davidson suggested, the "provinces will very quickly slip out from under the entire responsibility."[71] It was a gamble based on observations that Montreal, Winnipeg, Halifax, Saskatoon, Calgary, and Vancouver had proven more than willing to invest municipal funds. Davidson reasoned that the country would achieve better results from its CD program if the provinces matched some of this municipal money.

The matching funds program raised the hopes of municipalities seeking additional financial assistance, but the policy failed to achieve its immediate or long-term objectives. Despite extensive discussions with provincial authorities, most of the provinces were reluctant to agree with the federal program. By

November 1952, only three provinces had agreed to the matching funds program. Quebec rejected the proposal out of hand, citing federal responsibility as the key issue. Ontario's representatives argued that their own $50,000 allocation was sufficient and that Ottawa should deal directly with the municipalities. Worthington instructed his officials to persuade the provinces to ask for money for their smallest projects, even recovering the costs of postage, in order to create some proof of progress in CD and value for their expenditure. Projects that might have actually improved municipal preparedness, such as shelter systems or evacuation route signage, were considered too "fantastic" for federal funding. Worthington, toeing the line, insisted that Ontario and Quebec could be forced to participate if most of the provinces agreed to the Financial Assistance Program (FAP).[72]

The trouble with Worthington's assumption was that provincial authorities did not draw the media's attention to the federally approved projects for civil defence. Worthington's information officer, former newspaper editor Dan Wallace, speculated that this reluctance was because the provinces rarely gave credit to the federal government's contributions to provincial programs and would not do so for CD.[73] Instead, negative press reports about municipal organizations' financial difficulties continued into 1953. Worthington suggested that he should meet with the "responsible Press" so that editors would present both sides of the story to the public. Wallace counselled strongly against this course of action, stating that the press was "already sufficiently misinformed or intentionally ignorant about many other Federal-Provincial programs involving far larger sums of money."[74]

The first year of the FAP produced dismal results. Of the $1.4 million offered to provincial governments, $319,918 had been matched by provincial projects. British Columbia and Alberta were the only provinces to meet, or exceed, their portion of the matching funds.[75] The federal office sent statistics to provincial CD co-ordinators comparing their efforts with US state governments of similar populations. In every case, the state's request exceeded or equalled the funds made available.[76] Eventually, the numbers began to add up to an embarrassing figure. Of the $2.8 million allocated from 1951 to 1953, over $2 million remained unspent, largely because of Quebec and Ontario municipalities' exclusion from the program.

Informed by his frequent discussions with local CD leaders, which included Penhale, Worthington renewed his argument that a loophole had to be exploited to allow the federal government to deal directly with the municipalities. If the provinces were allowed to handle the transfer of money between the federal government and the municipalities, without having to contribute themselves, municipal CD organizations stood a chance of receiving some financial support directly from the federal government in a way that would still respect constitutional boundaries. While suspicious of the provinces, Davidson agreed that Worthington's proposal could dull the edge of municipal criticism and mitigate negative press about the federal-provincial dispute over financial responsibility generally and the matching funds program in particular.[77]

The new formula was announced in the House of Commons on 22 June 1954, along with a boost in the annual funding to $2 million. Gradually, Ontario signed on to the matching grants program on a limited basis. While Quebec refrained from accepting any funds for CD, the province did agree to relay money and equipment to those municipalities that were in need. The FAP became a central pillar supporting CD in later years, but in the immediate aftermath of the Korean War it appeared to come too late to repair the damage done by years of intergovernmental bickering. As Worthington mused in his diary soon after the policy was introduced, "the federal government can now back out very gracefully and throw the owness [sic] on the province, but that does not solve our problem, nor foster better progress in civil defence."[78]

Armistice in Korea

Even the most competent and well-organized municipal organizations faced looming problems by late 1953. Finances were thin and, in some cases, still nonexistent. Without an international crisis to keep them on edge, volunteers dropped out and moved on. The recruitment and retention of volunteers was a serious problem encountered by every local organization and was the subject of frequent discussions in international CD circles. A common conclusion reached was that CD was taken seriously by the public in times of great crisis, but only for short periods before its attraction waned.[79]

Civil defence organizers across the country attempted to use the Korean War to mobilize financial support and recruit volunteers, but this tactic became less effective as the war dragged on. Before the UN, China, and North Korea finally signed an armistice in July 1953, Canadian soldiers still fought, died, and were injured in the war, but the conflict failed to hold the public's attention. The United Nations and the Chinese traded artillery shells and raised raiding parties in static warfare fought in the mountains. Canadians at home rapidly lost interest in the faraway conflict and sputtering armistice talks. The war had little visible impact on their daily lives. Their cities were not under attack, and Canadians did not suffer from rationing or other shortages.[80]

The end of the Korean War precipitated some speculation about the continued usefulness of a CD program. Civil defence authorities were particularly concerned that the public would grow complacent without an immediate war risk. British Columbia's CD agency circulated a public warning: "Some of us may feel that because of the so-called 'peace moves' now being put forward by the new Soviet Government we can afford to sit back and slacken our efforts ... Surely we have not forgotten what the former proposals by the Russians for a truce in Korea led to."[81] When faced with questions about the practicality of peacetime CD, one Vancouver volunteer proclaimed over the radio that "we should forget about wars and threats of wars, and look upon Civil Defence as a strong right arm in reserve," for use in natural disaster.[82] The change in tone of Vancouver's publicity succeeded in keeping the organization alive, if only barely.

Even with its successful organization rooted in a pre-existing base of volunteers, Winnipeg began to face severe difficulties holding the attention of its members in 1953. The wardens' council meetings were sparsely attended by senior planners and volunteers, much to Penhale's frustration.[83] The organization had convinced volunteers to make a short-term commitment of their time for basic CD and first aid training, but finding committed volunteers who would remain as wardens was an enduring problem.[84] St. Vital, one of the areas hardest hit by flooding in 1950, managed to attract 181 volunteers for first aid courses, but none of these individuals volunteered to stay on as wardens. Penhale and other CD workers could see that their organization faced a decline in public interest and esteem with the end of the Korean War. Jack Bumsted, a Winnipeg historian, recalled that near the end of the war, CD was increasingly met with black humour and public apathy, as posters went up ridiculing CD wardens, with their helmets, ladders, and whistles, as "human hardware stores."[85] These posters advertised the equipment that wardens needed, including "one broom with short handle to stick up your ass for sweeping up when it is all over."[86]

The challenge of retaining volunteers was common everywhere in Canada, and by 1953 most planners diverted their organizations' meagre resources to purchase better publicity. By the end of the Korean War, Winnipeg's Advisory Committee used $6,000 of its annual allotment to hire an advertising expert to co-ordinate CD publicity events and maintain interest in the organization.[87]

Conclusion

Civil defence advanced unevenly across Canada during the Korean War. In those areas that self-identified as target areas, or that had experienced recent natural disasters, federal pressure to develop a CD organization was welcomed. Even in those areas where the effects of disaster or worries about the atomic threat were keenly felt, municipalities and the provinces balked at the high price attached to adequate preparations. Much of the organization across Canada depended to an extent on the individual initiative of organizers in the local communities, on the existence and interest of large voluntary agencies willing to co-operate with the new organization, and on the likely proximity to either nuclear or natural disaster. Successful organizers such as those in Winnipeg managed to work skillfully around municipal politics and co-operate with existing city departments and voluntary agencies in the community. Toronto and Montreal, by contrast, had large, promising organizations that stopped dead for want of funds, and their occasionally ham-fisted local co-ordinators feuded publicly with municipal and provincial politicians for more money. Inevitably, the press picked up on these disputes and the more important and still un-resolved issues of financial and ethical responsibility for CD. Unwelcome press attention, continuing municipal and provincial rebellion, and, as the Korean War gradually settled to an armistice, slackening public support for CD forced the federal government to intervene visibly with the FAP, which was designed to inject federal and provincial funds into local projects. The move helped to sustain civil defence, and the FAP also represented a tacit admission by the federal government that the provinces and municipalities could not prepare for nuclear war on their own. They required federal leadership and assistance to finance their CD agencies as well as to attract the public support necessary to attract volunteers for local CD services.

Publicizing Armageddon: Responsible Citizenship and Civil Defence, 1948-54

DURING THE FALL AND winter of 1953, an "On Guard, Canada!" civil defence (CD) convoy travelled to major cities across Canada. The exhibit, originally designed and displayed in the United States, was the first nation-wide publicity campaign launched by the federal government to convince Canadians of the need to adopt CD measures. The federal CD agency, in co-operation with its provincial and municipal counterparts, employed the exhibit to make the case that the long, watery, and frozen distances separating Canada from Cold War conflicts in Europe and Asia no longer protected citizens. The enemy, at a moment, could reduce their cities to rubble with atomic bombs, salt the earth with volatile biological agents, and poison their air with suffocating chemicals. To meet the horrors of modern warfare, young and old visitors were shown how to support CD in their homes and in their communities. Over 100,000 Canadians visited the exhibit, but public interest did not lead to any significant increase in the number of volunteers for CD services.

Civil defence authorities advertised more than just protective measures. Both the Canadian and American versions of the convoy attempted to depict CD as part of the core obligations of citizenship. Preparing a basement shelter and saluting the flag were equated visually with the defence of cherished values such as freedom of speech. The exhibition displays, and the way in which attendance was promoted and organized, depicted a hierarchical order of citizenship that valorized patriotic voluntarism and prescribed strict gender divisions, demonstrating to men and women how and where they could best fulfill their obligations to their community.

Citizenship and Civil Defence Publicity

The study of citizenship is a varied field, and in Canada some scholars have investigated the process by which the individual immigrant, or immigrant communities, seeks, finds, or is granted membership in the host community.[1] Citizenship is often defined as the contract between the state and its occupants characterized by imposed obligations (military service, taxation, and obedience to the law) in exchange for individual rights (freedom of speech, religion, and assembly) as defined by law. Citizenship may also be interpreted as a mark of pride and membership in a wider social network, traditionally linked to the confines of the nation-state.[2] Yet a unitary concept of citizenship in Canada was difficult to apply to a society divided by so many competing ethnic, cultural, and linguistic tensions.[3]

After the Second World War, Paul Martin, then the secretary of state, drafted the Canadian Citizenship Act with the aid of senior civil servants. He argued vigorously in the House of Commons that the act would serve as a marker of what a united Canada could accomplish.[4] Passed into law during a "Citizenship Week" in January 1947, the act was meant to encourage the concept of Canadian citizenship as a means of fostering national pride and consciousness of an identity that was notionally and legally different from the status already conferred on Canadians as members of the British Commonwealth.[5]

In Canada and the United States, CD agencies folded their publicity programs into the citizenship project by stressing that participation in CD was a responsibility that everyone had to bear in order to defend their hard-won rights. Publicity was the CD organization's first point of contact with the public, and it was mobilized to persuade Canadians to live up to their obligations by volunteering for their local CD corps. Canada's survival efforts depended on convincing the public to support the "self-help" defence strategy.

For the first few years following his appointment, Federal Civil Defence Co-ordinator Frank Worthington played the leading role in an unsophisticated campaign to publicize the needs and aims of his organization. He travelled extensively across Canada to address gatherings of veterans' groups, industrial preparedness associations, city councillors, teachers, students, and church groups. He eventually came to rely on a scripted "Basic Speech" for these events, which stressed the key points that were essential to familiarizing the public with his organization and its goals.

Worthington suggested in his addresses that support for CD would contribute to Western deterrence because it would demonstrate the civilian population's willingness to resist a Soviet attack.[6] As the Korean War deteriorated into a stalemate, Worthington's exhortations about each citizen's responsibility to participate became more pronounced. In a speech to the Canadian Hospital Council on 29 May 1951, he informed his audience that CD was "straightforward patriotism which requires voluntary time and the only wage which the patriotic man and woman will receive from this effort is the continuance of the Freedom and Liberty we now enjoy."[7] By September 1951, Worthington was insisting that CD's importance was equal to that of the armed forces, and he claimed that, without each of them, the defence of Canada would be completely "nullified."[8]

Worthington's personal endorsement of CD was meaningless without a budget or staff to produce publicity and training material on a national scale. Many local agencies had lost patience with the lack of direction and support from the federal planning body. Municipal planning staff began their own publicity programs in the winter of 1950. Retired navy commander F.L. Houghton, Halifax's CD director, commenced a weekly radio broadcasting campaign immediately after his appointment to inform residents of his progress in organizing their community for civil defence. Houghton argued that his publicity campaign would address "the impatience of the populace [for Halifax civil defence] to 'do something.'"[9] The director based his speaking engagements and fifteen-minute radio broadcasts on points lifted from transcripts of Worthington's speeches and, just as frequently, lifted themes from American and British CD manuals.[10] By late 1951, Houghton and other local directors grew impatient with their own limited programs and demanded publicity material to aid recruitment and public education.[11]

The federal agency responded by establishing a branch of the Department of National Health and Welfare's Information Services Division (ISD) in the federal co-ordinator's office, which was directed by retired Colonel Homer Robinson. This branch's responsibility was to disseminate the necessary information about CD across Canada as a part of the federal training and planning program. For assistance with the complex job of selling CD, the federal agency hired Sidney Denman, a representative of a Montreal advertising firm that had offered its services to craft publicity.[12] The ISD developed a logo, a CD slogan, "Civil Defence Is Self-Defence," and briefly considered commissioning a song for its volunteers. George Davidson, deputy minister of welfare, initially had little enthusiasm for CD publicity, and he told Worthington as much: "I can swallow a slogan and a symbol, but may God preserve us from a song. The atomic bomb itself could not be worse!"[13]

Davidson eventually warmed to CD publicity, if not a song, and by late October 1951 Denman and the staff of the ISD had approval for national publicity. Their program demanded that each province appoint public relations officers to provide timely press releases about CD news of national and local import and to co-ordinate loans of exhibitions and films. Another purpose of the national public relations plan was to minimize negative publicity over federal-provincial conflicts about financial responsibility for CD. Instead, public relations officers emphasized positive news of progress that described the numbers of volunteers enrolled to date, training courses completed, and federal initiatives.[14] The success of the publicity program was left to municipal public relations workers, who could promote CD locally to keep their organization relevant and in the public eye.[15]

In early 1952, the staff of the ISD advanced CD publicity by erecting exhibits at numerous events where they would obtain the most exposure to the public, but without committing the government to major expenditures. A display was designed and erected for the Canadian National Sportsmen's Show, which was held in the Toronto Coliseum Exhibition Grounds in March 1952.[16] The design itself was spectacular and eye-catching – the central panel was dedicated to a graphic treatment of an illuminated atomic bomb cloud flashing on and off over a city skyline. Alongside this panel was another panel that described the nature of CD. The answer to the question "Who is needed?" was consistent with the basic CD message: "Everybody. Self-help and mutual aid are the responsibilities of all good citizens."[17]

The CD agency's ability to conduct a national publicity campaign was limited by the federal government's unwillingness to commit major expenditures to peacetime CD. Only $4.2 million in federal funds was allocated to CD purposes in the 1951 fiscal year. Compared to the billions spent for defence mobilization and rearmament, CD was a budgetary afterthought for the Canadian government.[18] When the American Federal Civil Defense Administration (FCDA) offered the "Alert America" convoy to Canadian authorities in June 1952, Ottawa's officials seized an opportunity to launch a ready-made nation-wide publicity campaign at a fraction of the cost of developing their own. As Davidson explained to his doubtful minister, Paul Martin, on 16 October 1952, the cost of sending the convoy across Canada compared favourably with the department producing an educational film. He predicted that "the returns from this present project in terms of the impact it will make upon the public will be well worthwhile."[19]

The Alert America convoy was conceived in the United States as the result of the resounding success of a "Freedom Train" exhibit of artifacts that promoted the theme of the triumph of democracy over tyranny in American history.[20] Train cars contained 127 historic documents highlighting the evolution of American civil liberties, such as the Declaration of Independence, a copy of the Constitution, and Abraham Lincoln's Emancipation Proclamation. Also on display were artifacts of recent American military victories, such as the German and Japanese surrender articles. The Freedom Train travelled 37,000 miles across the continental United States between September 1947 and January 1949, visiting 322 cities. Over 3.5 million people visited the train, prompted by an immense advertising campaign in the press, on radio, and on television. The tour's promoters boasted that its popularity had cemented the spiritual resolve of the nation against Communism and foreign ideologies.[21]

In 1951, the American FCDA approached the Freedoms Foundation of Valley Forge, a coalition of advertisers and prominent citizens, to help promote awareness of the American CD program.[22] The Freedoms Foundation created three travelling exhibits, each composed of ten-truck convoys, which eventually visited eighty-two principal target cities, where they were viewed by over a million

FIGURE 7 Appeals to citizenship, such as the one contained in this recruiting poster, were central to Canada's civil defence publicity. *Source:* Library and Archives Canada, Paul Joseph Martin Fonds

spectators. At many of the stops on the route, the convoy was combined with CD exercises and civic parades. Like the Freedom Train, the logo and promotional material for the Alert America convoy drew heavily from American heritage. Visitors were greeted by a large silhouette of Paul Revere bent over his horse during his midnight ride. Generations of Americans had learned about Revere's exploits during the War of Independence. The use of his silhouette in the Alert America publicity was a warning that the time had arrived when all civilians were expected to do their duty and join up and stave off disaster.[23]

Canadian officials followed the success of the tour with interest throughout the summer of 1952 with an eye to their own education and training program.[24] At the conclusion of the Alert America tour, the FCDA offered to provide one entire exhibition to Canada for one year free of charge. The offer was made to mark the signature of a new Canadian-American memorandum of agreement that permitted their CD agencies to operate freely across borders in the event of an attack.[25] The new agreement was formalized on Parliament Hill on 24 July 1952 during a ceremony to hand over the convoy to Canadian authorities.[26] A small crowd was in attendance when the full convoy arrived on Parliament Hill the following day, where it was welcomed by Worthington, Davidson, and representatives from the US embassy. Worthington publicly expressed his confidence that he would have the exhibit moving within a month, but the contents of the convoy trucks were unceremoniously dumped into storage, where they remained for almost a year.[27]

Since the Canadian version of the Alert America convoy relied on the participation and expenditure of government departments, rather than on a wealthy, privately funded organization, Worthington's optimism had been altogether unrealistic. Any plans for the Canadian tour had to be approved by the Cabinet, and designers of the Canadian Government Exhibition Commission had to repair worn displays and "Canadianize" specific aspects of the exhibit. Worthington's office, the Defence Research Board, and the director of Atomic Energy of Canada Limited provided content advice. As a result of a cumbersome approval process, the Canadian convoy did not set out until September 1953, when a line of International Harvester trucks drove up the ring road outside Parliament towards its first destination in Montreal.

The exhibition, once unloaded and assembled, greeted visitors with a carrot and a stick. In the introduction, a utopian future, made possible with the development of atomic energy, was juxtaposed with a dystopian atomic holocaust.[28] The promise and threat of atomic energy were summarized in two panels that described the ongoing debate in the West about the state's control over atomic science. The first panel, entitled *Peacetime Use of Atomic Energy*, postulated the potential, fantastic applications of the atom to better everyday life in the near future, including atomic planes and cars. The Canadian version of this panel stressed Canada's pioneering research into cobalt-60 cancer therapy. In contrast, a large arrow bearing the words *"Or will it be this?"* pointed to a crumbling doorframe surrounded by a panel with images of destruction wrought by the atomic bomb at Hiroshima.

With this ominous warning, the visitor progressed to the next enclosure, entitled *The Five Warfares,* where, in graphic three-dimensional montages, they were shown the ways that external and internal enemies might attack their way of life.[29] The *Biological Warfare* display was an example of one of the internal threats, and it portrayed two sides of a farm field. On the left side of the divide, a faceless saboteur in a dark hat and trench coat knelt in the midst of a barren field, holding a vial filled with a bubbling substance. In the background lay the bare bones of livestock and a dilapidated farmhouse. On the right side of the display was a thriving farm, proving the value of preparedness. The *Incendiary Attack* display presented artwork of bomber aircraft dropping loads of high explosives over London during the Second World War.[30] The theme was familiar to Canadians because the resilience of the civilian population during the Battle of Britain had been used to great wartime effect as inspirational propaganda in Canada and the United States. Images of burned-out British cities provided CD organizers with the best-known example of the effectiveness of a prepared CD corps in saving lives and property. Many demobilized soldiers would have had vivid memories of these attacks based on their first-hand experience while awaiting the invasion or while they were on leave in Britain during the war, as would Canadians at home who learned about the British experience through letters home, newsreels, and radio accounts of CD efforts in burning cities.[31]

The *Destruction of City* display was the centrepiece of the civil defence convoy in both the United States and Canada. As the visitor entered, piped music swelled in dramatic tones. The lights were dimmed so that only a model skyline was visible, and the music rose to a crescendo, the sound of aircraft engines rumbled, followed by the scream of a falling bomb. A giant, multicoloured cloud then illuminated a second skyline of jagged wreckage with a purple glow, accompanied by the sound of an atomic explosion, flames, secondary explosions, and collapsing wreckage. After the "attack," the lights brightened, the nightmarish sounds faded into the background, and a reassuring recorded narration began: "You have just seen a small picture of the death and destruction that modern warfare can bring to the cities and farms, the churches and schools, the homes and families of our country. We want peace. We hope and pray and work to preserve our traditional freedoms and to share them with others in peace. But lasting peace can never be bought by weakness. Eternal vigilance is the price of

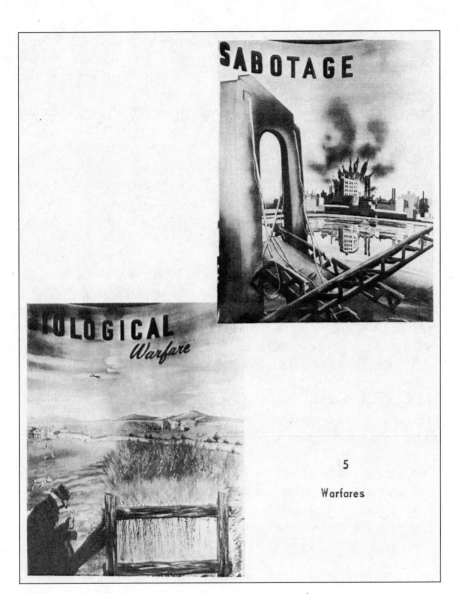

Figure 8   A saboteur poisons the field in the *Five Warfares* display. *Source:* Government of Canada/Library and Archives Canada, *For Your Information: Canada's Civil Defence Convoy*

freedom."[32] The rhetoric of achieving peace through strength was a staple of Cold War discourse. In this display, it was being effectively applied to CD, which its organizers hoped would contribute to the West's deterrent capability as much as rearmament.

Besides being promoted as a nuclear insurance policy, officials considered an effective system of CD to be part of the West's deterrent to war. The reasoning went that the Soviets would not risk a war they could not win, and a properly funded and organized CD could preserve the West's will and ability to carry on fighting even after an atomic attack. The rationale behind this assumption was always strained by the casual observer's comparison of the large amounts of capital expended on armaments versus the tiny amount of funding funnelled into CD measures.[33] The display's message also addressed the uncertainty that hovered over an otherwise peaceful home front. Its quasi-military tone would not have seemed out of place in the exhibit because, at most of the Canadian destinations, the On Guard, Canada! display was erected in local armouries and was complemented by displays of anti-aircraft artillery and flyovers from Royal Canadian Air Force (RCAF) jets.

The shaken visitor exited the "destroyed" city to learn how to exercise individual self-defence, at home and at work, along with basic survival tips such as building a basement shelter from concrete blocks. The displays clearly depicted the role of the family household in self-protection. A staple of the CD organization was the involvement of women, based on the assumption that the mother or wife would have to manage the home under attack, especially if it occurred while a man was working during the day. She would have to prepare to extinguish house fires and evacuate children to a shelter. In the *Transition Room* display, the role of the mother was emphasized. Standing in the rubble of their home, an awe-struck mother holds her unharmed baby and her son's hand.[34] Women in cities visited by the convoy were urged to see the exhibit by local CD directors and newspaper editorialists. An appeal that was published during the display's run in Calgary from Ray Smith, a local warden, sought out female volunteers: "Amongst the non-specialists required for help is the 'corner stone' of every city – the housewife. She, with her expert knowledge of home and child care, is an invaluable asset to any community and she can help in hundreds of ways."[35]

In yet another exhibit stressing the value of fire protection, a woman was depicted with a garden hose in hand, effortlessly extinguishing a fire in her home before it can spread to other houses. By managing small domestic fires on her own during an attack, the housewife could free skilled (male) firefighters to subdue major fires. This was domestic perfection carried to an extreme – a neat, ordered home with a concerned housewife could reduce property damage in a disaster. The image conjured by the exhibitry was actually based on evidence collected from model homes exposed to atomic bomb tests in Nevada. Federal Civil Defence Administration workers touring the model homes after the attack learned that messy, cluttered homes caught fire quickly and sustained more

FIGURE 9   Mothers were informed it was their role to guard the home and their children. *Source:* Government of Canada/Library and Archives Canada, *For Your Information: Canada's Civil Defence Convoy*

damage than homes that were kept clean.[36] Female preparedness in the home ensured that, in an attack, skilled male volunteers in the target area would be freed to do more "important" work on firefighting and rescue teams. Although the exhibit was designed by Americans, such manicured representations of women in the home were common in the contemporary Canadian media.[37] The summative effect of the imagery and public appeals that represented the patriotic female CD worker served to reinforce traditional gender roles while posing no threat to the feminine image of the individual volunteer. These representations did not reflect dissent within the CD organization about the role that female volunteers should be allowed to play. Even conservative volunteers belonging to the Imperial Order Daughters of the Empire aspired to more than providing CD in the home. In their annual report, the order pointed to a CD training course where women who had participated had excelled in every field including those typically reserved for men, such as rescue: "The course certainly proved that women have a major part to play in Civil Defence and also that they *can* play a part in every phase of CD."[38]

The mother might be the first line of defence, but the father was the head of the household. In the *Civil Defence Where You Live* display, a husband and wife were shown sitting in a spacious and comfortable basement shelter. To the left of this panel was an instruction to study CD booklets, over an image of a father reading them to his family. Below this panel was an instruction to "organize family into a fire-fighting team." The father and his son were rushing to douse a fire, while the mother and daughter were filling buckets of water. The men were in charge of the home when they were not at work and were, it appeared, the best qualified to organize the family to resist disaster.[39]

The visitor exited the exhibition through a final enclosure, entitled *Civil Defence Protects Our Way of Life,* which was altered from the American *Know Your Freedoms* display. The Canadian government's Exhibition Commission made the change so that the exhibit would better reflect Canada's distinct political culture. The finished space confronted the visitor with several large graphic panels depicting the rights of Canadian citizenship. In one panel, a child has her head bowed in prayer, symbolizing freedom of religion. In the second, the speaker of the House of Commons stands in Parliament, stressing the institutional foundations of Canadian society – the guarantors of the rights of citizenship. In the final panel, the visitor was shown the individual obligations of citizenship, through images of Boy Scouts taking direction from a CD worker or a policeman. This last room visually connected CD, loyalty, and good citizenship by linking the rights and obligations of membership in the community.[40] Unlike the American version of the exhibit, the Canadian convoy did not exploit visual symbols of the nation's heritage. Paul Revere's silhouette had been removed, and it was not replaced by any distinctly Canadian substitute. The convoy's most visible connection to Canada was devised in the planning stage, when it was renamed "On Guard Canada!" in August 1953 to distinguish the exhibition from its American origins.[41]

The Tour

On 18 September 1953, after fourteen months of planning and co-ordination, the convoy rolled out from Parliament Hill on a three-month tour of ten cities thought to be the prime targets for atomic attack: Montreal, Regina, Calgary, Vancouver, Edmonton, Saskatoon, Winnipeg, Windsor, Halifax, and Saint John. Toronto was conspicuous by its absence but only because the municipal authorities publicly refused to spend money to host the convoy.[42] Toronto mayor Allan Lamport, a political showboat always ready to supply the press with a witty quote, dismissed criticism from his colleagues by calling the CD program "a pig in a poke," which had lost its utility as hostilities had ended in Korea.[43] Arthur Welsh, provincial secretary and minister in charge of Ontario CD, supported Lamport's position that CD was a federal responsibility.[44] The editors of the *Globe and Mail* offered to pay for the convoy's showing in Toronto, but federal planners politely rejected the newspaper's initiative because they were not willing to spend more on publicity, and they did not want to give provincial officials a platform for their criticism.[45]

Other municipalities eyed the convoy's tour schedule with envy. In written protests to the federal authorities, local directors of municipal CD organizations and their city councils decried the decision not to include their cities and townships on the convoy route. Often these letters attempted to convince the federal authorities that their local organizations would be overcome by public apathy if the convoy did not stop in their towns. Co-ordinators argued that the mere presence or passage of the convoy through their jurisdiction would bolster Canadian loyalty and defeat Communist sympathizers.[46] To accommodate smaller centres, the convoy route was repeatedly changed to allow the trucks to stop in municipalities with active CD corps. In these towns, the road crews were welcomed by municipal councils and local Legion halls.

In the cities hosting the convoy, welcoming the exhibition was a more sophisticated affair, with attention-grabbing spectacles and effective advertising. Organizers in Montreal incorporated the convoy's arrival into a massive military parade, which had been arranged to open an international municipal congress in the city. Local CD workers and vehicles from the convoy and the municipality formed the tail end of the parade, which drew over 150,000 spectators.[47]

Other show cities held similar pageants of defence forces, with the blue and gold convoy trucks as the main attraction, followed by local CD workers in improvised ambulances and municipal firefighting vehicles.[48] Organizers in Winnipeg proclaimed a "Civil Defence Week" to coincide with the arrival of the convoy.[49] Calgary's opening ceremonies included air raid drills, where RCAF Mustang fighter planes flew low over the city on a mock strafing run. In Saskatoon, recently installed sirens wailed as the exhibition doors opened.[50]

Outside the military armories where the exhibits were usually assembled, CD volunteers put on live demonstrations of their trades for large audiences. The street theatre replicated the horrific conditions of war found in the exhibits inside, as Canadian Red Cross workers rushed about tending to casualties with simulated head traumas and broken limbs, while other volunteers rescued people from smoke-filled buildings with the assistance of the fire department. Local Boy Scout troops demonstrated crowd control and radio services.[51]

The activities of the organizers and volunteers bolstered the convoy's message, complete with its gender distinctions and prescriptions for voluntary involvement. The tasks allocated to the sizable number of volunteers who participated in the exercises outside and in crowd control inside were distinctly different for male and female volunteers. In the various rescue and firefighting demonstrations, men played a central role, rushing into smoke-filled buildings to save casualties, moving debris to uncover survivors, and running from one point in the evacuation chain to another as messengers. Male participation in CD, as advocated by the exhibits inside, was an active participation. Female volunteers were also outside, on the scene of destruction, but they were limited to bandaging "casualties" and providing blankets and hot food. Women in the disaster area were characterized as being maternal yet somehow unconnected to the chaos surrounding them.

A survey of newspaper and photographic coverage demonstrates that, within the exhibit grounds, gender roles were similarly divided. Male volunteers handled all aspects of crowd control, including shepherding groups of visitors from one display to the next. With few exceptions, male experts explained the technical aspects of the communications displays run by the Bell Telephone Company and a male voice provided soothing narration to the *Destruction of City* display.[52] Alternatively, female volunteers and Girl Guides acted as welcoming hosts to the throngs of visitors, handing out pamphlets, answering questions, and, most importantly, serving up coffee, tea, and biscuits.[53] Hostesses were seen as being instrumental in providing a relaxed atmosphere in which visitors could enjoy their food and converse about what they had just seen, and organizers clearly preferred that these hostesses be as attractive as possible.[54] To capitalize on the coffee and biscuit stands, the CD co-ordinator for Calgary placed local recruitment forms close to the garbage pails.[55]

Both the male and female volunteers, operating under a strict division of labour, were necessary to make the exhibit work smoothly. The gender roles of the volunteers would have been instantly familiar to visitors, since similar partitions were reflected in North American newspaper and magazine advertisements that sold the ideal household along with their products.[56] The important distinction made by the exhibit's promoters was that fulfillment of these roles extended beyond familial obligations – they were a gender-specific civic responsibility. For female volunteers, however, the home would have to come first.

The exhibit's aim to promote CD as an obligation of responsible citizens was achieved by an ordering of the audience.[57] Despite vigorous advertising to create wide public appeal, the exhibit was open to the public for a very limited time in the largest cities on the convoy's tour. Montreal hosted the convoy over four days, but the public was only admitted for eighteen hours. The rest of the time was set aside for special groups. The first night in Montreal was reserved for civic leaders and delegates to the International Municipal Congress. The second night was for CD personnel. The third was reserved for local women's groups, the fourth for industrial workers' groups, and the last night was for veterans. Only then was it open for general admission.[58] This exclusive schedule was made for an inherently pragmatic reason – to boost attendance figures – but it had a political significance that was complementary to the exhibit's message.[59]

By providing local chapters of national organizations such as the Canadian Legion or the Imperial Order Daughters of the Empire with special viewings, an incentive was given to the leaders of such organizations to endorse the convoy publicly, providing free "word of mouth" publicity to the exhibit and improving attendance with the members of their organizations. As historian Keith Walden has demonstrated, organizers had employed exclusive schedules known as "societies' days" to draw in community elites at fairs since the turn of the century.[60]

The composition of the audience, and the organizations that were selected to participate in a "ritual of approval" of the convoy exhibit, illustrate the premium that organizers placed on civic activity and involvement. The audience was structured hierarchically in terms of its contribution to CD as well as by the visitor's perceived status as a responsible citizen. Each of the groups that were invited to special showings by the municipal CD co-ordinator were active supporters of the local organization, which had already demonstrated their commitment to their obligations of citizenship in their communities. Advanced showings allowed exhibit promoters to bestow privileges on these organizations, as prestige in return for their commitment to responsible citizenship, and, at the same time, to benefit from the endorsement of community groups.[61]

Convoy organizers also hoped to underline the exhibit's educational benefits by inviting thousands of school children to the exhibition. Children were intended to leave with a sense of what they could expect in a future war and to understand their responsibility to defend themselves. For Canadian organizers, as for American, the *Destruction of City* display and other films in the exhibit could be used to "introduce tomorrow's citizens to the atomic world in which we appear destined to live," while the spectacular show hopefully set children talking to their parents about the exhibit and civil defence.[62] One of the problems with this strategy was that the organizers assumed that children would view the convoy as an educational opportunity, while many may have simply viewed it as entertainment or a break from monotony. In Calgary, Civil Defence Canada's press officer Harvey Adams complained that "convoy personnel had to be in attendance all the time to prevent [the] show [from] being wrecked by uncontrolled children," which suggests that their teachers may have viewed the convoy as an entertaining field trip rather than as a deadly serious education in nuclear war.[63]

As with the support of community groups, the support of industry was a trade in prestige and publicity. Co-operation with industry formed a key part of the CD agency's disaster planning.[64] The relationship between industry and CD was grounded in public relations as well as in national security. The federal agency planned for the protection of industry, but it could also declare publicly that business executives supported CD. Industries advised the government on aspects of CD and, in return, received publicity that portrayed Canadian industries as responsible citizens contributing to the defence of the country.[65] Some companies took CD preparations more seriously than others. John Labatt Limited Breweries, in co-operation with the National Brewery Workers Union no. 1, organized a Mobile Disaster Service. By September 1951, over 200 employees were qualified for rescue work. The disaster service carried out public rescue exercises and offered their services to nearby communities.[66]

In the name of public service, many companies provided significant resources for the On Guard, Canada! convoy, including free trucks, drivers, tires, and fuel used to move the convoy across the country.[67] Product placement and other means of advertising were the prices paid by the CD agency to secure the support of industry.

Local businesses provided most of the advertising for the convoy. Co-ordinated by each city's CD committees, this advertising embedded the convoy's arrival into the everyday routine of the residents. Such advertising reinforced the message that participation in CD was a vital act of community involvement. In most cases, industries paid for the convoy's advertsising costs in local newspapers. Companies received a credit for publishing the advertisement as a public service. In Halifax, public-spirited businesses and community organizations such as St. John Ambulance collaborated to finance the promotions.[68] Other local firms paid to design and publish their own advertisements in support of the convoy. Nova Scotia Light and Power promised that "all of our resources of men and equipment stand ready for any emergency!" while their mascot offered a jaunty salute to the words "civil defence."[69] In addition to newspaper advertising, store window displays, and short radio broadcasts, municipal organizers convinced local businesses to send out CD publicity to all of their customers.[70] In the press, on the radio, and in their daily routine, residents were reminded of the upcoming show and of their responsibility to play a role in community civil defence.

Strong endorsements of CD by public officials during the tour underpinned the convoy's message. Municipal, provincial, and federal organizers temporarily set aside their differences to insist, repeatedly, that the indiscriminate damage done by an atomic bomb demanded new responsibilities from those living in the community. Lieutenant-Colonel Arnold J. Lavoie, the provincial assistant co-ordinator for CD in Alberta, declared that preparations for nuclear war would be a permanent part of Canadian life, stating explicitly that participating in CD was a duty of citizenship.[71] Health minister Paul Martin provided the most eloquent expression of the convoy's message in an address to his hometown Lions Club in Windsor, where he, like Lavoie, proclaimed that international instability had created another permanent obligation of citizenship. Apart from the traditional duties of citizenship, respect for law in peace, and defence of the nation in war, Martin asserted that "we may be required for the first time to share in defending our own communities, our own families and our own homes against direct enemy attack. Thus, civil defence has added a third dimension to citizenship."[72]

It is not possible to know how visitors reacted to the exhibit, except what may be derived from reports written by local CD directors. Nine hundred and twenty-five visitors joined local organizations in Edmonton and Vancouver in the aftermath of the On Guard, Canada! convoy, while in other areas directors reported increased "interest."[73] Harvey Adams, who was consistently impressed by both the audience turn-out and interest, proposed during the Vancouver exhibit that a "civil defence train" would be a logical next step in the Canadian publicity program. Adams argued that a train would be able to visit those communities with CD organizations that had been excluded from the On Guard, Canada! schedule, including Toronto.[74]

Worthington abruptly rejected the idea of repeating the convoy exercise on 20 January 1954, after conferring with Davidson. In their view, the On Guard, Canada! exhibit did not achieve its aims. While there was considerable local publicity and some limited recruiting, the federal, provincial, and municipal expenditures on the project were too high to justify its showing to less than 200,000 visitors. The federal expenditure alone was over $30,000, and the more successful showings had cost the municipalities well over the $400 federal authorities had predicted would be necessary.[75] Worthington also contended that the exhibit had harmed CD's progress in Canada, since a sizable portion of his staff, and those of local organizations, had to be dedicated to the convoy effort. As a result, the production and publication of much-needed educational media, posters, pamphlets, and manuals had been delayed, and the work of the Transport Branch had been similarly curtailed.[76]

From 1953 onwards, federal CD publicity was issued by more subtle means. The staff of Information Services advised that a long-term publicity program was required, not a short burst of activity designed to grab headlines.[77] After the convoy had returned to the United States, information officers took immediate steps to build formal long-term relationships with the press and radio and television media groups.[78] While not immediately successful, this initiative did eventually lead to a national newspaper series and radio broadcasts in 1955. The initiative gave CD organizers at the local and provincial level the opportunity to publicize preparations and precautions in their area, which was an outlet that provided needed publicity to civil defence without the expense of spectacular exhibits such as the On Guard, Canada! convoy.[79]

Smaller exhibits travelled from Ottawa to support the efforts of provincial and municipal organizations, but none of these had the power or publicity of the convoy. Other efforts to promote CD also fell short, such as Civil Defence Canada's two cartoon mascots "Bea Alerte" and "Justin Case." In a series of colourful posters, the characters warned their guileless fellow citizens away from danger. In one poster, a stern Justin Case, in appearance and attitude almost certainly modelled on Frank Worthington, cautioned a young gambler: "You bet your life ... when you bet against disaster." In another, a calm, sharply dressed Bea Alerte advised that CD could save lives, while in the background a woman ran for her life as a smiling atomic bomb gave chase.[80] Amusing though they were, the mascots never had the popular cachet of the American CD mascot "Bert the Turtle" featured in the 1951 film "Duck and Cover." High-profile federal publicity campaigns eventually slowed to a crawl, however, until the government demanded that citizens start building shelters in their basements in the late 1950s.

FIGURE 10 Civil Defence Canada's mascot: Bea Alerte. *Source:* Canadian War Museum, 20040030-002

Conclusion

Late in the Korean War, favourable publicity was essential to convince Canadians of the need for the organization and to recruit volunteers for training. Canadian officials used the On Guard, Canada! convoy as part of a publicity campaign that sold CD as one of the core obligations of good Canadian citizenship. Through the innovative exhibit displays, exclusive showings to community groups, and the use of volunteers both within the exhibition and in demonstrations outside, officials promoted a hierarchical order of citizenship that accorded prestige to community elites and prescribed strict gender divisions that inextricably linked the role that women could play in disaster to traditional domestic household tasks. This message was taken beyond the boundaries of the exhibit through newspaper and radio advertisements that were supported by industry, street demonstrations, and special tours to schoolchildren.

Canadian organizations used an American exhibit to convey their message in large part because of the close co-operation and liaison between the two agencies at all levels of government to meet a shared threat. The American offer to share their convoy for free was also hugely convenient for Canadian officials, who otherwise lacked the resources to launch a national publicity campaign of the same scope on their own. Their failure to capitalize on the exhibition with additional publicity indicated a lack of will on the part of the government to continue their public relations campaign.

The federal government and Civil Defence Canada were always willing to discuss the organization in terms of the obligations owed to it by the public, but they never pledged an equivalent level of sustained financial or political support. The convoy's publicity blitz may have raised awareness about CD temporarily, but after it departed so too did the federal support for local activities that might have kept CD going as the Korean War ground to a halt and the organization lost its wartime urgency.

4

Evacuation and Celebration, 1954-56

FROM 1954 TO 1956, Canada enjoyed a period of political stability and remark-able economic growth. Canadians in ever greater numbers could afford to purchase homes and start families in the suburbs, and thousands did so, further fuelling the economy and changing the face of life in cities. Yet the arms race also accelerated, as the Soviet Union and the United States successively tested more destructive hydrogen bombs – weapons that were exponentially more powerful than those dropped on Hiroshima and Nagasaki.

The hydrogen bomb was a scientific breakthrough that unsettled military planners, the public, and politicians. In late 1954, the foreign minister, Lester B. Pearson, voiced his growing unease about the arms race. He warned an audience in Princeton, New Jersey, that "a war which begins on an island ... may soon spread to a world."[1] But what kind of war would it be? By February 1955, experts reporting to US President Dwight Eisenhower confirmed what the public already feared – war meant "death and destruction on a scale almost beyond knowing, and certainly beyond any sensibility to shock and horror that men have so far experienced."[2] Soviet observers reported that the size of the explosion "tran-scended some kind of psychological barrier," a destructive potential that lived solely in the imagination before the nuclear arms race made it a reality.[3]

The changing nature of the international and nuclear balance forced emer-gency planners around the world to revise their basic assumptions about policy and their strategies for survival.[4] Like most NATO members, Canada gradually abandoned its early Cold War "self-help" strategy for CD. Military and civilian planners had always maintained that the atomic bomb was, in principle, only different from conventional explosives in scale.[5] They had therefore recom-mended the combination of shelter, firefighting, and rescue that had been used extensively in Germany and the United Kingdom during the Second World War. Now, however, the city-killing hydrogen bomb offered a persuasive argu-ment against their plans. To begin, the United States and later Canada adopted a policy of planned evacuation, where success hinged on the swift but orderly exodus of residents from major urban centres prior to an attack.

The evacuation strategy changed the nature of CD not only inside cities but also in the surrounding rural towns and counties that would be expected to house, feed, and care for the waves of nuclear refugees. Planners slowly recognized that this new strategy called for national, not local, solutions. The industrial metropolis, to which so many Canadians had moved after the Second World War, was no longer the last line of defence. The agrarian countryside had taken its place. The breadbasket of the country would serve as a refuge for displaced urban populations. This change of strategy took place even as municipal governments disbanded their organizations, rebelling at the cost of maintaining CD in peacetime and at the fierce federal-provincial disputes over financial policy that were still unresolved.

Maintaining interest among the volunteers that were needed to co-ordinate evacuation and reception was still a vital challenge to CD. The lack of an immediate war emergency made nuclear drills an unattractive occupation of Canadians' free time, despite Civil Defence Canada's repeated appeals to their sense of civic responsibility. Evacuation exercises and headlines about hydrogen weapons did, however, prompt a brief resurgence of interest in CD. For the first time, CD exercises involved not just a handful of volunteers but also tens of thousands of citizens who were asked to "flee" their city. "Operation Lifesaver," an enormous public exercise that dispersed a quarter of Calgary's population to the safety of the countryside, was Canada's largest test case for evacuation. The exercise was meant to determine how to conduct an efficient, lawful, and safe evacuation of a city. Its organizers also sought to expand the reach of CD preparations from target cities to the rural countryside.

As a case study for evacuations, Operation Lifesaver made clear that evacuation created as many problems as it was meant to solve. Not least among these were the silences in the exercise's script, especially about the willingness of rural populations to share homes and food with refugees. The lethal and inconvenient effects of radioactive fallout also went entirely ignored. As the Canadian government belatedly came to grips with the implications of fallout by 1956, it became evident that the newly minted evacuation strategy was impractical and not nearly sufficient to ensure the survival of the country.

The Hydrogen Bomb and Civil Defence

The first hydrogen fusion bomb was detonated on the Eniwetok Atoll in the American Pacific Proving Grounds in 1952, followed eight months later by the first successful Soviet test. Photographs showed that the Eniwetok explosion completely destroyed the atoll, and smashed a crater 175 feet deep into the ocean floor. A second, much larger, "Bravo" test on Bikini Atoll produced a fifteen-megaton blast (the equivalent of fifteen million tons of TNT) that surprised and alarmed even those atomic scientists observing the blast. A 100-mile diameter mushroom cloud spread over ground zero, scattering pulverized and irradiated coral and sand over the ocean. Eighty-two miles downwind of the explosion, the entire crew of the Japanese fishing boat *The Lucky Dragon* fell ill from radiation sickness as the dust settled on their exposed skin. Their illnesses and deaths revealed the lethality of fallout, a hitherto underestimated radioactive by-product of nuclear blasts. In the first week of April 1954, alarming footage and photographs from the test were carried in newspapers around the world.[6]

News of the bomb's effects, coming so soon after Western intelligence agencies determined that the Soviet Union had successfully detonated a hydrogen bomb of its own in August 1953, shocked the Canadian public. Everywhere in the press, Canadians were presented with recently released aerial photographs of the undersea crater created by one of the American test shots in the Pacific.[7] Pearson's warning against the unrestricted pursuit of bigger and better bombs appeared beside images of total destruction and gave voice to concerns that the lure of technological advancement had overwhelmed good sense and international stability. An editorial cartoon published in the *Halifax Chronicle Herald* captured the anxious mood. The cartoon placed technology in the driver's seat; a robust, arrogant, anthropomorphized hydrogen bomb towered above the clouds, with a riding crop in one hand and the reins of "civilization" in the other.[8] A similar cartoon in *La Presse* depicted a boy holding a clutch of balloons labelled "Bombe H"; he cries out: "Misère j'ai oublié de prendre un billet de retour!" (I forgot to buy a return ticket!), as humanity's sinister discovery pulls him higher from the safety of the ground.[9]

The hydrogen bomb's arrival hit Civil Defence Canada particularily hard because it was coupled with the precipitous decline of public interest in the CD organization since the end of the Korean War. Civil defence planners were left struggling to find a role that was relevant to Canadians in peacetime, especially once they were aware of the scale of destruction and fatalities that would occur if hydrogen bombs were used. In British Columbia's *Civil Defence Circular* in early 1954, volunteers in Victoria lamented CD's apparent decline in the province.[10] The editorial board for the *Victoria Daily Times,* which supported the local organization, also noted this trend: "Many a citizen who would willingly man a gun in war time has no intention of spending in peacetime even one night a week or a month under a tin helmet, equipping himself for possible emergency."[11] One of the volunteers in Victoria's CD organization vented his or her frustration (male and female membership in CD being roughly equal) in the circular through a poem entitled *Epitaph ... 195?:* "Here lies the body of Tardy Tom/Who got in the way of an Atom Bomb/He might have survived through Common Sense/And taken a course in Civil Defence."[12] Retaining members proved to be as great a problem as recruiting them. As a sense of futility often prevented new recruits from joining the CD organizations, disinterest led the valuable, newly trained volunteers to leave their posts. The strength of CD organizations across the country slowly bled away. Federal training officers attempted to address the problem by changing the format of training courses to include entertainment that would at least sustain trainees' interest.

Diminished commitment and municipal politics led to the abandonment of CD in Victoria and Montreal, two key Canadian target cities. Victoria's CD organization did not long outlive the end of the hostilities in Korea. In October 1954, Victoria's city council abolished the city's program. Councillors blamed the federal government for a lack of financial support to maintain the organization in peacetime. Despite a plea from British Columbia's provincial authorities to preserve the voluntary organization, most of the city's nearly 4,000 remaining CD volunteers quit, leaving only a few dedicated hangers-on.[13] The situation repeated itself in Montreal. In late 1954, newly elected mayor Jean Drapeau and twenty-eight of his colleagues from the Civic Action League, a municipal political party, promised voters that they would stop wasting municipal money. Metropolitan Montreal's CD organization was an easy target. The city council abolished it as a waste of the city's time and money and promptly converted the municipality's fleet of CD transport vehicles into garbage trucks. Civil Defence Canada officials thought that Victoria's defection was unfortunate, but Montreal's was intolerable because it left one of Canada's most valuable target cities without a CD agency, even as a showcase.

Meeting with the Montreal City Council in early 1955, Worthington castigated its members for putting lives at risk. He argued that the federal government could not help the city on its own. Civil Defence Canada's principles of self-defence demanded sacrifice and investment by the city and its residents. To provide a historical example, Worthington claimed that "the early settlers of Montreal itself would have been massacred by the Indians had the citizens themselves not been prepared to defend themselves."[14] The co-ordinator threatened that the Soviets were at the gate, armed with thermonuclear weapons, and he hinted to councillors that many of the congratulatory letters they had received for disbanding the wasteful CD corps were written by domestic Communists.[15] The councillors were unmoved. Civil defence trucks continued to haul garbage in Montreal.

The most prominent Canadian defections were the result of the persistent fiscal and jurisdictional complaints that had dogged the organization since its post-war revival. In Victoria and Montreal, municipal councillors justified their decision in public by deriding CD as a waste of money and as an outmoded method of defence in the thermonuclear age. The federal government could not compel these cities to reinstate CD but could only appeal to the public to overrule their municipal governments. This situation stands in contrast to the response of the Home Office in the United Kingdom when Coventry's city council discarded its CD. Coventry's leaders had reasonably concluded that CD preparations could not defend its citizens against a thermonuclear attack. They chose instead to disband their organization to save money and to "strengthen the hands of international statesmen in their efforts to ban the hydrogen bomb."[16] Sir David Maxwell Fyfe, the British home secretary, responded by appointing commissioners to carry on Coventry's preparations at local expense, a power accorded to him by CD legislation passed in 1948.[17] Worthington and Paul Martin had no such power, so CD vanished for a time in Victoria and Montreal. Civil Defence Canada's public appeals to persuade doubtful Canadians of their organization's continuing relevance in 1954-55 were premature because they had no policy that could offer a realistic defence against the hydrogen bomb. The Cabinet Defence Committee (CDC) turned to an evacuation strategy as the answer, which placed previously unconsidered, but highly pressing, demands on the provinces and municipalities, especially in regions surrounding the target cities.

Towards an Evacuation Policy

The Department of National Defence was the first government institution to reach the conclusion that Canada's CD policies required reorientation. The need became apparent in 1953, during revisions to the Defence of Canada Regulations, which set the terms of the War Measures Act. These revisions expanded government involvement and control over the economy, civil liberties, and the armed forces during emergencies.[18] Revisions were overdue, made necessary by the transfer of responsibility for CD to the Department of National Health and Welfare two years earlier. Lieutenant-General Charles Foulkes, the chairman of the Canadian Chiefs of Staff Committee (COSC), wanted to ensure that his soldiers would be available for war in Europe and not preoccupied with digging out corpses on the home front. At the very least, he wished to avoid giving CD authorities (and, more importantly, the public) the false impression that the army would be prepared to step into the breach after a nuclear blast.[19]

During discussions at the COSC, Foulkes maintained that the "self-help" concept of CD – the model that had served London so well during the Blitz – was outmoded.[20] Canadian intelligence estimates about Soviet capabilities suggested that the army might be forced in any case to step in to help the country survive. The Joint Planning Committee supported these predictions. The Soviets' long-range thermonuclear bomber fleet, once clear of North America's air defences, would in all likelihood annihilate the CD organizations that planners had worked so hard to establish, along with the target cities that they were meant to defend. The Canadian armed forces would be the only standing force capable of salvaging life and property.[21]

On 15 January 1954, the COSC directed the Joint Intelligence Committee to inform CD authorities about the scale of the Soviet threat and to urge them to make changes accordingly.[22] The armed forces' leadership spent much of the next year devising a policy that would meet Canada's two general war aims. These were to prevent the destruction or serious disruption of North America's industrial potential and to prevent Soviet forces from overrunning Western Europe. Neither aim could be met if the other was neglected. The updated policy, finalized nearly a year later, made modest concessions towards increasing the Canadian army's presence in CD. More officers would attend CD training courses, and municipalities near Canadian bases could expect advice from military liaison officers, which would be offered mainly to ensure that local plans did not hinder mobilization.[23] Air Marshal Roy Slemon, chief of the air staff, later admitted during a meeting with Worthington and the deputy ministers of the Department of National Health and Welfare that, if the entire strength of the Canadian armed services was given over to CD, "even these resources would seem insignificant in the light of the magnitude of the problem."[24] The verdict from the armed services was clear: Canadian cities and towns could not expect much assistance from their armed forces in a thermonuclear war.

The federal government announced its findings in March 1954 at the fourth Federal-Provincial Conference on Civil Defence. That the conference was held at all indicated the gravity of the situation. Paul Martin, who had been tagged by a journalist as the "part-time minister for civil defence," did not share Worthington's enthusiasm for CD and had even less patience for dealing with provincial grievances. Martin had managed to delay the federal-provincial meeting for two years, but George Davidson, his deputy minister, patiently insisted that the matter could no longer be delayed because the country urgently required better CD preparations.[25] The conference took place at the new Canadian Civil Defence College in Arnprior, Ontario, on the site of a wartime British Commonwealth Air Training Plan station. The college consisted of thirty buildings converted for training purposes and rescue simulations at a cost of $250,000. In its first year of operation, 2,000 trainees visited the college from provincial and municipal CD agencies, the armed forces, and police and fire services.[26]

Although much of what was discussed at the conference dealt with financial responsibility for CD, half of the items on the agenda examined new developments in nuclear weapons technology and their implications for CD plans. The military appreciation of the international situation was a classified lecture based on the latest intelligence about Soviet capabilities, presented to a smaller group of delegates, most of whom were federal public servants. The film *Operation Ivy* was also screened at the conference to display the destructive power of the megaton blast.[27]

At the conference, the federal government laid out its initial proposals to alter CD strategy and basic assumptions. The federal CD office would amend the Financial Assistance Program to enable direct federal-municipal co-operation on projects where the province refused to co-operate. Previously, where the provinces had refused to commit matching funds to support municipal projects, federal monies were left unused and local agencies, especially in Ontario, Newfoundland, and Quebec were beggared. The federal government's concession, offered at the conference, was meant to bypass provincial obstruction to help these organizations fend off failure. In light of the changing threat, the federal government had little alternative but to commit more resources to help the cities survive war.

Paul Martin addressed the Arnprior conference with a detailed and frank speech about the threat to Canadians and the need for more concerted efforts to develop a civilian defence program that would defeat or mitigate the destructive power of the atom bomb. The minister listed off some of Canada's accomplishments in the CD field: over 160,000 registered volunteers, with more than 3,000 trained in federal courses, twenty-four target areas established and identified, over $2 million worth of materiel and supplies delivered to the provinces, 400 or more air-raid sirens installed in Canadian cities, fire hose coupling standardization under way in three provinces, and more than $9 million invested in stockpiling medical supplies. Yet Canadians, he warned, had much left to accomplish:

> Despite what we have done ... I doubt if we could honestly say that many of our Canadian target cities are even yet fully capable of coping in organized fashion with the dropping of an A-bomb of the 20 KT [kiloton] variety. But the 20 KT atom bomb that opened up in 1945 this awful new atomic world to us ... this bomb of 1945 is just a pop-gun in the 1954 arsenal of lethal man-destroying weapons ... No government at any level can stand aside and say that it takes no responsibility for its own people – and that, and nothing less than that, is what is now at stake ... All the provinces ... and *all our major cities* must take their fair share of this responsibility ... if we are not to fail in our elementary duty to the people whom we jointly represent.[28]

Journalists observing the opening of the CD college commented favourably on Martin's apparently decisive approach to changing strategies and predicted sweeping changes to his organization in the weeks ahead.[29] However, Martin's speech did not translate into immediate action.[30]

The minister was less concerned about the hydrogen bomb threat than by impending questions from the opposition benches about what CD was going to do about it.[31] After the conference had ended, Martin sought answers from his organization about how to respond to questions about the hydrogen bomb. At a departmental meeting on 28 April 1954, he complained that the information that had reached his desk about CD's answer to a hydrogen bomb attack was inadequate. The newest addition to the staff, Major-General Matthew Penhale, who had left his organization in Winnipeg to accept an appointment as commandant of the CD college, suggested an ad hoc committee to provide more definitive commentary on the necessary changes. Martin agreed and immediately appointed him to direct the committee with George Davidson's assistance. The Ad Hoc Committee to Study the Effects of the Hydrogen Bomb in Civil Defence Planning (Ad Hoc Committee) also included Dr. E.E. Massey, the Defence Research Board's (DRB) scientific advisor for CD, and several of Worthington's most capable staff. Their role was to evaluate how the average Canadian community would be affected in a thermonuclear attack and whether anything could be done in the next six months that could mitigate the damage. Martin wondered: "Should we adopt an all-out policy of telling the people everything, or should we soft-pedal the effects to avoid panic?"[32] The committee ultimately decided to disclose all of the available information about hydrogen bomb effects to the public, even if it provoked alarm.

The committee considered whether an evacuation policy could work for Canadian cities. When Canadian planners used the term "evacuation," they referred to a multi-phase withdrawal of the civilian population from cities. The first phase, known as "pre-attack evacuation," entailed the planned movement of vulnerable citizens from target areas, which would occur after the government announced a state of emergency. Civil defence officials believed that the ideal conditions for an evacuation included an extended period of international crisis that would serve as a strategic warning of possible nuclear war and that would provide local CD wardens with enough time to evacuate the elderly, the disabled, hospitalized patients, and some women and children from target cities to surrounding reception and mutual aid areas.

"Tactical withdrawal," the second phase, involved the movement of mass populations from target areas after officials had received warning of an impending attack. According to mental health specialists asked to advise the government about the psychological effects of an atomic or thermonuclear attack on mass populations, information and familiarity were vital to the evacuation process. Familiarity, experts agreed, bred acceptance and defeated panic. By this logic, cities and citizens were the same as soldiers learning a routine drill – in an emergency, training would suppress the human instincts for flight or panic. Persuading the population to accept either phase of the evacuation process meant a great deal more than learning rally points and proper traffic procedure. Experts did not believe that everyone would or could be evacuated. Volunteers and able-bodied men and women would have to endure the strain of sending children and loved ones away for possibly long periods of separation. Worthington's Advisory Committee of Social Scientists believed that those who were left behind after a pre-attack evacuation would be at the greatest risk:

> The stress of the tactical withdrawal situation will probably be so great that no amount of planning will be adequate to the task of control unless extensive efforts go into the education of the populace in developing the secondary motive of self-sacrifice. Death is the inevitable lot of man in any case and it can be – and often has been – faced without panic by those who were willing to die for a purpose greater than themselves. In the past, this has been for the glory of the courageous few; in the future it must become the accepted value of the majority. Such a populace will still desire self-preservation, but will in addition, still desire the preservation of their dependents and of their values still more.[33]

In the age of thermonuclear weapons, the principle of responsible citizenship in CD had a grim, mostly unspoken implication. Some citizens, possibly a large number, would have to sacrifice themselves so that others could survive. During the early Cold War, American, Canadian, and British CD planners reasoned that one of their agencies' main contributions to the preparation for a future war was public education, with the aim of controlling panic and fear. In 1949, Worthington had met psychiatrists from the Allan Memorial Institute at McGill University on the advice of the DRB to discuss a means of increasing the resistance of the civilian population to panic. Dr. James Tyhurst launched a study to examine how different racial and social groups reacted to danger and how to select leaders from a community preparing for disaster.[34] Tyhurst's earlier research about individual responses to community disaster indicated that citizens exposed to trauma underwent periods of reaction that influenced their behaviour during a crisis and their ability to cope in the aftermath of disasters.[35] The DRB project would extend his findings to predict possible reactions to a thermonuclear war and to propose methods to treat those individuals suffering from post-traumatic stress. The project lapsed for several years before it resumed in 1954, but the question of panic control and proper conditioning of the public remained a subject of study for the CD organization.[36]

Martin brought his department's evacuation strategy recommendations to Cabinet for approval in November 1954. He requested that the federal agency take on new responsibilities for CD. Martin argued that the government had to take over full responsibility for advance attack warning in order to ensure that warnings from the Royal Canadian Air Force's (RCAF) Air Defence Control Centre in St. Hubert, Quebec, would reach the cities in time for some evacuation to take place. The health minister asked for 200 additional staff for CD and the armed forces and a $10 million annual increase in CD expenditures. Cabinet approved these additional resources and determined that the RCAF would take over all of the key staffing positions to ensure uniformity as well as to ensure that the transmission of warnings giving cities advance notice was as reliable as possible.

Advance warning was necessary because cities would require as much time as possible to move people and vital equipment out of the blast's range. By early 1954, only a few cities had developed training courses or significant plans for evacuation. Martin endorsed the Ad Hoc Committee's recommendation of a two-year tour of Canadian target cities by federal officials in order to stimulate local planning and rehearsal for evacuation. He also requested authority to begin stockpiling equipment needed to billet and house millions of displaced people as well as funds to accelerate the medical stockpiling program.[37] Although the thrust of the CD policy required change, Martin argued against abandoning the federal training programs for wardens, police, and fire staff at the Canadian Civil Defence College because trained volunteers could still save the lives of Canadians caught in areas that were not completely incinerated by the bomb. His Ad Hoc Committee believed that disbanding the courses would reduce the appeal of CD organizations that focused on disaster training, a peacetime application for CD that many municipal agencies had adopted to survive local austerity measures.[38]

The CDC, meeting in December 1954, did not immediately move to adopt the Ad Hoc Committee's recommendations but instead authorized an extensive study of the evacuation policy by additional sub-committees, some administered by Civil Defence Canada and others by the Canadian army. The government had neither the resources nor the political will to quickly implement all that was required for an effective evacuation policy. Firefighting and rescue operations in a destroyed city would be difficult but developing a nationwide capability to accommodate entire cities of refugees was a problem of enormous magnitude and cost. Evacuation of Canada's major urban centres, even for a short time or a false alarm, would create conditions that could easily deteriorate into mass panic or cause a significant disruption to commerce. The unilateral adoption of an evacuation policy at the federal level would, in turn, have an impact on municipal costs and claims for compensation for improving road and transportation systems – costs previously dismissed as being unrelated to CD preparations under the terms of the Financial Assistance Program. The CDC delayed a decision on the matter as a result of these considerations.

The federal government did, however, act on a draft plan entitled "Evacuation of Selected Cities," which identified several major target areas that should be evacuated based on principles for the dispersion of Canadian cities agreed on by the COSC in late 1954. Civil Defence Canada did not yet know the best methods or planning processes that would help cities prepare for evacuation because the large-scale movement of the population was a new and untested strategy.[39] Worthington formed a "Federal Planning Team" that worked mainly in Ottawa to collect information about basic planning and procedures from the United States and the United Kingdom. The federal office contributed advice and information bulletins about evacuation and offered, in co-operation with their provincial counterparts, limited financial assistance for municipal evacuation studies and exercises.[40]

Other countries were engaged in the study of evacuation strategies for their urban centres. Canadian planners benefitted from ongoing bilateral and multilateral discussions with the United States and NATO. Most of Canada's information about the effects of the hydrogen bomb originated from the United States' Federal Civil Defense Administration, the Atomic Energy Commission, and through biannual meetings of the Canada-United States Civil Defence Committee. This committee comprised bilateral working groups that examined food distribution, standardization of firefighting equipment, joint billeting and assistance of refugees across the border, and other issues. Evacuation was also scrutinized by the North Atlantic Council's Civil Defence Committee in Paris, where individual NATO countries were struggling to standardize policy. NATO's Civil Defence Committee was an outgrowth of a Working Group on Civil Organization in Time of War, which first convened in the summer of 1952 to examine the overall effects of war on Western society, ranging from the problem of refugees and billeting to questions of sabotage and security. This group's focus was too broad, and so NATO's North Atlantic Council formed the Civil Defence Committee with a smaller mandate to act as a forum for the exchange of ideas about the technical and administrative aspects of CD with a goal of determining "common lines of action."[41] Canada's ambassador to NATO represented Canadian views at the committee's meetings.

Lord Ismay, the secretary-general of NATO, sought to co-ordinate and promote a common CD policy throughout NATO. He believed that failure to do so could undermine the will of Western Europe to stand fast against a Communist invasion: "The people of Western Europe have the bitter experience of the last war in their minds and ... are inclined to think that nothing – not even life under a communist dictatorship – could be worse than another experience of an aerial bombardment."[42] However, questions of national sovereignty, and the insistence by some countries on "common financing" for evacuation, made agreement on a standard response difficult, and the Civil Defence Committee ultimately abandoned its attempt to develop a common approach. Its divided reaction to the thermonuclear threat was a case in point.[43]

Most delegates to the North Atlantic Council recognized that the hydrogen bomb represented a shift in destructive power, but American secrecy delayed work on determining a common solution. As the Canadian member of the NATO committee commented, "very little appeared to be known of this weapon by any country but the United States and it is quite obvious that they alone have the secrets."[44] Further, most European NATO allies did not feel as threatened by the hydrogen bomb as North American representatives on the committee. Judging from the positions of their representatives at the NATO meetings, Europeans believed that their cities would not have to evacuate because they expected the Soviets to use tactical nuclear weapons against their military formations in order to avoid irreparably damaging the industrial potential of Western Europe. They gave at best tepid support to an evacuation strategy that was largely untested. At the end of 1954, in accordance with the CDC's tentative support for evacuation, the Canadian delegate informed the NATO Civil Defence Committee that Canada would hold a series of test evacuations in Canada, the largest set for Calgary in 1955.[45]

Operation Lifesaver

The first Canadian evacuations took place in the fall and winter of 1954 from St. John's, Newfoundland, and Brockville, Ontario. The primary aim of these exercises was to test whether the large-scale movement of the populace was possible on short notice. In Brockville, over 15,000 residents evacuated the city by car, bus, and truck without any road accidents or traffic jams. The exercise tested the ability of auxiliary CD police and existing emergency services to direct the flow of traffic and prevent congestions that would endanger the city's survival.[46] A secondary, but no less important, goal of these evacuations was to inform Canadians about what they could expect in an emergency and to tell them where to go, what to bring, and, most importantly, how to behave.[47] An orderly evacuation would save lives. A panicked evacuation could create traffic jams, dooming evacuees.

Calgary's CD authorities hoped that their exercise would instill in residents a sense of duty as citizens to support the local organization. The city's officials could not, however, prevent the exercise, and others like it, from taking on the atmosphere of a civic festival. The public, unable or unwilling to grasp the predicted devastation that nuclear war would bring to their cities, transformed the event into an adventure for the whole family. The resurgence of interest in CD in Calgary and elsewhere receded once the festival of evacuation and return ended.

Evacuation exercises were different than most CD tests. Most exercises were conducted in plotting rooms by officials who tested plans on maps and paper to refine existing procedures and new concepts. Often, these exercises were meant to co-ordinate responses between federal and provincial governments, between Canada and the United States, or, more rarely, between NATO countries. Exercises involving the public's participation were uncommon, but they attracted far more attention, which was not surprising. This type of CD activity should be understood as part demonstration and part spectacle. As theatre historian Tracy Davis has argued, exercises were "rehearsals" or "performances" designed to draw the unimaginable closer to reality.[48] Municipalities developed mock air-raid drills, evacuations, and mass care or feeding exercises to show the public the right way to do something in peacetime so that they would know how to behave properly in a war. Civil Defence Canada kept a close eye on the public's reaction to false alarms, for example, in order to measure the effect of fear on Canada's preparedness.

On the night of 21 May 1954, a fire in Winnipeg helped illustrate the point of public exercises. The fire set off an accidental sounding of Winnipeg's air-raid sirens. Thousands of residents immediately rushed to the phones, clogging telephone switchboards and police and fire dispatchers. The authors of the *Winnipeg Metropolitan Civil Defence Board Bulletin* classified the public response as "very close to panic" and bemoaned the short memory of residents who had been told repeatedly not to use the telephone in the event of an air raid: "Yes, a lot of people lost some sleep ... a lot of people got a scare – that was unfortunate. Now most of them had forgotten it – THAT IS TRAGIC."[49] Civil defence planners counted on realism in their plans to attract crowds of onlookers to the wider aim of educating the public about CD and creating greater support for local organizations.

On 11 February 1955, representatives from the federal government and the provinces of Alberta and British Columbia issued statements that Calgary and Greater Vancouver had been chosen to host the first large-scale "planned withdrawal" studies. These studies included plans for an exercise to evacuate 48,000 to 50,000 citizens from Calgary to determine solutions to various problems associated with the tactical withdrawal of the population of a large area. Calgary's CD planners divided the city into four sectors. Sector B, which was north of the Bow River and east of 4th Street NW, was chosen to host the evacuation study because of its blend of commercial, residential, and industrial neighbour-hoods. It was not publicly acknowledged that an evacuation of the northeast sector of the city would also be the easiest to carry off because the area had less traffic.[50] A second exercise was planned for Vancouver to simulate the total evacuation of an area on short notice.[51] The Canadian exercises followed on the heels of an announcement of similar mass evacuation exercises in the United States in the winter of 1955, the largest planned for schoolchildren in the city of Mobile, Alabama.[52]

The tactical withdrawal studies announced in February 1955 were designed to carry out an evacuation under near-ideal conditions in the provinces that the federal government considered to be the most prepared for atomic attack. They were not the first evacuation exercises held on Canadian soil, but they were certainly the most ambitious, requiring integrated, extensive planning and the co-ordination of all three levels of government, thousands of volunteers in different cities, and, above all else, the co-operation and assistance of nearly a quarter of the population of a major Canadian city.

Calgary was selected for the first major evacuation exercise because of the size of its organization and its complement of trained CD workers. Several Albertan municipalities had carried out exercises in previous years, most of which were positively received by the press, but this evacuation exercise was much more complicated than mock air raids held in small towns such as Ponoka, Alberta.[53] It was to be the largest evacuation in North America to date, with different aims than those held in Brockville and St. John's. Calgary's evacuation would succeed or fail based on the preparedness of its block warden system to register and inform the public and the willingness of individuals to participate. The evacuation's organizers also wanted to test the adjoining municipalities' ability to receive and support refugees. Evacuees would not be asked to leave the city's limits and return immediately, as had been the case in Brockville, but would travel in multiple convoys to mutual aid and reception areas in the sur-rounding countryside. Drumheller, which was nearly 140 kilometres away, was the planned destination for a significant number of the evacuees. As such, Calgary's exercise was also Drumheller's, where volunteers would have to register and care for thousands of citizens. Similar tests would accompany Calgarians as they arrived in sixteen other cities and towns, including Acme, Airdrie, Beiseker, Bowden, Carbon, Carstairs, Crossfield, Didsbury, Drumheller, Innis-fail, Irricana, Olds, Penhold, Rockyford, Strathmore, Three Hills, and Trouhu.[54] In May 1955, Calgary's Civil Defence Planning Committee officially named the evacuation "Operation Lifesaver" to underline the exercise's ultimate goal.[55]

Calgary's CD organization prepared for Operation Lifesaver without much federal assistance, relying on its own voluntary staff who travelled to the CD control centre (at a local golf club) in the evenings to plot how best to evacuate the city. The enormity of the job took G.O. Bell, the city's co-ordinator, by surprise. Even with a large number of enthusiastic and determined volunteers, the exercise occupied all of his time. In April, Calgary's post office delivered 10,941 preliminary notices, as wardens began a block-to-block canvass of homes. The notice was addressed to the male head of household. It explained the reason for the exercise and asked that he follow all of the directions of the CD workers and police during the evacuation. It would also issue a warning if the homeowner failed to comply: "You and your children (and it could just as easily be you and yours as anyone else!) might be trampled to death in a frenzied mob, or killed by the bomb because your progress out of the city was impeded by impassable bottle necks."[56]

The warden's survey, which followed the mail-out, provides a sense of the scale of work involved in preparing the city to evacuate. Bell and others believed that a survey of each household would take a short five-minute interview, but this estimate was dashed by experience. Each warden eventually canvassed over one hundred houses, explaining their jobs and the purpose of the exercise, and gathering information about how many lived in the household, where they worked, and whether they had their own transport for the evacuation or relied on a neighbour or public transit. On average, each interview took over half an hour to complete, but the face-to-face personal interaction between the public and the wardens might have accounted for the high percentage of respondents who co-operated.[57] In the neighbourhoods that the wardens visited, 92 percent of households agreed to participate in the exercise. According to Bell, the remaining 8 percent said that they could not participate for reasons of illness or because they had other obligations, not because they rejected the need for the exercise.

Calgary's city council played a significant part in developing public awareness and support for the exercise. Only two city councillors had voted against the planned exercise, calling it a waste of money and time. According to a federal observer, they were "somewhat appalled" at the high percentage of Calgarians who agreed to participate. Calgary's mayor Don MacKay, by contrast, publicly declared his full support for the exercises, stating that he "would prefer to hear that the evacuation was a success than to hear that Calgary had won the Grey Cup in 1955."[58] Municipal councillors gave Calgary's CD organization surprising control over the city's business for the exercise. It was planned for a half-day holiday on 21 September 1955, creating favourable conditions for businesses and industries to close down and send their employees to participate. Employers agreed not to penalize union members who left the job to participate, and unions agreed not to apply for overtime or travel pay.[59] School boards in the area were notified that they and their students were expected to participate in the exercise, and teachers instructed children to time how long it took them to walk home from schools, so that they had an understanding of how much time they would need to evacuate.[60] Calgary was given the right to refuse exemptions for offices and businesses that did not want to participate.[61]

Calgary's CD aggressively targeted volunteer community and charitable organizations that were likely to support Civil Defence Canada's overall message of defence through community service. Planners visited voluntary groups throughout the city, offering lectures about CD and evacuation and asking for the co-operation of their volunteers. In early May 1955, Calgary's exercise planning committee asked local ministers to promote the evacuation exercise during their sermons. As Bell later explained to Harvey Adams, "we feel the churches can do an immense public relations job for us."[62] The appeal had some success. Reverend John Pottruff of the North Hill United Church attended a lecture about CD presented to the Calgary Optimist Club (a service organization established in Calgary before the war) and was so moved that he wrote and delivered a sermon to his congregation, entitled "The September Evacuation – Is It Vital?" which provided full-blooded support for CD and the evacuation.[63] The dean of Calgary's Anglican Church promised the Civil Defence Planning Committee that he would promote the exercise in each of his monthly parochial letters leading up to September 1955.[64]

Community groups responded to the committee's outreach efforts with pledges to support Operation Lifesaver. The Canadian National Institute for the Blind's Calgary chapter was offered an exemption for the exercise, which the group indignantly turned down. The local chapter was eager to participate.[65] The planning committee also astutely sought out support from the largest community event in Calgary, the Stampede. The Stampede's Parade Committee offered a location for a CD contingent to set up, while provincial officials included CD films in the annual Stampede show. Calgary's Civil Defence Planning Committee chose to display *Operation Ivy*, a film about the American hydrogen bomb trials in the Pacific, which had been edited so that a Canadian spokesman delivered the final commentary.[66]

While planners in Calgary's organization were working overtime, federal and provincial CD agencies agreed to split the estimated $31,000 cost of the exercise evenly under the terms of the Financial Assistance Program. The provincial government was thoroughly engaged with exercise planning outside Calgary's city limits, working with rural municipalities to prepare them for their share of the "evacuees" and establishing a network of breakdown and recovery vehicles along the highways. The province contracted with the RCMP to ensure that all incoming traffic was stopped within fifteen miles of the evacuation area. The province also requested the assistance of the Canadian armed forces to establish a communications centre at RCAF Station North in Calgary to link with fixed radio stations in reception areas and with police radio bands.[67]

Federal government involvement was limited. However, the Department of Health and Welfare's Information Services Division (ISD) did become heavily involved in underwriting publicity to help Calgary's CD gain additional media coverage for the exercise. Harvey Adams, director of the ISD, offered his services to Bell in April 1955. Adams suggested that the exercise would benefit from a press office, which would provide journalists with greater access to CD head-quarters during the exercise. Adams believed that allowing journalists to report from the site would result in accurate and favourable stories about the exercise.[68] In the early 1950s, the press office had rapidly become an indispensable media relation's tool at Canadian exercises. The goal of including a press office adjacent to the operations room at the exercise was to permit information services to prepare an open forum for press investigation and enquiries, while simultan-eously exercising control over the type and amount of information packaged for journalists at such events.[69] In short, it aimed to create uniformity in the reporting of stories in the daily newspapers and radio broadcasts and to avoid the potential for embarrassment. The press office was used across government departments to co-ordinate major events, and it reflected the federal govern-ment's increasingly sophisticated public relations for all of its programs, includ-ing CD.

As early as 1949, the Directorate of Public Information at the Department of National Defence had advised Worthington to adopt the use of a press officer at CD events, in large part because of the department's own experience with natural disasters: "Reporters who cover the disaster can never find anyone of authority to discuss and get information from and, in the final analysis, gener-ally obtain their information from 'the village idiot.'"[70] The press officer policy was born from a natural mistrust of the media, and it meant that CD planners, many of whom were retired military officers used to giving orders, did not craft messages for consumption by the media and/or the public.[71]

Adams, a former journalist, understood the imperatives of the newsroom and worked tirelessly to promote Operation Lifesaver. Calgary's CD office was happy to have the help. Bell was displeased with the coverage that was being provided by the local press. The press frustrated Bell because, as he put it to Worthington: "They don't always publish just what I tell them – because they think they know best just how much the public wants to know."[72] He also noted that the press, intentionally or not, had a tendency to misreport his intentions. Bell was the only person in the city who was aware of the precise time at which the exercise would begin. The *Calgary Herald* interpreted Bell's authority (and his retired rank of lieutenant-colonel) to mean that he intended to impose martial law for the duration of the exercise. The story eventually found its way to the Canadian Press and the British United Press before Bell demanded a retraction.[73]

Federal assistance with print journalists was limited to advertising Operation Lifesaver to representatives of the Canadian Press, *Maclean's*, *Saturday Night*, and other news outlets, noting the exercise's scale and the international attention it was expected to garner from US and European observers.[74] Most federal assistance, however, was aimed at preparing material for Calgary's CD office to deliver over the radio. The office secured twelve ten-minute Sunday broadcasts on CXCL, one of the city's major radio broadcasters, from July to September 1955. Calgary's mayor agreed to introduce each broadcast to promote the exercise.[75] Recognizing the opportunity for extensive coverage that this arrangement presented, Adams offered to sponsor a series of six professionally written radio plays for the city's use in public education. Bell enthusiastically accepted and arranged for the CXCL radio hosts to perform the plays in the six weeks preceding the exercise.[76]

The radio series, entitled "Evacuation with the Davidsons," was first broadcast on 31 July 1955. Written on commission by a scriptwriter in Willowdale, Ontario, the radio series followed a fictional family from their first contact with Calgary's CD wardens to their final preparations for taking part in the evacuation. The series covered both general topics, such as the effects of the hydrogen bomb, the history of Canada's CD organization, the rationale for evacuation policy, and specific Operation Lifesaver subjects, such as where to go and what routes citizens in each sector were expected to follow. The final broadcast confronted the Davidsons with a comic figure, Calgary cowhand "Wishbone Wilson," who did not think much of CD and wanted no part of Operation Lifesaver. CXCL listeners were warned not to "miss the antics of this rugged individualist."[77] Before the episode was over, the Davidsons had informed Wilson of the errors of his ways.

The radio broadcasts corresponded to the city's own publicity and public service warnings issued through the mail and the newspapers in the weeks before the exercise was carried out. In late July, Bell published and delivered evacuation instructions to households and press offices throughout the city. In the instructions, he reminded readers that individuals had a civic duty to support the evacuation and that doing so would help prepare the country's defences. "Individualism," he warned, was not just a matter of personal preference but, rather, a direct threat to the survival of the community as a whole: "These instructions (may not fit in exactly with your personal wishes) ... [but] any attempt to disobey these instructions, and to substitute for them rules of your own making, can only result in the introduction of mob law and all its attendant evils. The majority cannot be sacrificed to the whim of any individualist."[78] Bell believed that community-centred attitudes would ensure survival. He hoped to enlist additional assistance from federal authorities, including the governor-general, Prime Minister Louis St. Laurent, Paul Martin, and Frank Worthington, to instill the values of collective defence in the neighbourhoods north of the Bow River. In the end, Martin and Worthington recorded messages for Calgary's CD in August 1955.[79] The federal office contributed publicity aids similar to those produced for the On Guard, Canada! convoy two years earlier, including information pamphlets and advertisement stickers that were posted on loaves of bread at the local grocery stores and delivered to Calgary homes attached to milk bottles. Federal officials also secured amenities for the press corps attending the exercise such as cold Coca-Cola.[80]

However limited, federal assistance to the exercise sparked disputes between Calgary and Alberta authorities that threatened to derail the exercise. CXCL was the only broadcaster to receive exclusive federal Operation Lifesaver publicity. Predictably, the radio station was heavily invested in the exercise's success. As a result, CXCL announcers preceded many August broadcasts with the claim that the station was "the official voice of civil defence." This boast annoyed two larger Calgary stations, which complained to provincial representatives. Provincial co-ordinator G.R. Howsam threatened to put a stop to the publicity drive, a move that was halted at the last minute through urgent correspondence between the federal CD office and the province. Bell later told his federal colleagues that he expected rivalries to develop between the radio outlets, but he complained that he "never expected the smouldering fire to be fanned by one [Howsam] who should have as much interest as anyone in seeing the Operation succeed!"[81]

The city and the province completed preparations for Operation Lifesaver in September 1955. Dozens of newly trained RCMP officers joined Calgary's city police to prevent looting in the abandoned city, as others prepared to seal the evacuation area for nearly twelve hours during the exercise.[82] Federal and provincial CD welfare planners worked with towns in Calgary's outlying areas to prepare first aid stations, as businesses in reception areas such as Innisfail eagerly prepared for an influx of potential customers. Some of the reception area towns established refreshment posts where evacuees could purchase food and drink for a nominal fee. Most of these were administered by local church groups.[83] Detailed maps of the evacuation zone and egress routes and destinations appeared in the local press. Alberta's CD organization printed large advertisements in the *Calgary Herald* that informed readers about insurance available to cover possible vehicle damage and personal injury during the evacuation. Several days before Operation Lifesaver was to begin, MacKay directed all of the city's employees to participate in the exercise and made a special plea to local businesses to follow his example.[84] A letter writer to the *Calgary Herald*, identified only as "Count Me Out," reacted by denouncing several Calgary employers who pressed reluctant employees to take part in the exercise. The writer questioned whether the evacuation exercise was as voluntary as advertised and noted Vancouver's reluctance to mount an evacuation of similar scale, citing the fact that "everyone knows the real reason is that Vancouver declined to have anything to do with this absurd experiment!"[85]

This letter to the editor was not the only warning that the exercise would not go as planned. On 17 September, Bell announced that Operation Lifesaver was finally ready, but several warnings indicated that the exercise might not secure the 92 percent participation that CD officials had predicted in April.[86] The first warning was a shortage of vehicles and drivers to transport Calgarians without vehicles out of the area. Both MacKay and the CD organization issued pleas to find 500 cars and drivers, but by 20 September only 130 drivers had offered the use of their vehicles. Without transport, CD workers would have to turn back prospective evacuees with no conveyance of their own. Bell assured the press that "in the event of real attack, trucks, taxis and other vehicles would be commandeered."[87]

Another hint of trouble was the embarrassing failure of an evacuation exercise in Halifax on 18 September 1955, where more cars entered than left the evacuation zone – an area destroyed in 1917 by the devastating explosion of a French munitions ship in the harbour.[88] Staff editors of the *Calgary Herald* lamented Haligonians' failure to co-operate with the CD effort. Not wishing to see the Calgary exercises stumble, the newspaper issued a statement of urgent support for Operation Lifesaver and emphasized that every Calgarian had a duty to take part: "It can be regarded lightly by those who are asked to participate, but this is not a very far-thinking or responsible attitude ... The citizens of northeast Calgary will have the opportunity to show that they have a deep sense of the responsibilities of Canadian citizens."[89]

An early winter blast on 19 September did the most damage to the exercise as well as to CD in Calgary generally. Over the two following days, nearly eighteen centimetres of snow carpeted highways and rural roads, causing a number of highway traffic accidents. The roads outside Calgary were a blend of both asphalt and gravel roads, many in poor condition even in good weather.[90] In the storm, they became sufficiently dangerous that Calgary's CD office conferred with the city and province. Mid-morning on 21 September, when sirens were supposed to sound and begin the largest evacuation in North American history, Bell, MacKay, and Howsam announced that Operation Lifesaver would have to be delayed for an entire week until the winter storm passed. Howsam publicly apologized over the radio for the delay but insisted that evacuation would be carried out according to Calgary's plan if a real attack was imminent, regardless of weather conditions.[91] Most of Calgary's news outlets were sympathetic to the CD agency, not surprisingly given their part in promoting the exercise, but they were less forgiving about MacKay's preposterous claims that the weather would also have forced the Soviets to call off an attack: "Wednesday's weather would never, never be protection against such attack ... The enemy will assuredly arrange things that way if he possibly can."[92]

International and provincial CD observers present for Operation Lifesaver returned home disappointed. Most CD planners quietly observed that the whole effort might have been wasted. Harvey Adams returned to Ottawa with most of his staff, leaving behind a junior representative. Adams was keen to promote other events in his calendar. Privately, he expressed the belief that the postponement endangered the exercise's success and Calgary's credibility.[93] Bell attempted to salvage public and civic support in the following week. He appealed again for voluntary drivers to assist on the new date and pressed volunteers to put in extra hours to call and register additional evacuees.[94]

Meanwhile, a political battle began between the city of Calgary and the provincial government. Shortly after the postponement, Bell lashed out at Edmonton for failing to respond to his requests to improve exit roads that "look like battlefields."[95] Bell's criticism mobilized provincial road crews to clear exit routes that were still blanketed with snow and to repair the worst stretches of road.[96] In the midst of a municipal election, Calgary's local politicians entered the fray shortly before the rescheduled exercise. Alderman P.N.R. Morrison publicly criticized the city's CD in general for embarrassing the city by postponing the original Operation Lifesaver exercise. He also cast doubt on the strategy of evacuation because the effort had been defeated by the winter weather, which could kill the unprepared just as easily as the bomb. Morrison earned biting criticism from the *Calgary Herald*'s lead editorial for his trouble:

> He is certainly going out of his way to try to destroy a project which has had enough trouble already ... People who know infinitely more than Mr. Morrison ever will know about modern warfare are desperately searching for the answer. The best they have so far is mass dispersal of humanity into the countryside. It is clumsly, terribly inconvenient, perhaps only partly workable. But it is something. And it is not small-time politics.[97]

Evacuation as Celebration

Despite the local disturbances and public criticism, at 10:50 a.m. on 28 September 1955 air-raid sirens wailed throughout northeast Calgary, announcing the beginning of Operation Lifesaver. Citizens left school and workplaces, departing for adjoining towns and cities. Launching the exercise over the radio, MacKay congratulated Calgarians for their civic pride, "those who are showing such a grand attitude of learning to help themselves and who, in so doing, are establishing a pattern that will help others."[98] This was CD in action, Canadians helping themselves and their neighbours to survive, fulfilling an obligation asked of them by the government. Evacuees marshalled at assembly points or exited the city in their own cars, following the prescribed routes to reception towns, the first arriving forty-five minutes after the sirens sounded. Civil defence observers scrutinized reception work in the town of Innisfail, charged with carrying out emergency feeding and welfare registration to simulate actual conditions in wartime. Volunteers in the town dug slit trenches in the reception area, lighting fires to heat improvised stoves and boilers to feed over 300 evacuees.[99]

Press coverage of the evacuation reveals how staged the evacuation was in practice. The *Calgary Herald* followed George Nenzel, his wife, and their five children as they prepared for the evacuation. Nenzel went to work as usual on the day of the evacuation, returning to his house by public transit after the sirens sounded to gather his family and depart. His wife had prepared meals for the entire family the evening before, including a pot of baked beans. She spent the morning packing supplies for departure. Only two of the five children of school age were sent to school, the others, who knew that an attack was coming, remained at home. The newspaper described the older children as being aware of the urgent need behind Operation Lifesaver and anticipated that the younger children, who were excited for a holiday from school, would appreciate the exercise's value in later years.[100]

The newspaper account makes clear that the gendered division of tasks each family was meant to practise during their preparations survived the change of emphasis in CD strategy from rescue and firefighting to evacuation. The husband and father, forewarned before the exercise, led the family in making preparations to leave, determining the evacuation route and managing transport roles. In this position, he filled the role of a CD warden for his family. His wife, by preparing food and packaging supplies to care for the family en route, was concerned for the welfare and nutrition of the family. Civil defence mass feeding and welfare positions were, as a rule, staffed entirely by female volunteers.

When the sirens sounded, the Nenzels calmly turned off all of their gas appliances and left their home in the family car, already parked beside the curb in readiness for the evacuation.[101] The family drove in a convoy to Airdrie, twenty-eight kilometres north of Calgary (a region that would have still been hit by some of the blast and heat waves from a five-megaton bomb detonating in downtown Calgary), along with a convoy of other evacuees, and were registered by a local welfare-welcoming committee. Surreally, the Nenzels ate their

Figure 11   The Nenzel family begins their journey out of the city. *Source: Calgary Herald*, Glenbow Archives, na-2864-974-1

homemade baked beans brought from home on plates purchased from an Airdrie department store (they did not want to eat from the pot) and watched a movie in the community hall before returning to Calgary after the "all-clear" was sounded at 3:05 p.m.[102] Similar reception events took place elsewhere, but at several of the largest events evacuees were fed pre-prepared meals before returning to Calgary. The entire evacuation and return to Calgary took most of the day, with only one person injured.[103] All three levels of the Canadian federal CD organization were thrilled with the results of the exercise, which was considered "a great success."[104]

Public participation in the evacuation was far lower than its planners had hoped. The exercise was originally devised to accommodate all of the approximately 40,000 residents living in the northeastern quadrant of Calgary. In their post-exercise assessment, the city's organizers blamed the week-long postponement of the exercise and persistent adverse weather for a low evacuation rate of less than 15 percent. Only 5,891 of the residents evacuated – that is, left Calgary by public or private transit.[105] Press accounts claimed that 10,000 had evacuated the subdivision, so it is likely that most of those who left their homes or businesses in Calgary's northeast locale chose to shop at businesses or visit friends or family in other parts of the city rather than take a long road trip out of town. In many cases, the siren was simply ignored by businesses that had ordered staff not to participate in the exercise.[106] Many more without vehicles did not care to spend the day with strangers. For example, one resident had been asked to share a single vehicle with four other adults and four children. He and others faced with similar travel conditions decided to abstain from the exercise. Families who did have cars but were burdened with small children similarly refused to make the trip. As one respondent told the *Calgary Herald*, "she could not see herself changing diapers in a cold car."[107] Some families simply could not leave behind pets as they had been instructed. Others were confused by unfamiliar siren signals.

Most who heard the initial blast assumed it was the "all-clear," as heard in countless Second World War newsreels, radio broadcasts, and films. Civil Defence Canada had, in the interests of cross-border co-ordination, adopted the American siren system, which used different signals and was roundly criticized by the Calgary CD organization and local press for the confusion.[108] An informal assessment of public reaction revealed that many of those who refused to participate (and cared enough to offer a justification) responded to the exercise with "disbelief, or distrust in the exercise and cynicism, or they offered the excuse that the exercise did not concern them."[109] MacKay and others claimed that the city had never actually promised that the full 40,000 would evacuate, quoting the more "realistic" figure of 25,000.[110] At the press conference announcing the results of the exercise, MacKay blamed local politics for undermining civic support for civil defence. However, MacKay contended that the turnout of a quarter of the intended evacuees was a formidable accomplishment, "considering business, illness and other handicaps."[111] Similarly, in their own assessment of the exercise, the city's CD office looked for a silver lining, supposing that the 15 percent who actually evacuated the city despite confusion over the exercise's postponement and the less-than-ideal conditions "represented the percentage of keen supporters of Civil Defence in the sector."[112]

Howsam had a much more serious message to convey. In his view, Operation Lifesaver had proved that evacuation could work but that considerable labour remained to ensure that a similar event could take place despite weather conditions. He demanded a much more extensive effort throughout the province to stockpile sufficient supplies in reception areas. Howsam pointed out that in Alberta Canadians could survive out in the open for only five months of the

year and that most individuals would not think to pack for a longer or permanent exile to rural areas. Complicating the matter further, he warned, was federal
uncertainty over which locations would be attacked: "We believe that under
certain unfavourable circumstances the best thing to do will be to take cover
and stay put – at least for the time being. It means that these top level decisions
to evacuate or to stay put will have to [be] made on the spot, based on the best
information that is available ... It will be necessary that the public retain a high
degree of confidence in the civil defence arrangements [to ensure survival]."[113]

A federally sponsored analysis of Operation Lifesaver offered several conclusions about the organization and administration of CD in target and reception
areas. The most important were the necessity of improving communications
between the target city and outlying areas, of less dependence on private transport and fewer assembly areas to accommodate those without cars, and of more
and better highways to connect cities and ensure a safe flow of traffic. A post-
mortem of the exercise also revealed several fatal flaws in its planning, not least
among them the complete lack of accounting for the protection of evacuees and
the reception area from the intense radioactive fallout that would inevitably
follow the detonation of a five-megaton nuclear warhead.

The purpose of the exercise had been to test the movement, registration,
feeding, and return of a large body of people, not to simulate a realistic pre-attack
evacuation scenario. This test was aimed at refining the skills of the professional
and volunteer planners as much as it was meant to condition the public's response
to air-raid sirens. However, the exercise involved such a large number of the
public as passive observers and active participants that it evolved into a civic
event. Far from being a grim reminder of the massive destructive power of the
hydrogen weapon, Operation Lifesaver was transformed into a celebration of
CD and community values. In the publicity and public appeals that preceded
Operation Lifesaver, the success of the CD organization's exercise was linked
directly to the protection of local culture and civic pride. In practice, the evacuation to flee nuclear attack was an adventure for most families. At many of the
reception towns-turned-refugee camps, local businesses and civic leaders
changed a nuclear nightmare into a site of a civic festival.

Mar Walker, a *Calgary Herald* reporter, observed CD staff at their headquarters
at Calgary's airport emerging with new-found respect for workers she had
previously characterized as "ex-army brass muddling along" and "a lot of civilians who want to wear uniforms and give orders."[114] She refuted in her column
"the general attitude that Operation Lifesaver was a cross between a civic holiday
and a Stampede Parade."[115] A festival atmosphere was not what Calgary's CD
office had hoped to achieve during the exercise. Yet its promotion of the exercise

over the radio, in film reels, and public lectures, as well as during the Stampede's parade, relied on elements of pageantry that had surfaced during the tour of the federal CD convoy. It thoroughly engaged community leaders and was championed repeatedly by Calgary's charismatic mayor. In many of his speeches, MacKay interpreted the evacuation as a challenge for Calgarians. Overcoming it would testify to the success of Calgary's CD organization and the city's sense of civic pride.

Calgary businesses, sensing an upcoming public holiday, attempted to profit from the exercise. Before the exercise was postponed, Nagler's Department Store paid for a full-page advertisement in the *Calgary Herald* to advertise "Operation Moneysaver," their three-day furniture and appliance sale. The ad promised "explosive value" and tastelessly pictured a bomber aircraft dropping prices.[116] Similarly, by integrating CD into the schedule of the Calgary Stampede, organizers linked the principles of CD to the principles of independence and mutual community assistance that had shaped many Albertan rural farming and ranching communities.

Operation Lifesaver took place shortly after the Golden Jubilee celebrating Alberta's entry into Confederation. Officials consciously linked appeals to participate in the exercise to Albertans' distinct rural culture and history.[117] Although Calgary was no longer a ranching and farming town, the very nature of the evacuation and reception exercise highlighted interdependency between town and country. An editorial cartoon appearing shortly after the evacuation depicted not a line of cars and modern families departing the city but, rather, a blend of farmers, ranchers, and settlers in covered wagons and, for a more modern touch, businessmen and football players running along a dusty trail.[118] Many who chose to evacuate approached the exercise exactly like it was a civic holiday, packing picnic baskets and loading up the car with family to go on an excursion to the countryside.

Citizens without a car, who had registered to evacuate by public transit, had lined up at bus stations well before the siren had sounded, with food and diversions in hand for the trip. Families questioned before the exercise said that they would take part in the evacuation if the weather improved, but grey and slushy conditions kept many celebrants of the community event inside or at friends' houses within Calgary. Evacuees typically travelled as family or neighbourhood units, with many declining to participate if they could not travel with people they knew. The Nenzels' run out to Airdrie and back was characterized by the papers as "an adventure to remember," with one of their younger daughters quoted as saying: "Gee, we had a swell time and saw a free movie!"[119] Churches in Crossfield treated nearly 500 evacuees to bingo games, and spontaneous tailgate parties erupted in parking lots when entire Calgary neighbourhoods

FIGURE 12   Volunteers prepare meals for evacuees in Innisfail, Alberta. *Source: Calgary Herald*, Glenbow Archives, na-2864–974-1a

arrived for registration amid sound trucks playing programs of recorded music. The visit of evacuees to Crossfield coincided with a travelling exhibition that was related to Alberta's Golden Jubilee, which both local and "refugee" school-children were invited to attend.[120] The first of the evacuees arriving back into Calgary, speaking to journalists, characterized the event as "just like a family picnic ... we took our own basket lunch, but there was plenty of food for every-one."[121] Civil defence and community representatives in Strathmore expressed disappointment to the press that only 299 of the 2,500 expected refugees arrived in their town, and at the lunch they attempted to unload their substantial stock-pile of sandwiches and refreshments.

Two days after the Operation Lifesaver exercise, editorialists and community leaders commemorated the evacuation as a testament to the co-operation be-tween the city and its countryside. Commenting once again on the importance of the exercise, the *Calgary Herald* stated that rural Albertans had passed an important test, and, in so doing, "many Calgarians, and there were many European-born people among them [were able to] sample real Western hospi-tality, returned home with high praise for the arrangements that had been made for their comfort."[122] Participants in the evacuation appeared to have ignored admonishments from Bell's office about how to behave, and how to avoid panic, because Operation Lifesaver was an opportunity to enjoy a day of paid leave from work, which permitted them to connect with neighbours and with residents of other communities. Many evacuees who opted to leave northeast Calgary decided to visit friends and relatives in parts of the city not affected by the exercise rather than to take part in the festivities in other cities. Stanley Fisher, a former Calgary resident and CD worker in the reception town of Acme, Alberta, was only able to express her disappointment that more people did not avail themselves of the chance to get away:

> There were sandwiches and all sorts of good things to eat ... I don't know what they'll do with the leftovers, maybe they'll have to put them in the deep-freeze until a real Hydrogen bomb attack comes and the people of Calgary have learned to appreciate them. All the people that I spoke to that went out enjoyed themselves thoroughly and almost everyone was a little disappointed that there weren't more there to enjoy the fun.[123]

Underlying the celebratory atmosphere accompanying Operation Lifesaver were assumptions about the role of rural municipalities in a nuclear war. In Canada and elsewhere, CD planners widely assumed that rural municipalities would be pleased to take on refugees from cities. In the United States, state CD programs in Iowa and Nebraska identified rural areas as the "moral base of the nation." The nation as a whole would survive because of the selfless hospitality of the countryside.[124] Jenny Barker-Devine, in her study of perceptions of rural America in evacuation and reception planning, describes a tendency to view rural regions as homogenous groupings prepared to render assistance to the cities. US federal planners insisted that such assistance was the result of a "higher responsibility to your fellow man than that which is written in the law."[125] Yet the image that emerged in planners' rhetoric of rural reception areas as both a breadbasket to the nation and the cradle of national survival during nuclear war was never backed with sufficient resources for rural municipalities to prepare adequately for these extended periods of mass feeding and properly billet the refugees.[126] The same was true in Canada.

Although Operation Lifesaver was the first exercise to attempt both evacuation and reception in North America, survival planning only went as far the evacuation plan in most cities. The aim of Canadian CD planning was to ensure the survival of as many citizens as possible. Since rural areas were not targets for attack, their needs were assigned a lower priority than those of target cities, which required extensive preparations in order for evacuations to work. Traffic systems, co-ordination of transportation, and bigger and better highways were the subjects most often discussed. The survival of the evacuees once clear of the cities was of secondary importance. What would happen to the inhabitants of rural areas was considered next – if at all – but the laudatory press coverage accompanying Operation Lifesaver reinforced the image of Calgary's rural areas as centres of hospitality that were grateful to receive refugees. When receptions were transformed into civic events by local CD planners and municipal author-ities, such depictions obscured the tensions that would inevitably arise in overcrowded rural towns during a nuclear war. Those who participated in, or read about, the exercise were left with the rosy impression of rural Alberta's hospitality, summarized by the press: "Calgarians now know that they can count on the surrounding countryside for real help if the need ever arises."[127] In aiding the city during the exercise, rural areas had passed a "unique test." Yet what of these towns' survival?

Evacuation Becomes Official Policy

Operation Lifesaver was the last public exercise of its type carried out in Canada, though dozens of smaller reception exercises and evacuation drills took place separately in major target areas after this event.[128] In June 1956, the CDC officially adopted as policy plans to evacuate Montreal, Hamilton, Toronto, Winnipeg, Ottawa-Hull, Edmonton, Windsor, Quebec City, Saint John, Halifax, Victoria, and Vancouver.[129] Paul Martin announced the policy change in the House of Commons, stating that "our Civil Defence Policy should now be based on the development and testing of plans for the orderly evacuation on short notice of the main urban areas in Canada should the possibility of attack on such areas by nuclear weapons appear to be imminent."[130]

Martin's announcement came nearly four years after the detonation of the first hydrogen weapon in the Pacific Ocean and nearly two years after the scale of the devastation resulting from that detonation was made public knowledge. The long delay between the identification of the threat and the official adoption of the policy was caused by an initial and persistent uncertainty about the ef-fectiveness of evacuation, and by worries about the damage that would be done to the economy by work stoppages in the event of a false alarm. However, the official announcement by Martin merely formalized a planning process initiated by federal and provincial governments over two years before. In the same month that Martin announced evacuation as the "new look in civil defence," the Ontario Department of Planning and Development's Civil Defence Branch published the *Ontario Provincial Survival Plan,* which made arrangements to evacuate the five major target areas identified by the CDC and their surrounding counties.[131] The plan was skeletal and did not include detailed and co-ordinated planning with the municipalities, but it was the result of statistical surveys of target cities and their rural neighbours that permitted the province to designate certain areas for evacuation and others as "stand-fast zones."

Martin's announcement was preceded by a flurry of exchanges between Civil Defence Canada and the provinces about the new *Federal Guide to Survival Planning*, which was based on recently released American information about hydrogen weapons and the results of evacuation exercises. Worthington's survival guide was first circulated to provincial authorities in January 1956 and was eventually used as the basis for federal-provincial joint planning for CD. The guide called for the development of plans based exclusively on evacuation, which the federal government advocated not "because it was the best of survival alternatives, but because there is no alternative."[132]

Worthington's plan accommodated existing plans for the air defence of North America, recognizing that the soon-to-be-constructed Distant Early Warning radar line would give some cities sufficient time to evacuate. His plan also acknowledged, but could not respond to, the fact that the air battle over Canadian soil would complicate survival plans greatly. Evacuation studies conducted at great cost, countywide reception plans, and other CD predictions could prove worthless if, as was likely, Soviet bombers dropped payloads on the wrong targets or those shot down randomly detonated their payload as they crashed. These variances were more permissible if the air battle was fought in the far north. In the populated south of Canada, it called into question the rationale for paying for a large CD organization.[133] Worthington's four-phase plan called for the pre-evacuation of invalids and dependents from Canadian target cities during a presumed period of strategic warning, the immediate planned withdrawal of the remainder of the population to reception areas, "action after blast," and immediate aid and rehabilitation of the survivors leading to reconstruction. The third phase is of most interest because it was the first federal plan to incorporate fallout.

In early 1955, the United States Atomic Energy Commission released many of its findings about the effects of radioactive fallout, revealing that it was a much larger threat than the US military and CD agencies had previously believed. Their report indicated that radioactive particles dispersed by the wind would be carried hundreds of kilometres downwind of the actual detonation, blanketing cities and towns that would normally not be considered targets with persistent lethal radiation that threatened exposed citizens and livestock and endangered the food supply. Canadian defence scientists had recorded the phenomenon of fallout as early as 1951 by measuring radioactivity in snow falling in Ottawa after bomb tests in Nevada, but their findings were communicated only to American defence officials and not to the public.[134] Reporting on the

Atomic Energy Commission's findings, the *Montreal Star* noted that "a great many people threw up their hands in despair."[135]

For Civil Defence Canada, the findings meant that planning assumptions had to be revisited to identify which areas of the country would face the greatest danger. The DRB began to study the implications of fallout for Canadian planning, charting weather patterns over Canada and likely attack patterns. They hoped to devise a flexible, scientific guide to help civilian agencies adjust their planning for survival as a war unfolded. The Department of National Defence directed DRB scientists to supply the federal CD agency's Planning Committee with information about what, if any, evasive action civilian populations could take against fallout. They also sought to determine how to monitor and provide "live" reporting on fallout patterns to the federal government and CD agencies during wartime.[136] The government's increasing dependency on knowledge of the weather and winds for survival planning eventually led to the conscription of the Federal Meteorological Service and the Department of Transport into CD planning.

Worthington's 1956 survival guide integrated the DRB's limited findings about fallout protection and evasion into "phase C" of the plan. Fallout forced changes to the established evacuation planning measures. Survival would depend on the ability of the government to immediately locate and evaluate of the size and height of explosions to determine how much fallout could be expected and its probable dispersal pattern, which could shift with the weather. In Worthington's plan, the evacuation of target cities to reception areas would continue "unless diverted by controlling authority to avoid 'fallout areas.'"[137] Most evacuation exercises conducted in Canada had, however, been based on the principle that, to avoid panic and confusion during an actual evacuation, citizens had to know their destination and the route on which to travel before an attack arrived, since the local CD authority would in all likelihood be unable to co-ordinate the evacuation after the bomb fell. In Operation Lifesaver, this problem was ignored. Civil defence headquarters operated from the safety of a Calgary golf club. For national evacuation operations to work, centralized control and distribution of information and instruction to evacuees would be necessary. The same was true for plans for reception areas. Worthington noted that some reception zones in the anticipated fallout areas would be directed to take shelter, although fallout shelter planning was in its infancy in 1956, and he advised that "remedial evacuation" might be necessary. When fallout was taken into serious consideration, Civil Defence Canada learned that the whole country, not just the target areas and their immediate neighbours, would need a contingency plan in nuclear war.[138]

Worthington subjected his plan to critique and revision through Project Q, a study of evacuation in Ottawa, Saint John, Vancouver, Winnipeg, and Toronto, taking into account all elements of fallout planning. Completed in September 1956, the Project Q report reinforced Worthington's findings about the possible disruptions that fallout would force on any survival effort, but it also demanded immediate development of shelter plans for Canada. The study advised that survivors and rescuers in fallout areas would be forced to "take the best cover available."[139] An extensive and protected communications system that could operate under government control during attack conditions was needed. Communications would direct evacuees to reception areas, provide warnings about the direction and intensity of fallout on the wind, advise whether shelter or evasion through remedial evacuation were the safest routes, and co-ordinate post-attack rescue efforts with civilian and military mobile columns. To survive, Canada would require a more centrally controlled and co-ordinated concept of survival operations than had previously been considered under the "self-help" and evacuation strategies. Project Q also recommended that the federal and provincial governments would need to have dispersed, protected headquarters to manage the type of survival operations envisioned.[140] The planners concluded their report with the admonition that "Civil Defence alone could not win a war but the lack of it could lose it."[141] The difficulties associated with evacuation under fallout conditions were vast and forbidding, but the projected casualties that Canada would suffer without any preparations were equally grim. Of the total population of 4,885,900 in the thirteen target cities directed to evacuate, it was estimated that 3,645,800 would be killed without any planning and a further 920,950 would receive "non-fatal injuries." Only 322,150 Canadians living near the target areas would be uninjured.

Conclusion

For Canadians working in CD, the period from 1954 to 1956 was a period of uneasy transition. New weapons demanded new strategies to deal with them and called into question the assumptions on which Canadian CD was based. With weapons that could demolish entire cities in a flash, Canadian agencies were not given much choice in which strategies to use. The best defence from the hydrogen bomb, it was said, was not to be there when it went off.[142] When Cabinet weighed all of their options, evacuation was the only strategy that offered a defence. The decision reached informally by the federal government in 1954 to test evacuation as a possible response to the devastating power of the hydrogen bomb, which was officially ratified two years later, was not an easy one to make. Investments in evacuation strategies meant coming to grips with the many obstacles to survival, both physical and psychological. Evacuations such as those held in Brockville, St. John's, Brandon, Calgary, Vancouver, and

Halifax were designed primarily to test the ability of large groups of civilians to exit and re-enter a city with speed and without undue loss of life. Most of these evacuations proved that, with proper direction and training, evacuation of a target city was possible. However, most of those cities tested were not major metropolises. Toronto alderman Donald Summerville, who was sent to observe Operation Lifesaver in September 1955, commented that the plan could work for Calgary only if the city stopped growing. It could not have worked, he surmised, in Toronto's urban sprawl.

The evacuations were also held in near-ideal conditions. The psychological conditions with which CD planners had to deal were cynicism, lack of interest, and apathy, but they never included the full-blown panic that would have crippled a city given three hours' notice of its imminent doom. Operation Lifesaver unfolded in an air of unreality. Calls for widespread public participation were in large part successful, but citizens transformed the evacuation into a civic event. If planners sought to condition the public with an exercise simulating wartime conditions so they would respond calmly in an actual emergency, these exercises can only be counted as failures.

Within a few years, most of the Canadian cities marked for destruction had secretly developed plans on paper about how best to remove their citizenry, and the provinces developed plans for the surrounding areas to receive them. Exercises proved that cities could be evacuated, imperfectly, but questions about how to protect vulnerable Canadians from the effects of radioactive fallout that would blanket most of the country went largely unresolved. The vastly increased lethality of thermonuclear weapons had a comfortable lead over the emergency planners who were trying desperately to catch up. By the time Civil Defence Canada drafted preliminary plans to cope with fallout, a new technology – intercontinental ballistic missiles – and a new government had intervened. Both would have a role in radically recasting for a final time the structure and strategy of Canadian CD, reversing years of work to encourage municipalities to go it alone by centralizing the "national survival" effort in the federal government, involving the Canadian armed forces to an ever greater extent, and diminishing the role of citizens in defending their homes.

5
Emergency Measures, 1957-59

ON 26 SEPTEMBER 1957, Major-General Frank Worthington drove to the Canadian Civil Defence College in Arnprior, Ontario, for the last time in his official capacity as the federal government's civil defence co-ordinator. After nearly a decade at the helm of Canada's CD organization, several Cabinet shuffles, and a number of minor controversies, Worthington's wife had successfully convinced him that it was time to retire. Clara Worthington observed a change in her husband that was brought on by frustration over CD's slow progress: "The spirits of the Federal Coordinator alternated between high anticipation and rock-bottom realization ... and it was becoming harder to bounce back after each new low ... In the army there had always been something to laugh at. Even in the stress of war, laughter had a generous share in the grief and grimness of the time, but Civil Defence was no laughing matter."[1]

Worthington had proven to be an efficient administrator and leader of his organization, despite his over-eagerness and occasional public relations errors. He had taken what remained of a skeletal wartime organization and transformed it into a national organization with over 150,000 registered emergency workers and voluntary staff. J.W. Monteith, Paul Martin's replacement as minister for national health and welfare in the new Conservative government, lavished praise on Worthington at the ceremony: "Despite many difficulties and setbacks, he has largely succeeded. As he takes leave of his heavy duties, he has the satisfaction of knowing that he carries with him the respect and indeed the affection of a growing army of civil defence officials and volunteers ... General Worthington will continue to be regarded as the father of civil defence in Canada."[2]

During his tenure, Worthington had urged municipalities and community groups to organize themselves for the worst in peacetime, since they could not depend on the armed forces or other government services to help them in the first stages of a nuclear war. As he had repeatedly argued, such was the cost of citizenship in the nuclear age. This principle of self-help in CD did not long survive his retirement. Expert studies and common sense alike had already dictated that no single municipality would be able to co-ordinate its own defence. After Worthington's departure, the Canadian government created a separate planning agency called the Emergency Measures Organization (EMO). Originally conceived to carry out Continuity of Government (COG) planning in secret, the EMO eventually assumed financial and operational responsibility for CD, as a result of a formal survey of Canadian nuclear war preparations that was commissioned by the Diefenbaker government and carried out by retired Chief of the General Staff (CGS) Lieutenant-General Howard Graham. Graham's survey also demanded the formal commitment of the armed forces to assume CD tasks formerly managed by volunteers in the municipalities. Civil Defence Canada, which had been formed to meet the threat from bombs and bombers, faced its obsolescence in the missile age. It was ultimately replaced by the EMO.

Sputnik and Civil Defence Planning

The world entered the age of the intercontinental ballistic missile (ICBM) on 4 October 1957, when the Soviet Union successfully launched *Sputnik,* the Earth's first artificial satellite, into orbit with an unmanned rocket. While US officials informed the public that they had advance knowledge of the launch, its success took the West by surprise. The press offered the public equal parts coverage and speculation about the satellite. Canadian newspapers carried extensive accounts of its launch and orbit.[3] US and foreign experts were quoted in the Associated Press reports, under the headline: "Soviet Moon Is Key to Military Victory." French General Pierre Gaullois told reporters that the Soviets' evident superiority in missile research "makes it possible for Russia to win the peace without ever having to make war."[4] The *Calgary Herald* revealed the direct implications of the Soviet innovation for North American survival: "Moscow to New York in 16 minutes. That is the rate at which the Russian satellite is moving, and that is the length of time it would take a satellite carrying a nuclear-equipped weapon that distance when – not if – it is possible to equip and launch such a weapon."[5]

The Canadian government declined to comment immediately about *Sputnik's* implications for CD. When asked to comment on developments, Minister of Defence George R. Pearkes merely quipped: "I cannot comment on that because it's out of this world," leaving the public to speculate about the satellite's wider implications.[6] Civil Defence Canada did not have plans prepared to counteract the ICBM, which added further complications to the already complex task of preparing Canadian cities to evacuate in advance of a Soviet-manned bomber attack. These plans, which in 1957 still depended on a three-hour warning period, had not yet even taken into full account the threat posed by the post-attack radioactive fallout that would poison much of the country.[7] Officially and in public, Civil Defence Canada and the armed forces both discounted the strategic impact of ICBM technology and its implications for survival planning.

In the December 1957 *Civil Defence Bulletin,* Worthington's acting replacement, Major-General G.S. Hatton, offered an early evaluation of the impact that the ICBM would have on Canadian CD efforts. He described the ICBM as an inaccurate weapon of war, subject to deflection from its target by the intense heat caused on re-entry into the atmosphere. He also insisted that the ICBM had not taken the organization by surprise, because it had been a subject of public discussion for several years. Consequently, he noted that CD was developed to meet the "present" threat – piloted bombers – while keeping an eye to the future. Hatton then attempted to justify the existing evacuation policy by explaining the concepts of tactical and strategic warning. Tactical warning was the short window of opportunity offered by the North American radar warning lines in northern Canada, which would be triggered by a manifest threat to Canadian airspace. The key to evacuation lay in the strategic warning given to NATO by intelligence gathered from Soviet diplomatic and military preparations that would be entailed in "so vast an undertaking as total nuclear war."[8] Hatton's article reflected contemporary strategic thought about the Soviet Union's nuclear arsenal in Canada and in the United States. The Joint Intelligence Committee, which reported to the Canadian Chiefs of Staff Committee (COSC), assessed the ICBM threat shortly after the *Sputnik* launch and predicted that, over a ten-year period, intercontinental missiles would prove less dangerous than the Soviet Union's massive operational bomber fleet and missile-launching submarines.[9] American intelligence gathered from U2 spy plane flights over Soviet territory would soon prove planners correct – the Soviet missile threat was overblown. By 1962, the Soviet Union had only four intercontinental ballistic missile launch sites in operation, each of which took more than twenty-four hours to prepare for an attack.[10]

Hatton wrote the *Civil Defence Bulletin* article to offer a justification for the federal evacuation policy in light of increasing public "conjecture ... about the effects of a war in which the ICBM is a major feature."[11] It was hoped that, armed with the arguments set forth in Hatton's editorial, volunteers would continue to organize for CD in communities where faith in the organization had been further shaken by the new threat of a "push-button" nuclear war. This article and others like it were written to shore up the "self-discipline, moral courage and public service" that Hatton believed volunteers would need to carry out their work.[12]

Before his promotion, Hatton had served as the deputy federal CD coordinator. He was a native of Peterborough, Ontario, and a graduate of the Royal Military College of Canada before joining the British army as an engineering officer. By the end of the Second World War, he had earned the rank of major-general, serving as a staff officer in the Middle East and Africa. After the war's end, he commanded British troops in the Netherlands and served as a senior administrative staff officer in the British army's northern and southern commands, where he worked with the United Kingdom's early post-war CD planners. In 1949, he co-operated with Sir John Hodsoll, Britain's CD chief, to carry out Operation Britannia between the United Kingdom's CD workers and the army. Hatton was also involved in most of the major thermonuclear studies undertaken by NATO's Supreme Headquarters Allied Powers Europe until 1954.[13] Like many senior British generals, Hatton was appointed in 1955 to serve out his remaining years before retirement on the Army Council of the Navy at the Army and Air Force Institute, which one author described as a "great consumer of gold watches" in the post-war years.[14] He joined Civil Defence Canada shortly after returning to Canada in 1955. Hatton would never be confirmed as Worthington's successor, partly because of his combative and unattractive personality, but mainly as a result of the reforms in CD that were pushed through by Prime Minister John Diefenbaker's Conservative government from 1957 to 1959.

Continuity of Government

During Diefenbaker's first term, he accelerated changes to CD planning and the organization's structure, but the St. Laurent government had laid the building blocks for these adjustments. Revelations about the destructive power of the hydrogen bomb prompted the Cabinet War Book Committee (WBC) to inform Cabinet in July 1956 that existing civilian emergency plans were "badly out of date and needed revision."[15] The WBC, composed of deputy ministers from the Departments of Defence, External Affairs, Health and Welfare, Agriculture, Transport, and the Privy Council, concluded that civil planning was "out of balance with military planning." The committee expressed its belief that the structure and planning of the Canadian military rendered it more capable of functioning during a nuclear emergency, but it concluded that the same could not be said for the CD corps in Canadian cities. The survival of the Canadian political system depended on the response of the military and CD community after the first hydrogen bomb was dropped.[16]

On the recommendation of the WBC, Cabinet approved the secondment of a small body of senior civil servants from the Departments of Transport, Defence Production, Trade and Commerce, Agriculture, National Health and Welfare, Finance, Defence, and External Affairs as well as relevant government agencies, especially the RCMP and the Central Mortgage and Housing Corporation, to study civilian war measures for a period of six weeks in the summer and fall of 1956. The Working Group on War Measures, as it was called, was mandated to study the civil measures necessary to prepare for the "new conditions" that were expected in a major war – namely the massive destruction of Canadian cities or their inability to function because of radioactive fallout.[17]

In late 1956, the Working Group on War Measures received briefings from the Department of National Defence's Joint Intelligence Committee and the Joint Planning Committee about the nature of the nuclear threat. To learn more about American preparations, committee members also hosted senior representatives from the US Office of Defense Mobilization, which was responsible for the civilian and military aspects of US wartime mobilization planning. Hatton sat with the Working Group on War Measures for several days to brief its members on the many difficulties he and Worthington had encountered with other federal government departments and with local and provincial authorities under existing planning arrangements.[18] In January 1957, the group communicated its findings to the WBC.

The working group's most important recommendation was its suggestion for the immediate establishment of a federal government agency responsible for co-ordinating all of the various aspects of civilian emergency planning between responsible government departments. A collective response was necessary because of the immense complexity of civil emergency planning for nuclear war, which had to integrate many of the functions of CD along with essential elements of national supply, housing, feeding, control and regulation of traffic, COG authority and record keeping, provision for national transport, and communications. The working group's report indicated that much of this work was merely an extension of each government department's peacetime responsibilities, but in the absence of a central co-ordinating agency, "there had been the tendency in departments to leave the solution of these problems to someone else."[19]

"Someone else" usually implied Hatton and his officials, who rarely received the support of other departments and struggled, like Worthington, to make CD a priority in interdepartmental committees. George Davidson, deputy minister of welfare, observed during the WBC's deliberations that the federal government's "present difficulties" were the result of "past piecemeal attempts."[20] The report from the Working Group on War Measures proposed the creation of the EMO to ensure conformity across government departments for civilian emergency planning. The working group's report, however, noted many areas where the EMO and Civil Defence Canada would inevitably overlap, possibly to the detriment of both.[21] In July 1957, discussion within the WBC touched briefly on this question: "Civil Defence of course is of primary interest to EMO, but until the new organization was well established it seemed best to deal with CD ... through a liaison officer. EMO would in a few months be in a better position to judge whether CD should be integrated within it according to [the] suggestion of the Working Group on War Measures."[22] Until the government could resolve Civil Defence Canada's future role, the EMO would assume responsibility for aspects of civil emergency planning that had not yet been assigned to existing departments for resolution, such as the control of road traffic and the relocation of government in an emergency.

Early in 1957, officials on the WBC recognized that the mere mention of shielding the government and senior members of the civil service from attack could stir up public opinion against CD. Chairman Major J.C. Morrison insisted that, while the establishment of a system for emergency government that could be carried on in the midst of nuclear war could not be feasibly carried out without attracting public attention, Cabinet ministers "were aware of the problem and while they were not prepared at this time to seek public support ... they had agreed to provide funds for continued planning."[23] The working group's final recommendations, forwarded to the WBC and subsequently to the Cabinet, were to quietly establish an EMO in the Privy Council Office, with a small staff of officials seconded from other government departments that would answer to Robert Bryce, clerk of the Privy Council, and ultimately to the prime minister. The expenditure associated with planning would be initially hidden from public view through supplementary estimates of various government departments, rather than a separate budgetary allocation that would draw attention from opposition parties in Parliament. The EMO would become a publicly acknowledged government agency only after staff had completed the initial planning.[24]

St. Laurent's Cabinet approved the expenditure on 4 April 1957, and shortly after assuming office Diefenbaker formally approved the creation of the EMO in June of that year.[25] In November 1957, Bryce summarized the organization's aims for the prime minister:

The work concerns mainly plans for carrying on the minimum essentials of government during the very chaotic weeks ... expected at the beginning of a major war, and for doing what is possible to prepare to meet the urgent needs of the public at such times. As you have said yourself, we cannot expect in another major war to have time to prepare after it starts. If the government approves, it is expected that a comprehensive "shadow" organization of volunteers [from the civil service] will be recruited and trained to take on duties in regional and local centres when emergency action may have to be taken on a few hours' notice.[26]

R.B. Curry, the national director of family allowances and old age security and the senior official directing welfare planning for Civil Defence Canada, began work as the head of the nascent EMO with a skeleton staff.[27] Over the course of the following year, the EMO laid the foundation for an entirely new system of planning to prepare government agencies for attack. For CD officials at the federal, provincial, and municipal levels, few of the EMO's plans had any immediate effect on their daily business. In fact, most officials were unaware that the system established under Worthington had fallen out of the government's favour, but there were ready indications that the scarce support for CD would be cut back and then cut back again. Reduced federal support for National Civil Defence Day in 1958 served as an example.[28] The federal CD organization provided financial support and millions of pieces of advertising material to the provinces for the first National Civil Defence Day in 1957, but during planning for the following year this support disappeared.[29]

During the more subdued National Civil Defence Day celebrations in 1958, the federal, provincial, and municipal governments presented the public with a rare united front. The organization gave no indication that it would soon be replaced by another agency. Throughout the day, the public heard slogans in support of CD that were developed by the Information Services Division and broadcast over radio stations throughout the country. These included traditional messages such as "plan today to survive tomorrow"; "ignorance is bliss, but not during a nuclear war"; "hoping won't stop an H-Bomb – ward off the threat by making Canada strong." Several made claims that even the federal government no longer officially supported: "Face the facts about disaster and you'll find civil defence is the only answer." The most consistent boast was that support for CD in Canada was growing, buoyed up by its citizen volunteers.[30]

The EMO was not included in any publicity, nor did any of its representatives participate in the celebrations or exercises. The celebratory atmosphere of National Civil Defence Day disguised deep fissures within the organization that had prompted a crucial re-examination of the basic goals and tasks of CD. Few of the commentators on CD mentioned the national inquiry into CD that had been underway for nearly six months, managed by Howard Graham.[31]

The Graham Report: A Turning Point

Graham's inquiry was launched by Diefenbaker's government early in 1958 following a Cabinet discussion about the reorganization of departmental functions and responsibilities. Monteith leapt at the opportunity to shed the Department of Health and Welfare of responsibility for CD.[32] He revived the WBC's suggestion that CD should be administered through the EMO, which had operated only as an interdepartmental government planning body and not as an agency for civil protection. The minister argued that the shift would improve efficiency, and he pointed to changes in the United States, where on 24 April 1957 responsibility for CD had been merged into the Office of Civil Defense Mobilization.

Monteith concluded his proposal to the prime minister with the advice that a minister without a portfolio could be given the "opportunity" to advance civil defence, a task he had found "particularly baffling and frustrating up to the present time."[33]

Monteith received permission to ask Graham to take over the position of federal CD co-ordinator from Hatton. Graham found Monteith's offer less attractive than an employment opportunity with the Toronto Stock Exchange, but he did agree to assess Canadian CD organizations from coast to coast.[34] Monteith gave Graham the mandate to provide a comprehensive review of existing policies at the local, provincial, and national levels and to suggest revisions of the CD strategy that would offer solutions to the ICBM threat. The response across the country to the announcement of Graham's task was immediate, if unintended. Civil defence committees and councils across Canada feared that their investment of money and time into new plans and equipment could be rendered obsolete by Graham's findings. This worry caused paralysis at all levels of decision making from the federal CD headquarters down to individual volunteers.

As the review continued, plans were put on hold, or starved out of existence, as provincial officials refused to dispense funds to programs that were under review. News of the review came at the worst possible time for some local organizations. In Toronto, after a long wait for provincial approval of their evacuation plans and routes of dispersal, the CD organization had installed twenty-five sirens and was beginning to enlist the media to promote CD. Pamphlets were being distributed to homes, enclosed with the monthly hydro bills, and, most importantly, local training appeared to be getting off the ground. Yet in early August 1958, the head of the Metro Toronto Civil Defence Committee, Alderman Donald Summerville, reported that CD had to be "laid over" until the results of the survey were known.[35] At the end of the month, Metro Toronto's co-ordinator, H.H. Atkinson, discovered that every last submission for funding had been rejected by the federal CD headquarters, including the shelter survey and signage, on the grounds that it could not be covered by "existing regulations."[36] By the beginning of February 1959, the financial implications of Graham's review were still unclear, and funding for the next year's CD program had not been given federal approval.[37]

Toronto and other municipalities eventually tired of waiting for Graham to complete his report, which had been postponed for several months while he co-ordinated the Queen's visit to Canada in the fall and winter of 1958 at the request of the government.[38] Graham later recalled Diefenbaker's reaction to his initial reluctance to work on the royal tour because of the pressing deadline for his CD survey. The prime minister had stated that "it wouldn't matter if that is delayed a bit."[39] Political scientist James Eayrs had a characteristically pungent reaction:

> [It is] more urgent than ever that Canadian citizens be instructed in the hazards of fall-out and provided with protection against them. Yet what is being done for civil defence? Who is General Worthington's successor? What has happened to General Graham's report? What, indeed, has happened to General Graham? That question, at least, may be answered. He is planning the visit of the Queen and Prince Philip. First things first.[40]

Cabinet had intended to present Graham's conclusions to the House of Commons and the Canadian public. In their last meeting of 1958, Diefenbaker and his ministers agreed that because the report dealt with purely municipal and provincial matters, it could "hardly be withheld." After a preliminary review of his findings, which he submitted in early 1959, their resolve faltered.[41] The report was never publicly released, nor does there appear to be any record of Graham's findings in any of the archives of Cabinet ministers or in the departmental records, although over fifty copies of the report were circulated.[42] The Diefenbaker government did not disclose the Graham report for several reasons. Prominent among these was Graham's own recommendation that the report ought to be kept secret. Graham believed that the document, which laid bare the confusion and lack of co-operation in CD across the country, would place national security at risk if it was made public. Nor did he wish to publish the comments of provincial and municipal officials that had been recorded in confidence.[43]

In an early draft of his autobiography, Graham revealed his personal impressions of the manner in which CD had proceeded in the provinces. In most of his interviews, provincial premiers and responsible ministers had little or no understanding of the organizations for which they were responsible. Civil defence was left entirely to the discretion of its provincial co-ordinators. Graham also found no evidence of interprovincial planning or protected communication facilities that could survive an attack and permit governments, federal and provincial, to co-ordinate rescue efforts across the country. Over five months, Graham visited every major CD centre, and several others besides, always in the company of the provincial co-ordinator. He strove to obtain the views of the provincial premiers, cabinet ministers, majors, and average citizens.[44]

On 21 January, after further study of the report, Monteith argued to his colleagues that "tabling the report with its criticism of the government and its comments on provincial situations was inadvisable and self-condemnatory ... The government would not escape criticism by tabling the recommendations alone."[45] Cabinet agreed not to release any of the recommendations or to publish the report but, instead, to await further study of the subject by Monteith and George Pearkes. Graham's principal finding was that CD required an urgent update and reform to be of any use to the public in a thermonuclear war. The ministers recognized that delay might lead to an erosion of public interest in CD, but Graham's recommendations were far-reaching. They included greater responsibilities for the armed forces at home, a suggested change in departmental management, and alterations in the relationship between the provinces and the federal government. All of these were serious changes that would take time to implement effectively.

The report appears to have been lost, but the reaction to it within government agencies and, in particular, within the newly established EMO is well documented, shedding light on the content and character of Graham's findings. According to Robert Bryce, clerk of the Privy Council, Graham came down firmly against the mixed policy of "evacuation and shelter" that had been periodically articulated since late 1953. Graham's criticism of the program was based on discussions held with the commissioner of the Canadian Red Cross, St. John Ambulance, the presidents of the Air Force Association and the Royal Canadian Legion, the Canadian Federation of Mayors and Municipalities, and the co-ordinator of CD for the United Kingdom, which all led to the conclusion that mass evacuation was both "impracticable and unacceptable by the population ... the danger of 'fallout' makes it desirable to stay put."[46] The harshest observations were reserved for the federal government itself, which remained reluctant to take full responsibility for CD. Graham concluded, like others before him, that the full resources of the country would be needed to fight a nuclear emergency.

Graham believed that a fit, trained, disciplined force would be needed to carry out any plan and that the Canadian army was the only organization remotely qualified to do so.[47] This opinion was contrary to the Canadian planning process for nuclear emergencies. Entangling the armed forces in a domestic rescue effort during the first stages of a war with the Soviet Union was precisely what the Canadian Chiefs of Staff had been arguing against since the Second World War. Graham called for plans with a national, rather than a regional, character, "covering all our resources in men and materials."[48] As a logical extension of this finding, he recommended that the funding responsibility for CD in Canada should reside totally with the federal government. This advice emerged from his consideration of the likely national distribution of fallout following an attack and of the complete opposition by municipal and provincial officials to CD expenditures that he had encountered during his survey.[49]

Although the implementation of Graham's recommendations would be very costly for the federal government, his report did not resemble municipal plans that called for extensive and expensive shelter systems and military installations.[50] He believed, like many defence observers, that the Soviet Union and the United States were so equally balanced that a full-scale nuclear war was unlikely and that even a limited nuclear exchange would be preceded by a lengthy period of tension that would permit some population dispersal.[51] However, his survey revealed that plans for the mass evacuation of cities hours or minutes before attack were disjointed, inconsistent, unrealistic, and not understood even by the local CD co-ordinators who had drafted them. His recommendations for federal and military responsibility were based on his experience as a military officer and his faith in central planning and authority.[52] As CGS, Graham had introduced survival operations into the Canadian army militia's training schedule – an unpopular decision – but one that reflected his belief that the army could not escape its domestic role in a nuclear war. His report reflected this preference.

Graham's findings were valid. Canada's CD was broken largely as a result of the intergovernmental obstacles it had encountered since 1948. Graham's advice to the government to increase the military's involvement in CD was a solution that could improve federal leadership, but the army could not substitute for the large body of trained, if ill-co-ordinated, CD volunteers. Rescue and reconstruction operations in an area destroyed by nuclear weapons required a much larger force than the limited numbers the Canadian army could provide.

Implementing the Graham Report

The government took the Graham report very seriously because an intensified superpower confrontation had unfolded in Europe in the fall of 1958. On 27 November of that year, Soviet premier Nikita Khrushchev delivered an ultimatum to the West to withdraw its garrisons from West Berlin. If they did not follow his instructions, he would sign a separate peace accord with the Communist German Democratic Republic (GDR) and allow the GDR to restrict Western access to the city. This action would have spelled an end to the democratic Western outpost in the GDR, in which the United States, the United Kingdom, and France had invested extensive military and economic resources. The announcement set off nearly four years of crisis and confrontation.[53]

Riding a wave of success since the *Sputnik* coup, Khrushchev took his gambit to meet several aims. The Soviet premier wanted to stave off an expected NATO decision to station intermediate-range ballistic missiles in the Federal Republic of Germany (FRG) and to shock European NATO allies into recognizing and dealing with the GDR directly as a sovereign state – a position that was unacceptable to the West, which was committed to the eventual reunification of Germany. In his retirement, Khrushchev explained the policy of squeezing Berlin as a way of "achieving a moral victory without war." His goal was to force nervous Western Europeans to urge the United States to concede to some of the Soviet Union's demands. The risks of provoking the Americans were worth the initial rewards: "We were also afraid of war. Only a fool would not be ... that does not mean you can buy yourself out of war at any price, the detriment of your country's prestige."[54] Yet neither the Soviet Union nor the GDR believed that the West would actually provoke a nuclear war over Berlin.[55] Officially, NATO stood by its policy to support West Berlin, threatening war if the West's access rights were abused by the Soviets.[56] Most NATO countries suspected that the Soviets would never actually eject the West from Berlin with armed force. No one, including the FRG, wanted a nuclear war over the city.[57] The federal government quietly prepared Canada for war as the crisis deepened.[58]

Against this backdrop, the federal government convened an Ad Hoc Committee on Civil Defence to study Graham's report and prepare recommendations for the federal government. Bryce chaired the committee, which was composed of members of the Privy Council Office, Davidson from the Department of Health and Welfare, the chairman of the COSC, and the CGS. Over several meetings between 30 January and early March 1959, these representatives considered the future direction of CD in Canada. The original point of contention was Graham's recommendation to transfer control of CD to the Department of National Defence. Bryce and other members of the committee rejected his advice because the WBC placed this responsibility on all government departments and agencies. Civil defence, Bryce argued, was one component of government machinery in a total war.[59]

Both Davidson, the deputy welfare minister, and Pearkes, the defence minister, rejected any suggestion that the federal government should assume more responsibility over CD. Bryce countered that the federal government would undoubtedly control most resources after a nuclear strike. His agency had found that the public had generally supported municipal and provincial claims that CD was a matter of national defence and, therefore, a federal responsibility. The public, after all, looked to the federal government for their safety. Bryce concluded that any successful future program would require greater federal involvement and visible support.[60]

Pearkes and Lieutenant-General S.F. Clark, Graham's successor as CGS, initially rejected any army responsibility in co-ordinating CD, but later conceded that the army could carry out operational tasks such as re-entry into attacked areas, search and rescue, engineering, and radiation monitoring under aid of the civil power provisions.[61] It was agreed at the first meeting of the Ad Hoc Committee on Civil Defence (also called the Bryce Committee) that emergency tasks would have to be divided between the civilian authority and the military.

An internal EMO report about the economic impact of a nuclear attack informed Bryce's plan for the division of governmental and departmental responsibility for CD. The report, entitled *Economic Problems under Nuclear Attack,* was based on the long-standing NATO assumption that any nuclear war would be won in the "shock phase" of the first thirty days following the outbreak of hostilities or nuclear exchange. The EMO identified critical shortcomings in the area of supply, transportation, manpower, finance, and accommodation, as production in all areas slowed or came to a stop in the ensuing chaos. Preparing industry in all sectors for attack with surplus parts, stocks, or fuel was one massive problem; another was determining how to distribute supplies after an attack. Even this assumption was based on "very shaky statistical foundations." Survival would be endangered further because nuclear war was unlike any other conflict in Canadian history – urgent jobs would need to be filled immediately, and any attempt at national registration before attack would be as demoralizing as it would be completely ineffective. There was, in short, no area of Canada that was prepared for attack or any area of federal government activity that would not be critically inhibited.[62]

The EMO report was based on an attack scenario in which every Canadian target was hit in the first stages of the war and in which intense radioactive fallout blanketed the rest of the populated areas in the country. In order to ensure the survival of the country, each federal government department, beginning with the responsible minister, would need to assume responsibility for carrying on essential programs in co-operation with their provincial counterparts. These programs would be organized through protected headquarters outside of target areas run by a skeleton support staff and administered by regional officers empowered by the Privy Council.[63] The EMO was to be responsible for planning, organizing, and financing local preparations for displaced people in wartime.[64] Bryce's plan recognized that municipalities could no longer be held fully responsible for the organization and maintenance of CD organizations but would require trained police and fire services capable of keeping civil order until help could arrive from the military. The Bryce Committee approved the draft plan on 23 February 1959.

The committee's final report to Cabinet incorporated many of Graham's recommendations, with minor adjustments made by the EMO. Since much of the population already believed that the federal government, not individuals, was responsible for each citizen's survival, the committee concluded that the federal government had to invest in a greater federal effort to provide "central planning in peacetime and central direction in war."[65] Committee members rejected Graham's argument that the Canadian army was the only force capable of directing CD planning and operations and proposed that with greater federal leadership, the provinces could be convinced to improve their own CD efforts. The committee recommended that the federal government should increase its share of spending for projects under the Financial Assistance Program from 50 percent to 75 percent in order to provide the provinces and the public with immediate evidence of the federal government's new role in CD. The Canadian army would not be solely responsible for CD, as Graham had recommended, but the committee accepted his argument that the army should have a greater role in re-entering wasted cities to rescue trapped citizens.[66] In the past, it had been assumed by the COSC that the armed forces in Canada would provide assistance to the CD organization during an attack, but the Bryce Committee's report formalized their involvement, with far-reaching implications for mobilization and training.

The Bryce report was forwarded to Cabinet and approved on 17 March 1959. It set a new direction for CD in Canada. After nearly a decade of federal-provincial-municipal disputes, the principle of local self-sufficiency had been set aside for a COG policy, which demanded a greater federal effort. Civil defence, which had been to that point intentionally civilian in its nature and composition, also moved towards militarization by giving the armed forces influence over CD planning and operations. The Bryce Committee also hoped that a substantial increase to the federal government's financial investment in CD measures would resolve the intergovernmental battles about money and jurisdiction that had done so much damage to the credibility of Civil Defence Canada over the past decade.

Yet the new plan ensured that jurisdictional battles would continue, not only between governments but also within the federal government itself. While Civil Defence Canada had once been administered by one government department, all government departments would now be expected to carry out one or more aspects of the national survival program. In his report, Bryce predicted that the diffusion of responsibilities might lead to breakdowns in communication between departments and cause other complications, but he assured Diefenbaker that the government could "make it work."[67] The infusion of funds for the Financial Assistance Program was not matched by greater expenditure for the federal planning office, which would have to conduct expanded operations with its small staff. Bryce informed R.B. Curry that he should not expect any new funds for the EMO. Instead, Bryce sought to obtain resources for the EMO through the first major cuts to the existing federal CD establishment in the Department of National Health and Welfare.[68]

The EMO Absorbs Civil Defence

Davidson, like Monteith, was eager to remove CD from his list of responsibilities and, in particular, to rid himself of the staff that had occasionally created negative press coverage and criticism of the minister. Bryce's report promised Diefenbaker that the shift of responsibility from Civil Defence Canada to the EMO would give the government an opportunity to be rid of Major-General G.S. Hatton. Hatton's bombastic personality had grated on his superiors, on his colleagues, and, most importantly, on provincial officials. In the fall and winter of 1958, Hatton had been involved in a number of running battles with Ontario municipalities, which led to accusations by municipalities against the province. The province of Ontario was already dissatisfied with the tripartite arrangement for CD and reacted with hostility against both the municipal officials and Hatton. One such case was especially embarrassing for the federal government. Following a natural gas explosion that partially destroyed a federal government office in October 1958, Diefenbaker and Monteith both expressed their support for the city of Ottawa's emergency services. Hatton, however, chose the moment to attack the city council for its lengthy refusal to establish a CD organization. Monteith censured Hatton after the city filed a complaint with his office.[69]

Bryce had spoken with Diefenbaker about Hatton, who had acted as Worthington's replacement for nearly two years. In the course of the conversation, Diefenbaker revealed that the army wanted nothing to do with Hatton, nor did the Department of Health and Welfare. Bryce and Diefenbaker concluded that Hatton would serve as a special advisor to the EMO until he could be quietly dropped.[70]

On 23 March 1959, Diefenbaker announced his planned reforms of the CD organization to the House of Commons. Newspaper coverage of his speech focused more on those parts of his speech that indicated that the Canadian army would be responsible for "national survival" operations in the future and ignored the important point that the rest of Civil Defence Canada's functions not given over to other government departments would be taken over by the EMO.[71] Affected federal government departments reacted to the announcement with confusion and bewilderment. The *Ottawa Citizen* reported that Canadian army representatives in Ottawa did not know how the military's new responsibilities would be applied and that Civil Defence Canada workers were concerned about their future.[72] Employees of the Canadian Civil Defence College were aware that Graham's report had been under study, but they were caught off guard by the prime minister's announcement.

Hatton's leadership following the announcement did little to inspire confidence in his federal colleagues. Jack Wallace, a veteran planner first recruited by Worthington in 1949, arrived late to the CD headquarters on the day of Diefenbaker's declaration, witnessed Hatton's reaction, and concluded that the man was out of touch with the rest of the organization. Wallace relayed the news to Matthew Penhale, the commandant of the Canadian Civil Defence College in Arnprior, that Diefenbaker's announced changes had resulted in "many long faces and weeping and gnashing of teeth."[73] The prime minister's speech clearly indicated that CD was changing and gave the EMO more influence than Civil Defence Canada had ever enjoyed.

Hatton was in Kingston and had not received advance notice about the planned changes. When he returned to Ottawa on 24 March, he reassured the staff that no significant changes would take place. Wallace concluded from his remarks that "[Hatton] is naïve ... it is quite apparent from the statement that a major re-organization is to take place."[74] Hatton, for his part, stated that he would establish three additional sub-committees to suggest which CD tasks could go to EMO and which might go to the Department of National Defence, in order to preserve his organization. Once more, Wallace was pessimistic: "I do not think that those who are responsible for policy are suddenly going to change and ask Civil Defence what things should be changed."[75] The impact was immediately clear to Wallace. Civil Defence Canada, as established under the previous Liberal government, was no longer in charge of the country's survival efforts. Just two weeks after the announcement, Wallace gloomily told Penhale, even the departmental mail had slowed to a few items per day.

Diefenbaker announced his program of reform to a group of confused and anxious provincial representatives in April 1959. It was the first time that the prime minister had attended a federal-provincial CD conference. His presence was required because the EMO was ultimately responsible to him, but his attendance was also meant to signify the importance that his government accorded to emergency measures. Provincial representatives were encouraged by Diefenbaker's plans to centralize responsibility for emergency measures in the federal government and by the announcement that the Canadian army would be doing most of the heavy lifting in case of attack. They were most eager to learn more about the federal government's promise to assume three-quarters of the cost of provincial and municipal programs.[76] Pearkes, who was also present at the conference, provided an unusually detailed assessment of the military threat from the ICBM and from thermonuclear weapons, based on NATO's own planning assumptions, which predicted a crisis period in 1961-63.[77]

The federal government's frank disclosure of problems and threats at the conference greatly impressed the provincial delegates. W.D. Black, the representative from British Columbia, called the conference the "biggest step forward in [civil defence's] history."[78] Every province's representatives at the conference agreed with the proposed division of powers, which asked for no new commitments from the provinces.

Diefenbaker's reform package was formalized in Order-in-Council 1959-56, which was approved on 28 May 1959. The "Civil Defence Order" (CDO), as it was identified, restructured federal responsibility for CD along departmental lines. The Department of National Defence assumed responsibility for Canada's air-raid warning system and agreed to create another warning system that would detect fallout patterns after an explosion had occurred. Most importantly, the CDO assigned responsibility to the armed forces for "controlling, directing and carrying out re-entry into areas damaged by a nuclear explosion or contaminated by serious radioactive fallout ... and the rescue and provision of first aid to those trapped and injured."[79] The armed forces would also assume emergency powers over "municipal and other services," meaning that the Canadian army would take over the operational control of municipal CD, fire, police, and public works during an attack. Planning for CD was given over to the EMO, which was responsible to the prime minister. The Department of National Health and Welfare only retained the obligation to assist provinces and municipalities with advice on emergency health and welfare planning. It also continued to operate the Canadian Civil Defence College in Arnprior, which trained federal and provincial employees and municipal volunteers in emergency measures doctrine. The CDO took effect on 1 September 1959.

Over the months following the CDO's implementation, Civil Defence Canada employees were slowly parcelled out to other government departments, given the option of working out in Arnprior (many refused), or being let go.[80] The most valuable employees were offered posts in the EMO. Wallace, who had served as the deputy commandant of the Canadian Civil Defence College, transferred to the EMO to serve as its assistant director under R.B. Curry. As federal departments grappled with their new responsibilities, and Civil Defence Canada employees faced an uncertain future, the decision-making process in Ottawa ground to a halt. This standstill, in turn, affected municipal CD organizations, many of which were left waiting for the government's new financial regulations to take effect.

Transition and Confusion

The period following the formal announcement of the new direction in CD was therefore marked by the same organizational paralysis that occurred during the period of Graham's survey. H.O. Waffle, the chair of the Metropolitan Toronto

Civil Defence Committee, wrote to Curry in August to complain that his volunteers were steadily leaving the organization because the municipality was no longer certain what role, if any, they were meant to play. "In other words," Waffle wrote, "we are maintaining an organization without knowing what our objectives are, or being able to explain them." In such an atmosphere, securing approval for financial projects was impossible, and the recruitment and retention of volunteers was "exceedingly doubtful."[81]

The situation was the same elsewhere. W.M. Nickle, Ontario's minister of planning and development, sent a letter of apology to Pearkes, the defence minister, after the Kingston area's CD organization folded in November. In his resignation letter, Brigadier-General C.D. Quilliam, Kingston's CD co-ordinator, likened his organization to "a bus full of passengers without any drivers." Without policy leadership, municipal interest in funding and in volunteering for the organization dwindled. The editors of the *Kingston Whig-Standard* bemoaned the loss of Quilliam and the failure of CD in a principal reception area.[82]

Confusion over direction lay at the root of these events, as provinces and municipalities struggled over their new roles. In some cases, they took little note of the responsibility of the armed forces, the new EMO, or the much-reduced role of the provinces in CD planning. In both British Columbia and Alberta, training carried on as usual, with the co-ordinators bound to operate under the terms of the existing provincial legislation for CD.[83] Other provincial organizations continued to look to Civil Defence Canada for leadership. When its office doors were closed after 1 September 1959, provincial CD offices faced a period of adjustment.[84]

The transition from CD to the EMO was not helped by a public protest from Hatton. Shortly after his involuntary transfer to the EMO, he published his letter of resignation "in the public interest" to declare that the new organization and its policies were "totally inadequate."[85] Hatton argued that the EMO was too small to carry out its tasks and that reliance on the army was far too great since it was not large enough to rescue Canadians if more than one target city was hit – hundreds of thousands of CD volunteers would still be needed and would have been trained under the old system. He also believed that the diffusion of CD tasks throughout the multiple government departments implicated in the CD order would render co-ordination in CD "ineffective in peace and disastrous in war." His and Worthington's experience in trying to obtain agreement on policy matters in interdepartmental committees had proven that more hands did not necessarily make light work. In Hatton's experience, interdepartmental involvement meant fewer resources and virtually ensured that confusion would reign in emergency planning. The "disgraceful" treatment of his staff in the CD office was further proof of the government's lack of commitment.[86] Yet Hatton's claim that he was resigning because millions of Canadian lives were at stake was mere posturing. His departure, like the absorption of Civil Defence Canada into the new COG program under the EMO, was already a foregone conclusion. If Hatton did not go willingly, Bryce would have pushed him out.

Conclusion

Observing her husband's optimistic reaction to his retirement, Clara Worthington remarked that Worthy had sloughed off CD "like an old skin, he emerged bright-eyed, vigorous, looking ten years younger."[87] Canada's CD organization also underwent a period of rapid transformation after Worthington's departure. The federal government needed to modernize its plans to accommodate the ICBM and because the evacuation strategy did not account for lethal fallout, which would have blanketed the entire populated area of the country and complicated local, municipally directed CD efforts. After much study, the Canadian government concluded that CD should provide for COG, and they decided to build a federal framework for the central planning and direction of survival operations during the worst period of a nuclear war. The Diefenbaker government rapidly implemented plans laid down by their predecessors, creating the EMO to begin national survival planning.

The creation of the EMO, which was kept secret for over a year, was a response to the changing international environment and internal politics. Although Civil Defence Canada carried on its operations as usual, even mounting two National Civil Defence Days in 1957 and 1958, which were public celebrations meant to raise awareness of nuclear war plans and encourage volunteers to join CD organizations in Canadian cities, these events papered over the cracks that were starting to appear in the organization's foundation and that remained after the celebrations passed. The Diefenbaker government's decision to reassess CD conditions across the country in the fall of 1958, carried out by former CGS Howard Graham, was both timely and responsible. Even though Graham's survey took place against the background of international tension over Berlin, the government's response to its recommendations was politically driven, and the report itself was classified for fear of embarrassing the government.

Graham's recommendations were so incendiary that they could not be ignored. During 1959, Diefenbaker and the EMO revised Canada's existing CD system based on Graham's findings, assigning new and important tasks to government departments and agencies, and assuming greater federal responsibilities for financing municipal and provincial CD. Yet Civil Defence Canada's period of transition was also characterized by stagnation. As government agencies struggled to understand their new responsibilities, no one could render decisions on the vital questions of CD financing, evacuation, and shelter planning.

The most important change was made to the balance between civil and military involvement in Canada's nuclear war preparations. Until 1957, CD in Canada had been animated by a principle of communitarian "self-help" where municipalities would depend on their own resources for survival in the first stages of a war. The most important of these resources was the body of civilian volunteers who gave of their time to help their communities survive. With Civil Defence Canada more or less disbanded by 1959 and the Canadian army assuming responsibility for most of the traditional CD tasks, the principle now was that cities would have to depend on outside help from Canada's military, which was suddenly thrust into the centre of Canada's nuclear survival effort. The role of the community volunteer began to fade into the background as soon as the extent of the military's involvement became clear. Additional reforms were necessary to meet the worst period of international crisis in the early Cold War, which lasted from 1959 to the Cuban Missile Crisis in October 1962.

6

The Survival Army, 1959-62

THE GOVERNMENT'S 1959 Civil Defence Order (CDO) had far-reaching consequences for which government departments were responsible for the Continuity
of Government program. The Canadian army assumed substantial obligations
for CD, and in the years between 1959 and 1963 it expended tens of millions of
dollars in a scramble to prepare a national warning system, to develop emergency
shelter and communications for government officials, and to prepare its soldiers
to fight the "re-entry battle" – the grim responsibility of entering bombed and
radioactive cities to save as many civilians as possible and to salvage damaged
infrastructure. For this task, the Canadian army turned to its citizen-soldiers
in the militia, who were located close to or in many of the target areas.

Army planners soon realized that all of Canada's regular and reserve forces
combined would be insufficient to make a significant contribution to the survival
of Canadians trapped under rubble or fighting fires in the remnants of their
bombed cities. Analysts estimated that hundreds of thousands of civilian volunteers were still required to ensure the country's survival. The small size of
Canada's armed forces preserved the role of municipal CD volunteers in the
new order of Canadian emergency preparedness planning. In peacetime, the
Canadian army devised plans for militia rescue columns to enter damaged cities
and assume command over whatever survivors remained, absorbing their greater
numbers into civil-military rescue cadres, under military discipline, to better
co-ordinate the survival effort. These plans were never made public, though the
government repeatedly insisted that CD volunteers were still needed in great
numbers to work with the military if war came.

The public's interest in CD periodically soared during the periods of intense
international crisis. The Canadian army's plans would in all likelihood have
remained on paper if the Soviet Union had not decided to press the West to
withdraw from Berlin in the summer of 1961. Faced with the prospect of imminent nuclear war, the Diefenbaker government launched an ambitious temporary program designed to resolve the military's manpower shortage. In the
fall and winter of 1961-62, the government authorized the Special Militia Training
Plan (SMTP) to recruit 100,000 civilians into the militia for a six-week training
course in survival. It remains as the only "crash course" in CD training to take

place in Canada during peacetime and, at a cost of $35 million, the largest government investment in CD since the Korean War. The SMTP, which attracted over 80,000 men, incorporated elements of past recruiting campaigns, but it encountered new problems. The public was skeptical that the force's recruits were committed to the defence of the country because they were drawn mainly from the ranks of the unemployed. And a program designed to provide for the civilian defence of the country was administered by the military, whose conception of the rights and obligations of its citizen-soldiers differed from those promoted by Civil Defence Canada and expected from its volunteers.

Civil Defence and the Canadian Army to 1959

To properly understand the importance of the entry of the armed forces into CD preparations and the SMTP, it is necessary to retrace the history of the Canadian army's commitments to CD in the early Cold War. For much of the 1950s, the army did not show much concern about the effects of a nuclear attack on Canada. Such a possibility was the concern of the air force, which developed capabilities to defend North American airspace against Soviet bomber fleets. The army's planning was directed at its primary tasks overseas, which, apart from its involvement in the Korean War, included the maintenance of the Canadian brigade serving in Germany and Canada's commitment to NATO's defence of Western Europe. Two brigades were kept at home, in reserve, to be deployed to Germany in the event of an outbreak of a third world war.[1]

Successive chiefs of the general staff were adamantly opposed to any diversion from the army's contribution to NATO's deterrent forces, especially the aid-of-civil-power role that an increased support for CD would entail. The army was meant for war, not rescue operations. However, despite its reluctance, the army had been implicated in CD planning at an early stage. The Canadian army, with its independent supply and logistics chains, engineering element, and supply of trained, physically fit men, was the most logical service in the Canadian armed forces to assist in rescue operations and reconstruction of cities following a nuclear attack.

The 1950 Canadian Army Policy Statement concerning "participation of the armed forces in civil defence," which was prepared by the Directorate of Military Operations and Planning, stated that the work to organize CD in Canada was primarily a civilian and municipal responsibility. The armed forces' support for CD was vaguely defined in the policy, which promised that the Canadian army would supply "mobile reserves in secondary role" and "provision of skilled personnel ... helping to clear debris [and] for restoration of communications and public services; treatment and evacuation of casualties in conjunction with

CD medical services."[2] The armed services' first domestic priorities were not centred on protection of the public but, rather, on the security of their own installations and establishments in Canada during the first phases of an atomic war. At the height of the Korean War in March 1951, the Directorate of Military Operations and Planning eliminated promises of army assistance to CD.[3]

Major-General F.F. Worthington had realized the limitations of the armed forces during a wartime emergency. Outwardly, he respected and supported army policy, but Worthington pressured the military to present clear commitments and limitations on the forces available to CD, rather than vague assurances in policy statements, because he did not want to give provincial politicians the mistaken impression that they could simply call out the army if Canada was attacked. If CD failed during the first stages of nuclear attack, however, Worthington suggested that the military could direct some, but not all, of its forces to prevent the country from falling into chaos. He listed as possible resources untrained soldiers and new recruits, then troops awaiting overseas deployment, and only as a last resort experienced, combat-ready soldiers, depending on the country's need.[4] The co-ordinator hoped that if the armed forces provided sufficient assistance to help create a strong national CD in peacetime, such efforts might prevent unnecessary or unwanted diversions during a war.[5] Chief of the General Staff (CGS) Lieutenant-General Guy Simonds, perhaps in response to Worthington's suggestion, later commented that the co-ordinator "would have loved to get his hands on my soldiers."[6] In 1952, Simonds rejected the proposal out of hand, and army policy maintained that it was "undesirable that troops under training ... should be involved in civil defence tasks, either as units or individuals, except as a last resort."[7]

Thermonuclear weapons forced the army to reassess its commitment. In February 1954, the Directorate of Military Operations and Planning reiterated the primary responsibility of the civilian authorities to prepare for nuclear attack, but added an important caveat:

> It is recognized, however, that these air attacks may create such wide-spread damage in target areas as to extend either beyond the capacity of the local civil defence organization or even to render it completely incapable of carrying out its task. While the Armed Forces are necessarily concerned with other important aspects of the national war effort and should not be needlessly deviated from their primary roles, yet because the alleviation of suffering and the restoration of civilian activity in a bombed area is of immediate importance to the war effort, they must be prepared as a temporary measure to come to the immediate assistance of the civil defence organization within bombed targets or even to assume completely the functions of that organization.[8]

As the federal CD agency took its first tentative steps towards an evacuation strategy, the Canadian Chiefs of Staff Committee (COSC) reluctantly authorized greater military involvement in CD planning. As a first step, the COSC instructed the commanding officers in Eastern, Quebec, Central, Prairie, and Western Commands to prepare emergency plans to assist provincial authorities.[9]

As part of this process, each area command surveyed Canadian CD agencies to assess their requirements. Area commanders in Ontario, Quebec, and the prairies expressed concern in their reports about the country's apparent unpreparedness for war. Central Command commented to Simonds that "the larger urban centres ... should be recognized as a major commitment for Central Command and one which will undoubtedly interfere with mobilization if enemy bombing activity is severe and continuous."[10] The General Officer Commanding (GOC) Prairie Command bitterly noted that the provisions of the most recent army policy statement could only apply if "a civil defence organization is, in fact, in existence and can operate ... Such is not the case in Prairie Command."[11] In every assessment provided by the GOCs, training installations and mobilized militia (reserve) forces were highlighted as the most important source of manpower to support CD organizations.

In February 1955, the area commanders' suggestions were incorporated into the annual policy statement, which outlined in clear terms that the armed forces should be prepared to "assume the functions of civil defence, as a temporary measure, in the event that the local civil defence organization has been overwhelmed."[12] Worthington's consistent emphasis on clearly distinguished roles for the armed forces and CD organizations was not founded solely on respect for the Canadian army's mission within NATO. He and other federal officials were also worried that the armed forces' involvement in CD could negatively affect enrolment of civilian volunteers and reinforce the impression of the provincial and municipal officials in Quebec and Ontario that CD precautions were an army responsibility. On seeing the 1955 policy statement, George Davidson, the deputy minister for welfare, sent an anxious note to Worthington asking whether it would be wise to "soft-pedal" the policy before releasing it to the provinces, given the "do-nothing" attitudes in Montreal, Ottawa, and Quebec.[13]

Worthington worked with Simonds to develop a joint announcement of the 1955 policy for Paul Martin, the health minister, and Ralph Campney, the defence minister. The guiding principles of civil-military co-operation in CD were laid out clearly to prevent the provinces from misinterpreting its impact on the need for continued local support: "The military are to assist civil authorities *but not replace them;* they will normally be employed in formed bodies under their own Officers and NCOs. GOCs are empowered to delegate troops in aid of Civil

Defence as to the task to be performed."[14] The supporting role of the armed forces was made clear when the policy was formally announced by Campney in the House of Commons: "They will not, therefore, become part of the Civil Defence Organization or assume any of its functions, but they will stand ready to provide assistance in an emergency, if called upon by the civil authorities."[15]

In April 1956, a General Staff Instruction introduced the first training regimen for "national survival" tasks. While area commanders were officially instructed to use both regular and reserve forces in support of CD if asked, George Urquhart's survey of earlier draft plans reveals that, in nearly every Canadian command, reserve forces were exclusively tasked with CD duties. The regular forces remained earmarked for deployment overseas.[16] Militia units were still trained for war, but their training programs increasingly reflected the demand for reserve forces specializing in communications and engineering duties, which were both essential for aid-of-civil power exercises. Some local commanders welcomed the new role, perhaps seeing the possibility for additional funding and more resources for their volunteer soldiers. As Lieutenant-Colonel W.R. Buchner explained, militia units were better suited for rescue duties because most major target areas were home to one or more militia units. Each had "close liaison with the key personnel and services in its locality and, being a cross-section of the community, it is in a unique position to assist in the re-establishment of the community's life and services after the disaster."[17]

As training progressed, the Canadian army began to fashion local militia groups into self-contained "mobile support groups," capable of assuming additional communication, reconnaissance, route clearance, rescue, traffic control, and first aid to bombed out areas where CD organizations existed and all functions of CD in those areas where the organizations did not exist or had been destroyed.[18] By May 1957, a policy for the mobile columns existed in draft that inextricably tied the assistance of the reserves to support of the "static [civilian] civil defence force which would have its hands full in executing the dispersal plan." The concept of mobile columns demanded unique units experienced in national survival operations, with their own leaders: "They require to be self-sustained and not dependent on other services."[19]

The decision to employ reserve forces in support of CD was not confined to Canada. In Denmark and the Netherlands, mobile columns were recruited from universal service conscripts. The columns were assigned officers, and they were maintained as a unit. The British army built up mobile columns from three-company units, selected from National Service conscripts, who trained for thirty days per year in national survival, with additional training provided to territorial army units.[20] By 1957, the United States had no formal armed forces mobile columns, but several state governments considered units from the National Guard for the role.[21]

The concept of reserve mobile columns was complementary to the Canadian CD evacuation policy. General evacuation planning for CD consisted of three phases: (1) the strategic evacuation; (2) the tactical evacuation, which were both managed by civilian volunteers; and (3) the "mop-up" or "re-entry" period, which was managed by the reserve forces. In the final stage, rescue squads were required to enter destroyed cities to salvage what life and industry they could. Under the armed forces policy, the reserve forces were responsible for re-entry, since Civil Defence Canada had admitted by 1956 that there was no organization in the country equipped for the task. However, the 1957 army policy statement read that military support for the third phase would only be temporary, because the armed forces could not "become needlessly diverted from their primary role." The armed forces warned local CD authorities that they might receive help with their evacuations, but "this should not be counted on ... and should be considered a bonus."[22]

The evacuation policy was badly dated by 1958 and tended to ignore the problem posed by the effects of radioactive fallout that could kill evacuees without shelter. Development and integration of intercontinental ballistic missiles into nuclear arsenals after 1957 also undermined the evacuation concept, which depended on the receipt of at least three hours' warning to empty the cities of as many people as possible. Under ideal conditions, the estimated warning of a missile launch was a little over fifteen minutes.

Graham's 1958 survey of CD, and the subsequent CDO, resolved and formalized government policy concerning the assistance of the armed forces in domestic nuclear war preparations. The Emergency Measures Organization (EMO) took responsibility for national CD planning, including the co-ordination of peacetime evacuation and shelter plans with the provinces. The armed forces were asked to provide attack and fallout warning and to lead re-entry and rescue operations in destroyed cities. As a consequence, they were also given the responsibility for directing emergency workers in and around the destroyed cities. In effect, the army would now be in charge of CD rescue efforts. Although the army had played a supporting, and largely ad hoc, role in CD for nearly a decade, government policy now forced the military to lead preparations for CD measures in peacetime.

The Manpower Problem
Before 1959, the army had pledged only 3,500 troops from the regular force for continental defence, and it had reserved the remainder of its strength for

deployment to Germany.[23] Most of these soldiers were located close to target areas. The militia's establishment was limited to just 45,000 part-time soldiers who could be mobilized in an emergency. In November 1959, defence minister George Pearkes clarified government policy. He stated that the army's new role had not eliminated the need for civilian rescue workers trained in CD by the provinces and municipalities. The federal reorganization had left municipal and provincial CD organizations more or less intact, although many local organizations had lost volunteers during the transition from Civil Defence Canada to the EMO.

The army believed that 300,000 civilian volunteers were still needed to salvage life from the ruins after a nuclear war.[24] This was not an arbitrary number but the result of detailed studies of requirements for national survival carried out in the United States and Canada. In February 1960, the CGS asked the new Directorate of Survival Operations and Planning (DSO&P) to study the needs of the army in light of the emphasis on re-entry and rescue operations in CD. The study built on the findings of the US Committee on Disaster Studies, the Defence Research Board's nuclear attack assumptions, and the Canadian Army Operational Research Establishment's assessment of the post-attack situation in Canada. The DSO&P concluded that, in an "average" scenario, all of Canada's major cities would be destroyed. Half of Canada's industry would be crippled, as would rail and air transport for lack of reliable fuel. Telephone, telegraph, and radio communications would be severely disrupted since most wire traffic was channelled through the major cities. The army would be left with fewer than two days' supply of food and less than one day's supply of gasoline. Nearly a million Canadians would be trapped in the rubble, requiring rescue.[25] Fighting fires alone would require seven times the personnel and resources then available in all of the Canadian target cities. In a near-ideal attack scenario, the army would only be able to rescue 19,000 people with their existing resources. The rest would succumb either to fallout or, more likely, to fires and smoke inhalation as many small conflagrations spread throughout the devastated cities.[26] These figures were never released for public consideration.

Canada's regular and reserve forces combined were not large enough to save a single bombed Canadian city. Winning the re-entry battle depended as much on trained and prepared personnel as the plans drafted by Civil Defence Canada in the 1950s. From February 1960, the DSO&P therefore argued for re-entry columns composed of a mix of civilian and military personnel. The military reasoned that they could provide leadership if civilians could provide the numbers. They also recognized that the maintenance of a large force of civilians trained in CD in peacetime was a task that neither Civil Defence Canada nor they could master. The DSO&P concluded that the army would be forced to depend on civilians who were willing to save lives *after* the bombs started falling.[27]

The DSO&P predicted that the re-entry force's greatest ally would be Canadians unharmed in the first attacks against cities. The military believed that survivors would not quit the outskirts of a destroyed city but, in some cases, would move towards the city centre. The DSO&P based this assumption on the conclusions of research projects commissioned by the US Committee of Disaster Studies as well as on their own observations of major natural disasters.[28] One such report pointed to "convergence behavior" among survivors of disasters, who flocked to the site of disasters to help, to satisfy curiosity, or merely to exploit the chaos.[29] The challenge facing the Canadian army, the DSO&P planners reckoned, was to harness the potential of "the convergers" to transform the civilian population's predicted curiosity, anxiety, and opportunism into useful work in support of the army's responsibilities for national survival. For all of the army's criticism of civil defence's outdated strategies, the DSO&P's conclusion was based on the same outdated British wartime experience with CD that had animated much of the civilian planning throughout the 1950s. In a July 1960 study, planners quoted extensively from Terence O'Brien's official history of British air-raid precautions during the Second World War, citing the fact that visible activity from the authorities persuaded volunteers to come forward and take part in their own defence.[30] The Canadian army directed the militia to supply leadership cadres to the projected "convergers."

The militia was ideally suited to absorb spontaneous civilian volunteers because of its top-heavy composition. With officers and non-commissioned officers comprising over a third of the personnel in the militia's mobile support column structure, labour was in short supply. Planners suggested that the small numbers of "career privates" in the reserve force provided an opportunity for units to integrate masses of disorganized survivors into civil-military cadres, boosting the numbers available for the mobile support columns while keeping the effort under military leadership. Through this process, the military hoped to increase the size of its mobile support columns from a company-sized organization to a battalion-sized rescue force composed of 120 soldiers paired with 380 additional civilian volunteers.[31] While the military expected that the "convergence" phenomenon would supply the numbers of survivors they would require for rescue, the DSO&P recommended that the public should be prepared for the task through education. With publicity, they hoped to encourage 20 percent of male Canadians between the ages of sixteen and sixty to join up "at the last moment" for rescue work.

Civil Defence Canada and the EMO were confronted by the same problem. Maintaining a large body of volunteers indefinitely was expensive and impractical. Civil Defence Canada asked the volunteer to become part of a standing defence of the city – part warden, part paramedic, part firefighter – and this role required substantial training and a commitment that most Canadians were unwilling to make. The military proposed a novel approach to the volunteer in survival operations. In response to the problems encountered by CD organizations, army planners recommended that the best course was to "accept the situation as it is and devise ways and means to get the basic training necessary across to as large a portion of the population as possible in conjunction with some normal everyday activity."[32] To do so, the military planners turned to the same stakeholders that had supported CD in the past recruitment drives, such as government departments, municipalities, national and local industries, and service associations such as the Canadian Legion, the Imperial Order Daughters of the Empire, St. John Ambulance, and the Boy Scout Association. For the program to succeed, the federal government would have to take the lead by supporting a highly visible program of public indoctrination in rescue.[33] "The only alternative," the DSO&P concluded, "is some form of compulsion."[34]

Over the following year, the military gradually increased its commitment to national survival. Defence Construction Limited and military engineers from the Army Works Service supervised efforts to dig out emergency government bunkers, notably the Central Emergency Government Headquarters, which was colloquially known as the "Diefenbunker," outside Ottawa.[35] This emergency shelter, completed in late 1961, was the evacuation site for the federal government and a skeleton civil service staff under the Continuity of Government program. It also contained a communication hub capable of reaching regional emergency headquarters built in each of the provinces. All regional emergency sites, as their communications facilities became operational, were staffed with a complement of military signallers.

Over 1960-61, the Canadian army also slowly extended the national network of warning sirens, replacing aging or underpowered sirens in Canadian target cities.[36] The army moved officers into the Royal Canadian Air Force's Air Defence Control Centre in St. Hubert, Quebec, which was linked with the North American Air Defence agreement. Military engineers established rearward links with the Federal Warning Centre in Ottawa, which was responsible for disseminating the military warning to the public.[37] Regular and reserve units reluctantly integrated national survival and rescue courses into their training programs, with much grumbling from the ranks about having to play "snakes and ladders" in a rescue role during the next war.[38] Distaste for the task suffused

FIGURE 13   The Halifax Rifles opted for a volleyball tournament instead of national survival training. Here, Private Barrett, the tournament's winner, receives an award cobbled together from the unit's survival issue. *Source:* George Metcalf Archival Collection, Canadian War Museum, 20000014-011_p7b

all ranks, from a staff officer who displayed a blank piece of poster board to illustrate his lack of progress in survival planning (he was promptly reassigned) to the men of the Halifax Rifles, who happily substituted volleyball for first aid training.[39]

To combat opposition within the military, the DSO&P launched an internal publicity drive to promote national survival training. Major-General A.E. Wrinch, who was responsible for co-ordinating the army's national survival efforts, delivered countless lectures at mess dinners and corps associations to explain the army's role. He and his advisors from the various army services (engineering, medical services, infantry, and so on) ensured that service publications carried at least one article about the principles of rescue and re-entry. Every edition of the *Canadian Army Journal* published between 1959 and 1962 devoted a special section to national survival. The journal featured frequent articles about the basics of panic and mass psychology and the results of episodes such as "Nimble Phoenix," which was a re-entry, casualty evacuation and decontamination exercise amid the imagined devastation of Saint John, New Brunswick, involving civilian emergency officials and much of 3 Canadian Infantry Brigade Group.[40]

On paper, the army organized twenty-two regular mobile support columns and a further forty-four militia mobile support columns from the existing forces, turning it into an organization that formed the basis for the military's concept of survival operations. Cabinet accepted the plan on 16 March 1961. It included provisions for regular and reserve units to take command of civilian workers. Pearkes made press announcements, explaining that the military would require hundreds of thousands of civilian volunteers to assist with rescue work in a war, but the government did not undertake any special public education program so the public did not learn that CD workers would fall under military command during a nuclear war.[41] The central requirement on which the military's effectiveness hinged was the efficient integration of civilian volunteers with military personnel during an emergency. In the two years following the implementation of Diefenbaker's 1959 CDO, neither the military nor the federal government undertook a concerted effort to present the problem to the public, and it was not addressed realistically in the military's own planning.

The 1961 Berlin Crisis and the Acceleration of National Survival

Nuclear war was closer than Cabinet would admit publicly. Economic conditions in the German Democratic Republic (GDR) had continued to decline since the first Berlin crisis in 1958, when Soviet Premier Nikita Khrushchev delivered an ultimatum to the West to withdraw its garrisons from West Berlin within six months or lose its access rights to the city. Khrushchev allowed this ultimatum to expire without incident. East Germany continued to lose skilled workers to the Federal Republic of Germany at a crippling rate. GDR leaders claimed the exodus cost them nearly a billion marks per year, and they sought assistance from the Soviet Union. Khrushchev was content to defer any decision until the Vienna summit in June 1961 with the new US president, John F. Kennedy.[42] Seeking to challenge the younger, less experienced Kennedy, Khrushchev renewed his ultimatum and the threat of war over Berlin.

Khrushchev's behaviour at the summit and his clumsy threats unnerved Kennedy, but it did not move the United States' position on its access rights to West Berlin. On 25 July 1961, Kennedy articulated the United States' intent to defend its rights and, by extension, democratic Berlin by force if necessary. With the support of Congress, Kennedy also announced an increase in the size of the American garrison in Berlin, in addition to raising the ceiling on the army's strength from 825,000 to 1 million.[43] Concurrent with the military increases, Kennedy sought a dramatic increase in CD spending to fund a nationwide survey of public buildings to locate fallout shelter spaces for Americans.[44] In Europe, Dean Rusk, Kennedy's secretary of state, urged NATO countries to bring their militaries up to strength in order to force Khrushchev to negotiate. As Rusk explained to nervous allies at the North Atlantic Council, "we do not propose to rattle the saber, we propose to show how quickly it can be drawn from the scabbard in defence of our obligations and rights."[45] The world, while not quite on the brink of war, edged towards it in the summer and fall of 1961.

Diefenbaker's own tentative, uncertain response to the Berlin issue is clear from the available Cabinet conclusions. His Cabinet did understand the very real threat of war if the Soviet Union allowed the GDR to squeeze the West from Berlin. In July, after long discussions in Cabinet, Diefenbaker, Douglas Harkness, the tough-minded defence minister, and Howard Green, the pro-disarmament secretary of state for external affairs, reached an uneasy consensus that Canada should support the United States' stand on Berlin, even if that meant going to war.[46] According to Canadian Institute of Public Opinion polls, most Canadians agreed. Approximately 60 percent of those polled favoured nuclear war if it was necessary to defend Berlin.[47]

As the crisis reached its peak in August, the United States persuaded its allies to increase their general military preparedness and funding for CD.[48] Diefenbaker's Cabinet met five times in late August to approve measures that would proclaim Canada's moral and military support for the United States and Berlin. At these meetings, Harkness presented a long list of actions the government could take to augment its military and passive defences. He recommended the immediate dispersal of food rations, military vehicle stocks, and emergency clothing from central warehouses to depots outside Canadian target areas. Harkness also requested more money to accelerate installation of air-raid sirens across Canada, and speed the purchase of radiation monitors that the Canadian army needed for re-entry operations. Cabinet approved these plans but rejected Harkness's suggestion to build 23,868 fallout shelters on Department of National Defence property. Cabinet members were concerned that Canadians would be angered if the government erected shelters for its employees rather than providing shelter spaces to those who could not afford to build their own.

Cabinet's uneasy backing of Kennedy's robust stand began to erode once the GDR closed off East Berlin. Green and others were convinced that the GDR's actions presented a possibility for negotiation. Clearly aware of the limited strength of Canada's armed forces in comparison to its allies, and of the divisions within Cabinet, Harkness recommended a very slight increase of 1,100 soldiers for the Canadian NATO brigade in Germany. Cabinet also agreed to raise the manpower ceiling of the Canadian armed forces from 120,000 to 150,000 during the crisis. This measure met Canada's NATO commitments. In the event of a conventional war with the Soviet Union, Canada would send two additional brigades and a headquarters to Europe.[49] Harkness and the other ministers recognized that if the crisis resulted in an immediate nuclear war in Europe, Canada's army brigades would be of little help to NATO and would be better employed at home to save Canadian lives.[50]

In the tense international situation, the government was prepared to enact measures to increase its emergency preparedness at home, but these would be done quietly. An innovative program introduced by Harkness during the Cabinet meeting on 21 August underlined the concern with which his department viewed the Berlin crisis. The Department of National Defence would introduce a large-scale public training course in national survival skills, a nationwide recruitment drive to enlist over 100,000 Canadians as paid privates for special militia survival training courses over the winter of 1961-62.[51] Harkness believed that the plan offered a temporary solution for the national survival program's greatest obstacle: a lack of personnel trained to look after the wounded and homeless in a nuclear war. The program represented the military's effort to overcome the problems that Civil Defence Canada had encountered in the "self-help" model of volunteer recruitment over the past decade. Canadians would be paid to undergo CD training for the first time. The proposal illustrated the fundamental changes brought about by the 1959 reorganization of CD. The military, for years opposed to any substantive role for its soldiers in civilian defence, would now be in charge of instructing the largest group of paid CD workers in Canadian history, who would in turn receive military indoctrination over the course of their training.

The SMTP, 1961-62

Cabinet agreed to Harkness's ambitious program not only because of the possibility of war over Berlin but also to address an unemployment crisis. Canada's slow economic performance in the late 1950s led to rising unemployment, with 356,000 Canadians affected by July 1961. The training program would benefit the government by temporarily lowering the number of unemployed men between eighteen and fifty-five and reducing the drain on Canada's unemployment insurance funds.[52] When he presented the SMTP to Cabinet, Harkness noted that the plan would be attractive to Canadians largely because the pay rate of an unmarried private in the militia was $20 per month more than the maximum payable unemployment insurance.[53] During Cabinet discussions about the SMTP, ministers sought to recruit as many unemployed as possible into the training courses to reduce unemployment figures. The government recommended that the National Employment Service should "suggest the availability of the programme" to those without work, stopping just short of refusing payment of unemployment insurance if the unemployed did not enlist.[54]

The SMTP's benefits as an unemployment relief measure made the significant expenditure easier for Cabinet ministers to accept. As the minister of finance Donald Fleming reflected on the program in his memoirs, "it was difficult to know whether the programme was worth $30 million because benefits were very hard to measure in the civil defence field, but the plan seemed to be a good one and unless civil defence was going to be useless in a nuclear war, such a programme as this should be undertaken."[55] At the time, Fleming had argued against further expenditures so soon after he had tabled the government's budget in the House of Commons. The additional defence costs, he lamented, defeated the government's larger goal of restoring stability to the economy.[56]

Like all other CD plans, the SMTP was an example of government contingency planning for nuclear war. The implementation of the SMTP was largely improvised. A slight objection to the plan emerged during discussion of its emphasis on military training as the foundation for rescue, firefighting, and first aid skills. Civil defence recruiting had traditionally required the citizen to contribute to the defence of the country in a non-military capacity, and volunteers had trained in their community with other civilians to prepare for this task. Civil defence was a means for the public to defend their community and, by extension, their country, without being subject to military control. Paying the public to undergo military discipline posed the risk of erasing the distinction between the citizen-as-defender and the country's profession of arms. Unpaid CD volunteers would no longer be offered the incentive to become local leaders contributing to their community's survival but, instead, would become line soldiers in a military organization. Paid military training would almost certainly diminish the CD volunteer's civic importance to the community. As a result, Cabinet ministers were divided in their views about how the public would respond to the military's prominent role in training civilians. Cabinet agreed that the SMTP courses should not emphasize the military aspects of training.[57]

The training plan was approved and announced to the public in the House of Commons on 7 September 1961. The first course was scheduled for 14 November 1961, with three to follow, each aiming to train 25,000 Canadians in survival skills. The trainees were under no obligation to join the militia after the six-week course was finished, but all were subject to a continuous call-out during the course. If a nuclear emergency appeared likely during the training period, the trainees would, in theory, be available for emergency survival duties. At the end of the course, trainees were given the option to enlist voluntarily in the militia.[58]

Publicity for the training program was the next step, first through advertising its existence to employers and then to the public through mail-outs, newspaper inserts, and public speaking. Colonel J.M. Houghton, the army's director of manning, co-ordinated the distribution of advertising materials across the country, including posters for shop windows, recruiting offices, and armouries. The Department of National Defence purchased radio advertisements on thirty-five English and thirteen French stations and ran a national newspaper advertising campaign in sixty-seven English and eleven French daily newspapers. Finally, a sixty-second television advertisement was prepared and broadcast after 1 December 1961. Much of the advertising was delivered to the public through brochures sent to the National Employment Services in target areas and surrounding communities, which lent greater weight to the perception, then and since, that the SMTP's real target was to reduce unemployment.[59] Although the program was honestly presented as a survival measure, the temptation to use it to relieve the jobless rolls proved hard to resist in some areas.

The SMTP was a military recruiting program, but its publicity employed similar messages as those used in past CD campaigns to attract unpaid volunteers and included traditional appeals to civic responsibility. A lurid mushroom cloud dominated the centre of the recruitment brochure, surrounded by sketches of Canadian militiamen consulting a map, sending radio broadcasts, carrying stretchers, and rushing to the scene of a bomb blast in a jeep. The recruiting drive's appeal was directed at local communities' volunteerism: "Take time out NOW to help your community and your country prepare for any future emergency."[60]

Harkness explained the program to the public in a letter published on the inside cover of the brochure. His message was more plaintive than most CD publicity. Almost apologetically, Harkness explained that, though the army was responsible for rescue services, it required reinforcement from trained civilians. The unwritten admission of the recruiting campaign was that the Canadian army was not capable, either in terms of its manpower or resources, of saving Canadian lives alone. The minister concluded his letter with an appeal to civic pride: "Will you lend a hand? Even if nuclear war does not come, as we pray it may not, I feel certain you will always be proud of having taken a little time out to ensure – whatever happens – that Canada can carry on."[61]

The language of the advertisments reflected the martial nature of the program. The militia reached out to young, unemployed single men using a campaign built around a traditional concept of military service as a masculine virtue of citizenship.[62] An advertisement in the *Montreal Gazette* on 20 October challenged applicants to become citizen-soldiers, willing to make "a man-size contribution to Canada's defence, the safety of your family and your own future."

The advertisement simultaneously challenged readers' masculinity, offered reminders of citizenship's obligations, and offered applicants a career in the military.[63] The SMTP recruiters were seeking men for rescue duties – a field in which women had never been permitted to train – and, as a military recruiting campaign, the advertisements were placed where they could reach the largest number of young and available men. In the *Globe and Mail*, the advertisement occupied the bottom corner of one of the Sports and Outdoor Life pages as well as multiple listings in the classified section at the end of the paper. These were locations that would be read by active young men as well as by the unemployed.[64]

The government supplemented its public advertising, which was primarily directed at the unemployed, with appeals to industry to provide skilled employees with special paid leave to encourage them to take the training course. The needs of the survival program included highly skilled industrial workers, community leaders, and municipal staff familiar with existing municipal and industrial infrastructure. The DSO&P had concluded earlier that industry provided the most fertile ground for national basic training in survival skills. Figures from the Department of Labour indicate that over 435 companies across the country carried out in-house training programs that involved over 500 people at a time. The military estimated that industry training programs alone could reach a minimum of 217,500 Canadians across the country.[65] The Department of National Defence sent out a letter under Harkness's signature to 8,000 recipient institutions, including all Canadian Crown corporations, civil service departments at the federal and provincial level, large industrial concerns, and small companies. The federal and provincial civil services, after some legal wrangling and disputes with the Treasury Board, agreed to the request, and so did many businesses across the country. The list of those responding in November 1961 included Algoma Steel, Calgary Power Limited, General Foods of Toronto, Atomic Energy Canada, the Reader's Digest Association of Canada, Inco, Prudential Insurance, the Canadian National Railways, and the city of Verdun, Quebec.[66]

The crisis, accompanied by growing unemployment, presented an ideal atmosphere for SMTP recruitment.[67] Local militia commands in Western, Central, and Eastern Commands scrambled to muster sufficient training staff across their areas of responsibility to deal with the expected influx of volunteers. They required 2,700 experienced trainers for the first intake of 25,000 recruits alone. The militia's strength was already strained, so they requested assistance from the regular forces. In the first week of enrolment, approximately 5,000 men had reported across the different commands, and by 3 November numbers had reached 12,376, of which nearly 20 percent had joined that day.[68] Advertising over press and radio and by word of mouth drew the press's attention, a development that benefitted and hounded the program over its entire course.[69] Press reporting on the SMTP not only attracted additional volunteers to the program but also highlighted its many shortcomings and gave dissatisfied citizen-soldiers an outlet to vent their grievances about the program's military bent.

A Band of Scavengers?

Speculation about the program's success emerged shortly after it was launched in the House of Commons. The Canadian Press published a story on 19 September quoting sources that claimed the militia had downgraded its recruiting standards to accommodate the influx of new trainees. The author suggested that the survival courses would be filled with rejects, many of whom would join just to get their teeth fixed under the militia's dental benefits.[70] The report had some basis in fact. The Canadian army had two recruiting standards dictated by the battle and base PULHEMS – an acronym for the military's medical classifications for Physique, Upper extremities, Lower extremities, Hearing, Eyesight, Mental capacity, and Stability. The battle standards were designed to find soldiers who would likely see combat, while the base standards sought soldiers to fill support roles. For the training program, the militia used the second standard because they could not afford to reject every candidate who did not meet the physical requirements needed for front-line infantry duties.[71] Rather, they valued quantity over quality. To counter press criticism, Harkness assured the public that his program would attract an "exceptionally high class of recruit."[72] He predicted that most recruits would be young men in their teens and early twenties, eager to make a contribution to the safety of their country but just out of high school and without winter employment.

Problems arose almost immediately as volunteers enlisted for the courses. One example demonstrated the gulf between federal CD planners and municipal officials designated to implement plans developed centrally. Carl Signoratti, president of Local 524 United Electrical, Radio and Machine Workers of America in Peterborough, wrote an excoriating letter to Diefenbaker about the abuse of the SMTP by municipal employees on the local welfare committee, who had refused to deliver welfare payments to unemployed persons who decided not to apply for the course. It is unknown how widespread the practice was, but in St. Boniface, Manitoba, at least forty welfare recipients were refused their cheques and forced to join the program.[73]

Newspapers in central Canada were critical of the survival training plan, especially when the number of recruits did not match the government's targets. The statistics did not help the government deflect their criticism. Nearly 12,000 applicants, of the approximately 18,000 who signed up for the first intake of recruits, were unemployed when their course began. A journalist from the *Montreal Gazette* spoke to ten recruits at the Craig Street Armoury on their first day. When asked why they had joined, five responded that they were unemployed, three cited the nuclear crisis, and two could not recall why they had applied.[74] In Montreal, fewer than half of the 2,500 men who had registered turned out on the first day. In Toronto, slightly more of the original intake attended, but absenteeism grew over the second and third days of the course.[75] The expected number of recruits was exceeded only in Atlantic Canada, which could be explained by the Eastern Command's relatively low quota (2,500) and the high levels of seasonal unemployment in the Maritimes during the winter months.[76] Few of the recruits for the program appeared to be as young, physically fit, or as committed to the program as the Department of National Defence had hoped.

Questions also emerged about the quality of the men who signed up for the program. Harkness and Diefenbaker received letters from the public, many of whom doubted that the strategy of paying citizens to train in CD would result in any benefits for the country's survival, especially when its success largely depended on the unemployed, who were considered by some Canadians to be of dubious moral character. Two graduates of the first course, in discussions with their local members of parliament, were very pleased with the concept of the course and their own training but "aghast" at the quality of their colleagues, of whom 20 percent were "graduates of reform school and ... after the course ended, unemployable in any other field."[77] Contempt for the "survival army" was particularly evident in newspaper coverage and in Diefenbaker and Harkness's correspondence. *L'Action Populaire* reported on 24 January 1962 that the Armoury mess catered exclusively to SMTP trainees on Friday nights, and "it appears that on the following Monday several of them show up at the Welfare Office for money to pay the rent or heat, having gone through all of their $43 pay at the Training Centre."[78]

For these critics, the government's new emergency workers were a liability. Letter writers thought of them as unemployed and unemployable, who were at best opportunists and at worst listless alcoholics. A letter written to opposition leader L.B. Pearson by a Royal Canadian Navy veteran, after he had attended the first day of the course, illustrates the sentiment:

I am sure, and I swear beyond a doubt – that any mental patient in Ontario could enroll for this course. They are picking up every derelict in the City of Toronto. I have never seen such an assortment of Alcoholics and Criminals [sic]! Men, and many beyond the age of boot training, are being given boot training. They could tell these guys anything ... and a medical by interns that couldn't detect a man with rabies. All the recruiting wants is numbers. If they paid these fellows on Monday instead of Friday they wouldn't have any next week ... As it stands many people would prefer to die a neuclear [sic] death than have this band of scavengers from the City Relief Rolls protect them.[79]

The perception that the training plan was unemployment relief in disguise proved unshakeable. Even those in favour of the program viewed it as a tool to stimulate the local economy. Communities affected by the slowing Canadian economy flooded the Department of National Defence with requests to extend the program and to establish recruiting courses in their areas, many of which were far removed from the target cities. While some localities requested courses as a means of exploiting the public's renewed interest in CD, most bluntly demanded courses to stave off unemployment.[80] Martin Merner, president of the United Steelworkers of America, demanded that national survival courses be continued in Sydney, Nova Scotia, until his union's members could obtain jobs in other fields.[81] Ted Outram, the city clerk of Peterborough, Ontario, writing some time after the courses had expired, asked if any similar courses would be introduced for the next year. "The information," he suggested, "will be most helpful in planning any make work jobs of a municipal nature at the expense of the municipal taxpayer."[82]

The government of Canada depended on the unemployed in large part to fill the ranks of the survival training courses, but the program failed to win the public's confidence for the very same reason. "Mr. Diefenbaker's Private Army," as it was called in Toronto, became the source of ridicule for an already beleaguered government. Reeve Norman Goodhead of North York, one of the training program's supporters, complained that the public's understanding of the force's purpose was buried in ignorance and a lack of appreciation of the necessity of additional manpower to help with rescue. "Everybody's survival is everybody's business," he argued, noting that criticism of the force's unemployed ranks missed the point entirely.[83]

Press and public criticism tended to equate "unemployed" with "unskilled" or "unscrupulous." The editorial board of the *Globe and Mail*, examining the goals of the survival program, commented that the government's reliance on the unemployed was at cross-purposes with its goal to develop a corps of trained CD workers that could provide the militia with the needed civilian leadership on which to build in an emergency. "While there would undoubtedly be some [leaders] among the chronically unemployed," the editorial suggested, "their already proved lack of success in civilian life would indicate that there would not be many."[84]

As the third round of courses came to an end, Herbert Herridge, a Co-operative Commonwealth Federation member of parliament for Kootenay West, British Columbia, joined the press in criticizing the government's survival army. On 19 March 1962, he conjured up an image that simultaneously criticized the training program and evoked memories of the Great Depression. Basing his comments on rumours heard from his constituents, Herridge claimed that many survival training recruits were drifters with no connection to the community: "They came into a city, took the course, and then went on [to take it] again."[85]

Herridge's characterizations were pure hyperbole. There is no evidence to suggest that a vast army of unemployed actually rode the rails looking for work in survival training courses. A journalist's examination of the first intake revealed that the recruits were older than the government had anticipated – an average of thirty-four to forty-five years of age – yet they came from a wide variety of occupations and backgrounds, from retired veterans to serving professionals: "There are real estate and car salesmen, carpenters and bricklayers. There are schoolteachers between courses at the university, a dentist who looks after his patients in the evening, a professional engineer ... an unemployed chef and an out-of-work crane operator."[86] Gay Del Villano, a training officer in Sault Ste. Marie, Ontario, later recalled the range of enlistees: "We had people who just came off the street, we had teens who were unemployed and whose families told them to go out and do something useful ... we had a lot from industry and business."[87] Del Villano admitted that some of his trainees were homeless, but nearly a third came from the Algoma Steel Corporation plant, a result of an informal arrangement made over the telephone with the plant manager.[88] The recruits offered skills from a cross-section of the professions the militia would seek to exploit during survival operations.

What is most interesting about the public's criticism of the program is that it hinged not simply on the employment status of the recruits but also on the perceived reasons for their enlistment. While most Canadians did not volunteer for CD and many questioned the strategies underlying national survival as a whole, few criticized the unpaid volunteers who composed the CD corps. Popular rejection of the SMTP was based in part on speculation that recruits were less committed to national survival efforts because they were paid to take the course and, therefore, were prepared to move on as soon as the next job became available. The public took no comfort from the temporary protection that the SMTP offered. The public's reaction also suggests that there was some value to the principle of civic voluntarism in the community. At the grassroots level, the volunteer was generally accepted as a component of social welfare, rooted in the area. While CD had not attracted great public participation, its volunteers were rarely so viciously criticized as the survival army, perhaps because the public believed that its unemployed ranks looked first to defend themselves and not Canadian communities. The public could support either a valid CD force capable of saving lives or an army that was able to fill that role. The SMTP was neither, and it did not enjoy lasting support.

The End of the SMTP

The problems with the program were entirely practical ones. The skills of the survival army were only at the government's disposal for a short six-week period. The government made no provision to keep track of the tens of thousands of Canadians it was training in civilian defence. Once the recruits had graduated, they were released from service, classed by the military as trained militiamen, but were not asked to make any further commitment to return to service in the event of an actual nuclear emergency. Discovering this failure of planning at the end of the program's run in 1962, Liberal defence critic Paul Hellyer denounced the program as "futile as well as the most expensive civil survival training that has ever been undertaken in Canada."[89]

The government's reply to this charge was that it had no more control over the Canadian army's reserve forces than it did over the survival trainees. If the whole of the militia decided to quit, the government would have little choice but to accept it. Harkness likened the demands for a permanent list of names to national registration, which was a step away from conscription.[90] The point of the training course was never to boost permanently the size of the militia but, rather, to provide a foundation of trained civilians with whom the Canadian army could work to rescue injured Canadians. The addresses, occupations, and names of the recruits, Harkness added, would be given to local EMOs for their use in the event of an emergency.

Another practical problem emerged over the content of the training courses. For members of the program, the militarization of CD was problematic enough without conscription. Cabinet had stipulated that survival training would take precedence over military indoctrination. According to the recruits themselves, however, the militia appeared to disregard Cabinet's instructions, placing a heavy emphasis on military discipline and tactics. Several correspondents who had signed up for the program to learn more about CD were dismayed at the heavy emphasis on drill and military culture. In a six-week course, recruits spent the first three weeks learning the basics of the parade square, military law, but only several days on first aid. The fourth week prepared them for a test of these skills, and intensive rescue training took place in the last two weeks. Corporal G.J. Andrews, an amateur poet who graduated from the program hosted in Belleville, confided in verse that the last week was partially dedicated

FIGURE 14 Special Militia Training Plan recruits practise evacuating a casualty from a second floor at the Lakeview armoury near Toronto, September 1961. *Source:* National Defence Image Library, CEN61-144-12

to preparations for the graduation ceremony, where "even the mediocre shine/ when on parade for one last time."[91]

Shortly after the first course, two graduates informed their member of parliament that their training reflected total ignorance of the plans for survival in the event of an attack, let alone the technical aspects of fallout and radiation detection equipment.[92] Cleveland Clifton of Vancouver sent a blistering letter to Major-General J.M. Rockingham, the commanding officer of the Seaforth Highlanders, and Harkness, with a copy to a local radio broadcaster. Clifton remarked that an otherwise worthy project had been "prostituted" by the inclusion of army routine: "It was said among us that while we hadn't had time to properly learn about rescue work and first aid, we can surely keep you amused while you are dying, with our unlovely ... postures and gesturing, a la left and right by numbers [sic]." He further commented that "in the event of a national emergency the only presenting of arms that I may do will be alongside the head of any of the gold braid boys who get in my way when I'm doing my best to cope ... But do cut out all this damned silly mighty army nonsense. It if weren't for Uncle Sam and the Royal Navy, the Swiss Army and a Pope's Guard could kick the hell out of us."[93] Clifton was not alone. Another trainee who quit after a week wrote to complain that the survival courses were "just plain old Militia in disguise."[94]

Some of the volunteers' disillusionment with the SMTP and the militia's CD role in general can be explained by the differing notions of the citizen's responsibilities to the state that were put forward by CD officials and the military. While both organizations asked volunteers to contribute their time to help prepare the country for the worst, Civil Defence Canada had always approached the issue of recruitment from the "self-help" model. Individuals were asked to sacrifice some of their time and, later, their money in defence of their community. The ability of volunteers to survive and help themselves, their families, and their communities was crucial because they would be able to step in for the state when services broke down or were overrun during wartime, as they inevitably would be. By enhancing their self-dependence, they would, by extension, help to ensure national survival and ease each individual community's eventual (if hypothetical) reconstruction. Civil defence manuals and training tried to make this connection clear so that volunteers understood that learning something as apparently simple as first aid was a component of national survival in the event of nuclear war. Civil defence was pitched to Canadians as a means of insurance necessary in the nuclear age. In effect, the civilian model of this type of citizenship taught the individuals that they were of prime importance to ensuring the survival of the country.

The military's approach to survival operations was an inversion of the responsibilities of citizenship. This was in part because, as geographer Deborah Cowen has argued, the soldier's citizenship was "exceptional." Concerns for the soldier as an individual were always secondary to the needs of the state.[95] In traditional war-fighting scenarios, the responsibility meant that, by virtue of his occupation, the soldier could be asked, and was expected to obey, orders that might lead to his own death. Applied to the CD role, the militia infantryman could be expected to enter areas with high risk of radiation poisoning and death by fire or building collapse. This ideal of obedience and self-sacrifice was one of the goals of military training. In contrast to the civilian model of survival planning, plans for self-preservation and family protection were secondary.[96] An example of this perspective is found in the notes for a staff re-entry exercise at a militia staff course held in Kingston in 1959. Instructors there informed attendees that it was their responsibility to have a plan for their family in peacetime. Their failure to do so would prevent them from passing the course because the military would consider them "non-effective" and a possible risk for absenteeism. They were asked to make the plan so that they would not be distracted when the state demanded their services as officers in the Canadian army.[97] During the Cuban Missile Crisis in 1962, David Chaplin was twelve years old. His father, a naval intelligence officer, was scheduled to head out to Argentia, Newfoundland, at the warning signal. He taught his son to shoot a Lee-Enfield rifle so that he could defend the house from looters if he was called away at the outbreak of war.[98]

Civilians who signed up for the SMTP expecting to receive civilian defence training found the military's version incompatible with their expectations. In the military's conception of national survival operations, the individual citizen was merely a means to an end, just like any soldier. The SMTP was an emergency measure designed to help the military cope with the possibility of an impending war. Although the aims of both the civilian and military civil defence organizations were compatible, their conception of the individual within their respective programs was less so, and this way of thinking had an impact on the success of the SMTP as a whole.

In all, more than 80,000 Canadians enrolled in the SMTP between November 1961 and May 1962. Members of the SMTP were only temporarily enlisted in the militia, though they had the option to enlist with their local reserves at the end of the course if they chose to do so. By the time the training program ended, over 14,000 of the trainees had enlisted in the Canadian army's reserve mobile columns for national survival. As historian G.W. Nicholson has argued, these trainees were joining an organization that was still in turmoil over its shift in role from a war-fighting establishment to an aid-of-civil-power role. The requirement to assist with CD undermined the historic appeal of the militia and led to a severe decline in enlistment and retention figures.[99] Most of the reserve columns depended on volunteers and were severely under-strength well before the federal government initiated the SMTP, not only due to the unpopularity of CD but also because of financial restrictions. First imposed in 1957, cuts to militia training hobbled many regiments and closed summer training camps.[100] Since many units ignored survival operations and instead carried out their war training, "without pay and on their own time," it is not surprising that, at the end of the Berlin crisis, their instructors were less than eager to apply CD lessons to so many possible recruits.[101]

The SMTP had served its purpose, however, by providing a large reserve of men who could have been employed in an emergency during the Berlin crisis.

Once that crisis had been resolved, the rationale for such a drastic program disappeared. No program like the SMTP was repeated, much to the chagrin of municipal planners seeking to cut their relief rolls. Nor did the army's emphasis on national survival long outlast the training program itself. By 1963, the situation had "normalized," much to the relief of militia regiments across the country, many of whose members blamed their aid-of-civil-power role for their declining recruitment and retention numbers. Although the Canadian army retained responsibility for fallout reporting and the maintenance of the national shelter system, the militia's responsibility for rescue was once again made secondary to forming a reserve for overseas deployment in the event of war.[102]

Conclusion

From 1959 to 1961, the federal government sought to invigorate Canada's flagging CD organization by taking on a greater level of responsibility for the passive defence of the country. Only the Canadian army possessed the strength in numbers, the technical prowess, and the logistical capability to feasibly carry out survival operations, and so the task fell to them. The military gamely tackled domestic preparations for nuclear war, though many of its members resented their relegation to a rescue role. By assigning the military in this way, the government had hoped to bolster the ailing CD organization and provide tangible evidence of their commitment to the survival of Canadian communities threatened with destruction. Army planners soon learned that their numbers would be insufficient to operate effectively under nuclear warfare conditions, and they advocated for a wider public education program to familiarize as many Canadians as possible with the skills needed for national survival. The military depended on these semi-trained survivors to increase their own numbers for re-entry operations.

The Diefenbaker government launched the SMTP as an answer to the manpower problem, in the midst of severe international tension over the 1961 Berlin crisis. Its cost was added to the tens of millions of dollars invested in other survival measures, such as the Continuity of Government bunkers and the national warning system. The SMTP was, in effect, a public indoctrination program designed to supply the militia with additional trained personnel to fulfill its obligations. The program was at once ambitious and entirely unprecedented in the history of Canadian CD preparations, reaching 80,000 Canadians.

In spite of some initial successes, the plan quickly became mired in intense media and political scrutiny. Many of the trainees objected to the SMTP's emphasis on military training, while the militia considered the program to be too civilian in orientation for those seeking a career in the military. The public did not view the SMTP as a credible means of protection during the Berlin crisis because the six-week program only highlighted the temporary and imperfect solutions available to the ever-present threat of nuclear war. The military, always reluctant to commit its resources to CD, slowly retreated from its national survival obligations in order to concentrate on its traditional objective of training forces to defeat the Soviet enemy. The public was again left to prepare its own defences.

The Path to a Shelter Program, 1949-59

The fallout shelter is the lasting icon of Cold War civil defence. The shelter, as seen in public screenings of CD films, advertisements in newspapers, magazines, and television exposés provided a public reminder of the promise of protection and the nuclear threat facing the world. The shelter attracted substantial public attention, curiosity, and scorn. In the United States, "shelter mania" briefly took over public discourse in the late 1950s and prompted a wave of public and private shelter building.

Yet, for all the notoriety of the shelter, the Canadian government did not seriously consider fallout shelters as a survival strategy until 1959. Planners believed that the shelter provided the only guarantee of protection against the radioactive particles that would cover most of the country after a major attack against North America. The government looked south to the more active, costly, and extensive American model of shelter planning and adapted Canada's approach to conform to US standards. This decision was followed with a sustained publicity drive to convince every Canadian to build his or her own fallout shelter. The campaign provoked anxiety, controversy, and satire but did not result in many shelters being built.

From 1948 to 1959, shelters were built primarily for their publicity value and not always by Canada's federal CD agency. Shelters were referred to vaguely in some plans because survival strategies repeatedly shifted from the self-help model, based on wartime air-raid precautions, to the rapid evacuation of Canadian target areas after the thermonuclear revolution. Uneven official support for the promotion and construction of shelters reflected the government's own uncertain and shifting priorities. One consequence of the government's indecision was that the public received little in the way of concrete information about the best form of protection.

Yet the absence of a coherent government policy did not prevent official CD promoters from featuring model shelters as highly visible components at municipal displays throughout the 1950s. More frequently, private contractors or press outlets built shelter displays to capitalize on the public's anxiety and attract consumers. Officials often co-opted these popular private shelter displays to provide a stamp of legitimacy and tangible evidence of government involvement in shelter planning – when in fact there was none. Canadian officials promoted model shelter displays during the 1950s with more enthusiasm than they accorded to developing accurate and current information about useable shelter designs. Model shelters were better used to advertise the Canadian CD policy of the day and, most importantly, to promote public participation in CD as a component of each citizen's obligation to defend his or her family, and by extension the country, during the Cold War.

Early Shelter Policy, 1948-52

In the transition from post-war to Cold War, the government did not act immediately to provide the public with official information about shelters, mainly because Civil Defence Canada officials were themselves learning about the best forms of protection. They discovered the effects of the bomb, as did most Canadians, from mass-circulation magazines, the press, and radio programs. Frank Worthington and his aides sifted through hundreds of articles on the subject from Canadian, American, and British sources. They concluded that the media's descriptions of the available countermeasures would not help the public prepare their homes for an attack.

It may seem puzzling that the officials responsible for creating Canada's defence against nuclear weapons would resort to clipping newspapers, but in the early post-war period CD planners had no more access to classified information about sensitive subjects than did the general public. American secrecy laws surrounded the science of nuclear weapons. Canada and the United Kingdom were wartime partners with the United States in the creation of the first atomic bomb, but after 1943 the Americans assumed full control of the project. The Canadian government was not privy to the results of post-war atomic testing and so was mainly dependent on information published in reports and by journalists who observed the tests. In 1946, the United States Congress passed the Atomic Energy Act (also known as the McMahon Act), which prohibited the release of information related to atomic weapons to other governments.[1] This restriction included Canada and the United Kingdom. The British and Canadian governments managed to negotiate a partial exemption to the ban on the release of classified data through a technical co-operation program, but it was not until 1953 that the Americans released detailed information about the "effect on human beings and their environment of blast, heat, and radiation from atomic explosions."[2] Canadian CD planners turned to open-source American government reports and to eyewitness accounts of the Hiroshima and Nagasaki bombings. From these documents, federal CD officials attempted to piece together a rough prediction of what the population would need. Worthington was assisted in these efforts by scientists from the Defence Research Board (DRB), several of whom were posted as liaison officers to research establishments in the United Kingdom and the United States.[3]

Difficulties in obtaining external information delayed the release of advice about shelters until 1951. Before this time, federal or provincial officials responded to public inquiries with copies of the American National Security Resources Board's *Survival under Atomic Attack*.[4] There was no similar Canadian publication available. When Civil Defence Canada published its first information booklet, its authors recycled most of the American information. The Canadian booklet, entitled *Personal Protection under Atomic Attack,* was nearly indistinguishable from its American counterpart.[5]

Personal Protection under Atomic Attack advised Canadians that shelters should be considered as an investment, and likened to home insurance. The booklet included costly designs for basement shelters, counselling homeowners to build heavy blast shelters. These shelters required foot-thick reinforced concrete walls or "a blast wall of earth held together with boards ... about two feet [thick]."[6] The recommended measures amounted to major (and costly) structural improvements, but CD officials maintained that reinforcing sections of existing buildings would be cheaper and easier than asking the public to erect specialized protective structures.[7] Furthermore, the possibility that war might break out without warning meant that the public could not count on the government to have the time to build large communal shelters.[8] The policy was consistent with those of the United States and the United Kingdom. Only a few countries developed a more interventionist shelter policy. In Sweden, builders were required to include shelters in new construction, while the government dug enormous shelter complexes into the sides of cliffs.[9]

Who should build shelters? Civil Defence Canada recommended that nearly everyone bore this responsibility, from individual homeowners (the primary audience for the booklet) and apartment-building managers responsible for building "one or more good-sized shelters in the basement" to theatre owners and members of school boards, who were asked to provide large communal shelters on their property for customers and students.[10] Due to the cost and technical complexity of blast shelters, governments were the only organizations that could realistically afford to build shelters of the type demanded by CD plans. Yet the federal government, focused on post-war economic performance and rearmament during the Korean War, refused to invest the millions of dollars needed to provide shelters that might never be used, and municipal and provincial governments were unwilling and simply incapable of doing so.

The booklet's prescriptions for widespread shelter construction were also puzzling because Canadian CD policy aimed to recruit thousands of volunteers trained to fight fires in bomb-damaged areas. This policy was derived from hard lessons learned during the bombing campaign of the Second World War. Fire killed more civilians and damaged more property than had high explosive bombs. An early CD review of property damage and personal losses through fire in Canada revealed that fire safety was a dangerous vulnerability in many Canadian cities. The near-total destruction of the villages of Rimouski and Cabano in fires in 1950 heightened the federal emphasis on fire defence. In an early memorandum describing the importance of fire defence, Worthington mused: "Fire services should be treated as a highly essential service on the level of military and treated the same with reference to manpower ... Likewise, personnel of the fire fighting services should enjoy the same prestige as personnel of the armed forces."[11] By the end of the Korean War, Worthington succeeded in standardizing basic fire-fighting equipment, and the federal government had provided British-made fire pumpers to some Canadian cities free of charge. No comparable support existed for shelter construction, at least not from government sources.

With no official designs forthcoming from the Canadian government, concerned citizens and businesses sought to obtain government approval for their shelter designs. In 1952, the Department of National Defence, the prime minister, and CD offices across Canada were inundated with proposals ranging from the modest, such as a Sault Ste. Marie hospital's request for financial assistance to fortify their basement, to the absurd. Albert Vachon, a private citizen living in Ottawa, sent his secret plans to Prime Minister Louis St. Laurent for comment. He planned to purchase a lot that was twenty-four kilometres outside Ottawa so that he could build a twenty-unit luxury apartment block underground. Civil defence officials replying to his proposal advised against the idea because "in order to recover the costs of the building, the rents for such apartments would have to be uneconomically high."[12] The most ambitious plan presented to the federal government came from William Rogers, a First World War veteran employed by the Atomic Bomb Subterranean Shelter Engineers, a company operating out of Wisconsin. Rogers attempted to sell CD domes, each housing 200 people and equipped with "atomic anti-aircraft batteries." What, precisely, these batteries would fire was not described in the correspondence.[13] Like other bids received by the CD office, Rogers's offer was politely declined.

More practical proposals also arrived from a plethora of construction and engineering firms, most of which sought to profit from a possible shelter market in Canada. A Montreal representative of a West German firm that had constructed large communal shelters during the Second World War offered secret formulas for heat-resistant concrete for the government's use in building shelters. A structural engineer from Toronto inquired if there were any legal restrictions on advertising his services as a builder of atomic shelters in newspapers. The federal CD office was wary, advising that "no builder should advertise as a builder of atomic bomb shelters."[14] Canadian officials reached this decision because they did not have sufficient information to design a structure strong enough to withstand an atomic blast. Civil defence officials had no objection to shelter advertising so long as firms did not mislead the public into believing their products had official government approval or make unsubstantiated claims about their shelters' protective properties. In any event, few prospective shelter builders advertised in Canadian newspapers during the early 1950s.

At the same time that Civil Defence Canada quietly discouraged private shelter firms from advertising, the organization embarked on an extensive publicity campaign that featured untested shelter designs prominently. At first, the tools available for publicity were instruction manuals and public lectures. However, technical manuals and speaking engagements could reach only a very specific, limited audience, and usually those in attendance were already involved in local CD corps. A model shelter display, on the other hand, capitalized on public anxiety and curiosity about the atomic bomb by creating a site for discussion, exploration, and, most importantly, media attention. Whether or not the shelter display conformed to extant CD policies, or even to safety standards, was less important than if the press gave the display a positive review. Such coverage, federal CD officials reasoned, could feasibly convince more people to join up with their local organization, even if that municipality had no plans or capability to build shelters.

Government was not the only agent interested in building a shelter display. At the same time as CD officials mounted their first public shelter displays, private builders entered the field. Through the 1950s, private citizens, newspaper outlets, engineering firms, and realtors erected shelters for public interest – out of patriotic fervor or for sale. These private shelters typically caught the federal government, provinces, and municipalities off guard. Civil defence agencies hurriedly took steps to associate themselves with private shelter displays to garner more attention for their organization. In the process, officials legitimized projects with which they often had little direct involvement in order to provide the public and the press with visible evidence of progress in CD planning.

Both government and the private sector advertised shelters at the Canadian National Sportsmen's Show in Toronto in 1952. The Canadian Government Exhibition Commission helped Civil Defence Canada erect a mock air-raid shelter, complete with supplies, in a prime location on the exhibition floor. At a different booth in the same show, a Waterloo-based insurance company promoted its disaster insurance portfolio, also using a bomb shelter. The company distributed its own CD publicity, which had been developed by a private advertising firm, and displayed a replica atomic bomb near the company's larger, more comfortable-looking version of the shelter on view at the Civil Defence Canada booth. Every day of the exhibition, the company held draws for the emergency equipment featured in its shelter.[15] Fewer visitors frequented the insurance company's exhibit than the federal display, but federal officials commended the company for its dedication to public service while asserting ownership over the entire subject of shelters and public safety. Federal representatives politely declined the company's offer of a $10,000 private donation to finance a joint publicity campaign.[16]

The first federal shelter display met with mixed reviews from the public. Almost a quarter of those drawn to the shelter display expressed their view that shelters were probably unnecessary, while a few demanded to know if they should begin building their own immediately.[17] According to reports from the attendants, those most interested in shelter displays were people from the "Old Country," recent immigrants from the United Kingdom and Germany who had survived large bomber raids during the war. However, the new arrivals also thought that their roomy basements already offered greater protection than their wartime air-raid shelters. The booth's shelter construction manuals tended to be ignored by the general public but were quickly snapped up by professional contractors interested in expanding their businesses.[18] Civil Defence Canada was satisfied with the results of its first attempt at shelter publicity and circulated versions of the shelter at the Calgary Stampede and the Pacific National Exhibition in Vancouver.[19]

Shelters in the Thermonuclear Age, 1953-56

With the possible exception of those shelters constructed in the basements of new federal buildings in Ottawa, very few shelters were erected by the time the United States detonated the first hydrogen bomb in 1952.[20] The weapon's effects rendered shelter strategies for built-up areas obsolete. A hydrogen bomb would detonate in the megaton range, an explosive power calculated in the millions of tons of dynamite. Ralph Lapp, an atomic physicist (and later activist-cum-CD consultant), explained the explosive power of a twenty-megaton bomb in dramatic terms during an interview with the Canadian Broadcasting Corporation: "It would be, for example, a continuous solid trainload of solid TNT ... train to train from let's say Toronto all the way to Moscow."[21] The bomb detonated over Hiroshima had the explosive power of approximately 15,000 tons of dynamite. The shock wave from a hydrogen bomb would dig an enormous crater at ground zero measuring sixteen kilometres in diameter. The occupants of basement shelters within that kill zone would be crushed and burned at the same instant. Areas that would have been left untouched by the blast wave of a Hiroshima-type atomic bomb would be flattened by a thermonuclear weapon, as far out as eight to sixteen kilometres from ground zero. Structures in areas that were much further away would be uninhabitable, weakened by the blast wave or engulfed in uncontrollable fires.

The minister of national health and welfare, Paul Martin, defended his department's CD precautions, publicly declaring that the hydrogen bomb had made co-operation between different levels of government more important than ever. He reassured the public that his staff was in the process of reassessing CD with "intelligent planning, sober judgement and a realistic assessment of the possible risk" from the hydrogen bomb. He urged Canadians to support their local CD corps.[22]

Privately, Martin instructed his staff to study urgently whether the inauguration of the hydrogen bomb had any impact on CD preparations. At the committee's meetings, shelter effectiveness was the subject of heated dispute. Dr. E.E. Massey of the DRB stated that evacuation was the only solution for Canadian urban centres, though shelters built deep underground might save those unable to leave their cities.[23] Martin's deputy minister, George Davidson, wanted a bold statement for future CD policy that did not mince words: if a bomb were dropped on any city, "every person within [the explosion's] radius would be wiped out," including those in shelters.[24] The committee eventually recommended an evacuation strategy, but its members did not entirely abandon the shelter policy. Those caught without shelter in vulnerable areas, they reasoned, had a much smaller chance of survival than those who did.[25]

During the years between 1954 and 1956, CD planners from the federal to the municipal levels were consumed with efforts to implement and perfect evacuation plans across the country. Shelter planning accordingly fell behind, and Canada depended on shelter research in the United States to keep pace with developments. Rather than develop a pretense of expertise about shelter construction, Worthington decided that Canadian organizations, if asked, should continue to pass American manuals to the public. The North Atlantic Council's Working Group on Civil Defence had also decided in 1955 that the Americans, the leading nuclear power with access to atomic test facilities, would take the lead in shelter research and divulge findings relevant to CD to other countries. Canadian representatives at the NATO body, which was originally formed to co-ordinate refugee policies in Europe, reported that their European allies did not seriously believe that nuclear weapons would be used in their territories. They believed that the Soviets valued Western Europe's industry and infrastructure too much to destroy it.[26]

Canada did pursue some shelter research in co-operation with the United States during the mid-1950s. Canadian defence scientists and CD officials benefitted from close working relationships developed with their counterparts in

American federal and state governments. Worthington and two of his best officials, Matthew Penhale and Jack Wallace, were invited with other international observers to attend Operation Cue in 1955. In this set of tests in the Nevada desert, the American Federal Civil Defense Administration experimented with shelter and reinforced housing by subjecting them to an actual atomic blast. The US government had constructed several houses of different structural strength – some with shelters and some without – at different distances from ground zero. Test officials also installed an electrical power station, radio and telephone towers, and large gas tanks. Workers distributed cars, trucks, and other vehicles throughout the fake city built for the test. Mannequins were placed in the houses in various domestic montages to see how well they would fare when the bomb hit. High-speed cameras recorded the devastation in slow motion, and the results were broadcast live, across the country, on radio and later on television and film. At the time of the blast, 5,800 civilian and military observers were present at the site, some of whom carried out exercises near ground zero shortly after the explosion.[27] The results were filmed and shared with Canada and the United Kingdom, as part of a tripartite agreement on defence research.

In Canada, the DRB was responsible for testing different types of shelter designs to determine Canadian standards. DRB engineers constructed a shelter at the Chalk River Nuclear Laboratories in Ontario to test its resistance to radiation. This laboratory complex was used for a number of CD activities. Reactor leaks in 1952 and 1958 irradiated sections of the facilities. Canadian CD officials joined clean-up operations alongside military personnel.[28] Atomic testing was not politically viable in Canada, but the DRB, in co-operation with the United States and the United Kingdom, hosted a series of large-scale conventional blast tests beginning in the late 1950s to determine blast effects on structures and equipment.[29] The engineering section of Civil Defence Canada (and later the Emergency Measures Organization (EMO)) constructed test shelters at the Canadian Civil Defence College in Arnprior, Ontario, to determine the best designs for proper shelter ventilation and comfort.[30] These studies, however, did not translate into a shelter policy to accompany the evacuation strategy.

The federal government and municipalities had stopped developing prominent CD displays featuring shelters by 1955. Nevertheless, public interest in the effects of the hydrogen bomb prompted a number of private citizens and organizations to mount their own sample air-raid shelters. And federal, provincial, and municipal organizations continued their policy of publicly supporting displays in major target areas. A promotional team from the *Toronto Telegram* assembled a sample shelter in front of Toronto's city hall in August 1955. Federal authorities learned about the proposed display in conversation with colleagues in the Ontario government a month before it was erected. The *Toronto Telegram* decided to construct the shelter independently to capitalize on public interest generated by a joint Canadian-American press conference about evacuation and shelter held between Paul Martin and Val Peterson, the head of the American Federal Civil Defense Administration.[31] With no approved Canadian shelter designs, Worthington advised the *Toronto Telegram* to build a shelter based on American blueprints. He insisted that the federal government participate to put to rest press criticism about the lack of federal-provincial co-ordination in CD matters.[32] Worthington promised the *Toronto Telegram* that all levels of government would collaborate, forgetting in his enthusiasm to check beforehand with his superiors or with his counterparts in the city and the province.[33]

Martin approached the project with his typical caution. The federal government would support the shelter only on the condition that it would not be used as a statement of CD policy. No federal or provincial speaker could endorse the *Toronto Telegram*'s model as an official shelter for construction in private homes. Ottawa did, however, take the display seriously enough to ask CD liaison officers from the DRB to review the publisher's building diagrams and make modifications to create as accurate a model shelter as possible.[34]

Built above ground at Toronto city hall out of nondescript concrete blocks, the shelter opened on 4 August 1955 to large crowds. Mindful of Martin's restrictions, speakers at the event never addressed the utility of shelters. Federal officials instead used the event as a platform to promote better co-ordination between the federal CD office and the province of Ontario. Worthington praised the newspaper's shelter as evidence of intergovernmental co-operation. It was a curious claim because the provincial authorities' contribution was minimal, and the city of Toronto's CD organization existed only on paper. Toronto's city council had disbanded the Toronto-York Committee on Civil Defence shortly after the Korean War, but reinstated plans in 1955 after Hurricane Hazel passed through the city and its environs, killing eighty-one and rendering 1,688 people homeless.[35] Seeing an opportunity to keep the planning momentum going, Worthington expressed his hopes to the new Metropolitan Toronto Civil Defence Committee chairman that the publicity from the *Toronto Telegram* shelter would create pressure on the city to invest more resources in the local organization.[36]

At the opening, Worthington congratulated the newspaper publisher for the shelter and thanked him for stimulating public interest in CD. He admitted that the shelter would not provide any protection to the residents of metropolitan Toronto but suggested that similar shelters might protect Canadians in the city's outskirts, where the blast wave from a thermonuclear weapon could possibly leave some houses standing. The survivability of the shelter was, however, less important to CD officials than its use as a promotional device, and in advertising their display the *Toronto Telegram* borrowed from the federal government's CD publicity line. The publisher touted the construction as "a fine example of participation in civil defence for which this newspaper and the City of Toronto may be justly proud." They were less restricted in claiming the shelter's utility, "the like of which will save many lives should an enemy attack take place."[37] The Canadian government representatives at the event borrowed liberally from recent speeches from Winston Churchill supporting CD, telling assembled visitors that "no city, no family, nor any honourable man or woman can repudiate their civil defence duties and accept from others help which they are not prepared to fit themselves to render in return."[38]

Both the *Toronto Telegram* and CD authorities were enthusiastic about the numbers of visitors attracted by the display. During the first month, 63,000 Toronto residents visited the shelter outside city hall, and the *Toronto Telegram* successfully lobbied to extend the display's life through the entire 1955 Canadian National Exhibition. Generous coverage in their newspaper ensured that those who did not visit the shelter could read about it. As part of the paper's exploration of the issue, journalist Gordon Donaldson, his wife, and their two goldfish spent a weekend confined in the shelter. "Things weren't quite so bad as we had feared," recalled Donaldson, "I did have a go at working the hand operated [ventilation] fan but it was too much like hard work. Cooking didn't raise the inside temperature unduly, and the fumes were carried away quite successfully up the exhaust vent. The two goldfish ... enjoyed their weekend fine."[39] The *Toronto Telegram*'s display was a publicity coup for the newspaper and CD alike, at no cost to any level of government. By their public endorsement, CD organizations had shamelessly presented a misleading display built by a private agency as evidence of the civil defence program's success, when shelter strategies were all but abandoned in planning by the mid-1950s.

The risks posed to Canadians by fallout gradually brought shelters back on to the government's agenda. Civil Defence Canada's evacuation strategy, which was officially adopted in 1956, was quickly revealed to be deeply flawed because it did not take fallout risks into account.[40] Nuclear explosions would scatter irradiated particles far downwind of the blast area, blanketing areas of the country once thought safe from Soviet attack with potentially lethal doses of radiation. By mid-decade, the government received reports from its own scientific advisors and from the American Atomic Energy Commission that dismissed the genetic and somatic risks of radiation from bomb tests. These reports were followed by independent, publicly available studies by the American

Academy of Science and the British Medical Research Council concluding that radiation from fallout posed risks not only to those exposed to it but also to their children.[41] By 1957, CD officials in the United States and Canada determined that, for the public to survive a war fought with thermonuclear weapons and intercontinental ballistic missiles, individual citizens would need to have immediate access to fallout shelters built in peacetime. There would not be enough time to obtain a shelter once the bombs began to fall. The public needed to be persuaded to dig immediately, and to do so Canada's CD agency would have to furnish them with accurate and current information about shelters. Yet planners had little to offer.

More Harm than Good, 1957-59

Stephen White, the federal CD office's chief engineer, quickly recognized his organization's critical lapse in shelter research during Civil Defence Canada's focus on evacuation planning. He believed that the standing policy of encouraging evacuation from target areas, while asking homeowners in untouched regions to build family basement shelters, would lead to a massive loss of life. Evacuees would die without proper shelter if those in safer areas had no room to take them in. In April 1957, White proposed to ask homeowners to build communal shelters to house upwards of fifteen people per basement. In the circumstances, he argued, financial assistance would have to be provided in order to persuade homeowners to either expand their existing shelters or build communal shelters. White submitted that until the problem was resolved, "we are doing more harm than good by attempting to exhort the public into any form of shelter and refuge program."[42] White's letter prompted another series of meetings between the CD office, the DRB, and the Department of National Defence to determine what, if any, updates the shelter policy merited.

White's group had more information at its disposal than the ad hoc committee that grappled with the impact of the hydrogen bomb on CD in 1954. By 1957, the American Atomic Energy Commission had published many of its findings about the effects of nuclear weapons and effective shelter designs.[43] The DRB remained the Canadian authority on shelters. Its scientists had amassed some information about the materials needed to withstand blast overpressures and provide adequate radiation shielding. The organization reviewed countless shelter designs received from US sources and independent Canadian designers.[44] Many of the key issues relating to the provision and construction of shelters in Canada depended on precise political direction as to who was responsible for the costs, maintenance, and surveyance of the shelters.[45] Outstanding questions included whether the government would alter the National Housing Act to establish requirements for shelter construction in new buildings or provide financial assistance to persuade individuals to build shelters in their existing homes. As Worthington's replacement, Major-General G.S. Hatton, observed to his superiors in November 1957, "before we can place the Civil Defence stamp of approval on [any] designs, it is necessary to know what government policy will be ... and [the] financial or material budget which would be fixed by such a policy."[46] Without a firm answer on these policy questions, both the CD organization and Canadians who sought answers about their protection were left guessing.

Municipal planners, who had greater contact with concerned citizens in their communities, noticed the federal confusion about shelter policy. Mary Cameron, a training officer in Vancouver, reported that anxious citizens could not understand why there were no approved Canadian shelter designs. With little to offer, she dispensed pamphlets from the early post-war period that did not discuss fallout and remarked that "some people are most insistent and believe we are simply withholding information from them."[47] The reply to her letter, arriving a month later, was sympathetic, surprisingly frank, and totally unhelpful: "At the moment we are not anxious to issue any instructions in regard to home shelters because of possible confliction with the evacuation plan."[48] Officials were invariably forced to respond to inquiries with vague assurances that study was ongoing, when the lack of policy had effectively paralyzed the approval process for any Canadian shelter designs. Toronto alderman Donald Summerville, director of the Metropolitan Toronto Civil Defence Committee, reflected that the federal government's indecision had undermined CD's legitimacy: "At present we have nothing tangible to offer the public which would be of much help to them. My personal view is that if, as we do, talk shelter, we must provide some answer which has the highest authority behind it, and also that further delay mitigates against civil defence and its objective."[49]

The continued absence of a shelter policy was not a sufficient deterrent to prevent the Information Services Division from using images of shelters in its publicity and advertising. The first in a series of posters published by the Information Services Division in 1958 looked at "refuge" and featured a fallout shelter. The division published the poster, which was displayed in post offices across the country, without consulting their colleagues in the CD office.[50] The shelter depicted in the poster angered Stephen White, who remarked that, in addition to being a "monstrous" violation of policy, it depicted a blast shelter design developed in 1949, which could not possibly protect against the effects of a thermonuclear weapon. White recommended the posters' immediate recall and destruction.[51] It was not the first time that outdated information had been permitted to pass as policy. Old, out-of-date CD manuals were routinely sent out, some bearing Paul Martin's signature. Lacking resources to print new manuals and a policy that would fill them with information, CD officials instead applied stickers bearing the new minister's name on old manuals.[52]

The federal government's uncertainty about shelter policy reflected its diminishing confidence in the overall structure of Canada's CD organization. During Major-General Howard Graham's national survey in the summer and fall of 1958, which was commissioned by Minister of Health J.W. Monteith to reassess Canada's CD policy and structure, shelter studies were put on hold along with other programs. Civil defence planners were forced to struggle with the most important questions about shelter policy: who should build shelters and what financial incentives would be offered to the public so that they could afford to do so – questions asked at the exact moment when higher direction on many essential aspects of the CD program was pending. These questions were given additional urgency by increasing international tension over Berlin, but Civil Defence Canada and the EMO could do little to hasten government decision making. In September 1958, an interdepartmental Civil Defence Policy Committee drafted urgent recommendations that Cabinet approve a new shelter strategy, yet committee members decided not to forward the recommendations, instead choosing to shelve the shelter question until after Graham completed his study.[53] On 2 April 1959, as Cabinet secretly considered how to implement Graham's findings, CD's chief engineer was once again forced to explain to a correspondent that the government had no shelter policy, two years after he expiated on the grave consequences of neglect.[54]

During the confusion over shelter policy in Canada, the United States continued to be the only source of official information for the Canadian public. In Canada, CD policy discussions took place in secret, but in the United States congressional committees summoned experts to testify publicly about their findings. The most important public forum on defence issues in the United States during these years was the Military Operations Subcommittee (or the Holifield Committee), named after its outspoken chairman, Congressman Chet Holifield. The committee reported annually on its investigations. In 1956, Holifield launched an extensive review of the US CD plan.[55] As a result of his investigations, Holifield submitted a bill to Congress for a national shelter construction program the following year. The Federal Civil Defense Administration followed suit and requested US $32 billion to start building shelters.[56]

The Holifield Committee leaked its findings to the media, convinced that complacency over shelters and nuclear deterrence had undermined US national security. Its recommendations for shelter construction rapidly became public knowledge both in the United States and in Canada.[57] US President Dwight Eisenhower heard a chorus of recommendations from his scientific and CD advisors to begin digging, yet he resisted pressure to begin a multi-billion dollar passive defence project. Instead, his administration adopted a shelter policy that focused on surveying existing structures for fallout protection and educating the public about the need to build private shelters. The US government did not wish to pay the bill and made clear in their press releases that private enterprise would direct the shelter effort.[58] The American government, after all, had to finance missile research and construction to compete with the Soviet Union and sustain its credible nuclear deterrent.[59]

In Canada, the first family fallout shelter was not built by the federal government but, rather, by a private company. In January 1959, the Consolidated Building Corporation neared completion of Regency Acres, a subdivision of residential homes in Aurora, Ontario. The subdivision was opened to accommodate workers moving north for Aurora's new pharmaceutical plant. Their first open house for their four-bedroom bungalow model home featured a fully stocked basement fallout shelter. Jack Fienburg, the corporation's president, asserted that "a fallout shelter is a prime necessity in the home of tomorrow ... and the home of tomorrow is being built today."[60] The shelter was a "luxury" item offered for an additional price of $1,500, slightly more than 10 percent of the total purchase price of the model home. Fienburg disclosed that the shelter was built without advice from Canadian CD agencies. The architect had relied instead on American and Swedish information.[61] At the opening ceremony for the fallout shelter, no one addressed the question of how effective fallout shelters would be in the event that Toronto was hit by a nuclear weapon. Perhaps the subject was too grim. Instead, Fienburg and Toronto mayor Nathan Phillips directed press attention to the shelter's peacetime application as a storage room for jam or pickles.[62]

The Regency Acres project reflected renewed public discussion about fallout shelters inspired by developments in the United States. In the aftermath of the Regency Acres opening, the Canadian press was particularly critical of the government's continuing delay in releasing shelter information. The *Financial Post,* in the first of a series of scathing editorials about CD, demanded solutions to questions left unanswered or only vaguely addressed since 1957:

> The Canadian public has arrived at the opinion that plans [for evacuation] are so absurd as to be farcical ... If carried out on the outbreak of a war, they would bring the nation's life and war effort to a halt. The government should let the people know whether evacuation plans are still theoretically in force, and, if not, what it thinks of the shelter plans that have been seriously discussed in the United States.[63]

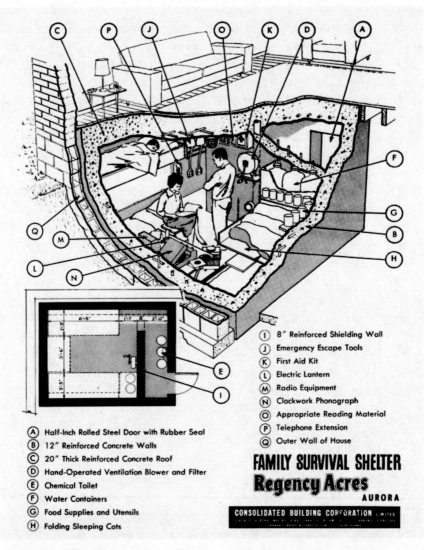

(I) 8" Reinforced Shielding Wall
(J) Emergency Escape Tools
(K) First Aid Kit
(L) Electric Lantern
(M) Radio Equipment
(N) Clockwork Phonograph
(O) Appropriate Reading Material
(P) Telephone Extension
(Q) Outer Wall of House

(A) Half-Inch Rolled Steel Door with Rubber Seal
(B) 12" Reinforced Concrete Walls
(C) 20" Thick Reinforced Concrete Roof
(D) Hand-Operated Ventilation Blower and Filter
(E) Chemical Toilet
(F) Water Containers
(G) Food Supplies and Utensils
(H) Folding Sleeping Cots

FAMILY SURVIVAL SHELTER
Regency Acres
AURORA

CONSOLIDATED BUILDING CORPORATION LIMITED

FIGURE 15   Canada's first custom-built fallout shelter for consumers in Aurora, Ontario. *Source: Toronto Telegram*, Clara Thomas Archives, York University

Other newspapers echoed this line of questioning, especially following the publication of the Civil Defence Order in March 1959, which delegated responsibility for CD to the EMO, other government departments, and the Canadian army. It did not, however, clarify what the government proposed to do about sheltering the population from radioactive fallout.[64]

In April 1959, the DRB completed its "lengthy and somewhat disturbing" appreciation of Canadian military and civilian defences and recommended substantial increases to CD funding.[65] The DRB's report stated that civilian losses in a nuclear war would be enormous but that they could be reduced if Canadians had some recourse to family or community fallout shelters. The Cabinet Committee on Emergency Plans (CCEP) subsequently met to determine the best shelter policy for Canada. It concluded from the evidence amassed in the United States and by the DRB that Canada's CD policy could no longer operate based solely on an evacuation strategy. The Cabinet ministers decided that the measure that would save the most lives in Canada was widespread construction of blast shelters.

Answers to most of the important questions about these costly shelters' vulnerability to fire and radiation, which were the government's greatest concerns, did not exist in the available research. Fallout shelters had been subjected to more study and, as importantly, were considered readily affordable to the average Canadian family. The CCEP therefore forwarded to Cabinet an urgent recommendation to launch an appeal to every Canadian to begin construction of a fallout shelter.[66] They favoured plans for family fallout shelters with an estimated cost of $200-300 and did not propose the construction of community shelters built to house groups larger than the average family household. This would prove to be the most controversial and unpopular aspect of the Canadian shelter policy because most Canadians quickly concluded that protection depended on the individual's ability to pay.

In Cabinet, the ministers noted that the Diefenbaker government had promised fast action on the CD portfolio when they launched the Graham survey. They agreed with the CCEP's decision that the public required more information about shelters. Ministers balanced this need against the possibility of frightening Canadians or of possibly upsetting the balance of international diplomacy by making visible preparations for war.[67] Cabinet decided that shelter policy would remain secret until it was approved by the provinces. It was a poorly kept secret. In advance of the October 1959 Dominion-Provincial Conference of Civil Defence, Minister of Defence George Pearkes leaked to the press some details about his intention to discuss cheap fallout structures that "any man who's handy with a saw and hammer can build in his basement or backyard."[68]

Pearkes issued an official statement of Canadian shelter policy to the press on 3 October 1959, a full seven months after the federal government restructured the Canadian CD organization. He informed every "prudent" householder to construct a shelter below ground, in which they could wait for forty-eight hours until authorities determined the likely fallout patterns.[69] In November 1959, the prime minister released a press statement to expand on Pearkes's appeal, advising homeowners who required financial assistance to apply to the Central Mortgage and Housing Corporation for home improvement loans under the National Housing Act. At the centre of the shelter policy was the family fallout shelter. The survival of the country would depend on the initiative, judgment, and enthusiasm of the average citizen, not on government action.

Conclusion

Shelter construction was not an important component of Canada's CD policy until 1959, despite the fact that shelters had featured prominently in government publicity for the preceding decade. What Canadians did learn about shelters in these manuals was usually copied directly from American sources. For Canadian CD planners, reliance on American input for shelter research was both convenient and necessary. Canada and the United States had shared vulnerabilities and worked closely in other aspects of defence research and policy. The United States was the only country with access to nuclear technology that could afford to carry out extensive testing, even though its secrecy laws prevented effective information sharing with its allies. Canadian officials, who always struggled to accomplish much within a small budget, would have wasted resources in reproducing American research.

Canada was slow to develop a strategy to shelter the public from radioactive fallout because of the dizzying advances in nuclear weapons technology. Canada and the United States grappled with the full implications of a war fought with thermonuclear weapons that could kill the population of entire cities, with or without shelter, and whose radioactive fallout could potentially kill survivors far downwind. Shelters were effectively embraced as a last line of defence for the civilian population.

Civil defence officials confused the issue by relying overly on shelters in their publicity to draw attention to their activities throughout the 1950s. Efforts to promote public evacuation exercises or firefighting and rescue demonstrations often featured examples of shelters, even if their presence ran contrary to official strategies for survival. Planners, it seems, could not resist the temptation to secure public attention to their cause, even if it meant appropriating displays mounted by private citizens, the press, and corporations. The fact that they did so primarily in target areas and in contradiction to the evacuation policy was inexcusable. Shelters built in Toronto or Montreal would only serve as tombs if an attack came. Even when shelters were identified as the best means to ensure the safety of the rest of the country in a war, those who were genuinely interested in shelter construction were left guessing and directionless as the government debated its policy for over two years. After 1959, the federal government's decision to urge individuals to go underground was followed by a vigorous and sustained campaign by spokesmen for the EMO, including the prime minister.

Irresponsible Citizens, 1959-62

From 1959 to 1962, the Diefenbaker government pursued a robust emergency preparedness campaign that was unprecedented in the history of Canadian civil defence. The government recommended private shelter construction by individual Canadian families, while pursuing its own Continuity of Government (COG) programs to ensure that when Canadians emerged from their shelters, a central authority would exist to direct reconstruction efforts. The Canadian government followed in the footsteps of the American government, which had launched a similar program during the first Berlin crisis in 1958.

The shelter issue did not have as much visibility in Canada as in the United States. Thousands of public buildings, banks, and schools in the United States were surveyed and marked as nuclear fallout shelters, and substantial monies were dispensed to stock them with supplies to feed the public. In Canada, officials carried out similar surveys, but the buildings were not marked outside of municipal planning rooms, and few funds were made available to stock them. Canadian publicity instead emphasized the importance of private shelter construction, through pamphlets, posters, lectures, and national television broadcasts. A handful of Canadian officials built their own backyard shelters to stimulate public interest and to deflect public criticism over the government's blast shelters that had been built at public expense. The best estimates of the Emergency Measures Organization (EMO) held that approximately 2,000 shelters were built in Canada by the end of 1962. The numbers may have been greater. Canadians who wished to avoid a property tax hike, or feared fending off their neighbours in the event of a disaster, might have built shelters in basements or backyards without informing municipal, federal, or provincial authorities. Governments were decidedly uneven in their surveying and reporting of shelter construction in Canada.

In letters to public officials, magazines, and newspapers, in calls to radio stations, and in public discourse, Canadians expressed their objections to going underground. These criticisms ranged from suspicions that the shelter program was a hoax designed to prolong the arms race or subdue public concern over fallout, to private doubts about the likelihood of survival in a $500 shelter, as well as a profound conviction that a world filled with radiation, possible starvation, and genetic mutations was not worth living in. The government, in turn, attempted to calm what they considered irrational fears and rebut the accusations of disarmament activists.

The most pressing and persistent obstacle to shelter construction was the problem that had faced CD organizers since the late 1940s. During the Berlin crises, most Canadians appear to have been convinced that either war would not take place or, if it did, they would not live to face the consequences. While this realization led some to protest vigorously for disarmament and negotiation, the vast majority saw no reason to take special measures or to expend substantial amounts of their own money to build a private shelter of dubious value.[1] When the crisis passed, so too did the public's call for government-funded mass shelters. Individuals who may have considered building a shelter to avert the worst no longer had the motivation to do so. Civil defence, national survival, rescue and re-entry, and basement shelters faded into the recesses of the public's consciousness, just as CD voluntarism and public interest had faded after the end of the Korean War. The public did not reject the government's prolonged campaign for shelter construction so much as ignore it.

Exercise TOCSIN and Shelter Publicity

The federal EMO information plan for the fiscal year of 1961-62 combined an ambitious mix of tried publicity tools and new means to reach the public. Traditional CD publicity, instruction manuals, and pamphlets figured heavily in the information campaign, as did scale model shelters circulated to each province for exhibition and televised public demonstrations. The EMO made greater use of television and radio broadcasts to publicize the government's policy than Civil Defence Canada had in the past. The EMO's information officer liaised with the Canadian Broadcasting Corporation (CBC) to recommend programs or features on topics dealing with national survival, but links with regional networks were left to the discretion of the provincial or municipal officials. Officials produced a half-hour program for Canadian radio stations, a short motion picture dealing with survival, and several twenty- to sixty-second film clips that were aired on television and in movie theatres. Short radio clips were also produced for broadcast on CBC and on other regional radio stations.[2]

The publicity program was designed to present the public with information about the Soviet threat and nuclear weapons effects as well as to familiarize Canadians with the rationale for emergency measures and existing government plans. Its aim was to help families prepare a plan for their survival in a nuclear war. The government wished to impress on the public that individuals had a twofold responsibility to the state: to ensure their own personal survival and to assist the government's reconstruction efforts after the war.[3]

The EMO's publicity campaign centred on the family fallout shelter, which had to be constructed by individual citizens. Yet these shelters were not incorporated into the national emergency measures exercises held in 1961: TOCSIN and TOCSIN B. The Canadian army and the EMO launched the TOCSIN exercises, named after an alarm bell, to test the federal and provincial government's COG program at protected sites across Canada. The exercises attracted more attention than any other publicity developed for CD because they were broadcast nationally over television and radio as they were carried out. The prime minister introduced and personally endorsed the exercise.

Canada's COG program involved the construction of blast and fallout-protected shelters, but these were meant to protect government officials, not the public. The Canadian army and Defence Construction Limited started construction on three major shelter systems across the country in 1958, and they continuted until 1963. These systems would house and protect a skeleton staff of military and government officials, who would direct the national survival effort from underground. The first, which was known as RUSTIC, was an interim fallout-protected shelter for 250 people established in older training and administration buildings at the Canadian army base in Petawawa, Ontario, which was over 150 kilometres outside Ottawa. RUSTIC acted as an interim headquarters, to be occupied by federal officials who would fan out from Ottawa to RUSTIC and smaller fallout-protected sites in wartime, decentralizing government activity to ensure that the country would not be left without leadership if the Soviets carried out a decapitation strike against Ottawa.[4]

However, the federal government could not direct the survival effort from the isolated RUSTIC sites alone. A series of underground and above-ground sites, which were designed to house the Canadian army's National Survival Attack Warning System (NSAWS), were approved in 1959 and given the code name BRIDGE. Situated from west to east, the shelters were located in Nanaimo, Penhold, Regina, Shilo, Borden, Valcartier, Gagetown, Debert, Charlottetown, and Holyrood. Of these sites, Nanaimo, Penhold, Borden, Debert, and Valcartier were located near predicted blast areas and built underground. The BRIDGE sites were equipped with military communications equipment to connect affected municipalities with the federal authorities that were coordinating nationwide rescue efforts. They also contained CBC studios for the production of emergency broadcasts of public information.[5] Each BRIDGE site housed over 275 people, including military personnel and an even blend of federal and provincial officials. Unlike RUSTIC, the BRIDGE sites were not considered a state secret. Officials encouraged publicity about the BRIDGE sites to provide the public with concrete evidence of government preparations for nuclear war.[6]

The government's most closely guarded secret was the construction of an "Experimental Army Signals Establishment" (EASE) in a former gravel pit in Carp, Ontario, located twenty-five kilometres outside Ottawa. The EASE project was a four-storey underground blast bunker built to house 575 people and the communication hub for the NSAWS. At full complement, it would have included several hundred military personnel, mainly signallers, and the prime minister, essential Cabinet ministers, and staff. The bunker could not accommodate families. Each occupant, including the prime minister, was required to develop family survival plans on his or her own, just like any other Canadian. Construction of the bunker was completed in late 1961, and soon after the Canadian army signal system moved there from the RUSTIC site in Petawawa. News of the bunker's existence broke nationally even before construction finished. The *Toronto Telegram*'s Ottawa reporter, George Brimmell, hired a private plane to fly over the site. Brimmell determined the building was a nuclear blast bunker by the nature of its construction and the equipment that was awaiting installation. His report and aerial photographs of the site were published in the *Toronto Telegram* on 11 September 1961, under a headline that announced: "This is the Diefenbunker!"[7] EMO officials were irritated by Brimmell's disregard for the site's security, and Diefenbaker was sufficiently embarrassed by the coverage that he had a private shelter built for his family at the prime minister's residence. He never entered the bunker.[8]

The TOCSIN exercises were the first test of the communication system that linked the RUSTIC, EASE, and BRIDGE sites under conditions of simulated attack. The Prime Minister's Office provided the official rationale for the May 1961 TOCSIN exercise in a press release:

> The aim of this series of exercises is to practise those emergency measures necessary for national survival and the continuity of government; to test those measures for which preparations have been made and to direct attention to whatever gaps in planning and preparation may still exist.[9]

The first 1961 TOCSIN exercise unfolded nationwide on 4-6 May and involved the ten provincial sites, the Canadian army, the federal Cabinet, staff of the EMO, and hundreds of municipal civil defence and emergency measures staff. The Department of National Defence and the EMO worked to give the press access so that reporters could maximize public interest in the emergency measures broadcasts. The press was permitted entry at every emergency government site, although journalists were forbidden from reporting anything they learned about fallout protection at each site, numbers and type of staff housed, and the communication and encryption systems.[10]

Across Canada, the exercise garnered extensive media coverage. A public information report prepared by the EMO revealed that Canadian newspapers published 842 stories on the 1961 TOCSIN project over two months.[11] According to the report, TOCSIN's radio broadcast of the exercise was heard in 49 percent of Canadian homes, but a broad audience was already tuned in to the radio to learn about the flight of United States Navy Commander Alan Shepard, the first American astronaut launched into orbit around the Earth in a manned spaceflight.

Partway through the news broadcast, on 5 May 1961, the Canadian Board of Broadcast Governors instructed all Canadian radio stations to replace their regular broadcasting with the TOCSIN program.[12] While much of the program revolved around the government and the armed forces' response to a simulated bomber attack, Diefenbaker, the EMO's officials, and provincial representatives directed their messages to the individual householder. Robert Curry, the director of the EMO, reflected mainly on the various emergency duties of federal government departments. He ended with a sombre reminder: "Please remember if, in spite of all efforts, nuclear war should occur, your own life and the life of this nation will depend very largely on the preparations you make ... If the time should come when the sirens have to sound in earnest and we are attacked, let us be prepared."[13] For its part, the federal government hoped that listeners would take the lessons of TOCSIN to heart and begin immediate preparations for nuclear war. Tommy Douglas, the premier of Saskatchewan, conscious of his supporters in the Co-operative Commonwealth Federation, asked the public to work for peace at the end of his TOCSIN address rather than "join in the numb fatalism of apathetic acceptance of catastrophe."[14]

Built into the 1961 TOCSIN schedule was the publication of *11 Steps to Survival*, an addition to the EMO's *Blueprint for Survival* series. This step-by-step instruction booklet was the most comprehensive guide to emergency measures issued by the Diefenbaker government, and subsequent editions remained in circulation more or less unaltered until the 1980s. Diefenbaker's introduction to the booklet set out the government's approach to the nuclear problem and its proposed international and domestic solutions:

Recognizing that nuclear war would be a catastrophe for all nations ... the Government has pursued a course of action designed to reduce world tensions, to bring about agreement providing for a settlement by peaceful means of international disputes, and to achieve disarmament with such controls as are necessary to preserve the security of all nations. Notwithstanding what has been and is being done, nuclear war is possible either by the intended actions of evil madmen or by miscalculation. Should such a tragedy happen, hundreds of thousands of

Canadians might be killed or injured and many cities and towns might be destroyed. On the other hand, many hundreds of thousands of Canadians who would otherwise perish could survive a nuclear war if preparations were made.[15]

Nowhere in the pages that followed did the Canadian government or its officials guarantee survival in the event of a nuclear attack. Readers were informed in a matter-of-fact tone that, if they followed the advice in the booklet, they could increase their chances to live through and after the catastrophe.

The fourth step to survival, "Have a Shelter," was given the most attention in the booklet. The reader was advised to build a fallout shelter, mainly to protect against radiation. However, the questions remained: who should build and where? The authors offered no definite solution to the problem: "The type of shelter required depends on the distance from the explosion. And unfortunately it is not possible to know this in advance. That is why each individual must make his own decision when selecting the type of shelter he wishes to have."[16] The booklet did not contain affordable designs for fallout shelters but promised future pamphlets about blast and backyard shelters.[17] The authors did include, however, brief guidelines for the construction of improvised fallout and blast structures in existing facilities. The government advised those who did not wish to leave potential target areas to build simple anti-blast shelters – for example, "you could ... dig yourself a trench in the yard."[18] This advice was accompanied by an unfortunately conceived drawing of a man apparently digging his own grave.

The remainder of the booklet contained information about stocking the shelter and seeing to its readiness. Father and husband played a dual role as family planner and guarantor of safety. Drawings accompanying the text portrayed an adult man maintaining the shelter much as he might a garage or home workshop and supervising other family members as they fitted out the shelter with fourteen days' worth of supplies. The booklet subtly hinted that a shelter was a father's responsibility, just as he was expected to provide his family with an income and security in peacetime.[19] In effect, within the isolated confines of the shelter, the father figure was meant to take on the role of the government – of leadership – while Canadian authorities directed survival efforts from the safety of their taxpayer-funded bunkers. According to *11 Steps to Survival,* isolated, presumably rural, or suburban family units were to be the nuclei of Canada's survival, linked together by the radio. After the war, families were meant to participate in recovery and reconstruction.

The booklet insisted that each householder purchase a battery-operated radio. The radio was the only means of mass communication that was likely to work after an attack because all of Canada's major telephone exchanges were located

IMPROVISED BLAST PROTECTION

FIGURE 16   Improvised blast shelter or digging one's own grave? *Source: Blueprint for Survival No. 4: Eleven Steps to Survival* (Ottawa: Queen's Printer, 1961)

in the very cities targeted for destruction.[20] The responsible citizen would receive instructions about when it was safe to emerge from the shelter and where help was needed in local rescue and reconstruction efforts. Planners underlined the importance of this link between the state and the sheltered citizen in the booklet: "It will be the only sure way that you know what is expected of you ... Follow whatever instructions are given implicitly. Your life will depend on your action."[21] The shelter, as described in *11 Steps to Survival,* was designed as an insurance policy; as a means to provide for the family in wartime; and as a way to serve the country as a whole. However, survival did not stem from concrete and sand alone; persuading Canadians to take shelter was central to the message being communicated by the EMO planners. Civic obligation would be the glue holding the country together after an attack. The responsibilities of citizens to their neighbours and to the remnants of a post-attack Canadian government did not end at the shelter door.

The EMO printed tens of thousands of the booklets, many of which were sent out directly to interested Canadians. Thousands had contacted the EMO with requests for information about survival measures in the summer and fall of 1961. The spike in interest was directly related to the brewing crisis between the United States and the Soviet Union over access rights to Berlin. The erection of the Berlin Wall in August 1961 dampened the international crisis, but the after-shocks of the Soviet Union's aggressive diplomacy and intimidation were felt well into the winter. The Diefenbaker government authorized a substantial rearmament and introduced the Special Militia Training Plan in August 1961. It was completed the following spring.

American interest in shelter construction also peaked in the summer and fall of 1961. In September, Canadians could read a special edition of *Life* magazine dedicated to fallout shelters, accompanied by a letter from US President John F. Kennedy. The issue, headlined "How *You* Can Survive Fallout," claimed that 97 percent of Americans could be saved by building fallout shelters, an assertion that was corrected in a later issue. This issue of *Life* was a bestseller, setting off a "shelter mania" in the United States, as concerned families looked about for plans and private builders sought to capitalize on the war scare. Kennedy had not intended to spark a national debate over the issue. The experience led Kennedy and his Office of Civil Defense Mobilization to be more circumspect about the national survival program.[22] "Shelter mania" crossed over the border briefly but was never as powerfully present in Canada as it was in the United States.

Khrushchev had backed down from his promise to resolve the Berlin crisis by force but had decided to open the twenty-second Party Congress in Moscow with a bang. On 30 October 1961, a Soviet bomber dropped a fifty-megaton *Tsar Bomba*, "king of all bombs," producing a forty-mile high mushroom cloud and immense devastation over the test area in Siberia. The force of the bomb, which was actually too big to be dropped by bombers or delivered by missiles to North America, was such that a person standing exposed to the blast 100 kilometres away would have received serious flash burns. Fallout from *Tsar Bomba* crossed over the Arctic, and the Canadian scientists detected a spike in radioactivity in the atmosphere over Canadian territory.[23]

News of the mega-bomb and fallout caused a war scare in Canada, and the Canadian government resolved to carry on with its second national emergency measures exercise of the year, TOCSIN B 1961.[24] Reacting to an announcement about the exercise, the Russian news agency accused the Canadian government of using the Berlin crisis as a pretext to stir up a war psychosis, "obviously influenced by the militarist quarters of the United States."[25] Yet Canadian planners were very conscious of the need not to alarm the public unnecessarily with an exercise that was primarily designed to refine procedures for emergency communications and fallout reporting.[26] The EMO had initially proposed that an expansion of the second TOCSIN exercise in 1961 could involve a mass public shelter drill of the type carried out in the United States. The Canadian army chief, Lieutenant-General S.F. Clark, opposed this proposal since group shelters had not yet been built nor was the public prepared to participate in such a drill. The Canadian government had never organized a mass shelter drill in the entire history of CD planning. Clark instead suggested using the exercise to publicize the desirability of surveying existing buildings for fallout protection and to promote the construction of private shelters in the home.[27]

In the end, the public was not asked to participate in shelter or evacuation drills for the TOCSIN B exercise, but the media coverage of the event was much greater than for the previous exercise. The intention of TOCSIN B was not just to test the emergency government dispersion and communication procedures but also to exercise the NSAWS, which included more than 2,000 air-raid sirens installed across the country. The planners urged the public who heard the air-raid sirens not to "become overly excited and rush to their telephones, as this would tie up phone lines, thereby possibly delaying fire or real emergency calls."[28] An intensive publicity drive preceded the exercise, with a particular emphasis on television to spread the message. In the first week of November 1961, the CBC carried three half-hour television specials about emergency measures and CD, focusing on shelters, nuclear weapons, radiation effects, and the national warning system. The CBC's English program *Target YOU,* which aired at 10:30 p.m., featured a twenty-minute interview with Curry.[29]

A few days before the exercise, Diefenbaker's jowly countenance interrupted television programming. The prime minister delivered a sober message about the exercise. He stressed that the simulated attacks were necessary to prepare the government and the population for the worst, and he reminded listeners that "in a nuclear war Canada ... would be a part of the battleground. In any case, Canadians will be exposed to the peril of radioactive fallout from the United States."[30] He argued that Canadians, if properly informed and prepared, could survive the attacks, but they bore a substantial personal responsibility to increase their own chances for survival. The address also provided a rationale for evacuating government officials to blast and fallout shelters nationwide since "only governments prepared and ready to act promptly throughout the nation can meet [survival] needs and maintain law and order."[31] Diefenbaker ended his speech by asking viewers to consider their own survival plans and whether building a shelter would help their family survive.[32]

TOCSIN's imaginary attack on Canada, which unfolded on 13 November 1961, was meant to help the public make up their minds. The attack lasted a short three hours and was carried out by a wave of bombers and missiles that levelled several major cities, killing a projected three million people.[33] Air-raid sirens blared in cities across the country to coincide with a national broadcast reporting on the attack and Canada's losses. Among the dead were John Diefenbaker and his wife, who were reported to have been killed by the blast over Ottawa while they were in their private family fallout shelter at the prime minister's residence.[34] The prime minister's fictional demise puzzled most of the

EMO and Department of National Defence planners, who wondered why Diefenbaker would deliberately choose not to enter the multi-million dollar bunker built for the express purpose of preserving the country's leadership. The public paid little attention to Diefenbaker's "death" because three million other Canadians were also killed in the simulated attack.

Diefenbaker's apparently strong personal endorsement for the high-profile TOCSIN exercise was remarkable, especially given his predecessor's tendency to ignore or downplay the government's survival efforts. During the early 1950s, Frank Worthington practically had to beg Paul Martin, the health minister, to promote CD, and only with great persistence was then-prime minister Louis St. Laurent persuaded to provide a written endorsement of CD for the organization's Christmas bulletin.[35] St. Laurent and others had not wanted to unnecessarily provoke Canadian anxiety over the international situation to energize CD. Either Diefenbaker did not share their caution, or he was persuaded that in 1961 the peril facing Canada was so great that emergency measures had to receive a greater degree of public attention. Regrettably, his personal accounts are silent on the matter.

In the weeks that followed, Diefenbaker was given many reasons to regret his public support of emergency measures. The TOCSIN exercise, meant to test the government's survival protocols and prompt individuals to consider their own plans, instead invoked a furious response from the Canadian public. Citizens, informed of their responsibility to plan for a post-apocalyptic future, railed against CD preparations, particularly the fallout shelter. The failure of the TOCSIN exercise revealed the failure of CD to convert individuals into responsible citizens.

Disarmament Activism against Shelters

National and local peace and disarmament organizations, whose membership comprised religious progressives, senior labour activists, Canadian nationalists, Communist party activists, and many private citizens, constituted the most outspoken critics of the shelter policy. The groups were opposed to the shelter policy on ideological and moral grounds and condemned the shelter exercises as an attempt to deceive Canadians and to prepare them for the inevitability of war. They believed that CD was an extension of the arms race – its "myth of protection" intended to numb the public to the actual horrors of thermonuclear war.[36] Although disarmament activists represented a minority of the population, their arguments drew strength from the international nuclear disarmament movement that grew in popularity in Canada in the late 1950s and early 1960s.[37]

National organizations in the Canadian peace movement, including the established Canadian Peace Congress and newer organizations such as the

Canadian Committee for the Control of Radiation Hazards (CCCRH) and the Voice of Women led the drive against shelters and national survival preparations. These groups, with chapters in most major cities, included members from many different local protest groups, such as the Toronto Committee for Disarmament. In the early 1960s, unmoved by critics who accused them of Soviet sympathies, these movements began to flex their political muscle by tapping into public support for international disarmament and an end to arms tests, which held out the hope of ending the nuclear arms race. In their petitions, public addresses, and correspondence, the Canadian peace groups subtly borrowed ideas and arguments from the British Campaign for Nuclear Disarmament and the American National Committee for a Sane Nuclear Policy.[38] In a January 1961 Gallup poll, 38 percent of Canadians wanted to ban nuclear weapons manufacture, and a further 52 percent wished to see international control and oversight of the weapons.[39] By August 1961, 80 percent of those polled answered that the United States should stop testing nuclear weapons.[40]

Disarmament movements also had an advocate in the Diefenbaker Cabinet. At the United Nations and in speaking engagements from 1960 to 1961, Secretary of State for External Affairs Howard Green promoted the arguments for international disarmament. In Cabinet, Green, who was opposed to nuclear weapons, clashed with Doug Harkness, the defence minister, over whether Canada should acquire warheads for its air defence missiles, a dispute that divided colleagues and ultimately confused Canada's defence policy. In public, Green crafted his statements with a nationalist outlook and a judicious sprinkling of anti-Americanism. Green suggested a move towards a neutral Canada, which had "only friends and no enemies."[41]

Peace activists who petitioned Diefenbaker and Harkness held up Green as an example of a sane statesman who shared their views about the necessity of disarmament. Green, meanwhile, publicly congratulated activists for their efforts to disseminate information about the effects of nuclear testing: "It is a great satisfaction to see our Peace workers, with whom I have the honour of being associated in a small way through the years, now beginning to be accorded the respect which is long overdue them."[42]

Disarmament groups, and Canadians who sympathized with their aims, believed that government survival preparations were designed to condition the public to fight a suicidal war. They were most vocal in Canadian cities doomed to destruction and particularly critical of fallout shelters. After a televised panel discussion held in the Montreal suburb of Notre-Dame-de-Grâce caught the attention of the EMO, the chairman of the community council of Notre-Dame-de-Grâce wrote to Minister of Defence Harkness to inform him that "the citizens find it controversial ... that the government's civil defence role to date is to tell the nation to '*build Shelters*.' But NDG [Notre-Dame-de-Grâce] and eight miles away will be total destruction and uninhabitable. Therefore, is 'Civil Defense fact or unintentional fraud.'"[43] J.W. Bailey, a training officer who argued for shelters at the meeting, reported that the gathering was decidedly hostile to civil defence measures. Peace advocate M. St. Germain "compared the federal government to the Nazis, alleging that the Canadian people are being deceived and misled in the way the Jews were in Germany."[44] The speaker appealed to mothers to forsake the shelter and spare their children the hardship of living underground while awaiting a slow death by radiation poisoning. Concluding his report, Bailey noted that the shelter policy's opponents, "students, beatnicks [sic] and pinks," were well organized and used emotional appeals that were more likely to impress the public than the government's less passionate expert advice.[45] Federal instructions soon followed from Jack Wallace, which instructed that local volunteers should not engage in public debates with opponents of planning. The debate offered activists a platform to attack shelter preparations and contributed to the public perception that local CD organizations were somehow opposed to peace.[46]

For the activists, diplomacy and peace were far better protection than shelters. In the Canadian Peace Congress's petitions circulated in 1961, shortly after the TOCSIN B tests, the eye-catching slogan along the footers read: "Disarmament is the only shelter that guarantees Survival! Sign against Atomic Death!"[47] Newspapers across the country received hundreds of letters to the editor that supported the peace groups' charges that the TOCSIN exercise and the shelter policy were a cruel hoax. In the *Toronto Daily Star,* correspondents wrote to condemn the exercise and the shelter policy alike as "the sickest civil defence joke of all ... calculated to prepare the public to accept a war nobody can win. The policy is a cruel deception of the Canadian people and should be exposed as such."[48] The *Toronto Star* published many such letters because of its own editorial board's support for disarmament. After the first TOCSIN test, the paper urged readers to sign a petition circulated by the CCCRH to demand an end to nuclear testing. Press support for the movements was important. It conveyed legitimacy and offered a platform for the dissemination of ideas. As political scientist Bernard Cohen posited, the news "may not be successful in telling people what to think, but it is stunningly successful in telling people what to think about." Press criticism kept the TOCSIN test and disarmament in the public eye, pressuring governments and individuals to take action.[49]

Peace groups' criticism of Canadian COG plans built on public outrage over the government's plans to construct shelters for its own refuge and not for the citizenry at large. To shelter critics and their supporters, the government's decision to build shelters such as the Diefenbunker constituted a failure of moral and international leadership. In dozens of letters to the EMO, the prime minister, the defence minister, and others, Canadians expressed their disdain for the government's efforts at self-preservation. The most trenchant letter to Diefenbaker was also sent to the *Vancouver Sun*, from Stephen and Mary Leskard, a couple with two young children in Vancouver. It synthesizes the distaste many Canadians felt both for the COG policy, fallout shelters, and for the national survival exercises as a whole:

> We are one of those families which died this morning during that "National Emergency Rehearsal" so aptly called "Operation Tocsin." In our dying moments we comforted ourselves with the thought that the people in the areas where the bombs were not falling perhaps had a chance to survive, and that in our own devastated city there may be enough Civil Defence and Civil Service people left to count the corpses and proclaim to the world that all is well and that Canada has saved its Government and its Land. We are so pleased that *only* three million Canadians died with us this morning, and that no more than possibly six million will die from the fallout. We sincerely hope that neither you nor any Civil Servants with access to Government shelters will be found dead, trampled in the rush to the entrance to the shelters, when those who got there first emerge in two weeks to mourn and bury the rest of us.[50]

Letters like those written by the Leskards moved some municipal councillors to eschew participation in national survival exercises, much to the consternation of local CD volunteers, who called for their removal for "disloyalty."[51] Like Diefenbaker, R.B. Bryce, director of the EMO, responded to criticism by building a fallout shelter at his Ottawa home at his own personal expense.

The government's decision, it was argued, indicated that it was prepared to spend millions of taxpayer dollars to ensure that Canada's leaders and civil service mandarins would survive a war. Most Canadians had no such guarantee, unless they were willing to pay for a family fallout shelter. Citizens wrote letters of protest to officials and media outlets to highlight the hypocrisy of the government's national survival policy. The EMO foresaw this genre of criticism during its preparations for the TOCSIN exercises. In the exercise press kit, officials attempted to explain why governments were provided for first: "In the Government's view the best chance for the populace to survive is if they are given leadership and guidance ... The preservation of a nucleus of government is basic to the welfare and survival of the people."[52]

Disarmament activists exposed the hypocrisy of the government's COG policies and its private fallout shelter campaign, but they cannot be credited for dismantling the government's shelter policy on their own. Their greatest

FIGURE 17   In this send-up of the TOCSIN exercise, Diefenbaker prepares to enter a government shelter as Minister of Defence Douglas Harkness works his air-raid alert. *Source:* Library and Archives Canada/Estate of Duncan Macpherson, reprinted with permission-Torstar Syndication Services

contribution was in placing the long-term health effects of radiation from bomb testing on the public agenda. In doing so, they highlighted the dangers of fall-out far more effectively than the EMO, a government agency, had been able to do. Disarmament groups attacked the shelter strategy as a symbol of acquiescence in an escalating arms race. It was never their goal to stop private shelter construction.

Private Shelters or Group Shelters?

The public's doubts about both the effectiveness and affordability of fallout shelters overcame their anxiety about nuclear war. Even Canadians who could afford to construct a shelter readily identified flaws in the government's suggested designs and had serious concerns about whether the shelter strategy could ensure their survival when, in the aftermath of a war, supplies were bound to be scarce and possibly irradiated.

The government's failure to deliver fallout shelter designs in a timely fashion created a number of practical obstacles to homeowners interested in building a shelter. Following Minister of Defence George R. Pearkes's first appeal to the public to start digging in October 1959, interested homeowners ran into problems immediately.[53] A *Toronto Star* reporter, Pat McNenly, took up Pearkes's challenge and built a shelter in his Etobicoke home, based on an example he had seen at a federal press conference. On completion, McNenly reported "my wife Helen and I proved an average couple can build the shelter ... but we also learned none of the building departments in the Toronto area want to have anything to do with the shelter under its present design." A building inspector was quoted as claiming that the shelter would have to be demolished before anyone was permitted in the house. The headline, "Inspectors Won't Pass A-Shelter," which was laid out in large type across eight columns, was an early defeat for the shelter construction campaign. The building inspector had been misquoted, but the damage was done.[54]

The McNenly episode revealed that conflict between municipal and federal levels of government over policy implementation continued to shape CD in Canada. Federal demands on homeowners to build shelters cost the government nothing, but municipal governments gathered taxes and conducted property assessments according to the size of homes and their amenities. A shelter counted towards a home improvement, leading to higher taxes. With such a limited tax base, municipalities were reluctant to make any changes to their own tax laws, a fact that had not been taken into account by the planners who devised the policy. The issue of municipal taxation forced homeowners to weigh the benefits of building a shelter against the cost of having to pay increased property taxes. In August 1959, Clarence Good wrote to inform his local CD organization in Victoria that he refused to build a basement shelter if it resulted in additional property taxes. He demanded federal intervention to stop "local authorities making money out of what is an urgent need."[55]

Officials from the EMO and the Department of Finance, fearing a public backlash, proposed a federal income tax exemption for homeowners building shelters. However, Curry recognized that the federal government would not be able to influence municipalities to reduce their own income, nor could they offer correspondents any guarantee against taxation for home fallout shelters.[56] Some city councils, as a result of public pressure, voluntarily excluded shelters from additional property tax assessments, but an early 1961 CBC poll revealed that only five of the thirty cities with a population over 30,000 excluded shelters from taxation.[57] The poll's researchers determined that the average homeowner who installed a shelter would have to pay an extra $144 a year in property taxes, a persuasive argument against taking on the cost.[58] Although the government offered loans through the National Housing Act, they were only meant to offset the costs of shelter construction. Municipal taxes could equal or exceed the loan's value, reducing the utility of the National Housing Act's loans as a financial incentive.[59]

During a period of economic recession and rising unemployment, the government's insistence on privately built and financed shelters appeared callous, unfeeling, and immoral.[60] Public criticism of private, costly shelters became more pointed in letters to government officials and the press as the Berlin crisis drew on. The aggrieved parties included mess hall staff at the Canadian army's Camp Borden, who could not afford to build shelters on their hourly wage of 89 cents; an unemployed man who wrote Diefenbaker to request a personal gift of $500; and an impoverished Quebec woman who lived in a rented house with no basement, whose complaint to the EMO was answered with a mailed pamphlet with instructions to build a basement shelter.[61] A Toronto resident who survived the bombardment of London during the Second World War lamented that the government's policy would ensure the survival of the richest.[62] Another writer protested "that money will be the deciding factor in whether one gets a chance to survive."[63]

Civil defence experts also criticized the government's position. Frank Worthington, four years into his retirement from the post of federal CD co-ordinator, provided the CBC television program *Close-Up* with an interview in January 1961. Worthington generally approved of Diefenbaker's reallocation of emergency preparedness responsibilities within the federal government, but he criticized the government's failure to provide shelter in the 80,000 homes owned by the government and lived in by servicemen and their families at military bases. The EMO, the Department of National Defence, and the Central Mortgage and Housing Corporation had attempted for years to resolve this embarrassing shortfall in the permanent married quarters (PMQs) built across Canada for military personnel by the Department of National Defence. The EMO asked the department in late 1960 to start construction of basement fallout shelters in PMQs "to provide a measure of protection for DND personnel and their dependents, and would also serve to set an example to other landlords and to private homeowners to do likewise." The Department of National Defence considered suggestions to build shelters in the basements of permanent married quarters for families, amortizing the cost over several decades and recovering it through hikes in rent, but it ultimately rejected this solution because service personnel moved frequently and would likely object strenuously to increased rents. Much to the frustration of the EMO, the issue was never resolved.[64]

Worthington blasted municipalities for taxing family fallout shelters. On the *Close-Up* program, EMO Director R.B. Bryce and Major-General Arthur Wrinch, director of the Canadian army's national survival program, offered a weak defence of the government's policy. When the interviewer brought up Worthington's critique, Bryce shrugged nervously. Clearly ill at ease with the question and visibly uncomfortable on camera, Bryce revealed that he had a fallout shelter. Wrinch did not, and could not, have a shelter. Like many Canadians, he lived in rented premises.[65]

Those who could build a shelter were not always successful. Arthur DeBrincat and his wife, homeowners from Burnaby, set out to construct a shelter at their home in Burnaby, British Columbia, in 1961. Two years had passed since the government had announced its shelter policy, but his local CD office could provide affordable and livable shelter designs. A letter to federal officials did not produce helpful information. DeBrincat found American designs and pamphlets but was told by municipal authorities that he could obtain a building permit only if a private engineer approved the plans beforehand. DeBrincat's bank manager told him that National Housing Act loans were only available for basement shelters. Backyard shelters did not qualify. DeBrincat was eventually disqualified for the loan because he maintained a healthy savings account. After several months of research, he gave up. In a letter to the prime minister, he pleaded: "Considering the present threatening situation, how long must we wait for help?"[66] By January 1961, the Central Mortgage and Housing Corporation had extended only two National Housing Act loans to Canadians for the purposes of building a family basement shelter.[67]

Despite the heated letters sent to Diefenbaker and EMO officials, the majority of Canadians did appear to think that fallout shelters were an answer to nuclear war, just not private shelters. Studies at the time indicated that most preferred the idea of large, communal public shelters paid for through taxation. Most appeared to agree with the long-held argument of several provinces that expenditure of public funds on CD was a federal responsibility, because shelters could be considered an investment in national defence. Political scientist James Eayrs summarized the public's attitude: "When civil defence becomes a central component of national security policy ... there can be no justification for thrusting responsibility for fall-out shelters upon the individual home-maker, as if it were a form of insurance policy or an extra coat of paint for the shingles."[68]

FIGURE 18 Survival of the richest? Many could not afford to build their own shelters. *Source:* Library and Archives Canada/Estate of Duncan Macpherson, reprinted with permission-Torstar Syndication Services

Criticism of the private shelter policy came from Canadians of all ages. Thirty-two teenagers at Tweedsmuir High School in London were commended by the local press for writing essays about the shelter debate for their civics assignment. The majority endorsed shelters as a precaution, but only a few accepted that individuals should bear the cost. The *London Free Press* editorialized: "Survival, the pupils agreed with total logic, should not be related to income or the ownership of homes."[69] Correspondence from adults tended to be more biting: "In a democracy individuals need not act independently in everything. If this were the case we would not need a Prime Minister ... Surely it is your responsibility to arrange a more adequate plan for our protection than tell us to build our own hole in the ground."[70] Canadians avoided taking individual responsibility for their survival by insisting on a collective solution. A review of Canadian opinion conducted in December 1962 indicated that 70 percent of individuals believed preparations were necessary, but the same number believed it was the obligation of the federal government to provide group shelters.[71]

Canadian officials noted the trend with great concern at the end of 1961, as international tensions abated. In a note to Bryce, Curry observed that "if people have not been moved to action under the attention given this subject ... during the period of the Berlin crisis, they are not apt to be moved in the months ahead when public interest in such questions may flag." He proposed extensive municipal surveys to locate shelter spaces in existing buildings, a solution that provided an answer for those seeking to determine how best to plan for a shelter if their family was not home at the time of the blast.[72] The government's response was that families spent most of their time at home, except during business or school hours.[73] The military suspected that the Soviets would likely attack at night, a time when most Canadian families would be under their own roofs.

In 1959, the government had initiated surveys of federal buildings to locate fallout-protected areas suitable for use as public shelters, but these shelter surveys were costly and took years to complete. For example, the fallout shelter survey for the city of Kingston was not completed until 1965.[74] Justice minister Davie Fulton proposed to meet the shortfall by using inmates in federal penitentiaries to construct cheap backyard shelters for the public. After a brief review by the EMO and the Department of National Defence staff, Harkness declined his colleague's offer. In the meantime, experts and laypersons raised pressing and difficult issues about the shelter program that had little to do with their affordability.

Doubts about the cost of the shelters were compounded by profound questions about whether Canadian society and values could survive a nuclear war and the two-week shelter period. Official CD literature released to the public mainly pertained to the construction and stocking of shelters with a fourteen-day supply of goods. Those who gave the matter some thought observed that this portrayal "implies that at the end of two weeks [the shelter occupant] just comes up and goes shopping for next week's supply," ignoring the deadly problem of radioactive isotopes in livestock, water, and crops following an attack and the certain destruction of Canadian supply and transportation systems.[75] The vast array of resources required to sustain life in cities, including electricity, refrigeration, water treatment, clothing, feeding, and transportation, would be severely disrupted in the event of an attack. If infrastructure was not destroyed outright, it could be rendered inaccessible if the areas were irradiated by fallout. While the government's Emergency Supply Planning Branch estimated that the productive capacity of Canada would deliver sufficient food stockpiles before

Figure 19   Fallout on the Farm. *Source: Fallout on the Farm,* Department of Agriculture 1961. Image provided by the Canadian War Museum.

an attack to sustain the population, it had no reply to the criticism made by provincial observers during the CBC program on the TOCSIN project that most distribution facilities were based in major target areas and were bound to be affected, except to say that the subject was under "very careful study."[76]

The government's solution to food production and distribution, found in the pamphlet *Fallout on the Farm,* provoked bitter attacks from farming communities for its naive optimism. Farmers were instructed to provide additional fallout protection and covered food and water sources for their livestock in barns, but they demanded to know who was to pay for these substantial costs. The pamphlet's authors also suggested that radioactive fallout on fields could be eliminated if farmers plowed the radioactive earth under with tractors. It was a simple solution that made no practical sense; farmers were depicted in the pamphlet driving tractors without fallout protection, shifting vast quantities of radioactive earth.[77] Criticism of *Fallout on the Farm* was sufficiently intense in his home base of Saskatchewan that Diefenbaker was forced to defend its authors in a difficult admission during the TOCSIN exercise: "The attitude of most critics of the booklet has been that the people who wrote it are stupid. In actual fact, of course, the scientists who wrote the booklet recognize the difficulties in some of the recommendations. They make them because there is no alternative to offer."[78]

The *Fallout on the Farm* controversy showed the limited and flawed nature of survival planning. If plans were thought to be stupid, this perception was added to by the respected critics, experts, scientists, medical doctors, or university professors who had more public credibility than the civil servants and volunteers that promoted the protective measures.[79] In their publications and public speaking, specialists readily exposed problems with the government's survival strategy and undermined public confidence in the CD plans. On 11 November 1961, Dr. Joseph Sternberg, a doctor of nuclear medicine at the University of Montreal, argued in *Weekend Magazine* that the Canadian government had not given sufficient thought to the duration of radioactivity's lethal effects nor to its pervasiveness. Sternberg borrowed heavily from his American colleagues and echoed the complaint of disarmament activists that CD measures appeared to be designed to "make people believe that a nuclear war would not be so bad after all."[80]

Civil defence planners in the provinces were frustrated by the public's respect for scientific opinion over the advice offered in the EMO publications. At a conference of provincial CD officials and army commanders in April 1961, A.C. Halmrast, provincial co-ordinator for Alberta, denounced "learned professors who are dealing with our young people putting up the idea that we should not be doing anything about this as it is all useless."[81] The opprobrium of the public scientist extended beyond the ranks of planners and volunteers. John Keyston, the vice chairman of the Defence Research Board, decried the tendency of Canadian scientists to voice their opinions about nuclear war and the long-term effects of fallout, when so few had access to classified information:

> The scientist who in practice does add emotional conclusions or implications to the scientific facts he imparts to the public is likely to maintain that he is not only a scientist but an educated, thinking citizen as well, [and] is entirely at liberty to speak his mind on any and every kind of inference, conclusion, moral, judgment, guess or hope he draws from his scientific knowledge. It is *not* for the scientist to take any part in garnishing his public educational pronouncements ... ask a scientist for his facts, and instead be given his feelings – that's the effect the nuclear environment seems to be having on most public-speaking scientists today.[82]

Scientific opposition to CD policies, furthermore, emboldened non-specialist critics to denounce shelter programs in public, citing "reports of qualified and unbiased scientists."[83]

Scientific opinion was divided on the shelter question, but the rapid decline of public confidence in survival planning put CD advocates back on their heels. On television, on the radio, and in public forums, CD officials were on the defensive, constantly challenged. W.D. Black, provincial co-ordinator for British Columbia, summarized the problem thus: "Some crack-pot in the community XYZ gets up and he gets all the headlines. What about our story? It is not being told."[84]

Fear, Shelters, and Society

Underlying many of the public's doubts about shelter policy were psychological factors that were unmistakably a product of the nuclear age. The very vocabulary created by Cold War rhetoric, such as "massive retaliation" and "mutually assured destruction," consistently communicated the fact that nuclear war would be the end of the world. The spectre of fallout – with its resulting invisible, lingering death – contributed to the public's perception of the nuclear weapon as a doomsday device. As scientists, public figures, and government officials debated casualty estimates and shelter effectiveness, nuclear war fiction and satire imagined a life after the bomb that seemed frighteningly real to many. The most important of these was Nevil Shute's *On the Beach*, originally published in 1957, serialized in newspapers and magazines, and later converted into a widely watched film in 1959.[85]

Shute depicted life in Australia several years after a war in the Middle East (presumably over the Suez Canal) that had spiralled out of control, with China and Russia employing highly radioactive cobalt bombs. Shute's fictional weapon had been the subject of serious study and debate since 1950, when it was first proposed by Leo Szilard, atomic scientist and one of the participants of the Manhattan project. Szilard predicted that an atomic weapon whose casing was salted with cobalt-60, an intensely radioactive isotope with an extremely long half-life, could theoretically kill far greater numbers by radiation poisoning over long distances than could be killed by blast, shock, and fire.[86] As a doomsday weapon, the cobalt bomb was a *diabolus ex machina,* a convenient rhetorical device for Shute and other authors to describe how a nuclear war would end all life.[87] Shute's work presented readers with his protagonists' horrible choice: die slowly and painfully from radiation poisoning or use government-issued suicide pills to preserve themselves and their newborns from such a fate? The film version of *On the Beach,* less nuanced than the book, was unambiguously anti-war and pro-disarmament, and its chilling end ensured that it remained in the public mind even after it departed theatres. A woman in Gowanstown, Ontario, evoked Shute's narrative when reacting to the TOCSIN exercises. She told the *Toronto Star* that the government should issue suicide pills to Canadians in the event of a war, to "ensure a painless, quiet and dignified death at a time when any delay would only mean days or weeks of a living hell in agony and beyond all human help."[88]

In addition to the flood of apocalyptic imagery in American literature and film, Canadian science fiction supplied its own versions of a chilling life after the bomb.[89] Short stories published in *Saturday Night* magazine recounted an alien expedition that discovered humanity's treasures preserved in a mountain shelter. The aliens were unable to discern what race had created the magnificent artworks stored in the mountain because radiation had exterminated all life on Earth.[90] Arthur Hailey's political thriller *In High Places,* which was serialized in *Maclean's* magazine in 1962, imagined a future prime minister of Canada, faced with an inevitable nuclear war, who was forced to consider moving the entire population of Canada to the North. The fictional leader was pressed by the United States to cede sovereignty over its air defence. Southern Canada was to be used as a defensive buffer zone where they could launch surface-to-air nuclear weapons at Soviet bombers.[91]

Civil defence officials never wished to cause panic in the public, and, as a result, they had self-imposed limits on what sort of scenarios they would choose to publicize. Science fiction authors entertained no such restrictions and were able to explore the horrors of nuclear war far more eloquently and imaginatively than the wooden, scripted narratives developed for CD exercises. However exaggerated and escapist these doomsday scenarios may have been, they enjoyed a much greater reach and audience than any Canadian CD manual, public lecture, or exercise. This was especially so because individuals in most cities in the country had the mistaken belief that their home was the likely target for a direct attack. Blair Fraser, a trusted political analyst for *Maclean's* hired by the CBC to host and narrate its national TOCSIN B television special, dryly noted in his (mostly bemused) commentary: "Thinking your town is bomb-worthy is a real mark of civic pride."[92]

Most Canadian planners believed that the targets of a Soviet first strike would be American strategic bomber bases, cities, and missile silos, with only a few locations in Canada intentionally targeted. This thinking lasted until the Cold War ended. Soviet records and accounts later proved that this assessment was accurate. As General Antoly Gribkov, deputy secretary of the Soviet Union's Defence Council, later explained: "Everybody understood it very clearly: that the ratio of forces was by far not in favour of the Soviet Union. In terms of warheads, we had a 1-to-17 advantage ... As for delivery vehicles that could hit the continental United States from the Soviet Union, we had only 25."[93] This information, paired with a Soviet strategy of pre-emptive attack after October 1961, meant that all Soviet assets were tasked with an attempt to destroy the United States' larger strategic arsenal before it could be unleashed against Soviet cities.[94] In such a scenario, Canadian territory would likely have been spared direct attack, but fallout would still threaten most Canadian population centres.

Most Canadians appear to have envisioned a post-detonation environment of nuclear ruin with few cities or towns remaining. Nearly half of the Canadians surveyed for a Peace Research Institute study in 1963 believed that, if a single five-megaton bomb was dropped on Toronto, half the population of Canada would die (11 percent believed this to be true) or everyone in Ontario would die (32 percent believed this to be true) – both estimates being a gross over-estimation of the power and lethality of the weapon.[95] A defence scientist then in residence at the University of Saskatchewan recalled with incredulity the belief commonly held by fellow students that the weapon was somehow magic, able to extinguish all life.[96] This public pessimism is reflected in correspondence from the public to officials and between CD planners. K.H. Watts, a volunteer in the Victoria area organization, lamented the "what's the use-ism" that was engendered by doomsday predictions in *On the Beach* and in other novels based on the "quite phony premise of an all-pervasive ever-lasting radiation fallout, along with panic and social disintegration."[97]

Satirists also found shelters a rich source of material. Max Ferguson, host of *Rawhide*, CBC Radio's hit entertainment show of the day, carried a number of features that ridiculed shelters, their proponents, and their builders between 1960 and 1961. In one episode, Ferguson presented "the Three Little Fallout Shelters," where CBC Radio employees, following Ottawa's orders, gamely built shelters on the lawn of the CBC building in Toronto. The character most influenced by the shelter pamphlets lamented to Ferguson's interviewer:

> If we can only get these lackadaisical Canadians, God love them, they're a voting people but they're lackadaisical, lathered up into a frenzy the way we got em down there [in the United States], get them thinking positively about nuclear war with a fallout shelter in every basement ... then the government in Ottawa has to get aggressive with Russia, just to justify building all these shelters [otherwise] it takes the fun out of things![98]

In another episode, Ferguson impersonated a Metro Toronto CD official. When asked what the individual who might not be able to afford a shelter could do to survive, the functionary mumbled: "That's a good question ... go under the kitchen chair, why, you could jump into bed, pull the covers over your head, go into the garden with your family, sit down, hold hands and sing a song?"[99] Ferguson depicted shelters as simultaneously impractical and costly, casting further suspicion on their purpose. Nor was his lampooning of Toronto's CD office far off the mark. When asked what the public without shelters should do in a war, John Pollard, the real Metro Toronto director, advised the public to take the best cover it could.[100]

Survival in an unimaginable war was just the first step. The public feared even more the political and social chaos that might follow an attack. In letters to newspaper editors or to public officials, Canadians likened the survivors of a nuclear exchange to the Morlocks, a cannibalistic subterranean race described in H.G. Wells's *The Time Machine*.[101] In the CBC television program *Close-Up*'s examination of the issue in January 1961, the program began and concluded with Norman Cousins, the Committee for a Sane Nuclear Policy's chairman, and his impassioned cry that he would rather die than poke around radioactive ash like a savage. Alan Munn, a Canadian dissenter, was also asked his opinion about the shelter policy. If a thousand "John Smiths" went into shelters, he replied, civilization would fall around them and "they would no longer be John Smith but Ugg Ugg of a thousand years ago." Most of the Canadians interviewed on the street in Aurora, Ontario, home of the first built-in family fallout shelter, dismissed the entire idea of shelters since they were all going to "get it" in any event.[102] The program's narrator agreed, ending the show with Albert Einstein's prediction that the fourth world war would be fought with sticks and arrows.

A key element of the shelter debate in the United States was the question of "shelter morality." American theologians – L.C. McHugh, Paul Ramsey, and others – wondered what would happen if humanity returned to a state of nature once the government retreated into nuclear bunkers or perished with the rest of civilized society. McHugh concluded that the survivors with shelters would be faced with angry and armed survivors outside, intent on gaining entry, and would thus be forced to "gun thy neighbor."[103] In the United States, some shelter owners appeared to take such warnings to heart and declared to the press their intention to mount machine guns and defensive positions outside their shelter to protect their family's chance for survival.

The American debate quickly entered Canadian discourse. In a lengthy, satirical letter to the editor, a man living in Don Mills proposed that "we must learn how to defend the shelters – not against the Russians, but against our friends and neighbours, the true enemy."[104] The writer suggested that the government offer practice dummies to interested families. In *Maclean's*, a sidebar about shelter construction in Canada pondered who was building shelters and where and deplored the lack of accurate information. The magazine speculated that those who were building shelters may have been hiding their efforts to prevent additional taxation and that some Canadians hired contractors to work secretly at night to prevent neighbours from learning about shelters under construction. *Maclean's* interviewed two men who had built shelters in Ontario. The first had built two shelters, a fake one that his unprepared neighbours could raid during an attack and a real one underneath where he planned to wait out the war. The second man, a retired policeman, was similarly unconcerned about his neighbours' welfare, confiding to the magazine that he had taught his wife how to shoot.[105]

The public feared not only the effects of nuclear weapons but also what they perceived to be the inevitable breakdown of public order and civility. Citizens suspected that the bonds that drew communities together in peace could not endure war. The family fallout shelter could not calm the public's fears of an apocalyptic societal collapse. In some cases, shelter publicity made things worse. Fear, long-lasting and deeply entrenched, had a permanent impact on how North Americans viewed their chances for their own personal survival.[106]

Retreat from the Shelter Policy, 1962

The EMO and its provincial counterparts were greatly concerned about the confluence of political, psychological, and practical objections to shelter construction. In particular, they sought to combat a perceived "common-sense" consensus that the individual had little chance of survival. The fallout shelter remained the only means of protection that the government could advise, and Canadians had rejected this advice. The majority of those who did support shelter construction did not believe that individual Canadians should be obligated to take on the building and supply costs. It was the government's responsibility, they argued, to provide for the protection of its citizens. The public demanded government-funded communal shelters. As Bryce explained to Diefenbaker in notes about the shelter policy, the predicted cost to protect twelve million Canadians in public shelters would be over $500 million. Whether through private investment or public taxation, Bryce concluded, "Canadians one way or another must pay."[107] Diefenbaker had no plans to spend that amount of money on CD, and neither did the public. R.B. Curry, director of the EMO, accordingly revised the government's shelter policy in the winter of 1961, with the help of Jack Wallace, his assistant director, and staff of the engineering division. In the revised policy, which was presented to R.B. Bryce on 29 December 1961, Curry described the existing plans as a failure: "People generally, in spite of the widespread interest that has been indicated by inquiries and otherwise, have not got concerned to the point where they have been willing to take action, provide the money required, and actually construct the recommended shelter."[108] The public had failed to build shelters, and their cumulative inaction threatened national survival.

The Americans had greater success, Curry reasoned, but even they had begun to shift their attention to providing shelter for their citizens in banks, courthouses, and other public buildings with reasonable fallout protection. Public demand and the action of Canada's allies all pointed to public, not private, shelters as the future course of action. Curry proposed a robust program to prepare the country for the worst by subsidizing shelters in federally owned buildings across the country. Congregate shelters could be installed in 4,000 large federal buildings. By December 1961, a survey of government-owned buildings was already underway, but Curry requested an immediate infusion of $100 million to hasten this slow, deliberate process. Civil Defence Canada had never received such financial support, and Wallace indicated that $100 million was, after all, only 6 percent of the current defence budget and that shelter construction could be justified as part of the deterrent to war.[109] Bryce, in handwritten comments on the proposed policy document, only expressed the view that to call the shelter policy a failure was "unfair" and to repeat that shelters in government buildings alone could not protect the public.[110] Curry shelved his policy and did not revisit it.

The EMO did, however, take several lessons from the shelter debates of 1961. It conceded that the organization had not provided satisfactory information to citizens living in targeted areas of the country and was sensitive to the criticism that government publications were unrealistic. The EMO's information services attempted to address both issues in its 1962 publication *Survival in Likely Target Areas*. This pamphlet informed city dwellers of the grim choice facing them under the government's "stay-put" policy. The government and its military planners believed that, whether Canadian cities were attacked or spared in the opening stages of a nuclear war, survivors would still require protection from fallout resulting from strikes against American cities or from explosions over Canadian territory. Canadians in target cities had to make their own individual choice after the air-raid sirens started wailing: try to find shelter in basements or evacuate with no guarantee of finding shelter from fallout in the countryside.

The EMO informed readers that the government would not be able to say with certainty how much time Canadians had before the first attack. If city dwellers chose to leave the city for the countryside, they had to have a plan to survive once they arrived. If they chose to remain, they should build a shelter. To help them make their choice, *Survival in Likely Target Areas* offered a more detailed explanation of the effects of nuclear weapons than had been provided in *11 Steps to Survival.* Each section of the new manual was accompanied with graphic imagery. The angular, impressionistic graphics of earlier publications were replaced with sketches that depicted humans suffering pain, fear, and shock. Live Canadian CD exercises frequently employed volunteers who were made up to simulate casualties, complete with broken bones, burns, and blood, but *Survival in Likely Target Areas* was the first Canadian government publication to depict nuclear war in such stark terms.[111]

Notwithstanding the new look of the EMO publications, the mainstay of the Canadian organization's message remained that adequate preparations carried out by individual citizens would mitigate damage to both cities and society, creating conditions in which the Canadian way of life could (and would) survive.[112] This notion had always been based on the government's prescriptive vision of a reciprocal, obligation-based citizenship developed to implement CD and other policies. In exercises, publications, and, more recently, the drive to build shelters, federal EMO and provincial CD agencies attempted to ensure the individual's co-operation by describing compliance with CD as one of the obligations of citizenship in Canada. Over the years following the shelter debate, however, the expectation that individuals would willingly contribute began to fade away – a consequence of the mainly psychological arguments developed against CD during the shelter debate. Two films proposed by the National Film Board for the EMO adapted CD publicity to meet the challenge posed by Canadians' fatalistic attitude towards nuclear war.

The first script, *You Survive,* was written for the EMO in 1962, but the film was never produced. The text offered two proposals to counter negative publicity surrounding the shelter issue. The first proposed that, despite Canadians' apparently earnest hopes to die in the first wave of an attack, they might survive anyway. The authors insisted that civilization could not collapse because of Canadians' sense of civic responsibility. The script opened on a man sitting dazed in a culvert on the outskirts of a city immediately after the detonation of a bomb, slowly emerging with the realization that what he had lived through was no exercise, as his thoughts turned to his family not far away. The narrator posed the question: "You're supposed to vanish in a puff of smoke, you're not supposed to care. But you're alive, and your family's waiting, what are you going to do next?" The authors claimed that most Canadians would survive the immediate aftermath of an attack by virtue of being far enough away from ground zero to escape immolation, explaining "mathematically, you couldn't count on not being around to face the consequences."[113]

The script then explored existing CD plans, the Canadian Civil Defence College in Arnprior, Ontario, and the thousands of volunteers who trained there annually. The volunteers were "citizens who accept the possibility [of destruction], who know that one man alone can do nothing, but that organized society will survive." The army and civilians were shown working together to save lives, and the filmmakers included a psychologist in the film to explain that civilization could not collapse into savagery because natural leaders would emerge in crisis situations to direct community efforts. The film was never produced because the EMO argued that the screenwriter placed too much emphasis on army operations, when the film was supposed to convince civilians to share the burden in national survival.[114]

Time to Live was written shortly after the Cuban Missile Crisis in 1962 and screened for the first time in early 1964. The producers explored several of the same themes as those found in *You Survive* but with more subtlety, nuance, and emphasis on the individual. Civil defence films prior to 1964 had based their approach on the assumption that viewers were either already volunteers or shared the organization's values. *Time to Live* was a significant departure from this approach. Its protagonists, the Macdonald family, assumed the role of everyday Canadians. The protagonists of *Time to Live* threw away every survival pamphlet they received and never planned for a disaster. In the film, the Macdonalds were visibly agitated, irritated with each other and their neighbours, and prone to making poor choices, such as bringing the household pet into the shelter. They, like most Canadians, had no shelter, but they did have a basement, where they decided to make their stand. To show that Canadian values would not disappear during an attack, filmmakers had the family take in their neighbour who was in desperate need of help.

Time to Live recognized that individuals were unlikely to build a shelter on their own. Given the declining role of the Canadian army in rescue operations, the rescue and re-entry columns promised in TOCSIN B publicity were not mentioned in the film. However, the producers developed three substantial points to challenge the anti-shelter consensus: (1) that Canadians outside of target areas would survive the attack and immediate aftermath; (2) that Canadians would wish to stay alive and help their community to survive; and (3) that even meager preparations for nuclear war might help individual families survive nuclear war. In the words of the producers, "the Macdonalds make it, but only just."[115] The film's producers accepted that most Canadians were irresponsible citizens, uninterested in preparations in peacetime, and portrayed the protagonists as such, rather than the idealized, responsible CD volunteer or family shelter builder.

Conclusion

Canada's shelter boom, if it can be called that, occurred between 1959 and 1961, coinciding with Western military preparations for a possible war with the Soviet

Union over Berlin. Adding to the growing public anxiety over international brinkmanship, the Canadian government launched a vigorous publicity program to convince citizens to invest in fallout shelters in the event that diplomacy failed. As a result, shelters were in the news, on the radio, and on the television. National broadcasts carried an endorsement of shelters by the prime minister, following Exercise TOCSIN, a thirty-minute simulation of Armageddon. Yet, in the end, only several thousand Canadians chose to build a family fallout shelter.[116]

Three factors informed Canadians' decision to reject the fallout shelter program. The international disarmament movement posed a serious challenge to CD and shelter advocates. The movement gained momentum in the late 1950s as a consequence of public health concerns over the long-term effects of radiation, which trumped suspicions of Communist subversion common in the early 1950s. Canadian disarmament and peace activists, like their allies in the United Kingdom and the United States, held forth that shelters were a disingenuous government program designed to lull the public into a false sense of security, while the great powers pursued the arms race. International experts, domestic politicians, and community activists all took part in the campaign to stop nuclear testing and promote disarmament. Peace and disarmament organization, and their supporters, effectively campaigned against the construction of shelters, much to the frustration of EMO officials.

The public did not necessarily need prompting from activists to raise doubts about the affordability, practicality, and effectiveness of fallout shelters. To many Canadians, the strategy made little sense and seemed both odious and impractical. Disputes among Canada's different levels of government over the right to tax shelters as home improvements drove up the cost to the individual homeowners. Renters and homeowners unable to pay for their own survival turned on the government's policy. Those in the public who found the family shelter policy unworkable demanded that the government should provide leadership and construct large communal shelters so that rich and poor Canadians could survive a war. Efforts launched in the United States to locate, mark, and stock communal shelters in public buildings, and the Canadian government's decision to build heavy blast shelters to ensure the safety of its officials, gave additional weight to the arguments of shelter critics.

The final and most difficult factor to measure, though perhaps the easiest to understand, was psychological. Nuclear war lived only in the mind. Caught up in a Cold War that was fought mostly "over there" in Europe and Asia, many hoped that nuclear war simply could not or would not happen. The alternative both horrified Canadians and strained their imagination. The majority of Canadians subscribed to the widespread belief that the world would end as soon as the first bombs fell. Any survivors struggling to rebuild a destroyed civilization, they reasoned, would surely envy the dead. The government never developed effective arguments to counter this perception, which was fuelled by popular discussion, science fiction, and satire. As early as 1962, the failure of the shelter-building campaign caused the government and the EMO to reassess the shelter policy and their approach to national survival as a whole. Most EMO officials concluded that Canadians did not build shelters because they did not want to think about nuclear war or CD measures.

9
Cuba, Confusion, and Retreat, 1962-68

On 17 October 1962, US aerial photo-reconnaissance revealed the existence of twenty-eight intermediate-range missile launch pads on the island of Cuba.[1] Four days later, US President John F. Kennedy authorized an immediate naval quarantine of Cuba to prevent more warheads, missiles, and launch equipment from reaching the island. The following day, Kennedy appeared on television to warn the public about the threat facing North America and to present the ultimatum he had delivered to the Soviets. Kennedy stated that the missiles were "capable of striking most of the major cities in the Western Hemisphere, ranging as far north as Hudson's Bay [sic], Canada, and as far south as Lima, Peru."[2] During the next thirteen days, global leaders frantically worked through diplomatic channels to resolve the crisis, intelligence experts assessed likely outcomes of military action short of a nuclear strike on Cuba, and the United States mobilized its military forces to prepare for a third world war.

In Canada, Prime Minister John Diefenbaker, deeply suspicious of the US president's leadership and his pride wounded by Kennedy's decision not to consult with him until shortly before the television address, initially refused to bring Canadian air and naval defence preparedness in line with the American mobilization. To the frustration of officials in Washington, Diefenbaker insisted on pursuing a multilateral solution to the crisis through NATO and the United Nations.[3] The issue nearly split his Cabinet, with Minister of Defence Douglas Harkness independently authorizing partial mobilization of the Canadian armed forces in line with Canada's obligations under the North American Air Defence (NORAD) agreement. For the Liberal Party in opposition, Diefenbaker's lack of leadership during the crisis dovetailed with the continuing debate over whether Canada should accept US nuclear warheads for the BOMARC missile system, which was purchased to replace the Avro Arrow. The question of Canada's contribution to the defence of North America ultimately brought down the Diefenbaker government in 1963.

The government, the Emergency Measures Organization (EMO), and the public were not prepared for a flashpoint such as the one that emerged over Cuba in the fall of 1962. Canada had based its planning for CD on the assumption that the country would have some strategic warning, defined by a prolonged period of international tension that would precede war. Emergency planners had hoped that a warning period would provide sufficient time to mobilize and implement CD programs and would allow the government to persuade individuals to make last-minute preparations for their own personal survival. The Berlin crisis, which had unfolded over three years, had impelled the Diefenbaker government to hasten its Continuity of Government (COG) program, train nearly 100,000 civilians in militia rescue tasks, and encourage Canadians to start building fallout shelters. They had little success.

Even under ideal circumstances, Canadian defence planners had long acknowledged that well over half of Soviet bombers and every ballistic missile that did not malfunction would penetrate North America's defences, killing millions. In a 1959 planning document, the Canadian Army Operational Research Establishment predicted that "in the early 60s due to the relative lack of air defence over Canada it would be most profitable for the USSR to use accurate, high yield [thermonuclear] aircraft-delivered weapons against Canada. These would result in very high casualties in the area attacked."[4] The same planners recognized that Canadian-American radar lines and air defence forces could detect an attack, but they did not possess sufficient numbers of aircraft to do more than provide an effective defence of North America's retaliatory nuclear arsenal. These assumptions reflected a belief that the numbers of bombers in the Soviet air force matched the more than 600 aircraft in the United States' Strategic Air Command capable of hitting the Soviet Union. The actual number of aircraft in the Soviet fleet by the end of the 1950s was approximately sixty long-range bombers and a similar number of intermediate-range aircraft with no realistic means of mid-air refuelling.[5] For much of the early Cold War, most of the Soviet nuclear arsenal was directed at the European theatre. The emphasis on active defence against a presumably equal enemy force meant that, in the prosecution of a nuclear war, civilian centres would have to be left unprotected, forced to attend to their own defence.[6]

Such was the challenge that Civil Defence Canada, and later the EMO national survival program, had been designed to meet. It failed the test. During the Cuban Missile Crisis, the system of passive defence was partially mobilized, but its response across the country was decidedly uneven and marked by confusion, ill-preparedness, and a lack of co-ordination. Despite over a decade of CD publicity and exercises, the citizenry had no conception of what they were supposed to do to escape immediate or lingering death from blast and radiation.

The country's civilian passive defences were nowhere near adequately prepared for nuclear war. There were simply not enough volunteers, full-time or part-time, to compensate for the massive damage to infrastructure and the enormous human losses that would accompany a single nuclear blast. By October 1962, the Canadian army and most federal and provincial departments had prepared a system of emergency government that could preserve the survival of the civilian leadership and, theoretically at least, direct the civilian and military survivors in their recovery efforts. Yet the EMO's emphasis on planning for COG had overlooked the plight of the governed. In the early Cold War, CD was organized around the complementary principles of "self-help" and responsible citizenship. Cities were expected to provide for their own survival with the voluntary contribution of their residents. With the adoption of national fallout shelter programs after 1959, the survival of the country depended on the willingness of individual families to prepare their own defences. The instructions to the public found in the government's survival instruction booklets were explicit: have a plan.[7] Few Canadians did.

What Do We Do?

Over the week following Kennedy's televised ultimatum to the Soviet Union, the press was rife with speculation about the severity of the threat, the appropriateness of the United States's response, and, to a lesser extent, the actions Canada should take.[8] Everyone recognized the real possibility of a nuclear war over Cuba. In a public statement issued after Kennedy's address, Diefenbaker asked Canadians not to panic: "This is a time for calmness. It is a time for a banishment of those things that separate us."[9] The Cabinet was deeply divided over how to respond to the crisis, although the ministers had agreed that a general public alert was both premature and likely to provoke panic.

Although the Cabinet could not agree to mobilize Canadian forces, the ministers quietly alerted the EMO on 23 October to ensure that key civilian officials remained in or near Ottawa, available to co-ordinate the civilian side of the Continuity of Government program. The Cabinet also secretly ordered the Canadian army to staff army command and federal and provincial emergency government headquarters on a twenty-four-hour basis.[10] Corporal Eric Brown, a signalman who in 1962 had recently been posted to the communications centre in the Diefenbunker in Carp, Ontario, returned from leave in Halifax to learn that he would be sealed inside the bunker for the foreseeable future. It was the first time that the bunker had been brought up to near its full capacity, complete with medical staff and members of the civil service taking up their posts.[11]

In the Canadian cities located close to the provincial regional emergency government headquarters, the preparations were a poorly kept secret. On 25 October, the *Winnipeg Free Press* reported that the emergency headquarters at Camp Shilo and Portage la Prairie were staffed twenty-four hours a day by specially trained signals officers "on temporary duty" and that Canadian army members were given telephone "fan-out" cards with names and numbers to call in the event of a general alert.[12] On the same day, Diefenbaker provided the only public acknowledgment that civil emergency measures had been called to alert. In a toothless statement to the House of Commons, the prime minister explained the activity as federal government departments merely updating their relevant plans in case of an emergency: "Our civilian departments have been instructed as a matter of urgency to bring up to date the measures which they would need to take in any emergency. They are doing so ... I do not think I should go any further into detail in dealing with the measures which we have taken or would be prepared to take, should circumstances require us to do so."[13] Few Canadians who read his statement, which was issued at the height of the crisis, would have understood what the government could actually do for them in the event of a war.

Finding no useful answers from their elected officials, Canadians turned to local, provincial, and federal emergency measures officials to ask what to do if an attack came without warning. The busiest people during the Cuban Missile Crisis were telephone switchboard operators and post office workers. Early on, Bell Telephone switchboard operators in Montreal reported hundreds of calls from residents seeking information about the municipal CD organization.[14] Public demands for information about emergency measures surged. Municipal CD officials received up to 1,000 enquiries by mail daily. In Toronto, phones rang every ten minutes. In Halifax, the volume of calls led E.J. Vickery, the local co-ordinator, to remind the public to stay off the telephones to avoid overwhelming switchboards that were needed in case of an emergency.[15] Some officials likened the public's anxiety to that which they had witnessed the preceding year during the Berlin crisis, but on a much grander scale and with greater urgency.[16]

The most common question asked by the public was: what to do? Civil defence and emergency measures offices responded by sending out 30,000 copies of the pamphlet *11 Steps to Survival* in response to public demand during the first few days of the crisis. This mailing also was a dramatic increase. From April to September 1962, considered by EMO regional officers as a period of "increased interest" in civil preparedness, the ten provincial EMO post office boxes together had received an average of only 1,000 requests per month.[17] As a public service, several newspapers reprinted the pamphlet in full within their pages.

Step 10 of the Canadian government's *11 Steps to Survival* informed readers to direct enquiries about emergency planning to their municipal organization.[18] Yet the status of municipal CD programs was uneven – most had shelved their planning during the 1959 reorganization of CD and had not resumed activities in any promising way before October 1962. Only a handful of municipalities could offer any constructive answers other than contact information for their federal and provincial counterparts or the provision of one of their rapidly diminishing stock of survival pamphlets. Others responded to the public's demand for guidance by dusting off dormant CD plans. Suddenly, many municipal officials and elected representatives realized that what they had been told by Civil Defence Canada and the EMO for years was true. In wartime, help would be in short supply. They would be responsible for the community's defence.[19]

Metropolitan Toronto's EMO announced that it aimed to establish a communication link between local staff and the national authorities, and it demanded a $100,000 infusion of federal funds to modify 100 schools in North York and Toronto into makeshift community fallout shelters.[20] Andrew Currie, a Canadian Football League official who also directed Winnipeg's EMO organization, asked the federal government for $10,000 to launch the city's police radio synchronization program, so that police in regions adjoining Winnipeg could share the same radio band. Currie also urged construction of an alternative radio site that could replace the police headquarters' broadcast station if it were destroyed in an attack.[21] In Truro, Nova Scotia, officials at the Board of School Commissioners established a committee to define regulations governing the evacuation of schoolchildren, with the publicly stated rationale that "some policy is better than no policy."[22] Under ideal circumstances, such programs would have taken months to implement. Their launch in a time of crisis revealed utter unpreparedness for a nuclear war.

Some municipal officials, unable or unwilling to respond to the public's concern, wanted the whole crisis to go away, and they took measures to proscribe public anxiety. At a meeting between Metropolitan Winnipeg's EMO officials and representatives from adjoining rural municipalities, the mayor of St. James tabled a motion to silence police and ambulance sirens. The mayor of St. Boniface accused emergency workers of abusing their vehicle sirens while on duty in residential neighbourhoods. Sirens during the night had "startled or provoked" residents, who called the city in panic to ask if the war had begun.[23] The motion, which was unsuccessful, illustrated the anxiety of the public and their municipal authorities and suggested that the public did not know the sound or meaning of the air-raid signals. In a real emergency, citizens who picked up their phones would have jammed switchboards needed to co-ordinate essential services.

Civil defence and EMO organizations had little to offer the public but direct and honest advice as the crisis deepened. On 27 October, when nuclear war appeared imminent as Soviet vessels bearing missile cargoes closed with the US naval cordon around Cuba, Winnipeg officials admitted that they had not prepared an evacuation plan for the city, nor did they have the resources to feed refugees if other cities were hit. Andrew Currie cautioned the public that they still had time to make a plan, warning "for the first few days or weeks it will be

FIGURE 20   Stan Williams, sixteen years of age, began digging a fallout shelter outside his home in Scarborough, Ontario, the morning after President Kennedy's broadcast about the Cuban Missile Crisis. *Source: Toronto Telegram*, Clara Thomas Archives, York University

every family for itself – go to the cottage, make plans to visit friends outside the city, make plans to share food ... Go at least 30 miles away, but no further than you can without gas ... Finally, don't adopt an attitude that all is lost once war is declared."[24] Metropolitan Toronto's police force had drafted more detailed plans about how its citizens could evacuate the city in just over a day, but, apparently, it had made no effort to publicize these plans, perhaps fearing a mass exodus.[25] Families considered leaving the cities for "early vacations" in rural areas during the crisis, but it is unclear how many Canadians, anticipating an attack, voluntarily evacuated from urban targets or how many just prepared to die.

Where Was Civil Defence?
The last-minute settlement between the United States and the Soviet Union on 28 October 1962 was the result of furious backroom diplomacy and aggressive naval strategy. It was a watershed moment in the Cold War. The American and Soviet leadership co-operated to install a direct line of communication to ensure

that the crisis would not repeat itself. So began a period of cautious rapprochement, leading to the policy of *détente*. In Canada, the emphasis of public enquiry quickly shifted from the question "What to do?" to criticisms of Diefenbaker's judgement and leadership during the crisis and to the divisive subject of arming the Canadian military with nuclear weapons.

At the height of the crisis, some outspoken public figures appeared on television to excoriate the government for not having done more to provide the public with the means to survive.[26] In its aftermath, few demanded answers about the EMO's lack of preparedness. Nor did the crisis result in public pressure for government-subsidized shelter construction programs. Many citizens had already concluded that such measures were hopeless. The public, which was the last to awaken to the need for individual and family plans for survival before the crisis, was also the first to fall back to sleep after its peaceful resolution. The pattern of public interest in emergency measures matches those observed during the height of the Korean War and the Berlin crises of 1958 and 1961.

Perhaps "forgetting" was the home front's survival mechanism. In the absence of prolonged crisis, the nuclear arms debate in Canada surfaced, and emergency measures fell to the backs of people's minds and to-do lists, becoming once again someone else's problem. In a 1963 study of public opinion commissioned by peace activist Norman Alcock's Canadian Peace Research Institute, the surveyors found a surprising lack of concern about nuclear war. Of those interviewed, 43 percent agreed with the statement: "There is nothing I can do. It is the government's responsibility since they have the power and information." A further 11 percent believed that the individual bore some responsibility to work towards peace but were happy to "let Joe do it." The results led the survey's authors to question "whether such feelings reflect realistic evaluation of the average individual's influence in complex modern society, or whether it is a convenient way to avoid one's responsibility."[27]

Federal and provincial emergency measures organizations were slower to let down their guard. For several weeks after the crisis, the Canadian army continued to staff government bunkers as the Royal Canadian Air Force and the Royal Canadian Navy conducted aggressive anti-submarine patrols of Canadian coastal waters. Cabinet did not immediately issue orders to reduce readiness in federal government departments either. Diefenbaker and Harkness directed R.B. Bryce, secretary to the Cabinet and head of the EMO, to keep key staff in government departments available "notwithstanding the relaxation of tension over the Cuban situation. It will not be necessary to be so strict in keeping key persons ... in Ottawa as it was last week, but care should be exercised."[28] By the end of November, these measures were gradually scaled back to peacetime conditions. Senior EMO officials, reflecting on the crisis, developed their own private assessments of the organization's response and were disturbed by its lack of co-ordination and public presence.

Jack Wallace, the assistant director of the EMO, issued the definitive criticism of his organization's progress. He outlined the agency's critical shortcomings during the crisis, not least the lack of established procedures to alert the public properly through the Canadian Broadcasting Corporation. The EMO did not have the authority to formally advise the provinces to increase their civil preparedness measures. Organizations across the country experienced shortages of printed materials and delays in obtaining republications of important pamphlets. Federal and municipal EMOs lacked co-ordination, resulting in public floundering and embarrassment in the press. Finally, the organization's inability to offer substantive advice to the public during the crisis undermined its credibility as an agency responsible for co-ordinating the country's survival strategy. Wallace concluded: "It goes without saying that of all the emergency preparations that have been made, the least has been done in the area of offering something substantial to the population, i.e., some type of shelter programme."[29]

Apart from the absence of shelters, the fundamental obstacle to national survival was a profound failure of communication not only between governmental EMOs but also between the EMO and the public, despite years of publishing news releases, information pamphlets, and radio and television broadcasts. N.S. Jones, in one of many scathing letters that the public sent to Diefenbaker after the crisis, concluded that "what civil defense organization we have seems to be a close-mouthed clique tucked away in some corner from where it must be sought if it exists at all in any effective form."[30]

What had happened to the over 279,000 Canadians that the federal government claimed as volunteers for civil defence?[31] There is some question as to whether a sizeable voluntary CD corps ever actually existed. A sizeable portion of the registered volunteers were actually full-time municipal employees. This group included all of the staff of municipal police and fire stations, all health workers, and every engineer with technical training, in some cases including contractors and equipment dealers. In 1956, full-time municipal employees, many of whom may never have known that they were considered "volunteers," comprised 42 percent of Canadian CD workers. Accurately tracking the personnel of any volunteer organization is difficult work, and CD corps were no exception. Most CD offices did not keep accurate data about who was actually serving in the organization at any given time. The numbers of citizens prepared to risk their lives to better the chances of national survival varied widely from place to place, often based on what officials considered to be a true volunteer.

The CD co-ordinator for the Greater Vancouver Area counted 15,000 people trained in basic first aid by St. John Ambulance as belonging to his organization. They had not been trained in first aid courses, but he considered them "available in an emergency." St. John Ambulance was officially considered a part of the national Civil Defence Health Services by way of a 1951 agreement, but the local organizer's definition of what constituted volunteering for CD stretched credulity. In a conservative estimate of municipal CD agencies' strength in Manitoba in 1957, provincial officials acknowledged that most of the volunteers they had listed in the estimate had not "formally enrolled" in civil defence. Counted among this number were citizens who had attended several CD courses but who had declined to sign an official enrolment form.[32]

Even for those citizens who had legitimately joined with CD or EMO agencies, many chose to leave during the confusion that followed the 1959 restructuring of CD in Canada, when the role of the unpaid volunteer was called into question. Those who remained were unable to do more than answer the public's questions during the crisis without federal direction. The federal government reserved strict control over the pre-attack alert system that governed civilian emergency workers, and supporting CD volunteers were to prepare reception centres, co-ordinate voluntary evacuation efforts, and implement other municipal or provincial emergency plans. Unless incapacitated, Diefenbaker alone reserved control over when and whether to issue the alert that would force the country's meagre CD resources to go into action. He was advised by Cabinet, the Canadian armed services, and the EMO. Civil defence's inaction, influenced by poor intergovernmental communications, limited resources, and public confusion, was also a by-product of Diefenbaker's characteristically cautious response to the Cuban Missile Crisis.

Diefenbaker could have authorized four states of government alert during the crisis, raising civilian levels of attack preparedness that corresponded to those developed for the Canadian Army's National Survival Attack Warning System.[33] These alert states were laid out in revisions to the government's *War Book,* a document that delineated federal government decision making and departmental responsibilities in wartime.[34] The Department of National Defence's *War Book* underwent significant revision before and during the Cuban Missile Crisis, leading to significant confusion over who was empowered to set the military on alert and at what time.[35] During the crisis, Diefenbaker's Cabinet authorized the civilian standby phase, which increased staff and readiness at the federal EASE and provincial BRIDGE sites. These preparations were not publicized to prevent public hysteria and alerting the Soviets that the government was going to ground, a possible indication of a first strike.[36] During the standby phase, federal and provincial agencies carried out secret preparations, but advice to municipal CD organizations was not part of the alert. As these agencies waited for direction from above, their officials did what they could to answer the public's questions. The crisis never reached the point where municipal agencies and their volunteers had to be called to action. The Canadian CD organization remained untested.

If a war had erupted over Cuba, Canada would have entered the emergency phase. EMO regional officers would advise provincial officials to begin their own emergency fan-out. Municipal CD organizations would be the last group alerted. Depending on the location, local groups could then begin their own telephone fan-out to call out their volunteers, if time permitted. The strategy was not likely to succeed. When the army tested the provincial fan-out network for the first time, it took more than an hour and a half to reach provincial colleagues.[37] Another flaw in this plan was obvious. Once a national alert was called, the volunteers that the EMO depended on to assist existing emergency services would immediately be faced with a fight-or-flight option – to stay and carry out the work for which they had trained (assuming they had any training) or to abandon their post to take care of their families. It also gave municipal CD organizations extraordinarily little lead time to begin co-ordination of services for the public. The public would make their own spontaneous decisions about what they would do as soon as the sirens started wailing, with the potential to create mass panic.

Wallace privately complained that the prime minister had not served Canadians well by refusing to discuss emergency measures immediately following Kennedy's televised address and by remaining silent on the matter throughout the crisis. "Such a broadcast," Wallace suggested, "would not necessarily have to endorse all that was said but it is clearly important that the Prime Minister at least offer words of caution to the public. Following Mr. Kennedy's speech, a great deal was left unsaid."[38] Diefenbaker not only remained quiet but he also went on the record requesting that others in the public realm do the same. The day after placing the Canadian government on standby, Diefenbaker responded to a question about CD preparations in the House of Commons by asking members of parliament not to ask questions. He revealed his unwillingness to provoke public alarm to increase readiness: "I think that in these hours and days of international sensitivity all of us will endeavour to exercise a restraint in asking questions which under normal circumstances would be appropriate but at this time might be considered as provocative or fear-producing."[39]

Perhaps Diefenbaker regarded a public alert, or even discussion of nuclear defence measures, as detrimental to his government's determination to see the crisis resolved through international negotiation. His hope for a multilateral solution to the crisis, informed by advice from the Department of External Affairs, formed part of the reason why the prime minister initially refused to raise Canada's military readiness to match that of the United States.[40] Diefenbaker had also feared the implications of surrendering Canadian sovereignty over defence, a charge that had been levelled against him by opposition Liberals when he signed the NORAD agreement in 1958.[41] His delay probably had less to do with his "pathological hatred of taking a hard decision," which his defence minister observed, than with the weighty international and domestic considerations tied up in the crisis.[42] Confusion over governmental responsibilities, conflicting personalities, and a Cabinet that was generally uninformed about strategic defence issues, however, created a void in decision making during the crisis that Diefenbaker did not rush to fill.[43]

Historians have almost universally condemned Diefenbaker's inaction during the crisis, but his stance on CD measures was both rational and responsible.[44] A publicized national alert may have resulted in a spontaneous exodus of citizens from urban target areas. Canada's CD organizations and its incomplete emergency communications system were not prepared for such an alert, which could alarm the public and possibly deepen international tensions. Diefenbaker's restraint in this regard was mirrored by Kennedy's. Both were faced with the dilemma that the Soviets could view ostentatious improvements to CD infrastructure or large public exercises as preparation for a first-strike nuclear attack under the guise of public protection. Had the crisis worsened, Diefenbaker might have formally authorized a public alert, but his caution during the standoff suggests that he would have acted only if the Americans sounded the alarm first.

The Best Defence: Go Nuclear

Diefenbaker's stance during the Cuban Missile Crisis enjoyed some sympathy from the press and neutralist and pacifist sections of public opinion, but most Canadians were outraged that their government appeared to be going against its long-standing commitment to co-operation with the United States in the defence of the continent.[45] They believed that, when the West needed to present a united front to the Soviets, security was more important than sovereignty.[46] Little of the invective directed towards Diefenbaker in the crisis's aftermath, however, faulted him or the EMO for not having a plan in place to help Canadians survive in a nuclear war. The question of Diefenbaker's leadership during the crisis, in the event, was quickly eclipsed by his government's internal debate over the nuclear warheads issue, which soon paralyzed government business and precipitated a federal election in early 1963. In the prelude to the election,

EMO officials were disturbed to learn that, even after sending out hundreds of thousands of pamphlets, orchestrating two (publicly reviled) Canadian emergency measures exercises, and answering thousands more nervous enquiries, 55.1 percent of Canadians indicated that they simply had no idea what to do in the event of a war.[47] There was no indication that the crisis had made Canadians any more interested in learning about the correct course of action. Nor did the EMO take measures after the crisis to address the public's lack of awareness.

In the aftermath of the Cuban Missile Crisis, Canadians showed more faith in the deterrent of nuclear warheads than in their largely disorganized passive defences that they bore a share in maintaining. Shelter and evacuation pamphlets gathered dust on kitchen tables or, more likely, in garbage bins. Those Canadians who wanted nuclear arms for their armed forces did so because Canada's conventional defences would have been useless against the large bomber forces that would have composed a sizeable part of the Soviet attack.[48] Nuclear weapons would not have stopped the attack, but at least they would plug an apparent and embarrassing gap in Canada's deterrent.[49] Canadians chose to augment their active defences rather than address the sizeable problems and lack of preparedness in their passive defences.

EMO officials at the federal level privately lamented the public's ignorance of civilian defence measures but could do nothing to halt the government's and the public's slack sense of urgency for emergency preparedness. Recommendations to improve public relations and promote the emergency measures and warning system ended up as a secondary consideration for emergency planners who, throughout 1963, delved into the invisible and unrewarding work of co-ordinating planning activities between disparate and disinterested government departments. As East-West relations improved over the following years – the nuclear arms issue "solved" by the acquisition of nuclear arms for Canadian units at home and overseas and disarmament activists mollified and (ironically) neutralized by the signature of an American-Soviet Partial Test Ban Treaty in 1963 – the importance of Canada's nuclear preparations recessed into obscurity, a process managed by Diefenbaker's successors.

Lester Pearson's government, which defeated Diefenbaker in the 1963 election, placed little importance on CD when compared to the major programs launched during the Diefenbaker years. The federal EMO had its budget reduced, and the responsibility for nuclear preparedness was kicked between departments, moved first from the prime minister's office to the Department of Defence Production in 1963, and then to the Department of Industry in 1965. Work continued on locating and assessing potential buildings that could serve as group fallout shelters, and some limited research began into how to build affordable blast shelters that might protect Canadians in the cities, but little came of either initiative because of the EMO's limited resources.[50]

Perhaps sensing the opportunity provided by a shift in government, the military quickly shed itself of its much-despised national survival tasks. The 1964 Suttie Commission, launched to reassess the role of the Canadian army reserves, made survival operations just one more aspect of war training. In order of importance, survival operations rated last behind support for the army, its role as a training force, and an internal security capability. A frustrated Jack Wallace, learning of planned cuts to national survival responsibilities, penned a sarcastic note to file: "DND should be invited to explain exactly how they propose to continue with the same policy and responsibilities when they are reducing training potential and their manpower capability so significantly. I submit that this [national survival] was not, contrary to the lip service which had been paid to it, as effective as we would wish."[51] The attack warning and communication systems remained in operation, but the rest of the armed forces largely abandoned their CD responsibilities.

During these years, public contact with the EMO decreased substantially, as emphasis in planning shifted gradually from nuclear preparedness to preparing for natural disasters. Although the EMO at the federal and provincial levels still pursued nuclear preparations, talk of emergency measures and CD gave way to the less alarming "civil emergency planning" soon after the 1963 election. In 1966, Charles Drury, Pearson's industry minister, who had inherited the EMO the previous year, laid out his plans for the future of Canada's passive defences in letters to his provincial counterparts. He announced that improved relations between the East and West and the marginal risk of nuclear war meant that many survival planning tasks could be safely placed on the back burner. Drury called instead for a new emphasis on civilian emergency planning for natural disasters. This was work that could be handled quietly within and between governments.[52]

With emergency plans no longer tied to nuclear war, Drury suggested that federal, provincial, and municipal planning departments could cut costs and programs, keeping only a trained core of planning officials to develop plans on paper. The public did not need to be involved. Drury reasoned that there was a need to inform the public of the reasons for emergency planning, but "past experience leads me to believe that the ability of our emergency organizations to respond effectively to the public need in times of crisis, provides greater benefits than trying to arouse them at times when the dangers are less apparent."[53] CD was to be streamlined, costs cut, and planning placed in reserve, safely away from the public. Cuts in Canada to the EMO matched those in the United

Kingdom, which in 1965 stripped away financing for recruiting and disbanded CD rescue and ambulance services. Soon after, the entire UK organization was placed on a care-and-maintenance basis.[54] By 1967, the EMO in Canada suffered a similar fate in a review of government spending and priorities. The organization moved again to become a sub-directorate of the Department of National Defence, its tiny budget frozen and its staff gutted.[55]

In a few short years, the focus of CD planning moved from individual and community preparedness, with all of the accompanying requirement for public information programs and demands for civic volunteers, to being just another function of the public service. In the absence of an immediate nuclear crisis, CD retreated from public life into a core of largely invisible emergency planning professionals, responsible for long-range planning, harmonizing interdepartmental and governmental procedures. The call for citizens to organize to defend their communities and their lives accordingly fell by the wayside. Canadian citizens, relieved of a Cold War responsibility they never accepted, went on with their lives.

Conclusion

FOR A BRIEF MOMENT in the fall of 1962, it appeared as though the uneasy nuclear balance with which Canadians had lived for so long would not hold. Civil Defence Canada, and later the Emergency Measures Organization (EMO), had sought to prepare the public for just such a crisis. Yet when it happened, people did not know how to protect themselves, nor were they equipped with the necessary resources to survive if the standoff had sparked a nuclear war. The long-standing organizational problems brought to light during the Cuban Missile Crisis served to illustrate the extent to which CD had failed since its introduction in 1948. Civil defence's failure was linked to the changing relationship between state and citizen, the impossible task of government planning for nuclear war, and the civil-military tensions it provoked within Canada's defence structure and the wider public.

From 1948 to 1962, civil defence had a public presence, reaching out to communities through an extensive publicity campaign, featuring films, instructional pamphlets, exhibits, and massive public exercises involving thousands of people. As a result of the structure of Canadian CD, based originally on the system used in the United Kingdom during the Second World War, progress depended heavily on the voluntary participation of Canadians at a grassroots, municipal level. The Canadian government sought to enlist the help of private citizens in preparing the defence of the country by equating support for CD with a civic responsibility each individual owed to the state. This concept of fulfilling the obligations of citizenship was present at every stage of CD development and was featured prominently in most of the organization's contacts with the public. Civil defence was most often promoted as a means to defend the community against an atomic attack and as a public good that would protect the values and rights that Canadians enjoyed as citizens of a liberal democracy.

The government's appeal to responsible citizens was most successful when organizers targeted and co-operated with existing national and local voluntary associations such as the Canadian Legion or municipal volunteer boards. Civil defence officials were concerned with gaining the support of these community elites – volunteers already active in the community whom officials believed could lend CD greater credibility and provide local leadership for the organization. Civil defence plans gave these volunteers a common purpose. Early policy envisioned local populations rushing to the scene of fires caused by nuclear explosions and pulling survivors out of the rubble. This communitarian strategy permitted CD officials to illustrate how individuals could demonstrate their usefulness to the community during a national crisis. Even as CD policy changed to evacuation thinking after 1954, volunteers kept their status as community leaders who would marshal fellow citizens to safety areas. The evacuation program expanded appeals from Canada's major urban areas to the rural countryside, whose residents were expected to offer up their homes and supplies to billet, feed, and care for nuclear refugees fleeing their doomed cities.

Revelations of the potency and lethality of radioactive fallout threw CD plans into confusion. In 1959, the government at last articulated a national survival policy, which placed emphasis on the private construction of family fallout shelters alongside a system of hardened blast facilities to provide for the continuity of government and preserve Canada's social order following an attack. Unlike the "self-help" and evacuation strategies adopted earlier, the national survival policy could not tie the individual citizen's effort to the communal good because survival had become a matter of personal initiative to provide shelter for the family's defence and not for the community. The role of existing volunteers within the organization was thrown into question. In the era of the intercontinental ballistic missile, the proud certainty of earlier CD strategies had disappeared. The government could not predict what areas of the country would be hit and which areas would be at risk from fallout. The best advice the government could offer to all Canadians was to have a plan and to build a shelter. The shelter policy transformed support for CD from an effort directed at preserving the community to a series of decisions that each citizen would be forced to make to provide protection for the family before an attack took place. With plans focused so intensely on individual family planning, rather than on community effort, the role of the volunteer withered away, and national and local voluntary associations gradually withdrew their support from the organization.

Yet the bond between the citizen and community defence did not disappear once the government began encouraging Canadians to build shelters. Shelter occupants were not meant to remain underground forever and were expected to keep an ear to the radio to learn what they were to do once they could rejoin the community. It was their responsibility to listen and respond through this radio link, which would be kept alive by government officials ensconced in their blast bunkers, so that the country could rebuild after families received instructions to emerge from their shelters. The connection between the individual volunteers and the survival of the country did, however, become increasingly tenuous as the nature and magnitude of the threat to Canada changed.

The professionalization of emergency measure planners also figured in the diminishing emphasis on civic voluntarism in CD publicity and planning after 1959. Apart from the shelter policy, government planning was directed at developing support systems that would remain standing during a war. This work did not so much require leaders able to communicate with their communities as it did a new class of public servant whose work was mainly concerned with harmonizing the intergovernmental and interdepartmental standards and procedures that made up the Continuity of Government plans. Community voluntary associations, once central to municipal CD agencies, lost their direction and importance as emergency plans became just "another function of government."[1] Increasingly, CD discussions were held in boardrooms, not city councils and church basements. The professionalization of CD planning, which intensified after 1963, pushed the organization from public view.

The failure of civil defence should also be considered a failure of policy and planning. The organizational structure that the federal government decided to implement after 1948 created an emergency planning system where financial and administrative responsibility was divided over three levels of government. The federal government could not compel its counterparts in provincial and municipal arenas to comply with the policies, advice, and guidance drawn up by Civil Defence Canada and the EMO in Ottawa. The decision whether to expend public monies to organize and maintain municipal CD was entirely voluntary. Most provinces and nearly every municipality objected to being saddled with the cost of preparations, especially once they learned that the price of efficient protection and infrastructure would dwarf their annual budgets.

Canada's CD program, like many of the federal government's post-war social programs, became entangled in a dispute over which level of government should bear the financial responsibility for emergency measures. The federal government likened the nature of peacetime CD planning to natural disaster contingencies – work best done using local resources directed provincially. The provinces and municipalities countered by pointing to the complexity and price of the task. Nuclear defence, they reasoned, was a matter of national defence and, therefore, a federal responsibility. For most of the 1950s, two provinces, Ontario and Quebec, refused to contribute at all to nuclear preparations. The situation led to ugly public disputes that undermined public confidence in CD and left Canadians without direction in times of crisis. The seriousness with which CD planners viewed the need to begin preparations is underlined by the fact that the federal government gradually retreated from its insistence that the provinces underwrite the costs. The federal government became more deeply involved at the local level in planning and financing CD preparations in target cities over the course of the 1950s, through the Financial Assistance Program and other means.

The limitations of CD planning were further exposed by the organization's slow response to rapid advances in weapons technology during the early Cold War. The first thermonuclear weapon was detonated in the Pacific Ocean in 1952, yet nearly four years passed before the federal government officially changed CD policy to reflect this revolutionary advancement. Intergovernmental disputes accounted for part of this delay, as the federal government coaxed reluctant partners to test and adopt new strategies. Planners also faced impediments in receiving accurate information about the weapon they were responsible for developing a defence against, a result of restrictive secrecy laws in the United States. Nor could changes in CD strategy, at the best of times, keep up with the changing nature and extent of the threat to lives and infrastructure. Gradually, technological revolutions stripped away planners' confidence that cities could be saved, that the cities alone would suffer, and, finally, that the public would have sufficient warning to take action in the event of an attack.

Civil defence organizations were also afflicted by the lack of sustained political support for their efforts. Civil defence intruded on the government's post-war agenda and found few political champions over the course of its existence. The St. Laurent government established the CD organization, but senior political officials who were unwilling to risk criticism or embarrassment were reluctant to offer public endorsements of civil defence. Minister of National Health and Welfare Paul Martin and the minister in charge of CD from 1951 to 1957, thought planning for nuclear war necessary but distasteful. J.W. Monteith, his successor, had even less desire to promote CD measures and happily shifted responsibility for the organization out of his department at the first available opportunity. Martin believed that rearmament and the CD effort extracted resources from his department that he wanted to direct towards his ambitious project to reform Canada's hospital insurance system. Monteith's enthusiasm for sport led him to spearhead a national fitness and amateur sports program, while he found the CD profile "particularly baffling and frustrating."[2]

John Diefenbaker, who after 1959 assumed political responsibility for Canada's emergency measures program, was the most active agent of national survival. During the Berlin crises, he oversaw a dramatic expansion in public spending on emergency measures and made repeated public appearances to explain the necessity of CD, fallout shelters, and national EMO exercises such as the 1961 TOCSIN project. Civil defence was an issue that Diefenbaker could have chosen to ignore, as St. Laurent had. Better CD measures would win few votes, and in view of the increasingly vocal anti-nuclear movement it carried political risk.[3] Diefenbaker deserves credit for his leadership, however imperfect, on the CD file. However, he was never able to explain this peculiar aspect of government planning to the public and suffered deep personal embarrassment when the media and voters lashed out at apparently lavish projects such as the Diefenbunker. So Diefenbaker balanced his support for emergency measures with caution, not wishing to provoke public anxiety that could further disturb his government's agenda. It was this caution that stilled Diefenbaker's tongue about CD during the Cuban Missile Crisis.

Diefenbaker's government accelerated organizational changes put in motion by St. Laurent's Cabinet to resolve the intractable intergovernmental divisions and the moribund planning process that plagued CD efforts. The Civil Defence Order (CDO) of 1959 made important concessions to the provinces about federal financing for local projects and brought about a number of important changes to Canada's CD structure and policies. However, the transition from Civil Defence Canada to the EMO left provincial and municipal CD agencies without central guidance or funding during a period of prolonged international crisis. The 1959 CDO also created severe problems for the Canadian military, which became responsible for large aspects of Canada's CD effort without the resources necessary to carry out its new and unwanted tasks adequately.

In 1948, Canada's CD planners had advocated a structure of passive defences that would prepare cities for nuclear war without the need for extensive military aid. Their rationale for this was twofold: the military was not large enough to handle the tasks associated with a nuclear CD on their own and the armed forces themselves did not want to assume responsibility for what they viewed as a civilian responsibility. Strategic thinking in the armed forces envisioned a short, sharp offensive strike that the country could absorb, so that the military could go on to fight, and presumably win, a conventional war in Europe. This thinking, both in Canada and elsewhere, went on despite evidence that the arms race would result in a much more destructive, perhaps apocalyptic, attack. For most of the 1950s, the Canadian army trained to fight the Soviet Union in Western Europe and carefully guarded its war-fighting capability against suggestions that their mobile force could be used to supplement or, if necessary, supplant Canada's CD volunteers.

After successive Cold War crises, the Canadian Chiefs of Staff Committee gradually recognized that their forces would have to offer support to CD and increase the home front's chance of survival. The CDO formalized this arrangement, placing the army in charge of blast and fallout detection, attack warning, and rescue. Rescue duties would require hundreds of thousands of soldiers and civilians to re-enter blasted cities to put out fires and extract injured Canadians trapped under debris. In the short term, neither CD corps nor the army derived much benefit from their new relationship. Volunteers in local CD agencies trickled away, alienated, with the belief that they had been replaced with hired help, even as defence ministers issued assurances that citizens' services were still required. The Canadian army's militia – the force tasked to create mobile rescue columns to save lives in bombed cities – in turn deeply resented the loss of its role as a reserve to Canada's NATO force. From 1959 to 1963, part-time soldiers gamely played along with rescue exercises that they derisively labelled "snakes and ladders," while membership in the militia dropped precipitously.[4]

At the foundation of Canada's CD establishment was the expectation that the public would contribute to its own defence. Although many Canadians across the country responded to this appeal, most did not. Citizens were willing to assume some obligations required of them by the government, such as taxation, in exchange for rights, privileges, and, increasingly after 1945, the services of the social welfare state. The public as a whole, however, did not accept responsibility for civil defence. Canadians never permitted personal responsibility for survival to be written into the contract between citizens and the state, despite repeated attempts by government officials to convince them of their civic duty to enlist for "self-help," train in evacuation tactics, or dig their own shelters. The public response to CD reveals that Canadians rejected the organization for a range of practical, political, and psychological reasons.

The majority of Canadians objected to CD efforts on practical grounds. From what they knew of Canada's planning, the public easily and often pointed to imperfect plans as an excuse not to participate. Firefighting and rescue made sense during a natural disaster, but these did not compare to the destruction of an atomic bomb. The public responded with incredulity to costly proposals to bombproof their cities. Evacuation plans were met with similar skepticism, as citizens living in cities compared their lived experience in rush hour traffic jams with plans to evacuate the entire population in under three hours. To many Canadians, these plans did not pass the litmus test of realism. The strongest evidence of the public's rejection of a CD policy on practical grounds was the failure of the government's fallout shelter program. Canadians who were asked to spend $500 for their own protection pleaded poverty. A third of the population pointed to their living situation in rented premises and wondered, when and if they emerged from their shelters, whether any food would be safe to eat.[5]

Disarmament activists and critics of the arms race used the public's doubts about the practicality of CD measures to some advantage. Peace groups argued at public gatherings and in petitions that CD was a hoax, meant to reassure the population that they could survive a nuclear exchange. Activists attacked the principle of preparing for nuclear war as evidence of the government's lack of commitment to work for peace. The pressure brought by these groups led some local city councils to refuse participation in exercises and embarrassed federal politicians about their role in the national survival program. Peace organizations promoted a campaign parallel to the EMO to convince the public that disarmament, not shelters, could ensure survival. These groups, with the assistance of the academy and a sympathetic press, placed the long-term health effects of nuclear fallout from weapons testing on the public agenda. Civil defence advocates, for their part, could offer no advice about how Canadians were supposed to survive the residual radiation that would contaminate the environment for thousands of years after a war.

Yet the greatest obstacle to the public's participation in CD was psychological. Canadians looked to atomic and thermonuclear weapons with a mixture of terror, reverence, and anxiety. Canadians asked to think about civilian defence first imagined an Armageddon portrayed in a constant flow of press and science fiction since the end of the Second World War. The bomb was not something against which a credible defence could be mounted. The world would change irrevocably from the peaceful existence Canadians knew into a burnt and poisonous landscape. It was a future that Canadians did not want and could not fully imagine. What was the use in evacuating a city only to die from exposure or radiation? What, they asked, was the point of digging a shelter when the world above it would be poisoned for generations? The government's CD offerings were never substantial enough to answer these questions, let alone dispel the public's fears, and so the call of CD officials for citizens to take on responsibility for their own defence went largely unanswered.

Canadians only turned their attention to preparedness during the most pronounced periods of international crisis. CD experienced a great expansion during the Korean War largely because of the public's concern that this conflict could spiral out of control, but interest in CD contracted sharply after the war ended peacefully. This pattern repeated itself again following the launch of *Sputnik* in 1957, intensified during the Berlin crises in 1958 and 1961, and built to its peak when war appeared certain over Cuba. However scorned CD might have been by the media and ideological opponents, the public was aware that it could fill a need for information and direction. The need, however, was seldom felt.

Notes

Introduction

1 "Civil Defence Heads Confer on Mock A-Attack," *Ottawa Evening Citizen,* 21 April 1952, 1.

2 T.H. Marshall, an early scholar of citizenship theory, argues in his well-known 1950 essay about citizenship and social class that the individual citizen takes an active part as a contributor to the civic order of which he or she is a part. As quoted in George Armstrong Kelly, "Who Needs a Theory of Citizenship?" in Ronald Beiner, ed., *Theorizing Citizenship* (Albany, NY: State University of New York, 1995), 95-96.

3 Canadian Citizenship Act, R.S.C. 1985, c. C-29.

4 Robert Bothwell, Ian Drummond, and John English, *Canada since 1945: Power, Politics, and Provincialism* (Toronto: University of Toronto Press, 1981), 91-101, 161-64.

5 Dominique Marshall, *The Social Origins of the Welfare State: Québec Families, Compulsory Education, and Family Allowances, 1940-1955,* translated by Nicola Doone Danby (Waterloo, ON: Wilfrid Laurier University Press, 2006), x-xvi.

6 Michael Ignatieff, "The Myth of Citizenship," in Beiner, *Theorizing Citizenship,* 67, 75.

7 Jonathan Vance, *A History of Canadian Culture* (Don Mills, ON: Oxford University Press, 2009), 357-64; Jane Jenson and Susan D. Phillips, "Regime Shift: New Citizenship Practices in Canada," *International Journal of Canadian Studies* 14 (Fall 1996): 115-16.

8 Jane Jenson, "Fated to Live in Interesting Times: Canada's Changing Citizenship Regimes," *Canadian Journal of Political Science* 4 (December 1997): 630.

9 D. Peter Macleod, *Northern Armageddon: The Battle of the Plains of Abraham* (Vancouver: Douglas and McIntyre, 2008), 89, 91-92.

10 J.L. Granatstein, *Canada's Army: Waging War and Keeping the Peace* (Toronto: University of Toronto Press, 2002), 3-6; James Wood, *Militia Myths: Ideas of the Canadian Soldier* (Vancouver: UBC Press, 2010), 10-13.

11 See the chapter "War and Citizenship, 1914-1917," in Wood, *Militia Myths,* 210-40.

12 As T.H. Marshall wrote, "if citizenship is invoked in the defence of rights, the corresponding duties of citizenship cannot be ignored. These do not require a man to sacrifice his individual liberty or to submit without question to every demand made by government." T.H. Marshall, *Citizenship and Social Class and Other Essays* (Cambridge: Cambridge University Press, 1950), 70.

13 Costia Nikitiuk, "Emergency and Organizational Legitimacy: The Dilemma of Emergency Planning in B.C.," *BC Studies* 38 (1978): 47-64; Marijan Salopek, "Western Canadians and Civil Defence: The Korean War Years, 1950-1953," *Prairie Forum* 14 (1989): 75-88; Sean Maloney, "Dr. Strangelove Visits Canada: Projects RUSTIC, EASE, and BRIDGE, 1958-1963," *Canadian Military History* 6, 1 (1997): 42-56; Bill Manning, "Beyond the Diefenbunker: Canada's Forgotten Little Bunkers," *Material History Review* 57 (Spring 2003): 79-92. Unpublished work includes: Steven Lee, "Power, Politics, and the Cold War: The Canadian Civil Defence Program and the North Atlantic Alliance 1945-1959" (MA thesis, Department of History, McGill University, Montreal, 1987); Anne Fisher, "Civil Defence in Canada 1939-1965: Garnering Support for War and Nuclear Weapons through the Myth of Protection" (MA thesis, Department of History, Lakehead University, Thunder Bay,

1999); Jennifer Hunter, "'Is it even worthwhile doing the dishes?': Canadians and the Nuclear Threat, 1945-1963" (PhD diss., Department of History, McGill University, Montreal, 2004), 315; André Lamalice, "En temps de guerre comme en temps de paix, gouvernement marquant, gouvernance marquée : la protection civile au Canada, 1938-1988" (PhD diss., Department of History, University of Ottawa, 2011).

14 David McConnell, *Plan for tomorrow ... Today! The Story of Emergency Preparedness Canada 1948-1998* (Ottawa: Heritage Research Associates, 1998), http://www.diefenbunker.ca.

15 The US Atomic Energy Commission (AEC), in consultation with the United States military, did censor the effects of fallout and fought to keep nuclear weapons' effects secret out of national security concerns and a fear of unnecessarily (and inconveniently) alarming the public. For example, AEC Chairman Lewis Strauss's decision to censor the effects of fallout that resulted from the BRAVO test remains controversial, and American disarmament and test ban advocates garnered much credibility in the late 1950s and early 1960s when they revealed flaws in the published findings of the AEC. Barton C. Hacker, "Radiation Safety, the AEC, and Nuclear Weapons Testing," *Public Historian* 14, 1 (Winter 1992): 49-52.

16 Michael J. Carey, "The Schools and Civil Defense: The Fifties Revisited," *Teachers College Record* 84 (Fall 1982): 122: "Extreme emotionalism could be the result of too much talk about the bomb. It was far better to give the American people Ike's pleasant and reassuring smile."

17 J.L. Granatstein and R.D. Cuff, "Looking Back at the Cold War: 1945-1954," *Canadian Forum* 52 (July-August 1972): 9.

18 Paul Boyer, *By the Bomb's Early Light: American Thought and Culture at the Dawn of the Atomic Age* (New York: Pantheon, 1985).

19 Ibid., xviii.

20 Ibid., 70.

21 Ibid., 333.

22 William F. Vandercook, "Making the Very Best of the Very Worst: The 'Human Effects of Nuclear Weapons' Report of 1956," *International Security* 11 (1986): 184. Guy Oakes, *The Imaginary War: Civil Defence and American Cold War Culture* (Oxford: Oxford University Press, 1994), 8-9.

23 Andrew Grossman, *Neither Dead nor Red: Civilian Defense and American Political Development during the Early Cold War* (New York: Routledge, 2001), xii. See also Stephen Whitfield, *The Culture of the Cold War* (Baltimore, MD: Johns Hopkins University Press, 1991), and Michael Hogan, *A Cross of Iron: Harry Truman and the National Security State* (Cambridge: Cambridge University Press, 2000). A Canadian equivalent to this study, though focused far more on the levers of government and policing than on the ephemera of culture, is Reg Whitaker and Gary Marcuse's *Cold War Canada: The Making of a National Insecurity State, 1945-1957* (Toronto: University of Toronto Press, 1994).

24 Laura McEnany, *Civil Defence Begins at Home: Militarization Meets Everyday Life in the Fifties* (Princeton, NJ: Princeton University Press, 2000). Other authors, such as Kenneth Rose in *One Nation Underground* (New York: New York University Press, 2004), have attempted to understand why certain programs, such as the shelter program, failed or succeeded. His work pointed to cultural influences in fiction and popular writing.

25 McEnany, *Civil Defence Begins at Home,* 5.

26 Ibid., 37.

Chapter 1: From World War to Cold War, 1945-50

1 William Lyon Mackenzie King Diary, 18 September 1939, 4-5, Library and Archives Canada (LAC), William Lyon Mackenzie King Fonds MG26 J13, http://www.collectionscanada.gc.ca/databases/king/001059-100.01-e.php?PHPSESSID=s79aiaqmp1hm9cjpnqilvpsse4.

2 Conference of District Officers, Commanding and Representatives of General Officers, Commanding-in-Chief and Chief of General Staff, 15 March 1942, LAC RG 24 C-1, Reel C-5283, File 8880-1.

3 Terence O'Brien, *Civil Defence* (London: Her Majesty's Stationery Office, 1955), 120-21, 292-317, 379-420.

4 William Richard Feasby, *Official History of the Canadian Medical Services, 1939-1945* (Ottawa: Department of National Defence, 1953), 513.

5 Privy Council Order 3962, 2 June 1941, LAC RG 24 C-1, Reel C-5283, File 8880-7.

6 Dr. W.L. Gliddon, Air Raid Precautions officer, to Colonel R.D. Gibson, 4 September 1941, LAC RG 24 C-1, Reel C-5283, File 8880-7.

7 Serge Durflinger, *Fighting from Home* (Vancouver: UBC Press, 2006), 80-81.

8 Canadian Bank of Commerce, *War Service Records, 1939-1945* (Toronto: Rous and Mann Press, 1947), 308-11.

9 F. Maclure Solanders to W.L. Mackenzie King, 31 January 1942, LAC RG 24 C-1, Reel C-5283, File 8880-7.

10 Premier W. Aberhart to W.L. Mackenzie King, 16 April 1942, LAC RG 24 C-1, Reel C-5283, File 8880-9.

11 George Brown to Alan K. Hay, 22 December 1941, and ACGS to the Directorate of Military Operations and Planning, 8 January 1952, LAC RG 24 C-1, Reel C-5283, File 8880-3.

12 Durflinger, *Fighting from Home*, 84.

13 Jeff Keshen, *Saints, Sinners, and Soldiers: Canada's Second World War* (Vancouver: UBC Press, 2004), 36.

14 Durflinger, *Fighting from Home*, 85; Keshen, *Saints, Sinners, and Soldiers*, 37.

15 It should be noted that even military stations along the St. Lawrence regularly violated blackout and dimout regulations during the war, even when German submarines operated in the gulf and the river. See Report HQS 0113-4 – Road Blocks – St. Lawrence Dimout, 12 March 1945, LAC RG 24 C-1, Reel C-5283, File 8880-5.

16 British Columbia Air Raid Precautions Advisory Council Pamphlet, 10 October 1943, LAC RG 24 C-1, Reel C-5283, File 8880-9.

17 Memorandum: Air Raid Precautions Federal District Area, 5 March 1943, LAC RG 24 C-1, Reel C-5283, File 8880-3.

18 In Verdun, Chief Warden Charles H. Barr, a Liberal Party organizer, "admitted as early as October 1941 that his organization's primary mission was to foster a 'win the war' attitude among the population." Durflinger, *Fighting from Home*, 87.

19 W.C. Mainwaring to I. Mackenzie, 24 August 1943, LAC RG 24 C-1, Reel C-5283, File 8880-3.

20 Chief of the General Staff to I. Mackenzie, 3 September 1943, LAC RG 24 C-1, Reel C-5283, File 8880-9.

21 Minutes of Joint Planning Sub-Committee of the Chiefs of Staff Committee, 5 October 1943, LAC RG 24 C-1, Reel C-5283, File 8880-9.

22 Minutes of the Meeting of the Joint Planning Sub-Committee of the Chiefs of Staff Committee, 3 October 1944; Cabinet War Committee Meeting, 5 October 1944, LAC RG 24 C-1, Reel C-5283, File 8880-9.

23 Brigadier-General A. Ross to I. Mackenzie, 25 January 1945, LAC RG 24 C-1, Reel C-5283, File 8880-9.

24 Editorial, *The Post: Official Organ of the Civil Defence Guild of British Columbia* 1, 2 (October 1945): 1.

25 William Lyon Mackenzie King Diary, 3 August 1945.

26 J.L. Granatstein, *Canada's Army: Waging War and Keeping the Peace* (Toronto: University of Toronto Press, 2004), 316.

27 James Eayrs, *In Defence of Canada: Growing Up Allied* (Toronto: University of Toronto Press, 1980), 7.

28 John Hersey, *Hiroshima* (New York: A.A. Knopf, 1946), 94-95.

29 David Bradley, *No Place to Hide* (Boston: Little, Brown, 1948), 165.

30 Granatstein, *Canada's Army,* 317.

31 *House of Commons Debates,* Second Session, Twentieth Parliament, Volume V (19 August 1946), 5059 (Douglas Abbott).

32 Ibid., 5057 (Henry Archibald). The Einstein article contended that "rifle Bullets kill men, but atomic bombs kill cities. A tank is a defence against a bullet but there is no defence in science against the weapon which can destroy civilization." *New York Times,* 23 June 1946.

33 During debates over amendments to the National Defence Act, in February 1947, Minister of Defence Brooke Claxton responded to a question about civil defence with a promise that "we have that in mind," but offered no concrete proposals about how defence would be organized. *House of Commons Debates,* Third Session – Twentieth Parliament, Volume I (17 February 1947), 521 (Brooke Claxton).

34 Chiefs of Staff Committee Meeting no. 384, 21 March 1947, LAC RG 24, Vol. 5256, File 22-7-1, pt 1.

35 Douglas Bland, *Canada's National Defence,* volume 1 (Kingston, ON: School of Policy Studies, Queen's University, 1997), 3.

36 *House of Commons Debates,* Third Session, Twentieth Parliament, Volume VI (9 July 1947), 5272 (Brooke Claxton).

37 Ibid., 5299.

38 Defence Research Board Meeting no. 4, 16 September 1947, LAC RG 24, Vol. 5256, File 22-7-1, pt 1.

39 Defence Research Board Meeting no. 5, 15 December 1947, LAC RG 24, Vol. 5256, File 22-7-1, pt 1.

40 Ibid.

41 Wallace Goforth, "If Atomic War Comes," *Maclean's,* 15 October 1947, 9.

42 Ibid., 66.

43 Ibid., 71.

44 Cabinet Document D177: Civil Defence Planning, 22 April 1948, LAC RG 24, Vol. 5256, File 22-7-1, pt 1. An earlier draft was much more aggressive in its wording of the threat: "No aggressor can hope to dominate the world unless he has knocked out the productive capacity of the North American continent."

45 Ibid.

46 Ibid.

47 Whitney Lackenbauer, "Guerrillas in Our Midst: The Pacific Coast Militia Rangers, 1942-1945," *BC Studies* 155 (Autumn 2007): 61.

48 Biographical Notes: Major-General F.F. Worthington, CB, MC, MM, CD, LAC RG 32, Vol. 853, File Worthington, F.F.

49 "Civil Defence Head Is Named," *Montreal Gazette,* 20 October 1948, clipping in file, LAC RG 25, Vol. 5492, File 50217-40, pt. 1.

50 "Modest First Move in Civil Defence," *Montreal Gazette,* 20 October 1948; "Just a Precaution," *St. John's Daily News,* 22 October 1948.

51 F.F. Worthington Diary, 22 November 1949, Directorate of History and Heritage (DHH) 112.3S4 (D29), pt 1.

52 B. Claxton to Premier J.W. Jones, Prince Edward Island, 21 March 1950, LAC RG 29, Vol. 693, File 110-1-1.

53 F.F. Worthington to B. Claxton, 4 December 1948, LAC RG 29, Vol. 698, File 110-3-1.

54 Report on Initial Civil Defence Discussions with Honourable L.E. Blackwell, attorney general of Ontario, 6 December 1948, LAC RG 29, Vol. 700, File 110-5-1.

55 Report on Initial Civil Defence Discussions with the Premier of Alberta, 20 December 1948, LAC RG 29, Vol. 706, File 110-8-1, pt 1.

56 Report on Initial Civil Defence Discussions with the Premier of Quebec, 29 November 1948, LAC RG 29, Vol. 698, File 110-4-1, pt 1.

57 F.F. Worthington Diary, 23 November 1949, pt 1.

58 F.F. Worthington to B. Claxton, 20 January 1950, DHH 112.3S4 (D29), pt 2.

59 Report on Initial Civil Defence Discussions with the Honourable J.H. Sturdy, Minister of Reconstruction for the Province of Saskatchewan, 17 December 1948, LAC RG 29, Vol. 704, File 110-7-1, pt 1.

60 F.F. Worthington Diary, 22 November 1948, 6 December 1948, and 14 December 1948, pt 1.

61 Ibid., 13 January-16 February 1949.

62 F.F. Worthington to B. Claxton, 17 March 1949, LAC RG 29, Vol. 52, File 100-1-1, pt 1.

63 Ibid.

64 Ibid.

65 Ibid.

66 Ibid.

67 Phases of Civil Defence Organization, 29 March 1949, LAC RG 2, Series 18, Vol. 247, File D-100-C, 1946-49.

68 J.D.B. Smith, Cabinet Defence Committee, 31 March 1949, LAC RG 2, Series 18, Vol. 247, File D-100-C, 1946-49.

69 A.D.P. Heeney to B. Claxton, 8 April 1949, LAC RG 2, Series 18, Vol. 247, File D-100-C, 1946-49.

70 F.F. Worthington to N. Robertson, 21 June 1949, LAC RG 2, Series 18, Vol. 247, File D-100-C, 1946-49.

71 Minutes of the First Meeting of the Civil Defence Joint Sub-Committee of the War Book Committee, 8 September 1949, LAC MG 32 B12, Vol. 25, File 15.

72 F.F. Worthington Diary, 10 September 1949, DHH 112.3S4(D29), pt 2.

73 Paul Dickson, *A Thoroughly Canadian General: A Biography of General H.D.G. Crerar* (Toronto: University of Toronto Press, 2007), 309.

74 *House of Commons Debates,* Volume 88 (17 March 1949), excerpt found in LAC RG 25, Vol. 5942, File 50217-40, pt 1.

75 C.C. Mann to W.J. McCallum, 23 September 1949, LAC RG 29, Vol. 726, File 112-T1.

76 Roger Greene, "Soviets Had One Bomb: Can't Catch Us: U.S.," *Globe and Mail,* 24 September 1949, 1.

77 Second Meeting of the War Book Civil Defence Sub-Committee, 4 October 1949, Appendix G – Toronto and York County Civil Defence Committee, LAC RG 29, Vol. 726, File 112-T1.

78 Ibid.

79 F.F. Worthington Diary, 13 October 1949, DHH 112.3S4(D29), pt 2.

80 Richard Goette, "Canada, the United States, and the Air Defence of Sault Ste. Marie Canal during the Second World War" (unpublished paper presented at the twenty-first Military History Colloquium, Waterloo, Ontario, 30 April 2010).

81 Report no. 53: Vancouver Civil Defence Plan, 26 October 1949, LAC RG 29, Vol. 707, File 110-9-1, pt 1; F.F. Worthington to C. Thompson, 28 November 1949, LAC RG 29, Vol. 707, File 110-9-1, pt 1.

82 F.F. Worthington to the Members of the Civil Defence Planning Committee, 17 October 1949, LAC RG 2, Series 18, Vol. 247, File D-100-C, 1946-49.

83 CSC 5-1-2: Memorandum for the Sub-Committee on Civil Defence to J.D.B. Smith, 20 October 1949, LAC RG 2, Series 18, Vol. 247, File D-100-C, 1946-49.

84 E.W.T. Gill to N. Robertson, 20 October 1949, LAC RG 2, Series 18, Vol. 247, File D-100-C, 1946-49.

85 F.F. Worthington to B. Claxton, 9 November 1949, LAC RG 25, Vol. 5942, File 50217-40, pt 1.

86 Ibid.

87 Ibid.

88 B. Claxton to Cabinet Defence Committee, 21 November 1949, LAC RG 25, Vol. 5942, File 50217-40, pt 1.

89 The deputy minister of health, G.D.W. Cameron, was reportedly "peeved" with Worthington's intrusions into the hospital planning field. F.F. Worthington Diary, 15 January 1950, DHH 112.3S4(D29), pt 2.

90 F.F. Worthington Diary, 9 March 1950.

91 Ibid.

92 Ibid.

93 Record of Decision – Civil Defence, 31 July 1950, LAC RG 29, Vol. 722, File 112-F1, pt 1.

94 Minutes of the Sixth Meeting of the Civil Defence Planning Committee, 16 March 1950, LAC RG 29, Vol. 718, File 112-C8.

95 F.F. Worthington Diary, 9 March 1950, pt 2.

96 Robert Bothwell, "The Cold War and the Curate's Egg," *International Journal* 53 (Summer 1998): 497-98. See also Robert Bothwell, *Alliance and Illusion: Canada and the World, 1945-1984* (Vancouver: UBC Press, 2007), 86-87.

Chapter 2: The Korean War and the Trouble with Civil Defence, 1950-53

1 J.L. Granatstein, *A Man of Influence: Norman A. Robertson and Canadian Statecraft 1929-1968* (Toronto: Deneau Publishers, 1981), 274; Robert Bothwell and William Kilborn, *C.D. Howe: A Biography* (Toronto: McClelland and Stewart, 1979), 253-54; Robert Bothwell, "The Cold War and the Curate's Egg: When Did Canada's Cold War Really Begin? Later than You Might Think," *International Journal* 53 (Summer 1998): 4.

2 *Civil Defence Manual no. 1: Organization for Civil Defence* (Ottawa: King's Printer, 1950).

3 C.E. Gerhardt to M.P. Cawdron, 24 January 1951, Library and Archives Canada (LAC) RG 29, Vol. 706, File 110-8-1, pt 1.

4 F.F. Worthington to A.B. DeWolfe, 4 October 1950, LAC RG 29, Vol. 696, File 110-2-1, pt 1.

5 Memorandum to Cabinet, 28 December 1950, cited in Bothwell, "The Cold War and the Curate's Egg," 412.

6 C.D. Howe, as quoted in Bothwell and Kilbourn, *C.D. Howe: A Biography,* 257.

7 Cabinet Conclusions, 28-29 December 1950, LAC RG 2, Vol. 2646, Reel T-2367.

8 Minutes of the Twelfth Meeting of Civil Defence Planning Committee, Appendix 'C' on the Summary of the Civil Defence Programme, 1951-52, 1952-53, 1953-54, 1954-55, LAC RG 24, Vol. 5256, File 22-7-1, pt 2.

9 The immediate rearmament costs in 1951 were $1.5 billion. Bothwell and Kilbourn, *C.D. Howe: A Biography,* 257. B. Claxton to Cabinet Defence Committee, 20 February 1951, LAC RG 2, Vol. 153, File D-100-C, pt 1.

10 David Bercuson, *True Patriot: The Life of Brooke Claxton, 1898-1960* (Toronto: University of Toronto Press, 1993), 210.

11 Seventy-First Meeting of Cabinet Defence Committee, 20 February 1951, LAC RG 25, Vol. 5942, File 50217-40, pt 2.1.

12 Dominion Provincial Conference on Civil Defence: Opening Statement by Honourable Brooke Claxton, Brooke Claxton Fonds, LAC MG 32 B5, Vol. 146, File "Dominion-Provincial Conference on Civil Defence 1951."

13 "Civil Defence," *The Listening Post* 10, 9 (November 1950): 1-2.

14 Civil Defence Annual Progress Report 1952, Paul Joseph Martin Fonds, LAC MG 32 B12, Vol. 26, File 17.

15 "L'Honorable Paul Martin est nommé Chef de la Défense Civile: Sept endroits susceptibles d'attaque atomique au Canada," *La Patrie,* 24 February 1951; "Ottawa Will Aid Civil Defences," *Halifax Chronicle Herald,* 24 February 1951; "Civil Defence Chieftain," *Windsor Daily Star,* 24 February 1951.

16 Statements Approved at a Meeting of the National Executive and Advisory Board and Presented to the Prime Minister and Members of the Federal Cabinet, 16 February 1951, LAC RG 29, Vol. 719, File 112-C18, pt 1.

17 "Civil Defense and Welfare," *Globe and Mail,* 28 February 1951, 6.

18 Paul Martin, *A Very Public Life: So Many Worlds* (Ottawa: Deneau, 1985), 146-47.

19 "Civil Defence," *The Listening Post* 10, 9 (November 1950): 2.

20 "Dominion's C.D. Policy 'Mystifies' All Ontario: Premier, Other leaders Would Like to Know If Ottawa Really Wants Precautions Taken," *Windsor Daily Star,* 28 February 1951.

21 Matthew Grant, *After the Bomb: Civil Defence and Nuclear War in Britain, 1945-1968* (New York: Palgrave Macmillan, 2010), 33-34.

22 P. Sauvé to P. Martin, 20 June 1951, LAC RG 29, Vol. 699, File 110-4-16, pt 1.

23 "House Passes Bill on Civil Defence," *Montreal Gazette,* 14 March 1951 [emphasis added].

24 F.F. Worthington to B. Claxton, Report no. 20/50: Visit of Civil Defence Coordinator to Manitoba, 27 November 1950, Directorate of History and Heritage (DHH) 112.3S4 (D29), pt 1.

25 A.C. Delaney to F.F. Worthington, 29 January 1951, LAC RG 29, Vol. 704, File 110-6-1, pt 1.

26 Local community groups began writing to the federal office soon after for guidance. Theo F. Cox, president of the Norwood Community Club, to F.F. Worthington, 20 July 1950, LAC RG 29, Vol. 704, File 110-6-1, pt 1.

27 A.C. Delaney, provincial civil defence co-ordinator, Manitoba, to F.F. Worthington, 29 January 1951, LAC RG 29, Vol. 704, File 110-6-1, pt 1.

28 Granatstein, *A Man of Influence,* 219; William Henry Pope, *Leading from the Front: The War Memoirs of Harry Pope* (Waterloo, ON: Laurier Centre for Military, Strategic and Disarmament Studies, 2002).

29 Matthew Penhale Diary, 12 July 1951, Matthew Howard Somers Penhale Fonds, LAC MG 31 B21, Vol. 9, File "Civil Defence – General – Record of Meetings and Emergency Personnel and Services."

30 The Role of the Boy Scouts Association in Civil Defence, 10 March 1951, and the Role of the Canadian Legion in Civil Defence, 7 December 1950, LAC RG 29, Vol. 676, File 108-3-3. See also *Civil Defence Manual no. 15: The Warden Service* (Ottawa: Queen's Printer, 1952), 17-19.

31 The Role of the Canadian Red Cross Society in Civil Defence, 26 January 1951, LAC RG 29, Vol. 676, File 108-3-3. For more information on the negotiations leading to this agreement, see Deanna Toxopeus, "1951 Agreement between the Red Cross and St. John Ambulance: Case Study of the Effect of Civil Defence on Canada's Health Care System" (MA thesis, Department of History, Carleton University, Ottawa, 1997).

32 The National Council of Jewish Women boasted over 4,700 members, many of whom had experience in the wartime Air-Raid Precautions organizations in Canada. Lucille Lorrie, president of the National Council of Jewish Women of Canada, to F.F. Worthington, 1 February 1951; Lyall Simpson, convenor of Citizenship and Community Service, to F.F. Worthington, 12 February 1951; A.C. Stirrett, grand secretary of the International Order of Odd Fellows, to N.J.M. Lockhart, grand treasurer, 9 April 1951, all contained in LAC RG 29, Vol. 676, File 108-3-3.

33 L.D. McPhail to P. Martin, 9 April 1951, LAC RG 29, Vol. 676, File 108-3-3.

34 Doug Smith, *Joe Zuken: Citizen and Socialist* (Toronto: James Lorimer, 1990), 126-27.

35 Ibid., 146.

36 P. Martin to C. Livingston, 21 March 1951, LAC RG 29, Vol. 676, File 108-3-3.

37 Matthew Penhale Diary, 18 July 1951.

38 Ibid., 1 August 1951.

39 Ibid., 22 August 1951.

40 Ibid., 19 September 1951.

41 "Speed Up Civil Defence or Kill It – Worthington," *Toronto Star,* 29 August 1951.

42 Larry Worthington, *"Worthy": A Biography of Major-General F.F. Worthington* (Toronto: Macmillan, 1961), 227-28.

43 Worthington also noted, with some amusement, that "press coverage was something terrific!!!" F.F. Worthington Diary, 29 August 1951, DHH 112.3S4(D29), pt. 2.

44 Martin, *A Very Public Life,* 146.

45 Editorial, *Montreal Herald,* 4 September 1951.

46 "Winnipeg Civil Defence 'Magnificent' Says Worthington," *Winnipeg Free Press,* 15 September 1951.

47 *Civil Defence Bulletin* (October 1951): 10.

48 "CD Volunteers Top 1500," *Winnipeg Free Press,* 22 September 1951.

49 Ibid.

50 Minutes of Meeting of the Advisory Committee, 5 September 1951, Matthew Howard Somers Penhale Fonds, LAC MG 31 G21, Vol. 9, File "Civil Defence – General – Record of Meetings." See also *Frank. R. Bigley, 1916-85,* http://www.gov.mb.ca/chc/archives/hbca/biographical/w/walker_frank_bigley_b1916.pdf.

51 "Aid Defence, Rotary Asked," *Windsor Daily Star,* 21 September 1951.

52 Howard Sykes, chairman of the Civil Defence Committee, Notre-Dame-de-Grâce, to F.F. Worthington, 19 January 1951, LAC RG 29, Vol. 698, File 110-4-1, pt 1.

53 F.F. Worthington to P. Martin, 9 March 1951, LAC RG 29, Vol. 698, File 110-4-1, pt 1.

54 F.F. Worthington to G.F. Davidson, 9 January 1952, LAC RG 29, Vol. 679, File 110-4-16, pt 1.

55 "City's $15 Million Defence 'Stuns' Ottawa's Planners," *Montreal Gazette,* 3 August 1951; "Montreal Defence Cost $363 Million," *Kitchener-Waterloo Record,* 3 August 1951.

56 "Ottawa Lag Blamed for Civil Defence Slow-Up," *Montreal Herald,* 12 July 1951.

57 G.F. Davidson to F.F. Worthington, 10 August 1951, LAC RG 29, Vol. 679, File 110-4-16, pt 1.

58 The Quebec government was no more willing to provide any expenditures for civil defence. P. Martin to P. Sauvé, 30 August 1951, LAC RG 29, Vol. 679, File 110-4-16, pt 1.

59 F.F. Worthington to G.F. Davidson, 9 January 1952, LAC RG 29, Vol. 679, File 110-4-16, pt 1.

60 R. Graham, city clerk in Stratford, Ontario, to L.S. St. Laurent, 16 July 1951, LAC RG 29, Vol. 700, File 110-5-1, pt 2.

61 "Let There Be No Misunderstanding," *Creston Review,* 1 November 1951.

62 "Civilian Defence Plans Complete," *London Free Press,* 5 November 1951.
63 "Council Says Ottawa 'Ducking Responsibilities in Civil Defence," *Windsor Star,* 7 November 1951.
64 Statements approved at a meeting of the National Executive and Advisory Board and presented to the prime ministers and members of the Federal Cabinet, 7 December 1951, LAC RG 29, Vol. 720, File 112 C18, pt 2.
65 Ibid.
66 Ibid.
67 J.H. Sturdy to P. Martin, 1 August 1951, LAC RG 29, Vol. 704, File 110-7-1, pt 1.
68 M. Penhale to R. Smith, 8 February 1952, Matthew Howard Somers Penhale Fonds, LAC MG 31 B21, Vol. 9, File "Civil Defence – General – Record of Meetings and Emergency Personnel Services."
69 Matthew Penhale Diary, 10 April 1952.
70 P. Martin to W.A. Matheson, 27 March 1952, LAC RG 29, Vol. 648, File 100-7-12, pt 1.
71 G.F. Davidson to F.F. Worthington, 5 April 1952, LAC RG 29, Vol. 648, File 100-7-12, pt 1.
72 F.F. Worthington to J.C. Jefferson and M.P. Cawdron, 19 November 1952, LAC RG 29, Vol. 648, File 100-7-12, pt 1.
73 J.F. Wallace to F.F. Worthington, 20 March 1953, LAC RG 29, Vol. 648, File 100-7-12, pt 1.
74 Ibid.
75 F.F. Worthington to Provincial Civil Defence Co-ordinators, 16 June 1953, LAC RG 29, Vol. 648, File 100-7-12, pt 1.
76 The states selected were Delaware, Vermont, Utah, New Mexico, North and South Dakota, New Hampshire, North Carolina, Arizona, Maine, Rhode Island, and Colorado. Only North Carolina did not meet or exceed the federal limits. Ibid.
77 F.F. Worthington to D. Wallace, 15 October 1953, LAC RG 29, Vol. 648, File 100-7-12, pt 1.
78 Report on the Federal/Provincial Conference, 28-29 April 1952, DHH 112.S9 (D29), pt 2.
79 Wing Commander Sir John Hodsoll, the director of Civil Defence for the Home Office in Britain, devoted an entire chapter to the matter on his retirement in the mid-1960s. He had been involved in one aspect or another of civil defence for nearly forty years. John Hodsoll, *Reflections on Civil Defence and Survival,* 1966, John Francis Wallace Fonds, LAC MG 30 E211, Vol. 4, File 14.
80 Granatstein, *A Man of Influence,* 330-32.
81 *British Columbia Civil Defence Circular no. 23,* 1 June 1953, LAC RG 29 Vol. 707, File 110-9-1, pt. 2.
82 *British Columbia Civil Defence Circular no. 25,* 1 December 1953, LAC RG 29 Vol. 708, File 110-9-1, pt. 3.
83 Meeting of Warden Committee, 23 January 1953, Matthew Howard Somers Penhale Fonds, LAC MG 31 B21, Vol. 9, File "Civil Defence – General – Record of Meetings and Emergency Personnel and Services," pt 2.
84 Ibid.
85 Jack Bumsted, "Flooding, Polio, and Nuclear Bombs: The Culture of Anxiety in Winnipeg in the Early Fifties," in Birk Sproxton, ed., *The Winnipeg Connection: Writing Lives at Mid-Century* (Winnipeg: Prairie Fire Press, 2006), 209.
86 K.L.P. Smithers to S. Denman, 12 November 1951, Paul Joseph Martin Fonds, LAC MG 32 B12, File 13.
87 Advisory Committee Meeting, 24 July 1953, Matthew Howard Somers Penhale Fonds, LAC MG 31 B21, Vol. 9, File "Civil Defence – General – Record of Meetings and Emergency Personnel and Services," pt 2.

Chapter 3: Publicizing Armageddon

1 Francisco Colom-Gonzalez, "Dimensions of Citizenship: Canada in Comparative Perspective," *International Journal of Canadian Studies* 14 (Fall/Autumn 1996): 95-109; James S. Frideres et al., "Becoming Canadian: Citizenship Acquisition and National Identity," *Canadian Review in Studies of Nationalism* 18 (1987): 105-21.
2 Desmond Morton, "Divided Loyalties? Divided Country?" in William Kaplan, ed., *Belonging: The Meaning and Future of Canadian Citizenship* (Montreal and Kingston: McGill-Queen's University Press, 1993), 50-51.
3 Ibid., 52-55.
4 Paul Martin, *A Very Public Life: So Many Worlds* (Ottawa: Deneau, 1985), 67.
5 Mildred A. Schwartz, "Citizenship in Canada and the United States," *Transactions of the Royal Society of Canada* 4, 14 (1986): 83.
6 A Basic Speech – Civil Defence, 14 February 1950 in Kingston, Library and Archives Canada (LAC) RG 29, Vol. 646, File 100-5-24, pt 1.
7 F.F. Worthington's speech to the Canadian Hospital Council, 29 May 1951, LAC RG 29, Vol. 646, File 100-5-24, pt 1.
8 Civil Defence Recruiting Week, speech in Winnipeg, 27 September 1951, LAC RG 29, Vol. 646, File 100-5-24, pt 1.
9 F.L. Houghton, Cabinet Defence Committee in Halifax, to J.F. Wallace, Information Services Division, 16 January 1951, LAC RG 29, Vol. 696, File 110-2-1, pt 1.
10 Ibid.
11 F.L. Houghton to W.J. McCallum, 18 October 1951, LAC RG 29, Vol. 696, File 110-2-1, pt 1.
12 P. Martin to Treasury Board, 9 August 1951, LAC RG 29, Vol. 56, File 100-5-1.
13 G.F. Davidson to F.F. Worthington, 29 March 1951, LAC RG 29, Vol. 726, File 112-J9.
14 Summary of Planning Discussion of Civil Defence Publicity – S. Denman and H.S. Robinson, 17 October 1951, LAC RG 29, Vol. 56, File 100-5-1.
15 Circular Letter X, "Public Relations," 30 October 1951, LAC RG 29, Vol. 56, File 100-5-1.
16 H.S. Robinson to A.D. Simmons, Canadian Exhibition Commission, 10 December 1951, LAC RG 29, Vol. 108, File 180-8-51; H.S. Robinson to K.B.F. Smith, 18 January 1952, LAC RG 29, Vol. 108, File 180-8-51.
17 T.C. Good, Canadian Government Exhibition Commission, to H.S. Robinson, 14 February 1952, LAC RG 29, Vol. 108, File 180-5-51.
18 *House of Commons Debates,* Fourth Session, Twenty-First Parliament, Volume III (11 May 1951), 2941 (Paul Martin). David Bercuson, *True Patriot: The Life of Brooke Claxton, 1898-1960* (Toronto: University of Toronto Press, 1993), 214-15.
19 G.F. Davidson to P. Martin, 16 October 1952, LAC RG 29, Vol. 108, File 180-8-55, pt 1.
20 Richard M. Fried, *The Russians Are Coming! The Russians Are Coming! Pageantry and Patriotism in Cold War America* (New York: Oxford University Press, 1998), 35.
21 Ibid., 432.
22 Ibid., 46. Robert Griffith, "The Selling of America: The Advertising Council and American Politics, 1942-60," *Business History Review* 57 (Autumn 1983): 398.
23 James M. Lindgren, "A Constant Incentive to Patriotic Citizenship: Historic Preservation in Progressive-Era Massachusetts," *New England Quarterly* 64 (December 1991): 597.
24 P. Martin to M. Caldwell, 3 July 1952, LAC RG 29, Vol. 56, File 100-5-13, pt 1.
25 E103612 – CTS 1951 No. 3, "Exchange of Notes Betweeen Canada and the United States of America Constituting an Agreement on Civil Defence Co-ordination, 27 March 1951." *Canada Treaty Information,* http://www.treaty-accord.gc.ca/text-texte.asp?id=103612.

26 Department of National Health and Welfare Press Release, 15 May 1952, LAC RG 29, Vol. 108, File 180-8-55.

27 "U.S. Mobile Civil Defence Unit to Help Alert Canadians of War," *Montreal Gazette*, 25 July 1952.

28 See Robert W. Rydell, *All the World's a Fair* (Chicago: University of Chicago Press, 1984), 184-89; Thomas Richards, *The Commodity Culture of Victorian England: Advertising and Spectacle, 1851-1914* (Stanford, CA: Standford University Press, 1990), 1-16; Keith Walden, *Becoming Modern in Toronto* (Toronto: University of Toronto Press, 1997), i-xvii; H.V. Nelles, *The Art of Nation-Building: Pageantry and Spectacle at Quebec's Tercentenary* (Toronto: University of Toronto Press, 1999), 12.

29 These were biological warfare, chemical warfare, incendiary attack, sabotage, and psychological warfare.

30 Images of these and other exhibits are found in the pamphlet *For Your Information: Canada's Civil Defence Convoy*, Paul Joseph Martin Fonds, LAC MG 32 B12, Vol. 25, File 21.

31 William C. Woodward, executive advisor to C.D. Howe during the war, wrote to a friend in Vancouver following an air raid on London: "The fire on Sunday night was something almost out of Dante's Inferno – so stupendous it was terrifying." W.C. Woodward to H. Darling, 3 January 1941, Canadian War Museum, George Metcalf Archival Collection, AL2008138.

32 Transcript of Narrative for "Destruction of City," [no date], LAC RG 29, Vol. 108, File 180-8-55, pt 1.

33 Bernard Brodie, *Strategy in the Missile Age* (Princeton, NJ: Princeton University Press, 1959), 296-99.

34 *For Your Information: Canada's Civil Defence Convoy*, Paul Joseph Martin Fonds, LAC MG 32 B12, Vol. 25, File 21.

35 Such editorials also offer interesting glimpses of the type of people who worked for the organization. Ray Smith, the author, lived in London during the Battle of Britain and the Blitz, and drew on his experience to stress how Calgary would fare in an attack. Ray Smith, "We're All in It," *Calgary Herald*, 9 October 1953.

36 "Jefferson Sees Improvement in Civil Defence Attitude," *Edmonton Journal*, 30 October 1953. See also the film *Operation Cue* (Federal Civil Defence Administration, Washington, DC, United States, 1955).

37 For instance, the pose struck by the female firefighter, grasping the hose daintily, was reminiscent of magazine advertisements for vacuum cleaners, in which housewives wearing aprons seemed to float behind their appliances. Valerie J. Korinek, *Roughing It in the Suburbs: Reading* Chatelaine Magazine *in the Fifties and Sixties* (Toronto: University of Toronto Press, 2000), 133.

38 55th Meeting of the Imperial Order Daughters of the Empire and Children of the Empire National Chapter Report, 1955, Imperial Order Daughters of the Empire Fonds, LAC MG 28 II7, Vol. 13, pt 1, 80-83.

39 *For Your Information: Canada's Civil Defence Convoy*, Paul Joseph Martin Fonds, LAC MG 32 B12, Vol. 25, File 21.

40 There are surprisingly few pictures of the civil defence convoy exhibits. As such, this "tour" was compiled by comparing a list of the exhibitions included in the convoy that was given to the Canadian government's Exhibition Commission in January 1953, with a later account by a journalist entitled "Defence Display Outstanding Show," *Saskatoon StarPhoenix*, 9 November 1953.

41 Fred Rowse: Field Officer's Interim Report on Initial Promotional Tour, 28 July 1953, LAC RG 29, Vol. 56, File 100-5-13, pt 2.

42 "Toronto Won't Pay $1,000: Convoy Not showing Here," *Toronto Daily Star,* 19 September 1953.

43 Donn Downey, "Mayor Gave City Sport, Planning," *Globe and Mail,* 24 November 1999, A26.

44 "Convoy Is a 'Pig in a Poke,' Mayor Tells Controllers," *Toronto Daily Star,* 1 October 1953.

45 "A Serious Matter," *Globe and Mail,* 25 September 1953. H. Adams to F.F. Worthington, 1 October 1953, LAC RG 29, Vol. 100-5-13, pt 6.

46 T.E.M. Smyth to F.F. Worthington, 21 August 1953, LAC RG 29, Vol. 57, File 100-5-13, pt 4; G.J. Monaghan to F.F. Worthington, 24 August 1953, LAC RG 29, Vol. 57, File 100-5-13, pt 4; C.A. Nesbitt to F.F. Worthington, 26 August 1953, LAC RG 29, Vol. 57, File 100-5-13, pt 4.

47 "Exposition au manège militaire," *Le Devoir,* 19 September 1953; "Canadian Civil Defence Convoy Due Here Saturday for Premiere," *Montreal Gazette,* 17 September 1953; D. Wallace to Civil Defence Directors in Halifax, Vancouver, Calgary, Edmonton, Regina, Saskatoon, Winnipeg, Windsor, Saint John, 22 September 1953, LAC RG 29, Vol. 57, File 100-5-13, pt 5.

48 "Canada's Mobile Civil Defence Show Opens Tomorrow Afternoon," *Evening Times-Globe,* 9 December 1953; "Street Parade to Open Civil Defence Show," *Halifax Chronicle Herald,* 3 December 1953.

49 M.H.S. Penhale to H. Adams, 24 September 1953, LAC RG 29, Vol. 57, File 100-5-13, pt 5.

50 H. Adams to F.F. Worthington, 15 October 1953, LAC RG 29, Vol. 57, File 100-5-13, pt 6; D.J. Fusedale to J.O. Probe, 12 November 1953, LAC RG 29, Vol. 57, File 100-5-13, pt 7.

51 "10-Car Civil Defence Convoy to Visit City in October," *Edmonton Journal,* 14 September 1953; "St. John Brigade to Give Displays," *Halifax Chronicle Herald,* 2 December 1953; "Thousands View Elaborate Display On Civil Defence," *Evening Times-Globe,* 11 December 1953.

52 "Jobs for All – Theme of Civil Defence Show," *Halifax Chronicle Herald,* 2 December 1953.

53 F.F. Worthington to General C.S. Stein, provincial co-ordinator for civil defence, British Columbia, 31 August 1953, LAC RG 29, Vol. 56, File 100-5-13, pt 5.

54 W.A. Croteau to F.F. Worthington, 14 August 1953, LAC RG 29, Vol. 56, File 100-5-13, pt 3.

55 G.O. Bell, director of Calgary's civil defence, to F.F. Worthington, 13 August 1953, LAC RG 29, Vol. 56, File 100-5-13, pt 3.

56 Korinek argues convincingly that such advertisements did not reflect reality but, rather, acted as a distorting mirror, depicting a comfortable world of middle-class consumers. Korinek, *Roughing It in the Suburbs,* 122.

57 Walden, *Becoming Modern in Toronto,* 37-39; Tony Bennett, *The Birth of the Museum: History, Theory, Politics* (New York: Routledge, 1995), 95.

58 "Canadian Civil Defence Convoy Due Here Saturday for Premiere," *Montreal Gazette,* 17 September 1953, 10.

59 Federal Civil Defense Administration (FCDA), Public Affairs Office, *Practical, Tested Suggestions for Your Local Promotion of the "Alert America" Convoy,* March 1952, LAC RG 29, Vol. 108, File 180-8-55, pt 1, 3-4.

60 Walden, *Becoming Modern in Toronto,* 192-93.

61 Bennett, *The Birth of the Museum,* 99, 101-2.

62 FCDA, *Practical, Tested Suggestions for Your Local Promotion of the "Alert America" Convoy,* 4.

63 Telegram: Harvey Adams to Worthington, 15 October 1953, LAC RG 29, Vol. 57, File 100-5-13, pt 6.

64 Executives advised the government on industrial plant protection and often sat in on policy committees dealing with transportation and communication. F.F. Worthington, "Civil Defence and Industry," *Industrial Canada* 53, 6 (July 1951): 165-68.

65 Ibid.; "Mobile Disaster Service Organized by John Labatt Limited," *Industrial Canada* 53, 6 (September 1951): 92-94.

66 Paul Henderson to Guy Dorval, 20 November 1952, LAC RG 29, Vol. 104, File 180-8-11.

67 F.W. Davies, Trailmobile Canada to J. Magee, Canadian Automobile Transportation Association, 3 October 1952, LAC RG 29, Vol. 108, File 180-8-55, pt 1.

68 *Halifax Chronicle Herald,* 3 December 1953, 13.

69 Ibid., 15.

70 In Vancouver, 10,000 stickers were pasted on laundry deliveries throughout the city, and the Coca-Cola plant included 500 counter cards in deliveries to its customers for display. E. Stead, public relations officer in Vancouver, to D. Wallace, 29 October 1953, LAC RG 29, Vol. 108, File 180-8-55, pt 2.

71 "Civil Defence Seen Permanent," *Edmonton Journal,* 30 October 1953.

72 "Civil Defence Has Added 3D to Citizenship – Martin," *Ottawa Evening Journal,* 26 November 1953, clipping in Paul Joseph Martin Fonds, LAC MG 32 B12, File "Civil Defence, September-December 1953."

73 Of these visitors, 525 were reported as enrolled in Edmonton and 400 in Vancouver. H. Davidson, civil defence director, Edmonton, to F.F. Worthington, 4 November 1953, LAC RG 29, Vol. 57, File 100-5-13, pt 7; Air Vice-Marshal F.V. Heakes, "The On Guard Canada Exhibit in Vancouver, B.C.," *British Columbia Civil Defence Circular* no. 25, December 1953.

74 H. Adams to D. Wallace, 17 October 1954, LAC RG 29, Vol. 108, File 180-8-55, pt 2; Draft Letter to N.R. Crump, vice president, Canadian Pacific Railways, to S.F. Dingle, vice president of Canadian National Railways, 20 January 1954, LAC RG 29, Vol. 105, File 180-8-19.

75 W.A. Croteau to F.F. Worthington, 14 August 1953, LAC RG 29, Vol. 57, File 100-5-13, pt 4; J.O. Probe to F.F. Worthington, 15 January 1954, LAC RG 29, Vol. 57, File 100-5-13, pt 8.

76 F.F. Worthington to H. Adams, 26 January 1954, LAC RG 29, Vol. 105, File 180-8-19.

77 G. Dorval to M. Berger, editor, *C-I-L Oval,* 19 March 1953, LAC RG 29, Vol. 104, File 180-8-10, pt 1.

78 B.M. Erb to H. Adams, 12 April 1954, LAC RG 29, Vol. 102, File 180-8-1.

79 M.F. Cheetham to G. Graham, 16 January 1956, LAC RG 29, Vol. 104, File 180-8-10, pt 2.

80 The Canadian War Museum holds a number of the posters in this series. See the accession lot numbered CWM 20040030 for the complete holding.

Chapter 4: Evacuation and Celebration, 1954-56

1 Lester B. Pearson, as quoted by James Eayrs, *In Defence of Canada: Growing Up Allied* (Toronto: University of Toronto Press, 1980), 265-66.

2 This was the first report of the Technological Capability Panel of Eisenhower's Science Advisory Panel, *Meeting the Threat of Surprise Attack,* issued on 14 February 1955. The panel concluded that US space presence and military satellites would help to meet the threat posed by missiles and bombers alike, advancing the space race. Report quoted in John Lewis Gaddis, *We Now Know: Rethinking Cold War History* (Oxford: Oxford University Press, 1997), 231-32.

3 N.A. Vlasov, as quoted in John Lewis Gaddis, *The Cold War: A New History* (New York: Penguin Books, 2005), 68.

4 British defence authorities argued in their 1954 White Paper that such preparations would be sufficient to permit the armed forces to fight a "broken-backed" war against the enemy in the field, while civil society worked to rebuild and recover. The definition disappeared from the 1955 paper as a result of revelations concerning the hydrogen bomb. Bernard

Brodie, *Strategy in the Missile Age* (Princeton, NJ: Princeton University Press, 1959), 160-61. For an analysis of the British response to the hydrogen bomb in civil defence planning, see Matthew Grant, *After the Bomb: Civil Defence and Nuclear War in Britain, 1945-1968* (London: Palgrave Macmillan, 2010), 77-98.

5   A Canadian army training manual about the influence of nuclear weapons on battlefield tactics asserted, for instance, that "nuclear weapons may now be considered as part of the normal armaments of the major powers." *Canadian Army Manual of Training: Notes on the Influence of Nuclear Weapons on Tactics (Provisional)* (Ottawa: Queen's Printer, 1956), 1. As Andrew Richter concludes in his study of the formulation of Canadian military strategy during the Cold War, the Department of External Affairs (DEA) never accepted this military argument. Pearson and others had held since early on in the Korean conflict that the atomic bomb was simply too terrible a weapon ever to be used casually by the superpowers. This view informed the DEA's early acceptance of deterrence as a credible nuclear strategy. Civil Defence Canada, tasked with planning for contingencies if deterrence failed, largely followed the American Federal Civil Defense Administration's "atomic weapon as conventional weapon" approach until the hydrogen bomb forced reconsideration of the matter. Andrew Richter, *Avoiding Armageddon: Canadian Military Strategy and Nuclear Weapons, 1950-1963* (Vancouver: UBC Press, 2002), 61.

6   "Moscow Wants H-Bomb Ban; Pearson Warns of Red Trap," *Winnipeg Free Press*, 2 April 1954.

7   "Pearson Voices Anxiety," *Ottawa Citizen*, 1 April 1954.

8   "In the Driver's Seat!" *Halifax Chronicle Herald*, 5 April 1954, 1.

9   "Misère j'ai oublié de prendre un billet de retour!" *La Presse*, 4 April 1954.

10 *Civil Defence Circular*, Library and Archives Canada (LAC) RG 29, Vol. 708, File 110-9-1, pt 3.

11 "Sacrifice Part to Save All," *Victoria Daily Times*, 18 March 1954.

12 Training and Operational Circular no. 1/54, 6 January 1954, LAC RG 20, Vol. 964, File 7-1200-2. Over a year later, a similar poem appeared in British Columbia's circular: "Here in peace lies Gloria Trent/Twenty-four hours on pleasure bent/Running around helter-skelter/Might have survived in an air raid shelter."

13 F.F. Worthington to G.F. Davidson, 8 October 1954, LAC RG 29, Vol. 708, File 110-9-1, pt 3.

14 F.F. Worthington to G.F. Davidson, 7 February 1955, LAC RG 29, Vol. 698, File 110-4-1, pt 2.

15 In his note to Davidson, Worthington argued that this assertion gave the city council some pause. Ibid.

16 "Cities and the Bomb," *The Economist*, 5 June 1954, clipping found in Paul Joseph Martin Fonds, LAC MG 32 B12, Vol. 25, File 1 "Civil Defence – H. Bomb."

17 Matthew Grant, *After the Bomb: Civil Defence and Nuclear War in Britain, 1945-68* (London: Palgrave Macmillan, 2010), 78-80.

18 Most of the necessary revisions pertained to Part 3 of the Defence of Canada Regulations, which regulated Public Safety and Order. Judge Advocate General to Chiefs of Staff Committee, 29 December 1952, LAC RG 25, Vol. 5943, File 50217-40, pt 3.1.

19 537th Meeting of the Chiefs of Staff Committee, 26 March 1953, LAC RG 25, Vol. 5943, File 50217-40, pt 3.1.

20 548th Meeting of the Chiefs of Staff Committee, 9 November 1953, LAC RG 25, Vol. 5943, File 50217-40, pt 3.2.

21 Assistance of the Armed Forces in Civil Defence, CSC 5-11-11, LAC RG 25, Vol. 5943, File 50217-40, pt 3.2.

22 Chiefs of Staff Committee Meeting, 15 January 1954, LAC RG 25, Vol. 5943, File 50217-40, pt 3.2.

23 Assistance of the Armed Forces in Civil Defence, 11 March 1954, LAC RG 29, Vol. 654, File C-102-3-2B.

24 559th Meeting of the Chiefs of Staff Committee, 12 March 1954, LAC RG 29, Vol. 654, File S-102-3-2A.

25 G.F. Davidson to P. Martin, 8 February 1954, LAC RG 29, Vol. 722, File 112-F1, pt 2. On Davidson's ability to defuse Martin's occasional tirades, see Knowlton Nash, *The Microphone Wars* (Toronto: McClelland and Stewart, 1994), 378.

26 F.F. Worthington to G.F. Davidson, 8 February 1954, LAC RG 29, Vol. 722, File 112-F1, pt 2.

27 F.F. Worthington to M.P. Cawdron, 16 March 1954, LAC RG 29, Vol. 722, File 112-F1, pt 2.

28 Notes for Monday, 29 March 1954, LAC RG 29, Vol. 722, File 112-F1, pt 2 [emphasis in original].

29 Arthur Blakely, "Obsolete," *Montreal Gazette,* 31 March 1954.

30 The editorial cartoon in the *Globe and Mail* following the conference depicted a jittery Canadian shaking in his armchair by the radio, surrounded by headlines *(H-Bomb Fired, Island Vanishes).* The radio announcement: "Flash! The last explosion is reported to have *moved* the Hon. Paul Martin to remark on civil defence" is greeted with a desperate "Oh! No!" poking fun at both atomic anxiety in general and Martin's reclusive profile on the subject of civil defence in particular. Editorial, *Globe and Mail,* 5 April 1954.

31 Civil Defence Meeting, 28 April 1954, and First Meeting of the Ad Hoc Committee to Study the Effects of the Hydrogen Bomb in CD Planning, 12 May 1954, LAC RG 29, Vol. 711, File 112-1-5.

32 G.F. Davidson to M. Penhale, 3 May 1954, LAC RG 29, Vol. 711, File 112-1-5.

33 Appendix B, First Meeting of the Civil Defence Advisory Committee of Social Scientists, 8-9 November 1954, Directorate of History and Heritage (DHH) 112.3S4 (D29), pt. 7.

34 Meeting with Dr. Line and Dr. Morton, 18 March 1949, LAC RG 29, Vol. 87, File 108-1-8.

35 J.S. Tyhurst, "Individual Reactions to Community Disaster: The Natural History of Psychiatric Phenomena," *American Journal of Psychiatry* 107 (April 1951): 764-69.

36 Unsigned letter to Dr. Aldwyn Stokes, April 1954, LAC RG 29, Vol. 87, File 108-1-8.

37 Many of these medical equipment stockpiles, including 165 field hospitals with 200 beds, packed into crates in strategic locations, remain in place. Renamed the National Emergency Stockpile System, most of the equipment is still of Korean War vintage. *Emergency Preparedness in Canada,* Report of the Standing Senate Committee on National Security and Defence, Volume 1, Second Session, 39th Parliament, 32, http://www.parl.gc.ca/Content/SEN/Committee/392/defe/rep/rep13aug08vol1-e.pdf.

38 Memorandum to Cabinet – Civil Defence in Canada, 1 November 1954, Paul Joseph Martin Fonds, LAC MG 32 B12, Vol. 24, File 5. See also André Lamalice, "En temps de guerre comme en temps de paix, gouvernement manquant, gouvernance manquée: la protection civile au Canada, 1938-1988" (PhD diss., Department of History, University of Ottawa, 2011), 135-37.

39 F.F. Worthington to C.R.S. Stein, 12 August 1955, LAC RG 29, Vol. 708, File 110-9-1, pt 4.

40 The federal policy was not, however, particularly well advertised. Major-General C.R.S. Stein, provincial co-ordinator for British Columbia, for instance, had never seen the "Evacuation of Selected Cities" plan, although two cities in his province (Vancouver and Victoria) were implicated. Stein also objected to the principle that municipalities would have to complete the "donkey-work" of planning an evacuation by themselves, when the latest army paper entitled "Assistance of the Armed Forces in Civil Defence," tasked the armed forces with providing support to civil planning. Worthington later replied that

the armed forces' obligations to the civil authority in this case extended only to the federal civil defence office. C.R.S. Stein to F.F. Worthington, 16 August 1955, LAC RG 29, Vol. 708, File 110-9-1, pt 4.

41 Report no. 3/53, Discussion with Federal Civil Defense Administration Officials on NATO Civil Defence Committee Meeting, 20 January 1953, LAC RG 25, Vol. 4876, File 50108-B-40, pt 1.

42 Memorandum for the Under-Secretary from M.H. Wershof, 13 March 1953, LAC RG 25, Vol. 4876, File 50108-B-40, pt 1.

43 J.M. Cook to B. Rogers, 30 October 1953, LAC RG 25, Vol. 4876, File 50108-B-40, pt 1.

44 Report on Civil Defence Committee Meeting, 4-5 May 1954, LAC RG 25, Vol. 4876, File 50108-B-40, pt 1.

45 Preliminary Report on Operation Lifesaver, LAC RG 29, Vol. 106, File 180-8-25.

46 F.F. Worthington to P. Martin, 24 October 1954, Paul Joseph Martin Fonds, LAC MG 32 B12, Vol. 24, File 13.

47 Ibid.

48 Tracy Davis, *Stages of Emergency: Cold War Nuclear Civil Defense* (Durham, NC: Duke University Press, 2007), 5.

49 See *Winnipeg Metropolitan Civil Defence Board Bulletin 15* (May-June 1954), found in Paul Joseph Martin Fonds, LAC MG 32 B12, Vol. 26, File 1. See also Exercises – General, 26 July 1956, LAC RG 29, Vol. 659, File 106-2-1, pt 1.

50 H. Adams to P. Martin, 30 June 1955, LAC RG 29, Vol. 106, File 180-8-25.

51 "Alberta and B.C. Cities Plan CD Withdrawal Studies," Press Release no. 1955-5, 11 February 1955, Paul Joseph Martin Fonds, LAC MG 32 B12, Vol. 26, File 3.

52 F.F. Worthington to C.E. Gerhart, 28 December 1954, LAC RG 29, Vol. 706, File 110-8-1, pt 3.

53 Civil Defence Progress Report no. 40, 22 August 1954, LAC RG 29, Vol. 706, File 110-8-1, pt 3.

54 H. Adams to G.R. Howsam, 28 September 1955, LAC RG 29, Vol. 106, File 180-8-25.

55 G.O. Bell to H. Adams, 24 May 1955, LAC RG 29, Vol. 106, File 180-8-25.

56 City of Calgary, Preliminary Notice, April 1955, LAC RG 29, Vol. 106, File 180-8-25.

57 G.O. Bell to Mayor D.H. MacKay, 4 July 1955, LAC RG 29, Vol. 707, File 110-8-1.

58 H. Adams to P. Martin, 30 June 1955, LAC RG 29, Vol. 106, File 180-8-25.

59 H. Adams to G.R. Howsam, 28 September 1955, LAC RG 29, Vol. 106, File 180-8-25.

60 Progress Report no. 48, LAC RG 29, Vol. 707, File 110-8-1, pt 4.

61 H. Adams to P. Martin, LAC RG 29, Vol. 707, File 110-8-1, pt 4.

62 G.O. Bell to H. Adams, 5 May 1955, LAC RG 29, Vol. 106, File 180-8-25.

63 G.O. Bell to H. Adams, 11 May 1955, LAC RG 29, Vol. 106, File 180-8-25.

64 Ibid.

65 H. Adams to P. Martin, 30 June 1955, LAC RG 29, Vol. 106, File 180-8-25.

66 G.O. Bell to H. Adams, 5 May 1955, LAC RG 29, Vol. 106, File 180-8-25.

67 H. Adams to G.R. Howsam, 28 September 1955, LAC RG 29, Vol. 106, File 180-8-25.

68 H. Adams to G.O. Bell, 6 April 1955, LAC RG 29, Vol. 106, File 180-8-25.

69 Information Services Division, *Public Information in Civil Defence* (Ottawa: Queen's Printer, 1957), 26-28.

70 F.F. Worthington, Notes on Meeting with Dr. Tyhurst, 5 August 1949, LAC RG 29, Vol. 87, File 108-1-8.

71 The problem was so persistent that the Information Services Division eventually published a guide to press relations for the use of provincial and municipal civil defence officials. See Department of National Health and Welfare, *Public Information in Civil Defence* (Ottawa: Queen's Printer, 1957).

72 G.O. Bell to H. Adams, 15 April 1955, LAC RG 29, Vol. 106, File 180-8-25.

73 Ibid.

74 H. Adams to G. Purcell, 14 July 1955, LAC RG 29, Vol. 106, File 180-8-25.

75 The radio station CXCL also absorbed costs from displaced advertisers to provide a running commentary on the exercise, with privileged access to the operations centre and officials. G.O. Bell to H. Adams, 27 April 1955, LAC RG 29, Vol. 106, File 180-8-25.

76 H. Adams to G.O. Bell, 12 July 1955, LAC RG 29, Vol. 106, File 180-8-25.

77 S. Brown to G.O. Bell, 23 August 1955, LAC RG 29, Vol. 106, File 180-8-25.

78 Instructions for Evacuation, July 1955, LAC RG 29, Vol. 106, File 180-8-25.

79 Martin, in the meantime, was engrossed by his duty as acting secretary of state of external affairs and his role in ongoing quadripartite disarmament talks at the United Nations in the summer of 1955. G. McCarty to G.O. Bell, 25 August 1955, LAC RG 29, Vol. 106, File 180-8-25.

80 J. McLennan, Coca-Cola, to H. Adams, 7 September 1955, LAC RG 29, Vol. 106, File 180-8-25.

81 H. Adams to G.R. Howsam, 8 September 1955, LAC RG 29, Vol. 106, File 180-8-25; G.O. Bell to H. Adams, 23 August 1955, LAC RG 29, Vol. 106, File 180-8-25.

82 Bill Gold, "Extra Police to Guard Area," *Calgary Herald,* 13 September 1955.

83 "Civil Employees Taking Part in Test," *Calgary Herald,* 14 September 1955.

84 Ibid.

85 "Letter to the Editor," *Calgary Herald,* 10 September 1955.

86 "All Is Ready for Lifesaver," *Calgary Herald,* 17 September 1955.

87 "Large Civil Defence Test Ready to Run Wednesday," *Calgary Herald,* 20 September 1955.

88 "Exercise Fails in Halifax," *Calgary Herald,* 18 September 1955.

89 "Calgary's Sense of Responsibility," *Calgary Herald,* 19 September 1955 [emphasis added].

90 Ray Guay, "Road Accidents 'Greatest Disaster,'" *Calgary Herald.* 15 September 1955. See also H. Adams to G.R. Howsam, 28 September 1955, LAC RG 29, Vol. 106, File 108-2-25.

91 "Operations Lifesaver Off: Exercise Delayed a Week," "Snow Beat Us, Say CD Heads," *Calgary Herald,* 21 September 1955.

92 "War Postponed because of Weather?" *Calgary Herald,* 22 September 1955.

93 H. Adams to N. Robertson, September 1955, LAC RG 29, Vol. 106, File 180-8-25.

94 "Weather Is Key to CD Scheme," *Calgary Herald,* 22 September 1955.

95 Bell was referring to the east-west connecting road between Calgary and Strathmore, which contained so many ruts and potholes that it often damaged tires. "Road Conditions under Fire by Civil Defence Officials," *Calgary Herald,* 24 September 1955.

96 "Outlook Good for Lifesaver," *Calgary Herald,* 27 September 1955.

97 Morrison earned biting criticism from the *Calgary Herald*'s lead editorial for his trouble: "Local Politics and Civil Defence," *Calgary Herald,* 27 September 1955.

98 "It's No Picnic, Neither Is War," *Calgary Herald,* 28 September 1955.

99 "Most Vital to CD Test," *Calgary Herald,* 28 September 1955.

100 "Five Children Add Problems, But Family Believes in Test," *Calgary Herald,* 28 September 1955.

101 "A Calgary Family Is Evacuated and Returns Home Safely," *Calgary Herald,* 28 September 1955.

102 Ibid.

103 The person in question was a member of the Queen's Own Rifles, who was burned by one of several smoke bombs detonated in northeast Calgary after the evacuation convoys had left.

104 "Defence Chiefs Satisfied Lifesaver Was a Success," *Calgary Herald,* 29 September 1955, 1.
105 Preliminary Report on Exercise "Lifesaver," LAC RG 29 1983-84/292, Box 22, File 580-10-1.
106 "Workers Stay on Job Despite Sirens' Blast," *Calgary Herald,* 28 September 1955.
107 "'Saver in Brief," *Calgary Herald,* 28 September 1955. Many similar accounts are found in "Success of CD Exercise Hinges on Weather," *Calgary Herald,* 27 September 1955.
108 "What's All This about Signals," *Calgary Herald,* 29 September 1955, 4.
109 Preliminary Report on Exercise "Lifesaver."
110 "Defence Chiefs Satisfied Lifesaver Was a Success," *Calgary Herald,* 29 September 1955, 1.
111 Ibid.
112 Preliminary Report on Exercise "Lifesaver," LAC RG 29 1983-84/292, Box 22, File 580-10-1
113 Ibid.
114 "'Doubting Thomasine' Does Turnabout on CD Opinion," *Calgary Herald,* 29 September 1955.
115 Ibid.
116 Advertisement, "Operation Moneysaver," *Calgary Herald,* 21 September 1955, 13.
117 James Opp, "Prairie Commemoration and the Nation: The Golden Jubilees of Alberta and Saskatchewan, 1955," in Norman Hillmer and Adam Chapnick, eds., *Canadas of the Mind: The Making and Unmaking of Canadian Nationalisms in the Twentieth Century* (Montreal and Kingston: McGill-Queen's University Press, 2007), 218.
118 Editorial cartoon, "They Went Thataway!" *Calgary Herald,* 29 September 1955, 4.
119 "Family (All Seven) Enjoyed Big Day," *Calgary Herald,* 29 September 1955.
120 "Trip to Crossfield Pleasant Excursion," *Calgary Herald,* 29 September 1955.
121 "'Big Picnic' in Opinion of Returnee," *Calgary Herald,* 30 September 1955.
122 "Rural Albertans Pass Unique Test," *Calgary Herald,* 30 September 1955.
123 "Hats Are Lifted to Rural Areas," *Calgary Herald,* 28 September 1955.
124 Jenny Barker-Devine, "'Mightier than Missiles': The Rhetoric of Civil Defense for Rural American Families 1950-1970," *Agricultural History* 80 (Fall 2006): 416.
125 Ibid., 422; "An Interview with Val Peterson," *Bulletin of Atomic Scientists* 10 (September 1954): 375-77.
126 Barker-Devine, "'Mightier than Missiles,'" 422.
127 "Rural Albertans Pass Unique Test," *Calgary Herald,* 30 September 1955.
128 Plans for Exercise East Coast, 29 April 1956, LAC RG 29, Vol. 659, File 106-2-1, pt 1.
129 Cabinet Defence Committee Decision, 13 June 1956, John Francis Wallace Fonds, LAC MG 30 E211, Vol. 5, File 5-7.
130 T.C. Rogers to H. Manning, 9 December 1957, LAC RG 29, Vol. 104, File 180-8-10, pt 2.
131 Less progress had been made for the evacuation of Ottawa-Hull because of the inability of the Ontario and Quebec governments to come to an agreement about the reception of nuclear refugees in the area. *Ontario Provincial Survival Plan,* Matthew Howard Somers Penhale Fonds, LAC MG 31 G21, Vol. 11, File "Ontario Provincial Survival Plan."
132 Ibid.
133 Ibid.
134 Letter from J. Arnell to A. Longair, appended to A.K. Longair, *Early Atomic Defence Research in Canada,* Chief Research and Development Report no. 4/79 (Ottawa: Department of National Defence, 15 March 1979).
135 "What Do We Do When the Bombs Fall?" *Montreal Star,* 28 February 1955.
136 Report of the Scientific Advisor to Federal Civil Defence Coordinator, LAC RG 24, Acc. 83-84/215, Box 13, File 5-1200-C9.

137 *Ontario Provincial Survival Plan,* Matthew Howard Somer Penhale Fonds, LAC MG 31 G21, Vol. 11, "File Ontario Provincial Survival Plan – operational plan."
138 Ibid.
139 Report of Project Q, John Francis Wallace Fonds, LAC MG 30 E211, Vol. 5, File 54.
140 Ibid.
141 Ibid.
142 Ottawa Board of Trade Civil Defence Newsletter #1, "What We May Expect," Canadian War Museum, George Metcalf Archival Collection, CWM 19840282-112.

Chapter 5: Emergency Measures, 1957-59

1 Larry Worthington, *"Worthy": A Biography of Major-General F.F. Worthington* (Toronto: Macmillan, 1961), 231.
2 Department of National Health and Welfare, "General Worthington Retires from Civil Defence Post," Press Release 1957-19, 13 September 1957, LAC RG 29 Vol. 646 File 100-5-25.
3 One such radio enthusiast interpreted the signals as Morse code advising against angering the "black bear." "'Hams' Across Canada Hear Satellite's 'Beep,'" *Toronto Star,* 5 October 1957.
4 "Soviet Moon Is Key to Military Victory," *Winnipeg Free Press,* 6 October 1957. See also "Feat Proves Reds Can Fire Missiles at U.S., Expert Says," *Toronto Star,* 5 October 1957.
5 "The Biggest Stick of All?" *Calgary Herald,* 8 October 1957.
6 "Satellite Crosses Canada: Red Sphere Circling World at Tremendous Speed," *Ottawa Journal,* 5 October 1957.
7 Revised Comments on the Assumptions of Civil Defence Planning, Report to the Joint Planning Committee by the Joint Planning Staff no. 5-11-1, 27 August 1958, LAC RG 25, Vol. 5944, File 50217-40, pt 6.1.
8 "Civil Defence and the Intercontinental Ballistic Missile," *Civil Defence Bulletin* 69 (November-December 1957), 2.
9 Draft Terms of Reference, Threat to North America 1958-67, 29 October 1957, LAC RG 24, Vol. 20853, File 7-26-9, pt 3. See also Andrew Richter, *Avoiding Armageddon: Canadian Military Strategy and Nuclear Weapons, 1950-1963* (Vancouver: UBC Press, 2002), 39, 52-53.
10 Jonathan Haslam, *Russia's Cold War: From the October Revolution to the Fall of the Wall* (New Haven, CT: Yale University Press, 2011), 197.
11 "Civil Defence and the Intercontinental Ballistic Missile," 2.
12 Ibid.
13 B.M. Greene, ed., *The Canadian Who's Who,* volume 9 (Toronto: Trans-Canada Press, 1959), 482.
14 Harry Miller, *Service to the Services, The Story of NAAFI* (London: Newman Neame, 1971).
15 Cabinet Conclusions, 31 July 1956, LAC RG 2, Vol. 5775, Reel T-12185.
16 Emergency Measures Organization (EMO), 16 January 1964, LAC RG 24, Acc. 1983-84/215, Box 192, File S-2001-50/53.
17 R.B. Bryce to J. Léger, 9 August 1956, LAC RG 25, Vol. 6039, File 50306-A-40, pt 1.1.
18 Working Group on War Measures, Memo to War Book Committee, 15 January 1957, LAC RG 25, Vol. 6039, File 50306-A-40, pt 1.1.
19 Minutes of the Internal Committee on War Book Committee, 30 January 1957, LAC RG 25, Vol. 6039, File 50306-A-40, pt 1.1.
20 Ibid.

21 Minutes of the Meeting of the Interdepartmental Committee on the War Book, 12 July 1957, LAC RG 25, Vol. 6039, File 50306-A-40, pt 1.1.
22 Ibid.
23 Ibid.
24 Ibid.
25 Report on Railway Transportation Forum, Canadian Civil Defence College, 5-7 November 1957, LAC RG 46, Vol. 1177, File W2106-0, pt 2.
26 R.B. Bryce to J. Diefenbaker, 12 November 1957, John Diefenbaker Fonds, LAC MG 26 M, Vol. 58, Reel M-7814, 49095-49098.
27 Record of Cabinet Decision, 4 April 1957, and R.B. Bryce to J. Léger, 30 May 1957, LAC RG 25, Vol. 6039, File 50306-A-40, pt 1.1.
28 H. Adams to Provincial Civil Defence Co-ordinators, 20 June 1958, LAC RG 29, Vol. 646, File 100-5-25.
29 In 1957, over two million posters, bus promotions, shopping bags, calendars, restaurant place mats, newspaper mats, and "dodgers" (slips inserted in mailboxes by door-to-door milkmen, laundry service, and Boy Scouts) had been produced by the federal government and distributed to the provinces free of charge, at a substantial expense. Civil Defence Day Newsletter, Suggestion no. 8, 28 August 1957, LAC RG 29, Vol. 646, File 100-5-25.
30 Civil Defence Day Newsletter no. 3, 29 July 1958, LAC RG 29, Vol. 646, File 100-5-25.
31 R.L. Beatty to C.L. Smith, 25 September 1958, LAC RG 29, Vol. 646, File 100-5-25.
32 It is possible that G.F. Davidson, the deputy minister for welfare, may have had a role in prompting the move, given his past reluctance to move in the field of civil defence.
33 J.W. Monteith to J. Diefenbaker, 9 May 1958, John Diefenbaker Fonds, LAC MG 26M, Vol. 48, File 140.
34 Howard Graham, *Citizen and Soldier* (Toronto: McClelland and Stewart, 1987), 243.
35 D. Summerville to Metro Toronto Civil Defence Committee, 11 August 1958, LAC RG 29, Vol. 727, File 112-T1.
36 H.H. Atkinson to D. Summerville, 28 August 1958, LAC RG 29, Vol. 727, File 112-T1, pt 5.
37 W.O. Waffle to J.W. Monteith, 2 February 1959, LAC RG 29, Vol. 727, File 112-T1, pt 5.
38 At a press conference, Toronto officials blasted the Diefenbaker government. "Metro Blast on CD Brings Ottawa Pledge," *Globe and Mail*, 30 January 1959.
39 Graham, *Citizen and Soldier*, 245.
40 James Eayrs, "Canada, NATO, and the Nth Power Problem," *Canadian Forum* 39 (April 1959): 6-7.
41 Cabinet Conclusions, 30 December 1958, LAC RG 2, Series A-5-a, Vol. 1899.
42 J.W. Monteith to G.F. Davidson, 13 January 1959, LAC RG 29, Vol. 1504, File 201-7-3.
43 Cabinet Conclusions, 10 January 1959, LAC RG 2, Series A-5-a, Vol. 2744.
44 First Draft of *Citizen and Soldier*, Book 7, Howard Graham Fonds, LAC MG 30 E524, File 10.
45 Cabinet Conclusions, 21 January 1959, LAC RG 2, Series A-5-a, Vol. 2744.
46 First Draft of *Citizen and Soldier*, Book 7, Howard Graham Fonds, LAC MG 30 E524, File 10.
47 R.B. Bryce, director of the EMO, to R.B. Curry, 9 January 1959, LAC RG 57 1989-90/216, Box 3, File 1020-2.
48 Ibid.
49 Graham, *Citizen and Soldier*, 245.
50 Ibid., 242.
51 Richter, *Avoiding Armageddon*, 68, 138.

52 Graham, *Citizen and Soldier,* 245.
53 John Lewis Gaddis, *We Now Know* (Oxford: Oxford University Press, 1997), 139.
54 Nikita Khrushchev, *Memoirs of Nikita Khrushchev,* edited by Sergei Khrushchev, translated by George Shriver, volume 3 (University Park, PA: University of Pennsylvania Press, 2004), 297.
55 *Cold War International History Project: Germany in the Cold War,* Comments on the Preparation of the Steps of the Soviet Government Concerning a Change in the Status of West Berlin, 4 December 1958, http://www.wilsoncenter.org/.
56 Robert Bothwell, *Alliance and Illusion: Canada and the World, 1945-1984* (Vancouver: UBC Press, 2007), 164-65.
57 Memorandum from Under-Secretary of State for External Affairs to Acting Secretary of State for External Affairs, 24 November 1958, Documents on Canadian External Affairs, volume 24, Document 302, http://www.international.gc.ca/department/history-histoire/dcer/details-en.asp?intRefID=6724.
58 Sean Maloney, *Learning to Love the Bomb: Canada's Nuclear Weapons during the Cold War* (Washington, DC: Potomac Books, 2007), 192.
59 Graham, *Citizen and Soldier,* 245.
60 Ad Hoc Committee on Civil Defence, 30 January 1959, LAC RG 57 1989-90/216, Box 3, Interim 284, File 1020-2.
61 Ibid.
62 Ibid.
63 War Organization, Civil Functions, and Plan 'B,' 5 February 1959, LAC RG 57 1989-90/216, Box 3, Interim 284, File 1020-2.
64 This recommendation was made with Bryce's comment that it was more palatable to fully fund provincial efforts but that federal control was the only way to ensure that the work would be done. Ibid.
65 Draft Report from the Ad Hoc Committee on Civil Defence, 9 March 1959, LAC RG 57 1989-90/216, Box 3, Interim 284, File 1020-2.
66 Ibid.
67 Memorandum to J. Diefenbaker from R.B. Bryce, 19 March 1959, LAC RG 57 1989-90/216, Box 3, Interim 284, File 1020-2.
68 Memorandum from R.B. Bryce to R.B. Curry, 18 March 1959, LAC RG 57 1989-90/216, Box 3, Interim 284, File 1020-2.
69 See "Hatton Remarks Draw Criticism," *Ottawa Journal,* 27 October 1958; "Civil Defence? The City Doesn't Need It – Mayor," *Ottawa Journal,* 31 October 1958. "See Fourteen-Month Delay in Rewiring Sirens," *Toronto Star,* 22 December 1958; "May Block Cash until Shakeup," *Toronto Star,* 27 December 1958; "Metro 'Frustrated,' Criticizes Ottawa," *Toronto Star,* 14 January 1959.
70 R.B. Bryce, Notes to Discuss with the Prime Minister Regarding New EMO Establishment, 7 April 1959, LAC RG 57 1989-90/216, Box 3, File 1020-2.
71 One of Diefenbaker's members of parliament, Dr. George Clark Fairfield, remarked on the press's interest in the new arrangements and particularly on their indifference to the EMO's much larger role, in his notes on the day's events. Notes, 14 April 1959, John Diefenbaker Fonds, LAC MG 26 M, Vol. 48, File 141.
72 "Atomic Defenders: Army Now Responsible for Canada's Survival," *Ottawa Citizen,* 24 March 1959.
73 J.F. Wallace to M.H.S. Penhale, 26 March 1959, Matthew Howard Somers Penhale Fonds, LAC MG 31 G21, Vol. 9, File "Civil Defence – Daily Diary – Management of CD College and Organization of Permanent Civil Defence Network 1958-1960."

74 Ibid.

75 Ibid.

76 Summary Record of the Dominion-Provincial Conference on Civil Defence Arrangements, 24 April 1959, LAC RG 25, Vol. 5944, File 50217-40, pt 6.2.

77 The assumptions circulated by NATO were evaluated and confirmed by the Department of National Defence's Joint Intelligence Committee, which suggested that the ballistic missile would be a serious threat as soon as 1960. Minutes of the Eleventh Civil Defence Policy Meeting, 29 September 1958, LAC RG 25, Vol. 5944, File 50217-40, pt 6.2.

78 Summary Record of the Dominion-Provincial Conference on Civil Defence Arrangements, 24 April 1959, LAC RG 25, Vol. 5944, File 50217-40, pt 6.2.

79 Privy Council Order 1959-656, 28 May 1959, LAC RG 2, Vol. 2233, File 790 H B.

80 M.H.S. Penhale to G.A. McCarter, 14 August 1959, Matthew Howard Somers Penhale Fonds, LAC MG 31 G21, Vol. 12, File "McCarter, G.A." See also Minutes of Meeting, 15 October 1959, LAC RG 29, Vol. 52, File 100-1-1, pt. 2.

81 H.O. Waffle to R.B. Curry, 14 August 1959, Douglas Scott Harkness Fonds, LAC MG 32 B19 Vol. 54 File 87-0.

82 W.M. Nickle to G. Pearkes, 23 November 1959, Douglas Scott Harkness Fonds, LAC MG 32 B19 Vol. 54 File 87-0; "Bus but No Driver: Unable to Rouse Interest in Civil Defence, Says Brig Quilliam" *Kingston Whig-Standard,* 20 November 1959; "We Lose a Good Man," *Kingston Whig-Standard,* 20 November 1959.

83 C.R. Boehm to R.B. Curry, 3 September 1959, LAC RG 57, Box 3, File 155-RO/00.

84 A.E. Cooney to R.B. Curry, 28 August 1959, LAC RG 57, Box 3, File 155-RO/00.

85 G.S. Hatton to J.W. Monteith, 22 September 1959, Lester B. Pearson Fonds, LAC MG 26 N2, Vol. 111.

86 Ibid.

87 Worthington, *"Worthy,"* 235.

Chapter 6: The Survival Army, 1959-62

1 Sean Maloney, *Learning to Love the Bomb: Canada's Nuclear Weapons during the Cold War* (Washington, DC: Potomac Books, 2007), 11.

2 Canadian Army Policy Statement no. 65, 27 September 1950, Library and Archives Canada (LAC) RG 29, Vol. 654, File C-102-3-2B.

3 Canadian Army Policy Statement no. 74, 10 March 1951, LAC RG 29, Vol. 654, File C-102-3-2B; Civil Defence Memorandum no. 5/52, G.F. Davidson to P. Martin, 11 March 1951, Paul Joseph Martin Fonds, LAC MG 32 B12, Vol. 24, File 7. The Directorate of Military Operations and Planning did, however, make provisions for increased peacetime liaison between the armed forces and the provincial civil defence agencies through the district and area army commands, a change welcomed by the Department of National Health and Welfare.

4 M.P. Cawdron to Lieutenant-Colonel W.H. Gillespie, 11 October 1951, LAC RG 29, Vol. 654, File C-102-3-2B.

5 F.F. Worthington, "Civil Defence and Armed Defence," *Current Affairs for the Canadian Forces* 7, 8 (15 October 1954), 30.

6 G.W.L. Nicholson, "The Canadian Militia's Introduction to Civil Defence," in Robert Bothwell and Michael Cross, eds., *Policy by Other Means: Essays in Honour of C.P. Stacey* (Toronto: Clarke, Irwin, 1972), 225-26.

7 Canadian Army Policy Statement no. 90, 17 January 1952, LAC RG 29, Vol. 654, File C-102-3-2B

8 Canadian Army Policy Statement (not yet approved), 11 March 1954, LAC RG 29, Vol. 654, File C-102-3-2B.

9   Minutes of the 559th Meeting of the Chiefs of Staff Committee, 12 March 1954, LAC RG 29, Vol. 654, File S-102-3-2A.
10 Appendix A to CCS 2090-1, 17 May 1954, LAC RG 29, Vol. 654, File C-102-3-2B.
11 Ibid. Saskatchewan, in particular, took few preparations for civil defence because provincial officials believed that the province contained no targets of any strategic value.
12 Chiefs of Staff Committee Paper no. 1(55), 14 February 1955, LAC RG 29, Vol. 654, File S-102-3-2A.
13 G.F. Davidson to F.F. Worthington, 15 March 1955, LAC RG 29, Vol. 654, File S-102-3-2A.
14 F.F. Worthington to P. Martin, 14 July 1955, Paul Joseph Martin Fonds, LAC MG 32 B12, Vol. 24, File 7.
15 Statement by the Hon. Ralph Campney, Armed Forces News Release 28-55, LAC RG 29, Vol. 654, File 102-3-2.
16 George Mackenzie Urquhart, "The Changing Role of the Canadian Militia, 1945-1975" (MA thesis, Department of History, University of Victoria, 1977), 73-74.
17 W.R. Buchner, "The Role of the Militia Unit in a Civil Disaster," *Canadian Army Journal* 11, 3 (July 1957): 62-63.
18 Instructions for Provincial Civil Defence Coordinators, 10 May 1956, Paul Joseph Martin Fonds, LAC MG 32 B12, Vol. 24, File 7.
19 Mobile Columns, Draft, 17 May 1957, LAC RG 29, Vol. 654, File 103-2-3.
20 In the United Kingdom, territorial army volunteers tasked with civil defence roles grumbled that they were no longer soldiers but "pick and shovel boys." Lieutenant-Colonel R.E.R. Robinson, "Civil Defence Training in a Territorial Army Battalion," *Army Quarterly and Defence Journal* 76, 2 (1958): 191-95.
21 Ibid.
22 HQC no. 2090-1 TD 7115, Assistance of the Armed Forces in Civil Defence, 25 April 1957, LAC RG 29, Vol. 654, File 102-3-2B.
23 J.L. Granatstein, *Canada's Army* (Toronto: University of Toronto Press, 2002), 349.
24 Statement by Department of National Defence, Armed Forces News 48-59, 5 November 1959, Lester B. Pearson Fonds, LAC MG 26 N2, Vol. 111.
25 Canadian Army Survival Operations – Re-entry and Maintenance of Law and Order, February 1960, Matthew Howard Somers Penhale Fonds, LAC MG 31 G21, Vol. 11. See also Canadian Army Operational Research Establishment Memorandum no. 59/4: The Post Attack Situation in Canada 1960-1970: Casualties and Resources, Directorate of History and Heritage (DHH) 81/256 EMO RO-376, Defence of the Canadian Population against Nuclear Attack, 28 January 1963, John Francis Wallace Fonds, LAC MG 30 E211, Vol. 3, File 3-10.
26 Canadian Army Survival Operations – Re-entry and Maintenance of Law and Order, February 1960, Matthew Howard Somers Penhale Fonds, LAC MG 31 G21, Vol. 11.
27 Ibid., pt I, 22.
28 Volunteers in National Survival, 29 July 1960, LAC RG 24 1989-90/212, Box 18, File 2100-6.
29 Canadian Army Survival Operations – Re-entry and Maintenance of Law and Order, 15-16, Matthew Howard Somers Penhale Fonds, LAC MG 31 G21, Vol. 11.
30 Volunteers in National Survival, 29 July 1960, LAC RG 24 1989-90/212, Box 18, File 2100-6.
31 "Re-entry Operations into a Damaged Area," *Canadian Army Journal* 15, 3 (Summer 1961): 6-8.
32 Volunteers in National Survival, 29 July 1960, LAC RG 24 1989-90/212, Box 18, File 2100-6.

33 Ibid.

34 Canadian Army Survival Operations – Re-entry and Maintenance of Law and Order, 16

35 K.J. Holmes, *History of the Canadian Military Engineers,* volume 3 (Toronto: Military Engineering Institute of Canada, 1997), 280-81.

36 Progress Report on Planning Activities, 10 April 1961, LAC RG 57 1984-85/658, Box 3, File 155-1.

37 Major General Arthur Wrinch, "The Army and National Survival," *Medical Services Journal* 16 (April 1960): 267.

38 Granatstein, *Canada's Army,* 350-51. See also G.W.L. Nicholson, "The Canadian Militia's Introduction to Civil-defence Training," in Michael Cross and Robert Bothwell, *Policy By Other Means: Essays in Honour of C.P. Stacey* (Toronto: Clarke, Irwin, 1972), 241-42.

39 See James Glassco Henderson, *The Nuking of Happy Valley and Other Tales Told in the Mess* (Victoria, BC: Trafford Publishing, 2001), 75-76; Canadian War Museum, George Metcalf Archival Collection 20000014-011, John E. Barnaby, *Short History of the Halifax Rifles 123 Armoured Regiment (RCAC),* volume 11, 1956-1958.

40 Harry B. Williams, "The Human Factor in National Survival," *Canadian Army Journal* 14, 4 (Fall 1960): 24-31; F. LeP. T. Clifford, "Exercise 'Nimble Phoenix,'" *Canadian Army Journal* 15, 2 (Spring 1961): 59-73.

41 Lieutenant-General S.F. Clark to M.H.S. Penhale and R.B. Curry, 17 March 1961; Concept of Re-entry into Damaged Areas, John Francis Wallace Fonds, LAC MG 30 E211, Vol. 3.

42 Frederick Taylor, *The Berlin Wall: A World Divided 1961-1989* (New York: HarperCollins, 2006), 123.

43 Ibid., 133.

44 John Lewis Gaddis, *We Now Know: Rethinking Cold War History* (Oxford: Oxford University Press, 1997), 146.

45 NATO to External, 8 August 1961, DHH 114.3Q1 (D14).

46 Cabinet Conclusions, 24 July 1961, LAC RG 2, Series A-5-a, Vol. 6177; Cabinet Conclusions, 17 August 1961, LAC RG 2, Series A-5-a, Vol. 6177. See also Denis Stairs, *Rogue Tory* (Toronto: Macfarlane, Walter and Ross, 1995), 415-16.

47 "Should Fight Berlin as Russ Won't Stop There," *Canadian Institute of Public Opinion,* 8 November 1961.

48 Cabinet Conclusions, 17 August 1961, LAC RG 2, Series A-5-a, Vol. 6177.

49 Ibid.

50 Cabinet Conclusions, 21 August 1961.

51 Ibid.

52 Donald Fleming, *So Very Near: The Political Memoirs of the Honourable Donald M. Fleming,* volume 2 (Toronto: McClelland and Stewart, 1985), 77.

53 Ibid.

54 Cabinet Conclusions, 22 August 1961.

55 Cabinet Conclusions, 28 August 1961.

56 Fleming, *So Very Near,* 372.

57 Ibid.

58 *House of Commons Debates,* Fourth Session, Twenty-Fourth Parliament, Volume VIII (7 September 1961), 8053-54; *House of Commons Debates,* Fourth Session, Twenty-Fourth Parliament, Volume VIII (12 September 1961), 8225.

59 Colonel J.M. Houghton to Director General of Military Training, 18 October 1961, Douglas Scott Harkness Fonds, LAC MG 32 B19, Vol. 57, File 87-6, pt 5.

60 The Canadian Army Militia Special Six-Week Training Program, Douglas Scott Harkness Fonds, LAC MG 32 B19, Vol. 57, File 87-6, pt 4.

61 Ibid.

62 Cross-cultural studies have suggested that the concept of an "achieved masculinity" is a key component to constructions of gender identity. See Joshua S. Goldstein, *War and Gender: How Gender Shapes the War System and Vice Versa* (London: Cambridge University Press, 2001), 252, 264-65, 269, 278; John H. Faris, "The Impact of Basic Combat Training: The Role of the Drill Sergeant," in Nancy Goldman and David Segal, eds., *The Social Psychology of Military Service* (London: Sage Publications, 1976), 13-27; Joanna Bourke, *An Intimate History of Killing: Face to Face Killing in Twentieth-Century Warfare* (New York: Basic Books, 1999), 99; Ruth Phillips, *Citizenship: Feminist Perspectives* (New York: Palgrave Macmillan, 2003), 31, 68-73.

63 "Take Time Out for Survival!" *Montreal Gazette,* 20 October 1961, 16.

64 "Earn and Learn," *Globe and Mail,* 24 October 1961, 30; "Take Time Out for Survival!" *Globe and Mail,* 25 October 1961, 21.

65 Volunteers in National Survival, 29 July 1960, LAC RG 24 1989-90/212, Box 18, File 2100-6.

66 All of the companies listed agreed to give their employees leave to take the course and make up any difference in salary so they would not be at a loss. See letters in file. Douglas Scott Harkness Fonds, LAC MG 32 B19, Vol. 57, File 87-6-1.

67 Dave McIntosh, "World Tension Sparks Survival Interest," *Montreal Gazette,* 6 November 1961.

68 D.M. Brown to D. Harkness, 3 November 1961, Douglas Scott Harkness Fonds, LAC MG 32 B19, Vol. 56, File 87-6, pt 1.

69 W.H. Dumsday, directorate of public relations, to D. Harkness, 27 October 1961, Douglas Scott Harkness Fonds, LAC MG 32 B19, Vol. 56, File 87-6, pt 1.

70 Canadian Press clipping, 20 September 1961, found in Douglas Scott Harkness Fonds, LAC MG 32 B19, Vol. 55, File 87-0, pt 4.1.

71 S.F. Clark to D. Harkness, 20 September 1961, LAC MG 32 B19, Vol. 55, File 87-0, pt 4.1.

72 Canadian Press clipping, 20 September 1961, LAC MG 32 B19, Vol. 55, File 87-0, pt 4.1.

73 "Survival Courses," *Globe and Mail,* 19 March 1961.

74 "Army's Recruiting Results Fall Well Below Objective," *Montreal Gazette,* 11 November 1961.

75 Ibid.

76 "CD Recruit Target Hit Only in East," *Winnipeg Free Press,* 8 November 1961.

77 A. Best to D. Harkness, 26 December 1961, LAC MG 32 B19, Vol. 56, File 87-6, pt 2.1.

78 "Très étrange façon d'entrainer les miliciens de 18 à 50 ans à des secours urgence," *L'Action Populaire,* 24 January 1962. The following week the newspaper printed a retraction, saying the original story had been based on exaggerations and lies. "L'exaggeration et faussetés en marge de l'entrainement des miliciens de 18 à 50 ans pour secours d'urgence," *L'Action Populaire,* 31 January 1962.

79 A. Lovell to L.B. Pearson, 7 November 1961, Lester B. Pearson Fonds, LAC MG 26 N2, Vol. 3, File 141.

80 M.D. Macleod to R.L. Hanbridge, 10 February 1962, Douglas Scott Harkness Fonds, LAC MG 32 B19, Vol. 56, File 87-6, pt 2.2.

81 M. Merner to D. Harkness, 12 April 1962, LAC MG 32 B19, Vol. 56, File 87-6, pt 3.3.

82 T. Outram to F. Stenson, 4 October 1962, LAC MG 32 B19, Vol. 56, File 87-6, pt 3.3.

83 "Goodhead Says Survival Force Misunderstood," *Globe and Mail,* 11 November 1961, 14.

84 "A Confusion of Issues," *Globe and Mail,* 11 November 1961, 6.

85 *House of Commons Debates,* Fifth Session, Twenty-Fourth Parliament, Volume II (19 March 1962), 1963 (Herbert Herridge).

86 James Senter, "Touches of Bilko, but Force Taking Shape," *Globe and Mail,* 11 November 1961, 1.
87 University of Victoria Oral History Program, Interview with Major Gary Del Villano, 5 March 2011.
88 Ibid.
89 *House of Commons Debates,* Fifth Session, Twenty-Fourth Parliament, Volume II (20 March 1962), 1973 (Paul Hellyer).
90 Ibid., 1973-74.
91 Corporal G.D. Andrews, "The SMTP Recruit" [no date], Douglas Scott Harkness Fonds, LAC MG 32 B19, Vol. 57, File 87-6, pt 3.1.
92 A. Best to D. Harkness, 26 December 1961, LAC MG 32 B19, Vol. 57, File 87-6, pt 3.1.
93 C. Clifton to Commanding Officer of the Seaforth Highlanders, D. Harkness, and J. Webster [no date], LAC MG 32 B19, Vol. 57, File 87-6, pt 2.1.
94 J.P. Bruck to Major-General J.P.E. Bernatchez, Vice-Chief of the General Staff, 5 December 1961, LAC MG 32 B19, Vol. 57, File 87-6, pt 2.1.
95 Deborah Cowen, *Military Workfare: The Soldier and Social Citizenship in Canada* (Toronto: University of Toronto Press, 2008), 17.
96 LAC RG 24 83-84/167, Box 4351, File 9700-8, Vol. 1, cited in Cowen, *Military Workfare,* 114.
97 *Militia Staff Course, Part II – 1959,* Exercise Jericho DS Notes – Requirement 1, Canadian War Museum, George Metcalf Archival Collection, CWM 19840282-123.
98 Phone interview with David Chaplin, Public Safety Canada, 30 November 2010.
99 Nicholson, "The Canadian Militia's Introduction to Civil Defence," 221.
100 Howard Graham, *Citizen and Soldier* (Toronto: McClelland and Stewart, 1987), 240
101 Granatstein, *Canada's Army,* 351.
102 Nicholson, "The Canadian Militia's Introduction to Civil Defence," 242.

Chapter 7: The Path to a Shelter Program, 1949-59

1 Atomic Energy Act, 1946, P.L. 585.
2 Exchange of Military Atomic Information, 6 January 1955, and Agreement between the Government of Canada and the Government of the United States of America for Cooperation Regarding Atomic Information in Mutual Defence Purposes, 22 July 1955, Library and Archives Canada (LAC) RG 24 83-84/215, Box 428, File S-9245-30/2-1, pt 2.
3 F.F. Worthington to Commander E.H. Robertson, 23 January 1950, LAC RG 29, Vol. 674, File 108-1-12; D.J. Goodspeed, *A History of the Defence Research Board of Canada* (Ottawa: Queen's Printer, 1958), 82.
4 United States, National Security Resources Board, *Survival under Atomic Attack* (Washington, DC: US Government Printing Office, 1949).
5 Canada, Department of National Health and Welfare, *Personal Protection under Atomic Attack* (Ottawa: King's Printer, 1951).
6 Ibid., 33-40.
7 M.P. Cawdron to A. Vachon, 19 May 1952, LAC RG 29, Vol. 678, File 108-4-3, pt 2.
8 F.F. Worthington and E.A. Gardner, chief architect, *The Maximum Use of Existing Structures for Shelter,* 17 March 1953, LAC RG 29, Vol. 678, File 108-4-3, pt 2.
9 "Defence Headquarters in Giant Mountain Shelter – Five Storied Mountain Shelters under Stockholm Boroughs," *Aftonbladet,* 23 July 1951, clipping, LAC RG 29, Vol. 678, File 108-4-3 pt 2.
10 *Personal Protection under Atomic Attack,* 19-23.
11 F.F. Worthington to F.R. Scott, 9 August 1949, LAC RG 29, Vol. 673, File 108-1-4, pt 1; H.W. Armstrong to W.J. MacCallum, 20 July 1950, LAC RG 29, Vol. 673, File 108-1-4, pt 1.

12 A. Vachon to L. St. Laurent, 19 May 1952, LAC RG 29, Vol. 673, File 108-1-4, pt 1; M.P. Cawdron to F.F. Worthington, 28 May 1952, LAC RG 29, Vol. 673, File 108-1-4, pt 1.

13 W. Rogers to Canadian Civil Defence Administration, 16 November 1953, LAC RG 29, Vol. 673, File 108-1-4, pt 1.

14 Dr. J. Hartman, Western Enterprises, to F.F. Worthington, 29 July 1952, LAC RG 29, Vol. 673, File 108-1-4, pt 1; H. Shiff to Department of National Defence, 5 August 1952, LAC RG 29, Vol. 673, File 108-1-4, pt 1; A. Zsolt to Department of Civil Defence, 15 October 1952, LAC RG 29, Vol. 673, File 108-1-4, pt 1.

15 H. Robinson to K.B.F. Smith, 5 March 1952, LAC RG 29, Vol. 108, File 180-8-51.

16 G. Dorval to H. Robinson, 26 May 1952, LAC RG 29, Vol. 108, File 180-8-51.

17 Report on the Civil Defence Exhibit at the Canadian National Sportsman's Show, 14-22 March 1952, LAC RG 29, Vol. 108, File 180-8-51.

18 Ibid.

19 Homer Robinson, Director of Information Services, to A.D. Simmons, Canadian Exhibition Commission, 10 December 1951, LAC RG 29, Vol. 108, File 180-5-51.

20 E.A. Gardner to F.F. Worthington, 14 September 1953, Paul Joseph Martin Fonds, LAC MG 32 B12, Vol. 24, File 16.

21 *Close-Up*, 8 August 1961, CBC Digital Archives, http://archives.cbc.ca/war_conflict/cold_war/topics/274/.

22 Department of Health and Welfare, "Honourable Paul Martin Makes Statement of Civil Defence and the H-Bomb," *Civil Defence Bulletin* 35 (June 1954), clipping, Paul Joseph Martin Fonds, LAC MG 32 B12, File 1 "Civil Defence – H. Bomb."

23 E.E. Massey, Ad Hoc Committee to Study Effects of Hydrogen Bomb on CD Planning, Paper no. 8, 14 May 1954, LAC RG 29, Vol. 711, File 112-1-5.

24 First Meeting of the Ad Hoc Committee to Study the Effects of the Hydrogen Bomb in Civil Defence Planning, 12 May 1954, LAC RG 29, Vol. 711, File 112-1-5.

25 Colonel M.P. Cawdron, Paper no. VII – Implications of a Thermonuclear Explosion on Canadian Civil Defence Planning, LAC RG 29, Vol. 711, File 112-1-5.

26 F.F. Worthington to Brigadier A.S. Todd, 26 July 1955, LAC RG 29, Vol. 678, File 108-4-3, pt 3. R.B. Bryce to J. Léger, 6 June 1955, LAC RG 25, Vol. 4876, File 50108-B-40, pt 1.

27 See "Marine Corps Participation in Desert Rock VI," news release, Matthew Howard Somers Penhale Fonds, LAC MG 31 G21, Vol. 12, File "United States Atomic Energy Commission, Nevada Test Site, Operation Cue 1955," pts 1 and 2.

28 Wilfrid Eggleston, *Canada's Nuclear Story* (Toronto: Clarke, Irwin, 1965), 238-40. See also John Clearwater, *Atomic Veterans: A Report to the Minister of National Defence Regarding Canada's Participation in Allied Forces' Nuclear Weapons Trials and Decontamination Work* (Ottawa: Department of National Defence, 2007).

29 Oral History Interview with Archie Pennie, Canadian War Museum, George Metcalf Archival Collection, 31D10 Pennie.

30 G.S. Hatton to Heads of Branches, 16 September 1955, LAC RG 29, Vol. 678, File 108-4-3, pt 3.

31 F.F. Worthington to D. Summerville, 26 July 1955, LAC RG 29, Vol. 678, File 108-4-3, pt 3.

32 Gordon Sinclair, "Civil Defence: As Useful as a Pea Shooter," *Liberty* (April 1955): 6-7. F.F. Worthington to D. Summerville, 26 July 1955, LAC RG 29, Vol. 678, File 108-4-3, pt 3.

33 F.F. Worthington to W.M. Nickle, provincial secretary, 26 July 1955, LAC RG 29, Vol. 678, File 108-4-3, pt 3.

34 F.F. Worthington to P. Martin, 26 July 1955, LAC RG 29, Vol. 678, File 108-4-3, pt 3.

35 F.F. Worthington to D. Summerville, 26 July 1955, LAC RG 29, Vol. 678, File 108-4-3, pt 3. Metropolitan Clerk to D. Summerville, 2 March 1955, LAC RG 29, Vol. 726, File 112-T1.

36 For the federal reaction to Hurricane Hazel and attempts to link it to better CD prepara-
    tions, see André Lamalice, "En Temps de guerre comme en temps de paix, gouvernance
    manquant, gouvernance manquée: la protection civile au Canada, 1938-1988" (PhD diss.,
    Department of History, University of Ottawa, 2011), 140-42.
37 *Toronto Telegram* brochure for shelter [no date], LAC RG 29, Vol. 678, File 108-4-3, pt 3.
38 Speech at demonstration specimen shelter, Toronto, 4 August 1955, LAC RG 29, Vol. 678,
    File 108-4-3, pt 3.
39 G. Donaldson to F.F. Worthington, 31 August 1955, LAC RG 29, Vol. 678, File 108-4-3,
    pt 3.
40 Analysis of Survival Plans Project Q, September 1956, John Francis Wallace Fonds, LAC
    MG 30 E211, Vol. 5, File 5-1.
41 "Academy of Sciences Report: Radiation Declared Harmful to Victim, All Descendants,"
    Globe and Mail, 13 June 1956. See also Paul Martin, "Health Hazards of Radiation and
    Nuclear Test Explosions," 27 July 1956, Paul Joseph Martin Fonds, LAC MG 32 B12, Vol.
    26, File 16.
42 S.N. White to G.S. Hatton, 30 April 1957, LAC RG 29, Vol. 678, File 108-4-3, pt 4.
43 Samuel Glasstone, *The Effects of Nuclear Weapons* (Washington, DC: Atomic Energy
    Commission, 1957).
44 Summary of Proceedings Held to Discuss Shelter and Refuge Policy, 29 May 1957, LAC
    RG 29, Vol. 678, File 108-4-3, pt 4.
45 G.S. Hatton to G.F. Davidson, 14 November 1957, LAC RG 29, Vol. 678, File 108-4-3, pt 4.
46 Shelter Policy – Decisions to Be Made [no date] LAC RG 29, Vol. 678, File 108-4-3, pt 4.
47 M. Cameron to Colonel L. Smith, 6 January 1958, LAC RG 29, Vol. 678, File 108-4-3, pt 4.
48 L. Smith to M. Cameron, 3 February 1958, LAC RG 29, Vol. 678, File 108-4-3, pt 4.
49 D. Summerville to G.S. Hatton, 29 August 1958, LAC RG 29, Vol. 678, File 108-4-3, pt 4.
50 Resumé – Civil Defence Informational Activities – 1957-1958 [no date], LAC RG 29, Vol.
    102, File 180-8-1.
51 It is unclear whether any action was taken on the issue.
52 J. Pratt to J.W. Monteith, 25 May 1959, John Diefenbaker Fonds, LAC MG 26 M, Vol. 48,
    File 141.
53 Report to the Joint Planning Committee by the Joint Planning Staff: Civil Defence Planning
    Assumptions, 27 August 1958, LAC RG 25, Vol. 5944, File 50217-40, pt 6.2; Minutes of the
    Eleventh Civil Defence Policy Meeting, 29 September 1958, LAC RG 25, Vol. 5944, File
    50217-40, pt 6.2.
54 S.N. White to A. Fontaine, Judge of Sessions of the Peace, 2 April 1959, LAC RG 29, Vol.
    678, File 108-4-3, pt 4.
55 B. Wayne Blanchard, *American Civil Defense 1945-1984: The Evolution of Programs and
    Policies* (Emmitsburg: Federal Emergency Management Agency, 1985), 5-6.
56 Ibid., 6. See also Deterrence and Survival in the Nuclear Age, 7 November 1957, OSANSP,
    NSC Series, Policy Papers Subseries, Box 22, File NSC5724(2), accessed at George
    Washington University National Security Archive, 8 October 2007, http://www.gwu.
    edu/~nsarchiv/NSAEBB/NSAEBB139/nitze02.pdf. See also Valerie Adams, *Eisenhower's
    Fine Group of Fellows* (Lanham, MD: Lexington Books, 2006), 173.
57 Ralph E. Lapp, "Civil Defense Shelters: An Interview with Congressman Chet Holifield,"
    Bulletin of Atomic Scientists 14, 4 (1957): 130-32.
58 Federal Civil Defense Administration News Release no. SR 571, 7 May 1958, LAC RG 29,
    Vol. 678, File 108-4-3, pt 4.
59 Stephen Schwartz, "Overview of Project Findings," *Atomic Audit: The Costs and Con-
    sequences of U.S. Nuclear Weapons since 1940* (Washington, DC: Brookings Institution

Press, 1998), 6 February 2009, http://www.brookings.edu/projects/archive/nucweapons/schwartz.aspx.

60 "Build Shelter for Fallout into New Home," *Toronto Telegram,* 16 January 1959.

61 Ibid.

62 "Reeve Waffle Ruffled," *Toronto Star,* 17 January 1959. Their sales pitch reflected those of other shelter salesmen in the United States, who appended the jam preserve or root cellar function to the list of a fallout shelter's other uses. See *CBC Radio: Assignment,* 6 November 1958, CBC Digital Archives, 6 June 2009, http://archives.cbc.ca/IDC-1-71-274-1462/conflict_war/cold_war/clip3.

63 "What Civil Defence Plans?" *Financial Post,* 7 February 1959, 6

64 "New Look in Civil Defence," *Globe and Mail,* 25 March 1959, 6.

65 Defence Liaison Division to Doug Lepan, 10 April 1959, LAC RG 25, Vol. 5944, File 50217-40, pt 6.2.

66 Proposed Shelter Policy [no date], John Francis Wallace Fonds, LAC MG 30 E211, Vol. 4, File 13.

67 Cabinet Conclusions, 28 September 1959, LAC RG 2, Series A-5-a, Vol. 2745.

68 "May Use Housing Act in Building Shelters for Civil Defense," *Globe and Mail,* 30 September 1959, 17.

69 "Pearkes Advises All Canadians Build Basement Fallout Shelters – No Use Driving Away If Bomb Is Dropped," *Globe and Mail,* 3 October 1959.

Chapter 8: Irresponsible Citizens, 1959-62

1 In his 1958 essay, Eayrs commented on the public's attitude: "A greater obstacle than ignorance of the facts is the inability to look them in the face ... Caught up in a wave of prosperity, preoccupied by forecasts of a still more gilded future, the Canadian citizen (in 1958) had little inclination to dwell upon the thought that the twentieth century, which Laurier with such apparent prescience predicted would belong to him, might end with there being no one at all for it to belong to." James Eayrs, *Northern Approaches: Canada and the Search for Peace* (Toronto: Macmillan Company of Canada, 1961), 50-51.

2 J.F. Wallace to the Regional Officers 28 of the Emergency Measures Organization (EMO), 13 February 1961, John Francis Wallace Fonds, Library and Archives Canada (LAC) MG 30 E211, Vol. 3, File 3-1.

3 Ibid.

4 Sean Maloney, "Dr. Strangelove Visits Canada: Projects RUSTIC, EASE, BRIDGE, 1958-1963," *Canadian Military History* 6 (Spring 1997): 42-56.

5 Ibid., 51

6 Ibid., 50-51. "Nuclear War Bunker Plan Now Ready," *Globe and Mail,* 20 January 1961; "Watch for Big War Citadels Contract Soon," *Financial Post,* 21 January 1961.

7 "This Is the Diefenbunker!" *Toronto Telegram,* 11 September 1961.

8 Maloney, "Dr. Strangelove Visits Canada," 49.

9 Office of the Prime Minister, Press Release, 1 March 1961. Found in "Exercise Tocsin 1961," Douglas Scott Harkness Fonds, LAC MG 32 B19, Vol. 56, File 87-5, pt 2.1.

10 Security Guide for Exercise TOCSIN 1961, Douglas Scott Harkness Fonds, LAC MG 32 B19, Vol. 56, File 87-5, pt 1.2.

11 Instruction to EMO Regional Officers 82, 9 June 1961, LAC RG 57 1983-84/212, Box 17, File 2550-61, pt 1.

12 "Defence Test Cuts Space Shot Off Air," *Toronto Daily Star,* 5 May 1961.

13 Script – TOCSIN 1961, LAC RG 57 1983-84/212, Box 17, File 2550-61, pt 2.

14 Ibid.
15 EMO, *Blueprint for Survival No. 4: 11 Steps to Survival* (Ottawa: Queen's Printer, 1961), 1.
16 Ibid., 19.
17 Ibid., 20.
18 Ibid., 21.
19 Ibid., 36.
20 John Pallett, chief government whip, took part in a TOCSIN exercise as the federal commissioner for Ontario. He registered surprise that the BRIDGE site at Borden was not connected directly to the RUSTIC site at Petawawa. The emergency bunkers relied on radio once the "attack" took out the teletype exchange in Toronto. J. Pallett to J. Diefenbaker, 29 May 1961, LAC MG 26 M, Vol. 48, File 141 – Exercise TOCSIN.
21 *11 Steps to Survival*, 38.
22 B. Wayne Blanchard, *American Civil Defense 1945-1984: The Evolutions of Programs and Policies* (Emmitsburg, MD: Federal Emergency Measures Agency, 1985), 9.
23 The federal government was sufficiently concerned about the public's state of mind to issue an order asking agencies such as the Dominion Observatory not to speak to reporters about the explosion. "Scientists Muzzled on Bomb," *Ottawa Citizen*, 31 October 1961. See also "A Quick, Reliable Guide to the Little Scientists Now Know about Fallout," *Maclean's*, 18 November 1961; "Windsor's Early October Fallout Count Tops Nation," *Toronto Star*, 25 October 1961, 5.
24 "Warns of Danger of Fallout 'Panic,'" *Toronto Star*, 26 October 1961; "Fallout Danger Slight in Canada, States Scientist," *Globe and Mail*, 26 October 1961.
25 Canadian Press clipping, 25 September 1961, Douglas Scott Harkness Fonds, LAC MG 32 B19, Vol. 55, File 87-0, pt 3.2.
26 Much of the point of these exercises was to develop proper communications procedures in order to ascertain, quickly, what parts of the country had been hit, what resources survived to serve the survival effort, and what to do so with the least risk of miscommunication.
27 S.F. Clark to R.B. Bryce and D. Harkness, 11 September 1961, Douglas Scott Harkness Fonds, LAC MG 32 B19, Vol. 55, File 87-0, pt 4.1.
28 "It's Only Mock Alert, Not 'Wells's Doomsday,'" *Toronto Star*, 1 November 1961.
29 Emergency Public Information Services Report Exercise Tocsin B-1961, LAC RG 57, Vol. 64, File 2500-2, pt 1.
30 Address on National Survival Exercise Program for Television, 9 November 1961, John Diefenbaker Fonds, LAC MG 26 M, Vol. 177, File "Shelters."
31 Ibid.
32 Ibid.
33 In the exercise, Douglas Harkness, minister of national defence, received first notice of the impending crisis from the Canadian Chiefs of Staff Committee. Harkness alerted the prime minister, who ordered Cabinet Secretary R.B. Bryce (Curry's superior) to advise continuity of government teams to prepare for evacuation to safe locations. An advance party of sixty such officials left for the RUSTIC site at Petawawa, Ontario, two hours later. At 6:30 p.m., the chief of general staff advised Diefenbaker to sound the national alert.
34 Report of Regional Officer Ellen Fairclough, 13-14 November 1961, John Diefenbaker Fonds, LAC MG 26 N2, Vol. 7810, File 141.
35 P. Martin to L. St. Laurent, 30 November 1954, Louis St. Laurent Fonds, LAC MG 26 L, Vol. 222, File D-12-1.
36 Norman Alcock, "Necessity for Peace Research Institutes," *Our Generation against Nuclear War* 1, 1 (Autumn 1961): 4-8.

37   Joseph Levitt, *Pearson and Canada's Role in Nuclear Disarmament and Arms Control Negotiations, 1945-1957* (Montreal and Kingston: McGill-Queen's University Press, 1993), 229-30.

38   See Milton Katz, *Ban the Bomb: A History of Sane, the Committee for a Sane Nuclear Policy, 1957-1985* (New York: Greenwood Press, 1986).

39   "Increase among Those Who Say 'Ban the Bomb,'" *Canadian Institute of Public Opinion,* 7 January 1961.

40   "The Vast Majority Want Nuclear Tests Stopped," *Canadian Institute of Public Opinion,* 23 August 1961.

41   *House of Commons Debates,* Fourth Session, Twenty-Fourth Parliament, Volume VIII (11 September 1961), 8169-74 (Howard Green).

42   Howard Green, as quoted by E. Symons to J. Diefenbaker, 12 December 1961, John Diefenbaker Fonds, LAC MG 26 M, Vol. 177, File D-70-8.

43   P. Farrell to D. Harkness, 20 October 1961, Douglas Scott Harkness Fonds, LAC MG 32 B19, Vol. 55, File 87-0, pt 1.

44   J.W. Bailey to J.F. Wallace, 29 November 1961, LAC RG 57 1984-85/658, Box 3, File 155-1.

45   Ibid. P. Oiders to J. Diefenbaker, 27 June 1961, John Diefenbaker Fonds, LAC MG 26 M, Vol. 177, File D-70-8.

46   Instruction to EMO Regional Officers 194, 3 January 1962, John Francis Wallace Fonds, LAC MG 31 E 211, Vol. 3, File 3.4.

47   Unsigned Petition found in file, John Diefenbaker Fonds, LAC MG 26 M, Vol. 177, File D-70-8.

48   "Only Means of Survival Is Positive Policy for Peace," *Toronto Daily Star,* 17 November 1961.

49   "Petition against Nuclear Arms," *Toronto Daily Star,* 11 May 1961. See also Hugh L. Keenleyside, *The Memoirs of Hugh L. Keenleyside,* volume 2 (Toronto: McClelland and Stewart, 1981), 550. Rowland Lorimer et al., *Mass Communication in Canada,* 6th edition (Don Mills, ON: Oxford University Press, 2008), 121-22.

50   S. and M. Leskard to Prime Minister J. Diefenbaker, 5 May 1961, John Diefenbaker Fonds, LAC MG 26 M, Vol. 48, File 140 [emphasis in original]. Stephen Leskard was born Stephen Laśkiewicz, his father served as the mayor of Lublin and fled with his children when the Germans invaded in 1939. The family fled through Romania to France, where they escaped to the United Kingdom with 25,000 other Poles at Dunkirk. Stephen, seventeen at the beginning of the war, trained as an officer with the Free Polish forces and returned to France on 21 June 1944, as part of the 1st Polish Armoured Division, which fought alongside the Canadians in the closing stages of the Falaise campaign. After the war, he studied art and emigrated to Canada, where he met Mary at an artists' group in Whitby, Ontario. Mary, born in 1925, worked at General Motors during the war on aircraft components. The two married in Banff, Alberta, and remained on the West Coast. He worked as a freelance commercial artist and changed his name to Leskard because art directors could not pronounce his name. Stephen and Mary watched the exercise unfold on television and were baffled at the contradictory advice given to different cities about how to survive an attack. They expressed their frustration in their letter, one of many written to public figures over the years. Phone interview with Mary Leskard, 29 September 2010.

51   M.C. Kaye to J. Diefenbaker, 11 November 1961, John Diefenbaker Fonds, LAC MG 26 M, Vol. 49, File 141.

52   Possible Questions from the Press at Exercise Tocsin 61 [no date], Douglas Scott Harkness Fonds, LAC MG 32 B19, Vol. 56, File 87-5, pt 2.

53   J. Pratt to J.W. Monteith, 25 May 1959, John Diefenbaker Fonds, LAC MG 26 M, Vol. 48, File 141.

54 Note appended by Brigadier H.L. Meuser to "Inspectors Won't Pass A-Shelter," *Montreal Gazette*, 10 November 1959, clipping, Douglas Scott Harkness Fonds, LAC MG 32 B19, Vol. 55, File 87-1.

55 Squadron Leader C. Good to G. Pearkes, 17 August 1959, Douglas Scott Harkness Fonds, LAC MG 32 B19, Vol. 55, File 87-1.

56 M. Lambert to J. Diefenbaker, 19 May 1961, John Diefenbaker Fonds, LAC MG 26 M, Vol. 48, File 140; R.B. Curry to R. Roberts, 25 August 1959, Douglas Scott Harkness Fonds, LAC MG 32 B19, Vol. 55, File 87-1.

57 G.S. Doherty, city clerk of Edmonton, to J. Diefenbaker, 4 December 1961, John Diefenbaker Fonds, LAC MG 26 M, Vol. 48, File 141; "More Bomb Shelters Seen as Best," *Hamilton Spectator*, 23 September 1961.

58 Ross McLean et al., *CBC Close-Up: Three Feet of Earth*, video recording (Toronto: Canadian Broadcasting Corporation, Television, 31 January 1961).

59 Instruction to Emergency Measures Organization Regional Officers 202, 9 January 1962, Jack Francis Wallace Fonds, LAC MG 30 E211, Vol 3, File 3-4.

60 Mrs. W. Davidson to J. Diefenbaker, 10 September 1961, John Diefenbaker Fonds, LAC MG 26 M, Vol. 48, File 141.

61 Camp Borden Mess Hall Staffs to G. Pearkes, 3 October 1959, LAC MG 26 M, Vol. 48, File 141; V. Grenier to D. Harkness, Douglas Scott Harkness Fonds, LAC MG 32 B19, Vol. 55, File 87-1, pt 1.

62 D. Harrop to J. Diefenbaker, 12 August 1960, John Diefenbaker Fonds, LAC MG 26 M, Vol. 48, File 141. A year later, another British-Canadian raised the same point to the prime minister. M.C. Kaye to J. Diefenbaker, 11 November 1961, LAC MG 26 M, Vol. 49, File 141.

63 K. Tremblay to J. Diefenbaker, 10 November 1961, LAC MG 26 M, Vol. 49, File 141.

64 C.F. Johns to Joint Services Accommodation Committee, 30 November 1960, LAC RG 24 1983/84-167, Box 7053, File C-2-533-15.

65 Ross McLean et al., *CBC Close-Up: Three Feet of Earth*.

66 Arthur DeBrincat to Diefenbaker, 24 September 1961, John Diefenbaker Fonds, LAC MG 26 M, Vol. 49, File 141.

67 Ross McLean et al., *CBC Close-Up: Three Feet of Earth*.

68 James Eayrs, "Survival and Civility," *Northern Approaches* (Toronto: Macmillan, 1961), 47.

69 "Pupils Decry Shelter Need," *London Free Press*, 25 November 1961, clipping found in file, John Diefenbaker Fonds, LAC MG 26 M, Vol. 49, File 141.

70 J.M. Griffiths to J. Diefenbaker, 14 November 1961, John Diefenbaker Fonds, LAC MG 26 M, Vol. 49, File 141.

71 Regional Officers 348 of the EMO, Survey of Newspapers and Television Programme TELEPOL, 7 December 1962, John Francis Wallace Fonds, LAC MG 30 E211, Vol. 3, File 3-4.

72 Proposal for a revised shelter policy, 29 December 1961, John Francis Wallace Fonds, LAC MG 30 E211, Vol. 4, File 4-13.

73 R.B. Curry to Mrs. P.A.C. Chaplin, 11 October 1961, John Diefenbaker Fonds, LAC MG 26 M, Vol. 48, File 141.

74 "The Kingston-Frontenac Shelter Survey," *Emergency Measures Organization National Digest* (February 1965), 1-5.

75 Dr. A Russell to J. Diefenbaker, 20 November 1961, John Diefenbaker Fonds, LAC MG 26 M, Vol. 49, File 141.

76 S. Fleming to R.B. Curry, 20 July 1960, and reply from J.C. Morrison, director of the Emergency Supply Planning Branch, 2 August 1960, John Diefenbaker Fonds, LAC MG 26 M, Vol. 49, File 141.

77 While it may have made little practical sense, the advice was not without some scientific merit. Following the 1986 Chernobyl disaster, farmers plowed fallout deep into the soil. Since many plants' roots grow only a few inches deep, the simple method prevented some of the radioactive isotopes from entering the food chain. Jessica Leeder, "Warning about Contaminated Crops Raises Spectre of a Lasting Nuclear Legacy," *Globe and Mail*, 22 March 2011.

78 Script – TOCSIN 1961, LAC RG 57 1983-84/212, Box 17, File 2550-61, pt 2.

79 See Michael Egan, *Barry Commoner and the Science of Survival: The Remaking of American Environmentalism* (Cambridge, MA: MIT Press, 2007), 47-79; Catherine Carstairs and Rachel Elder, "Expertise, Health, and Popular Opinion: Debating Water Fluoridation, 1945-1980," *Canadian Historical Review* 89 (September 2008): 345-46.

80 Joseph Sternberg, "Fall-out Shelters Are Not the Answer," *Weekend Magazine*, 11 November 1961, 11.

81 Proceedings of the Provincial Ministers and Commanders Conference, 17-18 April 1961, Directorate of History and Heritage (DHH) 73/1114.

82 Nuclear Weapons, Public Opinion and the Scientist, 12-14 August 1960, John Francis Wallace Fonds, LAC MG 30 E211, Vol. 6, File 6-11 [emphasis in original].

83 N. Lyon to J. Diefenbaker, 22 July 1959, John Diefenbaker Fonds, LAC MG 26 M, Vol. 48, File 141.

84 DHH 73/1114.

85 To date, it is estimated that *On the Beach* has sold over four million copies.

86 Peter D. Smith, *Doomsday Men: The Real Dr. Strangelove and the Dream of the Superweapon* (New York: Allen Lane, 2007), 380.

87 Philip Wylie's novel *Tomorrow*, published in 1954, also features a cobalt bomb, as does the 1970 film *Beneath the Planet of the Apes*. Ibid., 384-85.

88 "Will Ottawa Provide Suicide Pills for Children?" *Toronto Daily Star*, 17 November 1961.

89 For an excellent discussion of American atomic fiction and its critical reception, see Kenneth Rose, *One Nation Underground: The Fallout Shelter in American Culture* (New York: New York University Press, 2004), 38-77.

90 Robert Wolf Emmett, "Who Destroyed the Earth?" *Maclean's*, 1 January 1955.

91 Arthur Hailey, "In High Places," *Maclean's*, 6 January 1962. In the story, the US government agreed to transfer resources to Alaska to assist the Canadian government in building a new national home in the North.

92 Thom Benson and Blair Fraser, *Camera Canada – TOCSIN*, video recording (Toronto: Canadian Broadcasting Corporation, Television, 1961).

93 As quoted in John Haslam, *Russia's Cold War: From the October Revolution to the Fall of the Wall* (New Haven, CT: Yale University Press, 2011), 200-1.

94 Ibid., 199.

95 John Paul and Jerome Laulicht, *In Your Opinion: Leaders' and Voters' Attitudes on Defence and Disarmament* (Clarkson, ON: Canadian Peace Research Institute, 1963), 41.

96 Interview with Dr. John Anderson, 20 May 2010, George Metcalf Archival Collection, Canadian War Museum, file 31D11: Anderson.

97 K.H. Watts to A. De B. McPhillips, 22 January 1961, LAC MG 26 N2, Vol. 3, File 140.

98 "The Three Little Fallout Shelters," *Rawhide*, Canadian Broadcasting Corporation Radio, originally broadcast on 22 July 1960, CBC Digital Archives, http://archives.cbc.ca/war_conflict/cold_war/topics/274.

99 "Nuclear Warfare Can Be Fun," *Rawhide*, Canadian Broadcasting Corporation Radio, originally broadcast on 9 November 1961. CBC Digital Archives, accessed 5 February 2009, http://archives.cbc.ca/war_conflict/cold_war/topics/274.

100 J. Pollard, as quoted in Bryan Palmer, *Canada's 1960s* (Toronto: University of Toronto Press, 2009), 71.

101 W.W. Rose to the Editor, *Weekend Magazine,* 15 January 1962, Douglas Scott Harkness Fonds, LAC MG 32 B 19, Vol. 55, File 87-1.

102 Except for one Canadian who, puzzlingly, told the interviewer "I'm in the Militia, so I'm taken care of." Ross McLean et al., *CBC Close-Up: Three Feet of Earth.*

103 L.C. McHugh, "Ethics at the Shelter Doorway," *America,* 30 September 1961. See also "Religion: Gun Thy Neighbor?" *Time,* 18 August 1961, http://www.time.com/time/magazine/article/0,9171,872694-1,00.html.

104 John Seeley, "We Must Learn How to Kill Our Friends and Neighbours," *Toronto Daily Star,* 22 November 1962.

105 "Who's Building Shelters and Where?" *Maclean's,* 2 December 1961. This theme recurred in other *Maclean's* examinations of the shelter issue, "Guns to Repel the Neighbours," 18 November 1961, 73.

106 Fully a third of Americans surveyed by Nehnevasja were firmly convinced that society *would* fall apart after the first atomic bomb fell. Jiri Nehnevasja, "Issues in Public Acceptance of Civil Defense," *Emergency Measures Organization National Digest,* (February 1965), 17-21.

107 Points for p.m. in discussion with R.B. Bryce [no date], John Francis Wallace Fonds, LAC MG 30 E 211, Vol. 4, File 4-13.

108 R.B. Curry to R.B. Bryce, 29 December 1961, John Francis Wallace Fonds, LAC MG 30 E 211, Vol. 4, File 4-13.

109 J.F. Wallace to R.B. Bryce, 29 December 1961, John Francis Wallace Fonds, LAC MG 30 E 211, Vol. 4, File 4-13.

110 Handwritten comments on document, R.B. Curry to R.B. Bryce, 29 December 1961, John Francis Wallace Fonds, LAC MG 30 E 211, Vol. 4, File 4-13.

111 *Blueprint for Survival No. 5: Survival in Likely Target Areas* (Ottawa: Queen's Printer, 1962), John Francis Wallace Fonds, LAC MG 30 E 211, Vol. 2, File 2-32.

112 Some Questions and Answers about Nuclear War and Related Subjects, Matthew Howard Somers Penhale Fonds, LAC MG 31 G21, Vol. 10.

113 George Halverson, "You Survive" screenplay, found in LAC RG 29, Vol. 1009, File 115-1-4, pt 1.

114 Handwritten comments on "You Survive," LAC RG 29, Vol. 1009, File 115-1-4, pt 1.

115 Walter Hewitson and George Salverson, *Time to Live,* video recording (Ottawa: National Film Board of Canada, 1964). See script in LAC RG 29, Vol. 1009, File 115-1-4, pt 1.

116 Regional Officers 286 of the EMO, 3 July 1962, Matthew Howard Somers Penhale Fonds, LAC MG 30 E211, Vol. 3, File 7.

Chapter 9: Cuba, Confusion, and Retreat, 1962-68

1 "Major Consequences on Certain US Course of Action on Cuba, 20 October 1962," George Washington University National Security Archive (NSA), http://www.gwu.edu/~nsarchiv/nsa/cuba_mis_cri/19621020cia.pdf.

2 "Radio-TV Address of the President to the Nation from the White House, 22 October 1962," NSA, http://www.gwu.edu/~nsarchiv/nsa/cuba_mis_cri/621022%20Radio-TV%20Address%20of%20President.pdf.

3 Peter T. Haydon, *The 1962 Cuban Missile Crisis: Canadian Involvement Reconsidered* (Toronto: Canadian Institute of Strategic Studies, 1993), 121-26. Norman Hillmer and J.L. Granatstein, *For Better or For Worse: Canada and the United States into the Twenty-First Century* (Toronto: Thomson-Nelson, 2007), 204.

4 Canadian Army Operational Research Establishment Memorandum no. 59/4, July 1959, Directorate of History and Heritage (DHH) 81/256.

5 Richard Rhodes, *Arsenals of Folly: The Making of the Nuclear Arms Race* (New York: Vintage Books, 2007), 85-86.

6 Andrew Richter, *Avoiding Armageddon: Canadian Military Strategy and Nuclear Weapons* (Vancouver: UBC Press, 2002), 55-56.

7 Emergency Measures Organization (EMO), *Blueprint for Survival No. 4: 11 Steps for Survival* (Ottawa: Queen's Printer, 1961), 33-38.

8 "Kennedy masse des forces d'assaut face à Cuba," *La Presse,* 22 October 1962. Of these reasons, the editorial board appeared to prefer the second. "Stupéfaction dans le monde" and "Ce n'est pas la guerre mais," 23 October 1962.

9 "No Time to Panic, Diefenbaker Warns," *Winnipeg Free Press,* 23 October 1962.

10 Cabinet Conclusions, 23 October 1962, Library and Archives Canada (LAC) RG 2, Series A-5-a, Vol. 6193, 2-4; interview with Eric Brown, January 2009, Canadian War Museum, George Metcalf Archival Collection, 31D10 Brown.

11 Interview with Eric Brown, January 2009.

12 "Warning Centre Reinforced," *Winnipeg Free Press,* 25 October 1962.

13 Excerpt forwarded in Instruction to EMO Regional Officers 25 October 1962, John Francis Wallace Fonds, LAC MG 30 E211, Vol. 5, File 5-15.

14 "La psychose de la guerre se propose," *La Presse,* 24 October 1962.

15 "Civil Defence Busy Answering Calls," *Halifax Chronicle Herald,* 27 October 1962.

16 Instruction to EMO Regional Officers 348, 7 December 1962, John Francis Wallace Fonds, LAC MG 30 E211, Vol. 3, File 3-7.

17 Instruction to EMO Regional Officers 355, 22 November 1962, John Francis Wallace Fonds, LAC MG 30 E211, Vol. 3, File 3-7.

18 EMO, *Blueprint for Survival No. 4: 11 Steps to Survival* (Ottawa: Queen's Printer, 1961), 32.

19 Instruction to EMO Regional Officers 348, 7 December 1962.

20 "La psychose de la guerre se propage," *La Presse,* 24 October 1962.

21 "Police Radio Tie-up?" *Winnipeg Free Press,* 26 October 1962.

22 "No Civil Defence Alert," *Halifax Chronicle Herald,* 26 October 1962.

23 "May Muzzle Sirens," *Winnipeg Free Press,* 26 October 1962.

24 "CD Advises: Be Intelligent," *Winnipeg Free Press,* 27 October 1962. Editorials reflecting this advice were published across the country, many of which emphasized the lack of government direction of post-war survival efforts. A sampling of titles includes: "Plans for Emergency Still Needed," "People Want to Know What to Do," "No Panic Here, Every Man for Himself," and "Direction from the Top Needed."

25 Voluntary Dispersal Routes from the Metropolitan Area to Destinations in the Province of Ontario, 19 April 1962, LAC RG 57, Vol. 21, File 2306-2.

26 Bryan Palmer, *Canada's 1960s: The Ironies of Identity in a Rebellious Era* (Toronto: University of Toronto Press, 2009), 67-70.

27 John Paul and Jerome Laulicht, *In Your Opinion* (Clarkson, ON: Canadian Peace Research Institute, 1963), 35.

28 R.B. Bryce to E.A. Driedger, 2 November 1962, John Francis Wallace Fonds, LAC MG 30 E211, Vol. 3, File 3-9.

29 J.F. Wallace to R.B. Curry, 21 November 1962, John Francis Wallace Fonds, LAC MG 30 E211, Vol. 5, File 5-15.

30 N.S. Jones to J. Diefenbaker, 2 November 1962, John Diefenbaker Fonds, LAC MG 26 M, Vol. 558.

31 *Canada Year Book 1959* (Ottawa: Census and Statistics Office, 1959), 1176.

32 G.A. McCarter to G.S. Hatton, 20 February 1959; M.W. Turner to F.F. Worthington, 17 September 1956; A.S. de Wilden to F.F. Worthington, 10 June 1957; A.E. Gagné to G.S. Hatton, 2 April 1959, all contained in LAC RG 29, Vol. 676, File 108-2-3, pt 3.

33 The alert states were themselves the subject of much discussion on the Interdepartmental Advisory Committee of Emergency Planning (IACCEP), which had finalized the general tasks accompanying each level of alert, but was still working with the military to harmonize their terminology with the army and to better correspond with the alert states of the North American Air Defence system. Third Meeting of the IACCEP, 17 July 1962, LAC RG 29, Vol. 1014, File 115-3-4, pt 1.

34 IACCEP no. 8/62, 13 July 1962, LAC RG 29, Vol. 1014, File 115-3-4, pt 1.

35 Brad Gladman and Peter Archambault, *Confronting the "Essence of Decision": Canada and the Cuban Missile Crisis,* Centre for Operational Research and Analysis Technical Memorandum no. 2010-250 (Ottawa: Defence Research and Development Canada, November 2010), 39-45.

36 Third Meeting of the IACCEP. The final phase, emergency, issued during a period where attack was considered imminent, completed the transition of officials into emergency government sites and began the national alarm system, alerting the public to the likelihood of attack.

37 J. McKay Hitsman, *The Canadian Army's Role in Survival Operations,* Army Historical Section Report no. 96 (Ottawa: Arrmy Historical Section, 29 October 1962), 43, http://www.cmp-cpm.forces.gc.ca/dhh-dhp/his/rep-rap/doc/ahqr-rqga/AHQ96.pdf

38 J.F. Wallace to R.B. Curry, 21 November 1962, John Francis Wallace Fonds, LAC MG 30 E211, Vol. 5, File 5-15.

39 *House of Commons Debates,* First Session, Twenty-Fifth Parliament, Volume I (24 October 1962), 884 (John Diefenbaker).

40 Patricia McMahon, *The Essence of Indecision: Diefenbaker's Nuclear Policy, 1957-1963* (Montreal and Kingston: McGill-Queen's University Press, 2009), 149.

41 Robert Bothwell, Ian Drummond, and John English, *Canada since 1945: Power, Politics, and Provincialism* (Toronto: University of Toronto, 1981), 246-47; Robert Bothwell, *Alliance and Illusion: Canada and the World, 1945-1984* (Vancouver: UBC Press, 2007), 168-69.

42 Unpublished memoir, Douglas Scott Harkness Fonds, LAC MG 32 B 19, Vol. 57, File "The Nuclear Arms Question," 11.

43 Gladman and Archambault, *Confronting the "Essence of Decision,"* 10.

44 McMahon, *The Essence of Indecision,* xii.

45 Hillmer and Granatstein, *For Better or For Worse,* 204-5.

46 Canadians, however, appeared to favour political, rather than military, support to this united front. Paul and Laulicht, *In Your Opinion,* 26.

47 Instruction to EMO Regional Officers, 348.

48 Paul and Laulicht, *In Your Opinion,* 84.

49 In fact, the successful resolution of the Cuban Missile Crisis by diplomacy proved that serious crises could be resolved by negotiation and made nuclear weapons a less threatening option for Canadians. McMahon, *The Essence of Indecision,* 153.

50 In response to public criticism in 1961 about the lack of a viable shelter for city dwellers, the EMO staff requested assistance from the Defence Research Board to develop cheap shelters that could withstand blast waves from a thermonuclear weapon. At that point, their designs were based on drawings from private contractors with no idea about blast loading, derived from American and British pamphlets. The Defence Research Board did its best to accommodate the cash-strapped organization's needs, but in 1964 the EMO cancelled blast shelter tests in favour of fallout shelters. Chief of Station, Suffield

Experimental Station to Director, EMO, 12 February 1964, LAC RG 24, Vol. 24016, File DRBS1678-05. See also Gerard Bowers, "Kingston-Frontenac Fallout Shelter Programme," *Emergency Measures Organization National Digest* (February 1965): 1-5.

51 Notes on Re-organization in the Militia, 17 January 1964, John Francis Wallace Fonds, LAC MG 30 E211, Vol. 4, File 4-6.

52 C. Drury to T. Earl Hickey, 2 September 1966, LAC RG 57, Vol. 60, File 2300-2.

53 Ibid.

54 Matthew Grant, *After the Bomb: Civil Defence and Nuclear War in Britain, 1945-1968* (London: Palgrave Macmillan, 2010), 174-90.

55 David McConnell, *Plan for Tomorrow, Today! The Story of Emergency Preparedness Canada, 1948-1998* (Ottawa: Heritage Research Associates, 1998), 24, http://diefenbunker.ca/pages/uploads/1/Plan_for_tomorrow_todayP1.pdf.

Conclusion

1 *House of Commons Debates,* Second Session, Twenty-Fourth Parliament, Volume II, 1959 (23 March 1959), 2129-30 (John Diefenbaker).

2 Paul Martin, *A Very Public Life: So Many Worlds* (Ottawa: Deneau, 1985), 146-47. J.W. Monteith to J. Diefenbaker, 9 May 1958, John Diefenbaker Fonds, Library and Archives Canada (LAC) MG 26 M, Vol. 48, File 140. See also "Was in Diefenbaker Cabinet," *Globe and Mail,* 21 December 1981, 13.

3 Patricia McMahon has argued that Diefenbaker and his Cabinet "balanced defence priorities, on the one hand, with political popularity, on the other. Over time, the latter came to take priority." *The Essence of Indecision: Diefenbaker's Nuclear Policy, 1957-1963* (Montreal and Kingston: McGill-Queen's University Press, 2009), 29.

4 J.L. Granatstein, *Canada's Army: Waging War and Keeping the Peace* (Toronto: University of Toronto Press, 2002), 350-51; see also John Francis Wallace Fonds, LAC MG 30 E211, Vol. 4, File 4-6.

5 In 1961, federal statistics estimated that 66 percent of Canadians owned private homes. Eugene Flichel, "Home Ownership in Canada Back on an Upward Curve," *Housing Finance International* 2 (May 1987): 9-10.

Bibliography

Archival Sources

Library and Archives Canada

Record Groups
Civil Service Commission
Department of External Affairs
Department of National Defence
Department of National Health and Welfare
Department of Public Works
Department of Transport
Emergency Measures Organization
Privy Council Office

Manuscript Groups
Brooke Claxton Fonds
John Diefenbaker Fonds
Howard Graham Fonds
Douglas Scott Harkness Fonds
Imperial Order Daughters of the Empire Fonds
Louis St. Laurent Fonds
Paul Joseph Martin Fonds
Lester B. Pearson Fonds
Matthew Howard Somers Penhale Fonds
John Francis Wallace Fonds

Directorate of History and Heritage
F.F. Worthington Diaries

Canadian War Museum, George Metcalf Archival Collection

Document Collections
Major John E. Barbary Papers
Captain Harold Lester Joseph Corbett Papers
William Culham Woodward Papers

Oral History Program Interviews
John Anderson
Eric Brown
Archie Pennie

Newspapers, Magazines, and Bulletins

Calgary Herald (1953, 1955, 1957)
Canadian Army Journal (1958-64)
Canadian Institute of Public Opinion (1958-62)
Civil Defence Bulletin (1951-60)
Edmonton Journal (1953, 1961)
Emergency Measures Organization National Digest (1963-65)
Evening Times-Globe (1953)
Globe and Mail (1948, 1951, 1953, 1956, 1959-62)
Kingston Whig-Standard (1959)
L'Action Populaire (1962)
La Patrie (1951)
La Presse (1953-54, 1962)
Le Devoir (1953)
London Free Press (1951)
Maclean's (1946-48, 1959-61)
Montreal Gazette (1948, 1951-54)
Ottawa Citizen (1954, 1958)
Ottawa Journal (1953, 1958)
Saturday Night (1945)
Toronto Star (1951, 1953, 1957-61)
Toronto Telegram (1955, 1961)
The Listening Post (1951-52)
The Post: Official Organ of the Civil Defence Guild of British Columbia (1945)
Weekend Magazine (1961)
Windsor Star (1951, 1954)
Winnipeg Free Press (1951, 1954, 1957, 1962)

Films

Benson, Thom, and Blair Fraser. *Camera Canada – TOCSIN*. Video recording (60 minutes). Toronto: Canadian Broadcasting Corporation, Television, 1961.

Hewitson, Walter, and George Salverson. *Time to Live*. Video recording (28 minutes). Ottawa: National Film Board of Canada, 1964.

Kehoe, Isobel, and Nicholas Balla. *Operation Life Saver*. Video recording (15 minutes). Ottawa: National Film Board of Canada, 1956.

McLean, Ross, Doug Leiterman, Robert Crone, and John Kennedy. *CBC Close-Up: Three Feet of Earth*. Video recording (60 minutes). Toronto: Canadian Broadcasting Corporation, Television, 1961.

Other Sources

Alcock, Norman. "Necessity for Peace Research Institutes." *Our Generation against Nuclear War* 1, 1 (Autumn 1961): 4-8.

American Jewish Archives. *Introduction to the Abraham L. Feinberg Manuscript Collection.* http://www.americanjewisharchives.org/aja/FindingAids/Feinberg.htm.

Barker-Devine, Jenny. "'Mightier than Missiles,' The Rhetoric of Civil Defense for Rural American Families 1950-1970." *Agricultural History* 80, 4 (Fall 2006): 415-35.

Beiner, Ronald, ed. *Theorizing Citizenship*. Albany, NY: State University of New York, 1995.

Bennett, Tony. *The Birth of the Museum: History, Theory, Politics*. New York: Routledge, 1995.

Bercuson, David. *True Patriot: The Life of Brooke Claxton, 1898-1960*. Toronto: University of Toronto Press, 1993.

Bland, Douglas. *Canada's National Defence,* Volume 1: *Canada's Defence Policy.* Kingston, ON: School of Policy Studies, Queen's University, 1997.

Bond, Brian. *War and Society in Europe, 1870-1970.* Montreal and Kingston: McGill-Queen's University Press, 1998.

Bothwell, Robert. *Alliance and Illusion: Canada and the World, 1945-1984.* Vancouver: UBC Press, 2007.

–. "The Cold War and the Curate's Egg: When Did Canada's Cold War Really Begin?" *International Journal* 53 (Summer 1998): 407-18.

Bothwell, Robert, Ian Drummond, and John English. *Canada since 1945: Power, Politics, and Provincialism.* Toronto: University of Toronto Press, 1981.

Bothwell, Robert, and Robert Kilborn. *C.D. Howe: A Biography.* Toronto: McClelland and Stewart, 1979.

Bourke, Joanna. *An Intimate History of Killing: Face-to-Face Killing in Twentieth Century Warfare.* New York: Basic Books, 1999.

Boyer, Paul. *By the Bomb's Early Light: American Thought and Culture at the Dawn of the Atomic Age.* New York: Pantheon, 1985.

Bradley, David. *No Place to Hide.* Boston: Little, Brown, 1948.

Brodie, Bernard. *Strategy in the Missile Age.* Princeton, NJ: Princeton University Press, 1959.

Bruce-Briggs, B. *The Shield of Faith: A Chronicle of Strategic Defense from Zeppelins to Star Wars.* New York: Simon and Schuster, 1988.

Buchner, Lieutenant-Colonel W.R. "The Role of the Militia Unit in a Civil Disaster." *Canadian Army Journal* 15, 3 (July 1957): 62-63.

Canada. Information Services Division. *Canada Year Book.* Ottawa: Queen's Printer, 1959-63.

–. Senate of Canada. Committee on National Security and Defence. *Emergency Preparedness in Canada,* Report no. 13, Volumes 1-4. Second Session, 39th Parliament, 2008.

Canadian Bank of Commerce. *War Service Records, 1939-1945: An Account of the War Service of Members of the Staff during the Second World War.* Toronto: Rous and Mann Press, 1947.

Canadian Broadcasting Corporation Digital Archives. "Nuclear Warfare Can Be Fun." *Rawhide,* 9 November 1961, http://archives.cbc.ca/war_conflict/cold_war/clips/1465/.

–. *Close-Up,* 8 August 1961, http://archives.cbc.ca/war_conflict/cold_war//topics/274/.

–. "The Three Little Fallout Shelters." *Rawhide,* 22 July 1960, http://archives.cbc.ca/war_conflict/cold_war/clips/1475.

–. *CBC Radio: Assignment,* 6 November 1958, http://archives.cbc.ca/IDC-1-71-274- 1462/conflict_war/cold_war/clip3.

Carey, Michael J. "The Schools and Civil Defense: The Fifties Revisited." *Teachers College Record* 84 (Fall 1982): 115-27.

Carstairs, Catherine, and Rachel Elder. "Expertise, Health, and Popular Opinion: Debating Water Fluoridation, 1945-1980." *Canadian Historical Review* 89, 3 (September 2008): 345-71.

Clifford, F.L.T. "Exercise Nimble Phoenix." *Canadian Army Journal* 15, 2 (Spring 1961): 59-72.

Colom-Gonzalez, Francisco. "Dimensions of Citizenship: Canada in Comparative Perspective." *International Journal of Canadian Studies* 14 (Fall/Autumn 1996): 95-109.

Cowen, Deborah. *Military Workfare: The Soldier and Social Citizenship in Canada.* Toronto: University of Toronto Press, 2008.

Davis, Tracy. *Stages of Emergency: Cold War Nuclear Civil Defence.* Durham, NC: Duke University Press, 1997.

–. "Between History and Event: Rehearsing Nuclear War Survival." *Drama Review* 46, 4 (Winter 2002): 11-45.

Department of External Affairs. *Documents on Canadian External Relations.* Ottawa: Queen's Printer, 1948-60.

Department of National Defence. *Canadian Army Manual of Training no. 1-43: Notes on the Influence of Nuclear Weapons on Tactics (Provisional).* Ottawa: Queen's Printer, 1956.

Department of National Health and Welfare. *Civil Defence Manual no. 1: Organization for Civil Defence.* Ottawa: Queen's Printer, 1949.

–. *Civil Defence Manual no. 4: Personal Protection under Atomic Attack.* Ottawa: Queen's Printer, 1952.

–. *Civil Defence Manual no. 13: Operations and Control of the Civil Defence Services.* Ottawa: Queen's Printer, 1952.

–. *Civil Defence Manual no. 15: The Warden Service.* Ottawa: Queen's Printer, 1952.

–. *Public Information in Civil Defence.* Ottawa: Queen's Printer, 1957.

Dickson, Paul Douglas. *A Thoroughly Canadian General: A Biography of General H.D.G. Crerar.* Toronto: University of Toronto Press, 2007.

Durflinger, Serge. *Fighting from Home: The Second World War in Verdun, Quebec.* Vancouver: UBC Press, 2006.

Eayrs, James. "Canada, NATO, and the Nth Power Problem." *Canadian Forum* 39 (April 1959): 6-7.

–. *In Defence of Canada: Growing Up Allied.* Toronto: University of Toronto Press, 1980.

–. *Northern Approaches: Canada and the Search for Peace.* Toronto: Macmillan, 1961.

Egan, Michael. *Barry Commoner and the Science of Survival: The Remaking of American Environmentalism.* Cambridge, MA: MIT Press, 2007.

Eggleston, Wilfrid. *Canada's Nuclear Story.* Toronto: Clarke, Irwin, 1965.

Emergency Measures Organization. *Blueprint for Survival no. 1: Your Basement Fallout Shelter.* Ottawa: Queen's Printer, 1961.

–. *Blueprint for Survival no. 4: 11 Steps to Survival.* Ottawa: Queen's Printer, 1961.

–. *Blueprint for Survival no. 5: Survival in Likely Target Areas.* Ottawa: Queen's Printer, 1962.

–. *Simpler Shelters.* Ottawa: Queen's Printer, 1962.

Faris, John H. "The Impact of Basic Combat Training: The Role of the Drill Sergeant." In Nancy Goldman and David Segal, eds., *The Social Psychology of Military Service,* 13-27. London: Sage Publications, 1976.

Feasby, William Richard. *Official History of the Canadian Medical Services, 1939-1945.* Ottawa: Department of National Defence, 1953.

Fisher, Anne. "Civil Defence in Canada, 1939-1965: Garnering Support for Deterrence through the Myth of Protection." MA thesis, Department of History, Lakehead University, Thunder Bay, 1999.

Fleming, Donald. *So Very Near: The Political Memoirs of the Honourable Donald M. Fleming,* Volume 2. Toronto: McClelland and Stewart, 1985.

Flichel, Eugene. "Home Ownership in Canada Back on an Upward Curve." *Housing Finance International* (May 1987): 9-10.

Frideres, James S. et al., "Becoming Canadian: Citizenship Acquisition and National Identity." *Canadian Review in Studies of Nationalism* 14, 3 (1987): 105-21.

Fried, Richard M. *The Russians Are Coming! The Russians Are Coming! Pageantry and Patriotism in Cold War America.* New York: Oxford University Press, 1999.

Gaddis, John Lewis. *We Now Know: Rethinking Cold War History.* New York: Oxford University Press, 1997.

Garrison, Dee. *Bracing for Armageddon: Why Civil Defense Never Worked.* New York: Oxford University Press, 2006.

George Washington University National Security Archive. *Deterrence and Survival in the Nuclear Age.* http://www.gwu.edu/~nsarchiv/NSAEBB/NSAEBB139/nitze02.pdf.

–. *The Cuban Missile Crisis: 40th Anniversary.* http://www.gwu.edu/~nsarchiv/nsa/cuba_mis_cri/.

Gladman, Brad W., and Peter M. Archambault. *Confronting the Essence of Decision: Canada and the Cuban Missile Crisis.* Centre for Operational Research and Analysis Technical Memorandum 2010-250, Defence Research and Development Canada, Ottawa, November 2010.

Glasstone, Samuel. *The Effects of Nuclear Weapons.* Washington, DC: Atomic Energy Commission, 1957.

Glazov, Jamie. *Canadian Policy towards Khrushchev's Soviet Union.* Montreal and Kingston: McGill-Queen's University Press, 2002.

Goldstein, Joshua S. *War and Gender: How Gender Shapes the War System and Vice Versa.* London: Cambridge University Press, 2001.

Goodspeed, D.J. *A History of the Defence Research Board of Canada.* Ottawa: Queen's Printer, 1958.

Graham, Howard. *Citizen and Soldier: The Memoirs of Lieutenant-General Howard Graham.* Toronto: McClelland and Stewart, 1987.

Granatstein, J.L. *Canada's Army: Waging War and Keeping the Peace.* Toronto: University of Toronto Press, 2002.

–. *A Man of Influence: Norman A. Robertson and Canadian Statecraft 1929-1968.* Toronto: Denau, 1981.

Granatstein, J.L., and Robert Cuff. "Looking Back at the Cold War: 1945-1954." *Canadian Forum* 1, 11 (July-August 1972) 9.

Grant, Matthew. *After the Bomb: Civil Defence and Nuclear War in Britain, 1945-1968.* London: Palgrave Macmillan, 2010.

Griffith, Robert. "The Selling of America: The Advertising Council and American Politics, 1942-60." *Business History Review* 57, 3 (Autumn 1983): 388-412.

Grossman, Andrew. *Neither Dead nor Red: Civilian Defense and American Political Development during the Early Cold War.* New York: Routledge, 2001.

Hacker, Barton C. "Radiation Safety, the AEC, and Nuclear Weapons Testing." *Public Historian* 14, 1 (Winter 1992): 31-53.

Haslam, Jonathan. *Russia's Cold War: From the October Revolution to the Fall of the Wall.* New Haven, CT: Yale University Press, 2011.

Haydon, Commander Peter T. *The 1962 Cuban Missile Crisis: Canadian Involvement Reconsidered.* Toronto: Canadian Institute of Strategic Studies, 1993.

Henriksen, Margot. *Dr. Strangelove's America: or How Americans Learned to Stop Worrying and Live with the Bomb.* Berkeley, CA: University of California Press, 1997.

Hersey, John. *Hiroshima.* New York: A.A. Knopf, 1946.

Hillmer, Norman, and J.L. Granatstein. *For Better or For Worse: Canada and the United States into the Twenty-First Century.* Toronto: Thomson Nelson, 2007.

Hogan, Michael. *A Cross of Iron: Harry Truman and the National Security State.* Cambridge: Cambridge University Press, 2000.

Holmes, John. *The Shaping of Peace: Canada and the Shaping of World Order, 1943-1957,* Volume 1. Toronto: University of Toronto Press, 1982.

Holmes, K.J. *History of the Canadian Military Engineers,* Volume 3. Toronto: Military Engineering Institute of Canada, 1997.

House of Commons Debates. Ottawa: Queen's Printer, 1945-63.

Hunter, Jennifer "'Is it even worthwhile doing the dishes?' Canadians and the Nuclear Threat, 1945-1963." PhD diss., Department of History, McGill University, Montreal, 2004.

Jenson, Jane. "Fated to Live in Interesting Times: Canada's Changing Citizenship Regimes." *Canadian Journal of Political Science* 30, 4 (December 1997): 627-44.

Jenson, Jane, and Susan D. Phillips, "Regime Shift: New Citizenship Practices in Canada." *International Journal of Canadian Studies* 14 (Autumn 1996): 111-35.

Jockel, Joseph. *No Boundaries Upstairs: Canada, the United States, and the Origins of North American Air Defence, 1945-1958.* Vancouver: UBC Press, 1987.

–. *Canada in NORAD, 1957-2007: A History.* Kingston: School of Policy Studies, Queen's University, 2007.

Judt, Tony. *Postwar: A History of Europe since 1945.* Toronto: Penguin Press, 2005.

Kahn, Herman. *On Thermonuclear War: Three Lectures and Several Suggestions.* Princeton, NJ: Princeton University Press, 1961.

Kaplan, William, ed. *Belonging: The Meaning and Future of Canadian Citizenship.* Montreal and Kingston: McGill-Queen's University Press, 1993.

Katz, Milton. *Ban the Bomb: A History of Sane, the Committee for a Sane Nuclear Policy, 1957-1985.* New York: Greenwood Press, 1985.

Keenleyside, Hugh L. *The Memoirs of Hugh L. Keenleyside,* Volume 2. Toronto: McClelland and Stewart, 1981.

Keshen, Jeffrey A. *Saints, Sinners, and Soldiers: Canada's Second World War.* Vancouver: UBC Press, 2004.

Khrushchev, Nikita S. *The Memoirs of Nikita Khrushchev,* Volume 3, edited by Sergei Khrushchev and translated by George Shriver. University Park, PA: University of Pennsylvania Press, 2004.

Kincade, William H. "Repeating History: The Civil Defence Debate Renewed." *International Security* 2 (1978): 99-120.

Korinek, Valerie J. *Roughing It in the Suburbs: Reading* Chatelaine Magazine *in the Fifties and Sixties.* Toronto: University of Toronto Press, 2000.

Lamalice, André. "En temps de guerre comme en temps de paix, gouvernement manquant, gouvernance manquée: La protection civile au Canada, 1938-1988." PhD diss., Department of History, University of Ottawa, 2011.

Lee, Steven. "Power, Politics, and the Cold War: The Canadian Civil Defence Program and the North Atlantic Alliance 1945-1959." MA thesis, Department of History, McGill University, Montreal, 1987.

Levitt, Joseph. *Pearson and Canada's Role in Nuclear Disarmament and Arms Control Negotiations, 1945-1957.* Montreal and Kingston: McGill-Queen's University Press, 1993.

Lindgren, James M. "A Constant Incentive to Patriotic Citizenship: Historic Preservation in Progressive-Era Massachusetts." *New England Quarterly* 64 (December 1991): 594-608.

Lorimer, Rowland et al. *Mass Communication in Canada,* 6th edition. Don Mills, ON: Oxford University Press, 2008.

Macleod, D. Peter. *Northern Armageddon: The Battle of the Plains of Abraham.* Vancouver: Douglas and McIntyre, 2008.

Maloney, Sean. *Learning to Love the Bomb: Canada's Nuclear Weapons during the Cold War.* Washington, DC: Potomac Books, 2007.

–. "Dr. Strangelove Visits Canada: Projects RUSTIC, EASE, BRIDGE, 1958-1963." *Canadian Military History* 6 (Spring 1997): 42-56.

Manning, Bill. "Beyond the Diefenbunker: Canada's Forgotten 'Little Bunkers.'" *Material History Review* 57 (Spring 2003): 79-92.

Marshall, Dominique. *The Social Origins of the Welfare State: Québec Families, Compulsory Education, and Family Allowances, 1940-1955.* Translated by Nicola Doone Danby. Waterloo, ON: Wilfrid Laurier University Press, 2006.

Marshall, T.H. *Citizenship and Social Class and Other Essays.* Cambridge: Cambridge University Press, 1950.

Martin, Paul Joseph. *A Very Public Life,* Volume 2. Ottawa: Deneau, 1985.

McConnell, David. *Plan for Tomorrow ... Today! The Story of Emergency Preparedness Canada 1948-1998.* Ottawa: Heritage Research Associates, 1998, http://diefenbunker.ca/pages/uploads/1/Plan_for_tomorrow_todayP1.pdf.

McEnany, Laura. *Civil Defence Begins at Home: Militarization Meets Everyday Life in the Fifties.* Princeton, NJ: Princeton University Press, 2000.

McMahon, Patricia. *Essence of Indecision: Diefenbaker's Nuclear Policy, 1957-1963.* Montreal and Kingston: McGill-Queen's University Press, 2009.

Miller, Harry. *Service to the Services: The Story of NAAFI.* London: Newman Neame, 1971.

Minifie, James. *Peacemaker or Powdermonkey.* Toronto: McClelland and Stewart, 1960.

Morton, Desmond. *A Military History of Canada,* 3rd edition. Toronto: University of Toronto Press, 1992.

Nelles, H.V. *The Art of Nation-Building: Pageantry and Spectacle at Quebec's Tercentenary.* Toronto: University of Toronto Press, 1999.

Nicholson, G.W.L. "The Canadian Militia's Introduction to Civil Defence." In Robert Bothwell and Michael Cross, eds., *Policy by Other Means: Essays in Honour of C.P. Stacey,* 219-45. Toronto: Clarke, Irwin, 1972.

Nikitiuk, Costia. "Emergency and Organizational Legitimacy: The Dilemma of Emergency Planning in B.C." *BC Studies* 38 (1978): 47-64.

Noakes, Jeffrey. "Under the Radar: Defence Construction Limited and Military Infrastructure in Canada, 1950-1965." PhD diss., Department of History, Carleton University, Ottawa, 2005.

Northcutt, Susan Stoudinger. "Women and the Bomb: Domestication of the Atomic Bomb in the United States." *International Social Science Review* 74, 3 (1999): 129-39.

Oakes, Guy. "The Cold War Conception of Nuclear Reality: Mobilizing the American Imagination for Nuclear War in the 1950s." *International Journal of Politics, Culture and Society* 6 (1992): 339-63.

–. *The Imaginary War: Civil Defence and American Cold War Culture.* Oxford: Oxford University Press, 1994.

O'Brien, Terence. *Civil Defence.* London: Her Majesty's Stationery Office, 1955.

Opp, James. "Prairie Commemorations and the Nation: The Golden Jubilees of Alberta and Saskatchewan, 1955." In Norman Hillmer and Adam Chapnick, eds., *Canadas of the Mind: The Making and Unmaking of Canadian Nationalisms in the Twentieth Century,* 214-33. Montreal and Kingston: McGill-Queen's University Press, 2007.

Pal, Leslie A. "Identity, Citizenship and Mobilization: The Canadian Nationalities Branch and World War Two." *Canadian Public Administration* 32 (December 1989): 407-26.

Palmer, Bryan. *Canada's 1960s: The Ironies of Identity in a Rebellious Era.* Toronto: University of Toronto Press, 2009.

Paul, John, and Jerome Laulicht. *In Your Opinion: Leaders' and Voters' Attitudes on Defence and Disarmament.* Clarkson, ON: Canadian Peace Research Institute, 1963.

Phillips, Ruth. *Citizenship: Feminist Perspectives,* 2nd edition. New York: Palgrave Macmillan, 2003.

Pope, William Henry. *Leading from the Front: The War Memoirs of Harry Pope.* Waterloo, ON: Laurier Centre for Military, Strategic and Disarmament Studies, 2002.

"Re-entry Operations into a Damaged Area" *Canadian Army Journal* 15, 3 (Summer 1961): 2-10.

Rhodes, Richard. *Arsenals of Folly: The Making of the Nuclear Arms Race.* New York: Vintage Books, 2007.

Richards, Thomas. *The Commodity Culture of Victorian England: Advertising and Spectacle, 1851-1914.* Stanford, CT: Stanford University Press, 1990.

Richter, Andrew. *Avoiding Armageddon: Canadian Military Strategy and Nuclear Weapons.* Vancouver: UBC Press, 2002.

Rodgers, Thomas E. "Billy Yank and G.I. Joe: An Exploratory Essay on the Sociopolitical Dimensions of Soldier Motivation." *Journal of Military History* 69, 1 (January 2005): 93-121.

Rose, Kenneth. *One Nation Underground: The Fallout Shelter in American Culture.* New York: New York University Press, 2004.

Rydell, Robert W. *All the World's a Fair: Visions of Empire at American International Exhibitions, 1876-1916.* Chicago: University of Chicago Press, 1984.

Salopek, Marijan "Western Canadians and Civil Defence: The Korean War Years, 1950-1953." *Prairie Forum* 14 (1989): 75-88.

Schwartz, Mildred A. "Citizenship in Canada and the United States." *Transactions of the Royal Society of Canada* 4, 14 (1986): 83-96.

Schwartz, Stephen. *Atomic Audit: The Costs and Consequences of U.S. Nuclear Weapons since 1940.* Washington, DC: Brookings Institution Press, 1998.

Shute, Nevil. *On the Beach.* Toronto: Random House of Canada, 1957.

Smith, Denis. *Rogue Tory: The Life and Legend of John G. Diefenbaker.* Toronto: Macfarlane, Walter and Ross, 1997.

Smith, Doug. *Joe Zuken: Citizen and Socialist.* Toronto: James Lorimer, 1990.

Smith, Peter D. *Doomsday Men: The Real Dr. Strangelove and the Dream of the Superweapon.* New York: Allen Lane, 2007.

Sprockton, Birk, ed. *The Winnipeg Connection: Writing Lives in Mid-Century.* Winnipeg: Prairie Fire Books, 2006.

Taylor, Frederick. *The Berlin Wall: A World Divided, 1961-1989.* New York: HarperCollins, 2006.

Tillotson, Shirley. *Contributing Citizens: Modern Charitable Fundraising and the Making of the Welfare State, 1920-1966.* Vancouver: UBC Press, 2008.

Toxopeus, Deanna. "1951 Agreement between the Red Cross and St. John Ambulance: Case Study of the Effect of Civil Defence on Canada's Health Care System." MA thesis, Department of History, Carleton University, Ottawa, 1997.

Urquhart, George Mackenzie. "The Changing Role of the Canadian Militia, 1945-1975." MA thesis, Department of History, University of Victoria, Victoria, 1977.

Vance, Jonathan. *A History of Canadian Culture.* Don Mills, ON: Oxford University Press, 2009.

Vandercook, William F. "Making the Very Best of the Very Worst: The 'Human Effects of Nuclear Weapons' Report of 1956." *International Security* 11 (1986): 184-95.

Walden, Keith. *Becoming Modern in Toronto: The Industrial Exhibition and the Shaping of a Late Victorian Culture.* Toronto: University of Toronto Press, 1997.

Whitaker, Reg, and Gary Marcuse. *Cold War Canada: The Making of a National Insecurity State, 1945-1957.* Toronto: University of Toronto Press, 1994.

Whitfield, Stephen. *The Culture of the Cold War.* Baltimore, MD: Johns Hopkins University Press, 1991.

Williams, Harry B. "The Human Factor in National Survival." *Canadian Army Journal* 14, 4 (Fall 1960): 24-28.

Woodrow Wilson International Center for Scholars. *Germany in the Cold War.* Washington, DC: Cold War International History Project, 2008, http://www.wilsoncenter.org/.

Worthington, F.F. "Civil Defence and Armed Defence." *Current Affairs for the Canadian Forces* 7, 8 (15 October 1954) 5-30.

–. "Civil Defence and Industry." *Industrial Canada* 53, 6 (July 1951): 165-68.

Worthington, Larry. *"Worthy": Biography of Major-General F.F. Worthington, C.B., M.M, M.C.* Toronto: Macmillan, 1961.

Wrinch, Arthur. "The Army and National Survival." *Medical Services Journal* 16 (April 1960) 267.

Index

Note: "(f)" after a number indicates a figure

"public scientists," 193-94; fallout detection, 107; liaison with United States, 157-58, 173; panic study, 85; recommendation for nuclear CD, 21-24

Department of Defence Production, 40, 113, 216

Department of Industry, 216-17

Department of Justice, 31, 192

Department of National Defence, 45; absorbs EMO, 218; early responsibility for CD, 21-22, 24, 28, 30-31, 159; Graham Report, 121, 125-26; intelligence provided to CD, 81, 107, 114, 166; Korean War expansion, 41-42; press policy, 93; refusal to build shelters on property, 141, 189-90; War Book revisions, 213. *See also* Canadian army, Royal Canadian Air Force, Royal Canadian Navy, *and* Special Militia Training Plan (SMTP)

Department of National Health and Welfare, 247*n*3; Graham Report, 121; Information Services Division, 60, 93; responsibility for CD, 29, 31, 41-42, 82; transfer of CD to Emergency Measures Organization, 113, 116, 124-26

Department of Transport, 29, 107

deterrence, 9, 41, 59, 65, 68, 131, 167-69, 200, 216, 239*n*5

Diefenbaker, John, 111, 113, 115, 187(f), 189; 1958 Royal Tour, 117-18; Berlin crisis, 141; criticism of, 215-16; Cuban missile crisis, 205, 207; decision-making, 213-15, 262*n*3; Diefenbunker, 177; Operation TOCSIN, 178-79, 182, 255*n*33; personal fallout shelter, 177, 182-83; support for EMO, 124-26, 171, 174, 194, 222-23

Diefenbunker. *See* blast shelters *and* continuity of government

disarmament, 11, 141, 175, 178, 183-87, 194-96, 203, 216, 224-25, 227*n*15

Distant Early Warning (DEW) Line, 106. *See also* attack warning

Douglas, Tommy, 178

Drury, Charles Mills, 28, 217

Duck and Cover, 12, 74

Duplessis, Maurice, 27, 43

Eayrs, James, 118, 190, 254(f)

Edmonton, Alberta, 33, 69, 73, 97, 105

Einstein, Albert, 21, 198

Eisenhower, Dwight, 77, 168

Emergency Measures Organization, 168, 173-75; absorbs CD, 124-26, 135; criticism of, 127-28, 186-87, 207; established, 110-11, 114-16; mandate altered, 216-18; reaction to Cuban missile crisis, 207-12. *See also* Continuity of Government, fallout shelters, *and* Operation TOCSIN

Emergency Preparedness Canada, 10

Emergency Supply Planning Branch, 192-93

Eniwetok Atoll, 78

evacuation, 3-4, 29, 35, 38, 50, 54, 162; exercises, 88-89, 92-93; flaws in plans, 100-1, 106-8; implications for rural areas, 104-5; policy, 82-87; "stay-put" policy, 101, 110, 119, 200. *See also* Operation Lifesaver

fallout. *See* nuclear weapons

Fallout on the Farm, 193-94

fallout shelters, 4, 156; adopted as official policy, 171-72; disarmament activism against, 183-87; estimated numbers built, 210(f); futility in target areas, 172, 184, 200-1; group shelters v. private shelters, 191(f), 191-92, 209; *Life* magazine, 181; morality debate, 198-99; National Housing Act loans, 166-67, 189-90; national survey, 140-41, 174, 200, 216; private marketing initiatives, 159-60, 169-70, 170(f); promotion, 158, 160-61, 163-65, 167, 179-81, 203; psychological opposition to, 195-97; satire, 197-98; taxation of, 188-90

Federal Civil Defence Administration (US), 46, 61-63, 87, 163-64, 168, 239(f)

Ferguson, Max, 197

Fienburg, Jack, 169

fire-fighting, 1, 3, 24, 38-39(f), 68, 86, 136, 224; purchase of equipment, 70, 159; standardization, 27-28

Fleming, Donald, 143

Fletcher, C.H.F., 48-49

Foulkes, Lieutenant-General Charles, 22, 81

Fraser, Blair, 196

Freedom Train, 61

Frost, Leslie, 42

Serge Marc Durflinger, *Veterans with a Vision: Canada's War Blinded in Peace and War*

James G. Fergusson, *Canada and Ballistic Missile Defence, 1954-2009: Déjà Vu All Over Again*

Benjamin Isitt, *From Victoria to Vladivostok: Canada's Siberian Expedition, 1917-19*

James Wood, *Militia Myths: Ideas of the Canadian Citizen Soldier, 1896-1921*

Timothy Balzer, *The Information Front: The Canadian Army and News Management during the Second World War*

Andrew Godefroy, *Defence and Discovery: Canada's Military Space Program, 1945-74*

Douglas E. Delaney, *Corps Commanders: Five British and Canadian Generals at War, 1939-45*

Timothy Wilford, *Canada's Road to the Pacific War: Intelligence, Strategy, and the Far East Crisis*

Randall Wakelam, *Cold War Fighters: Canadian Aircraft Procurement, 1945-54*

Printed and bound in Canada by Friesens

Set in Helvetica Condensed and Minion by Artegraphica Design Co. Ltd.

Copy editor: Stacy Belden

Proofreader: Jean Wilson